Chronically Ill Children and Their Families

Problems, Prospects, and Proposals
from the Vanderbilt Study

Nicholas Hobbs
James M. Perrin
Henry T. Ireys

Foreword by *Julius B. Richmond*

Chronically Ill Children and Their Families

Jossey-Bass Publishers

San Francisco • London • 1985

CHRONICALLY ILL CHILDREN AND THEIR FAMILIES
Problems, Prospects, and Proposals from the Vanderbilt Study
by Nicholas Hobbs, James M. Perrin, and Henry T. Ireys

Copyright © 1985 by: Jossey-Bass Inc., Publishers
433 California Street
San Francisco, California 94104

&

Jossey-Bass Limited
28 Banner Street
London EC1Y 8QE

Library of Congress Cataloging in Publication Data

Hobbs, Nicholas.
Chronically ill children and their families.

(Jossey-Bass social and behavioral science series)
(Jossey-Bass health series)
Jossey-Bass health series.
Bibliography: p. 361
Includes index.
1. Chronically ill children.   2. Chronically ill
children—Education—United States.   3. Chronically ill
children—Services for—United States.   4. Chronically
ill children—Government policy—United States.
I. Perrin, James M. (James Marc)   II. Ireys, Henry T.
III. Title.   IV. Series.   V. Series: Jossey-Bass
health series. [DNLM: 1. Chronic Disease—in infancy &
childhood.   2. Public Policy—United States.
WS 200 H682c]
RJ380.H63   1985   362.1'9892   85-14698
ISBN 0-87589-655-3

Manufactured in the United States of America

The paper in this book meets the guidelines for
permanence and durability of the Committee on
Production Guidelines for Book Longevity of the
Council on Library Resources.

JACKET DESIGN BY WILLI BAUM

FIRST EDITION

Code 8533

A joint publication in
The Jossey-Bass
Social and Behavioral Science Series
and
The Jossey-Bass
Health Series

Contents

Foreword   xi
Julius B. Richmond

Preface   xvii

Acknowledgments   xxv

Note to the Reader   xxxi

The Authors   xxxvii

1. Introduction: Severe and Chronic Illness in Childhood   1

2. Changing Patterns of Childhood Illness   32

3. Effects of Chronic Illness on Children, Families, and Communities   62

4. Identifying Educational Needs and Employment Opportunities   102

5. Health and Social Services: Problems and Prospects   127

6. Defining the Costs of Care   169

7.   Patterns of Paying for Care   189

8.   Preparing Professionals for New Roles   231

9.   Directions for Research: Areas of Promise   257
     and Guiding Principles

10. Role of Values in Shaping Professional Ethics   282
     and Public Policy

11. Principles for Assessing Public Policy Options   314

12. Chronically Ill Children in Families: Policy Choices   331
     and Recommendations

     References   361

     Name Index   391

     Subject Index   397

Foreword

From the heartlands of these United States come forth extraordinary creative efforts for children everywhere. No one personified these efforts with greater impact than Nicholas Hobbs. Advocacy for children should not be permitted to go out of style. We had a rich heritage of child advocates in the early decades of this century. I refer to the Jane Addamses, the Abbott and Breckenridge sisters, the Julia Lathrops, Florence Kelleys, and Alice Hamiltons who were so influential during that early period. They succeeded in establishing the United States Children's Bureau as a result of the recommendations of the first White House Conference on Children and Youth in 1909, the first child guidance clinics, the children's courts, the infant health and welfare stations, the first schools of social work, and they promoted legislation for the abolition of child labor. Those were vintage years for children! Indeed, the very institutions that they founded almost replaced individuals as advocates.

But not for Nicholas Hobbs. For him there was no rest as long as one child was troubled, neglected, or abused. He provided the leadership for the rest of us—over the years, in many ways, and in many forms. But let us have him speak for himself. At a

Note: This statement is a revised version of Julius B. Richmond's remarks at the dedication of the Nicholas Hobbs Laboratory of Human Development at George Peabody College, Vanderbilt University, on January 14, 1983.

conference sponsored by the Hogg Foundation of Texas, reflecting on social changes in our society, he observed,

> We are fiduciaries for our future common good, trustees of our most precious resource, the children of the nation. The concept of children as private property, exempt from formal community concern, must yield to a larger interest, our future as a people. We need a quickened community conscience responsive to the needs of all our children, rich and poor alike. And we need to find ways to serve children through strengthened families.

Nicholas Hobbs taught us that the welfare of the child and the family cannot be fragmented. Thus he led us through many advocacy efforts that have had a profound integrative impact on the lives of our people. And it is difficult to choose from among them. For example, he served as vice-chairman of the Joint Commission on Mental Health and Illness in the late 1950s and early 1960s, which gave rise to the Community Mental Health Centers Act and helped set in motion a revolution in the care of the mentally ill that is still in progress.

As a member of President Kennedy's Panel on Mental Retardation, he contributed to the establishment of the Mental Retardation Research Centers to further our knowledge and to further the development of the University Affiliated Facilities programs for the training of personnel to improve the care of retarded persons in our communities.

As vice-chairman of the Joint Commission on the Mental Health of Children, he was a force for improving programs and not only for building buildings; he insisted that health and mental health are indivisible; he called attention to the need for potent advocates for children at every level, but especially at the local level.

Successive administrations found Nicholas Hobbs an essential participant in major policy deliberations. By 1977 he was again on a Presidential Commission on Mental Health. The matter of updating the programs of the first commission was primary. A new Mental Health Systems Act emerged that was designed to enable communities to tailor their programs for the mentally ill in ways unique to their needs. It was enacted by Congress; and while current circumstances have impeded implementation, these proposals will be back.

And most recently Nicholas Hobbs served on the Select Panel for the Promotion of Child Health. His contributions helped in generating recommendations to assure that child health services of high quality become universally accessible. In the pluralism of our society he struggled to prevent individual vulnerable children from falling between the cracks.

From all of these ventures I observed that Nicholas was a national resource for children in action. The message in this observation is that leadership is effective when it is born of experience and tempered with a deep sense of history and respect for the views of others. He taught us how to translate rich local experience into recommendations for national policy.

And we send forth another message: that we must treasure and recognize inventors of institutional change. Nicholas Hobbs is not only what sociologists might call a change agent. He had what Erik Erikson would call a sense of generativity; when existing institutions were not meeting society's needs, he invented new ones. For example:

When research and training programs for the mentally retarded were needed, he invented the Kennedy Center at George Peabody College, of which the Nicholas Hobbs Laboratory of Human Development is a part.

When it was clear that there was tragic neglect of emotionally troubled children in our society, he invented Project Re-ED, and he demonstrated the value of perseverance in the study of children through his publication in 1982 of *The Troubled and Troubling Child,* a twenty-year follow-up of Project Re-ED.

When he perceived that children were being ill-served by our processes of classification, he invented the Project on the Classification of Exceptional Children, which published volumes of enduring value to all who work with children and families. And characteristically, he personally wrote the summary volume, which he poignantly entitled *The Futures of Children.* The first paragraph tells it all. He said,

This book is about the classification of exceptional children. Its title, *The Futures of Children,* implies that classification is

serious business. Classification can profoundly affect what happens
to a child. It can open doors to services and experiences the child
needs to grow in competence, to become a person sure of his worth
and appreciative of the worth of others, to live with zest and know
joy. On the other hand, classification, or inappropriate classification, or failure to get needed classification—and the consequences
that ensue—can blight the life of a child, reducing opportunity,
diminishing his competence and self-esteem, alienating him from
others, nurturing a meanness of spirit, and making him less a
person than he could become. Nothing less than the futures of
children is at stake.

     And when he felt the need for more sustained attention to
national public policy concerning families and children, he invented the Center for the Study of Families and Children within the
Vanderbilt Institute for Public Policy Studies.
     He also saw the need to develop more effective programs for
children with chronic illness—a sensitivity, in part, to the fact that
many of the acute disorders of childhood were being brought under
control. This volume, reporting these studies, will be an enduring
resource and guide for all who work with children with chronic
illnesses.
     Any one of these achievements would have been sufficient for
one career, but he encompassed them all!
     There is a conceptual inventiveness to all of these activities.
Each of these developments was far ahead of its time. Indeed, a few
years ago some of us were musing about this aspect of Nicholas's
career and concluded that if one wanted to know what the future
trends in child care and research programs would be, we should
look at what he was thinking and doing today. There is an element
of clairvoyance to how he moved over time.
     Underlying all of these remarkable abilities has been a
commitment to values—the highest values in our society as he
perceived them. These values begin with a deeply held conviction
that the proper nurturing of its children is the most basic value of
a society. This commitment caused him invariably to drive himself
beyond the call of duty. He always came to meetings having done
his homework and taking home more work than his share.

These values have been reflected in his international concerns. He believed that as an affluent society we should be prepared to help improve the lives of people everywhere. He demonstrated this concern by taking time from his usual activities, at the request of Sargent Shriver, to help establish the Peace Corps. He put in place selection and training processes that have stood the tests of time in those programs.

We treasure Nicholas's commitment to high intellectual standards—particularly through his long service to George Peabody College, and to Vanderbilt University, which he served with such distinction as provost. During his tenure as provost, in the period of great student unrest in this nation, I had occasion to talk with him (often far into the night) during meetings in Washington. He always expressed concern and respect for students and struggled hard to understand their ferment and discontent more deeply. He responded in most sensitive ways. The splendid record at Vanderbilt in dealing with these problems reflected in no small measure his perceptiveness and responsiveness.

The respect he held for every human being was evident in his long efforts for a truly integrated society, including his many interuniversity activities and his service on the Board of Trustees of Fisk University.

His capacity to contribute to the work of people in other disciplines was evident in his appointment to the faculty of medicine at Vanderbilt and by his election to membership in the Institute of Medicine of the National Academy of Sciences.

We treasure the values of Nicholas Hobbs; we treasure his capacity to serve all children and all families through research and scholarship, through education, and through service programs with creativity, generativity, and inventiveness.

This volume represents Nicholas Hobbs's last complete project and reflects his collaboration with colleagues James M. Perrin and Henry T. Ireys. It demonstrates again the role of Nicholas Hobbs in shaping public policy. Here, the issues raised by chronic illness in childhood as developed by the leading workers in the field are carefully redefined in a broad context, integrating the information known about them in a fashion that heightens public consciousness and broadens and deepens our knowledge base.

Underlying social values are delineated and broad principles to shape public policy are presented. From this flows guidance to help the nation respond to children and families in a more caring way.

Boston, Massachusetts   Julius B. Richmond, M.D.
August 1985   *John D. MacArthur Professor of*
                                 Health Policy
                                 Harvard University

Preface

This book presents the findings from a study of public policies affecting chronically ill children and their families. The chronic illnesses of childhood include many different conditions, some of them quite rare, many of them unfamiliar to the general public. Diabetes, severe asthma, leukemia, cystic fibrosis, sickle cell anemia, hemophilia: these are examples of chronic illnesses that strike children. Twenty-five years ago, a study of public policies affecting children with these illnesses would have been of little use. At that time, most chronically ill children faced the prospect of an early death. The illness took its course and there was little that medicine could do about it. Developments in basic science and in medical care over the last two decades have altered the situation entirely. The large majority of children with chronic illnesses now live well into adulthood.

Along with this remarkable progress have come new problems and demands. Families face years of financial and emotional burden from caring for their ill child; physicians trained to cure must learn new ways of treatment for a child with a long-term but incurable illness. Nurses, who previously focused on acute, in-hospital care, now work with families in many home and community settings to provide a wide array of both traditional and new long-term nursing services. Schools must now integrate into regular classrooms children with illnesses that are frightening to teachers and peers; communities seek ways of embracing these children;

society as a whole must discover how to pay for the ever-accelerating costs of their care.

For each illness, the number of affected children is small. Collectively, however, children with a severe, ongoing illness number over a million individuals, up to 2 percent of the nation's children. Since most of them live in families, the number of persons actually affected by the presence of a childhood chronic illness is far higher. Because of the complexity of their medical care and the broad array of services that they need, these children claim more financial, professional, and family resources than their numbers would suggest.

This book takes its place in the continuing public debate about medical care in this country. Unfortunately, the debate has often overlooked the children with whom this book is concerned. Although the public periodically hears from an organization that is championing a particular cause on behalf of one group of children, the general issues of caring for seriously ill children remain largely unknown. Moreover, chronically ill children have received relatively little sustained attention from policy makers. A patchwork of service and financing programs now exists to meet the needs of these children, but from a national perspective coverage is spotty, eligibility criteria uneven, and care disjointed. Among the tangle of programs, some families with a chronically ill child find what they need; others fail to do so, many of them defeated by health, school, and community programs ill-equipped to meet the needs of children with chronic illnesses. Even within the community of physicians, nurses, social workers, and other professionals concerned with child health care, children with serious health problems have often taken second place to other concerns pressing for national attention. Furthermore, programs (such as the Crippled Children's Services) that have historically focused on these children have largely escaped close evaluation. The time has come for policy makers to turn their attention to children who have chronic illnesses, to their families, and to supporting effective programs for them.

In the quest for developing an effective public response to the needs of these children, policy makers, professionals, and parents all have a similar task: finding and organizing the disparate information relevant to the problem. This book, we hope, will assist with this task by defining the various aspects of the problem; by examining the strengths and weaknesses in current patterns of care, financing, professional training, and research; by analyzing various policy options; and by specifying elements of the best choice.

The issues raised in the following chapters are sufficiently broad to require the attention of everyone concerned with the welfare of chronically ill children. Families, community leaders, legislative staff, pediatricians, social workers, public health officials, teachers, child health advocates, agency officials, and the many other lay and professional groups who work on behalf of these children will need to participate collectively in the development of reasoned and effective policy. This book has been written with all of these groups in mind.

That multiple groups must work collectively to address the problems that face these children and their families is reflected in the range of agencies that have supported this project. The initial grant (No. MCR-470444) was provided by the Office of Maternal and Child Health in the U.S. Department of Health and Human Services. Subsequently, the Office of Special Education and Rehabilitative Services in the U.S. Department of Education contributed substantially to the study's support. As the project moved toward its completion, the Robert Wood Johnson Foundation added funds to those available from the federal agencies for the partial dissemination of findings and recommendations through regional and state conferences. The conferences, held in every area of the country between 1982 and 1985, were attended by over one thousand persons, including state agency personnel, educators, legislators and legislative staff, nurses, mental health professionals, physicians, parents, lawyers, economists, epidemiologists, social workers, and child health advocates. The breadth of experience of the individuals who came to these conferences underscores the fact that a broad-based public response to chronic illness in childhood is possible.

Who are the children with chronic illness? What distinguishes them as a class of citizens worthy of special consideration in policy development? Chapter One addresses these and related questions. It presents brief summaries of eleven selected illnesses as a means of conveying the breadth of potential problems. The descriptions of these illnesses are presented as representative of the broader class of conditions. Despite the enormous variation in the underlying disease processes among the illnesses, for policy purposes, all children with chronic illness should be considered as part of a single class because this strengthens the likelihood of a coordinated national public policy effort.

Chapter Two takes the reader from an overview of childhood chronic illness to more specific information related to current patterns of care, how these patterns have evolved, and where the challenges lie ahead. Estimates of the numbers of affected children, the distribution of the illnesses, and the relationship between disease severity and medical care requirements are covered. Rarely do problems of national importance emerge suddenly, and the policy problems posed by childhood chronic illness are no exception. This chapter traces the evolution of improvements both in basic science and in health care delivery as a means of framing current patterns of care within a historical context.

Chapter Three tells about the reciprocal effects of chronic illness on child development, families, and communities. Most children and their families shoulder the burdens of a chronic illness remarkably well; many do not. However, the lives of almost all families are taxed unnecessarily by the perversity and capriciousness of health care systems, unpredictable public programs, and suspicious communities. This chapter portrays the specific issues that arise as children, families, and communities negotiate the demands of chronic illness.

The questions involved in educating chronically ill children in an appropriate fashion and preparing them for employment are addressed in Chapter Four. Traditional responses to ill children on the part of local school districts, together with legislatively mandated practices, create categories for educational placement that fit poorly with the actual educational needs of these children. Few programs currently account adequately for these needs.

The health care system itself is the subject of Chapter Five. The most striking characteristic of health care for chronically ill children is its inconsistency. Medical and health services vary enormously from one location to another. Even within one hospital, medical care may be superlative, but the accompanying supportive services dismal. A narrow vision of medical care, interprofessional issues, a single-disease orientation, poor training, and splintered advocacy efforts all contribute to unacceptable inconsistencies and barriers in the care of these children and families. New programs are emerging to address these problems, and the last section of this chapter describes several new efforts.

For the purposes of developing policy for chronically ill children, a knowledge of costs and financing is essential. Chapter Six presents estimates of the costs of care for these children and describes the sources of cost. Experts agree that these costs are high, but accurate estimates are surprisingly scarce. The currently available information is assembled in this chapter.

Chapter Seven deals with the financing of care. Private insurance, Medicaid, and special state programs all contribute to the financial support of these children's care. Despite the varied potential sources of payment, children often remain without coverage and many services needed by them and their families remain unavailable because no payment can be found. Recent initiatives in reforming the system of financing care threaten to ignore once again the needs of these children and their families.

Chapter Eight attends to a part of the problem often overlooked: the task of preparing health care professionals to assume new responsibilities. One of the most striking characteristics of a childhood chronic illness is its interrelationship with aspects of child development, family life, medical care, issues of medical ethics, cultural differences in beliefs about health and illness, and community acceptance. Professionals must acquire some facility in responding to all of these areas as they develop skills relevant to chronic illness care.

Research in childhood chronic illness, including a discussion of its past characteristics and future possibilities, is the focus of Chapter Nine. In the past, the majority of research support has gone to biomedical studies focused on specific diseases and on narrow medical problems. It is time to match support in this area with support for research in other promising areas, including health services, the interrelationship between development and illness, prevention of family and social problems, medical ethics, and improved strategies to measure outcome and family functioning. The chapter concludes with a discussion of general principles to guide research efforts.

Chapter Ten examines the role of values in the making of decisions regarding the care of chronically ill children and in allocating resources to support that care. Issues of values infuse every effort to assist children with special needs, yet often values remain unacknowledged or unexamined. This chapter lays out the nature of ethical decisions related to childhood chronic illness and how such decisions may be expressed through the allocation of resources.

Following directly from the discussion of values, Chapter Eleven presents general criteria and principles that can guide the development of policy options and that can assist in choosing among them. The principles are intended to underlie policies for chronically ill children regardless of the specific health conditions affecting them.

The final chapter presents a series of policy choices. These choices vary widely in terms of the extent of effort required to implement them and their relative strengths. To each option we apply with broad strokes the principles outlined in Chapter Eleven. The analyses lead to a strong endorsement of the option calling for a national, community-based program for chronically ill children and their families. The chapter discusses this option at length, detailing elements that such a program would include: an appropriately broad range of services, planning and coordination of care, establishing a community base, reasonable eligibility criteria and sufficient avenues for access to the program, and adequate financing. A family-centered, community-based approach would serve chronically ill children well and would lead to the health care that they and their families deserve.

This book provides a needed synthesis of the background and issues that affect the daily lives of children with chronic illnesses and their families. It comes at a time of major reconsideration of public responsibility for the health of mothers and children in general and for those citizens whose health conditions create high costs and great family burdens. The organization and financing of medical and health services are currently undergoing major transformations that may enhance or inhibit the healthy survival of chronically ill children. This book focuses on the special needs of the 1 to 2 percent of children in the United States with severe chronic health conditions and offers guidance to policy makers in legislative or executive positions, to health professionals who interact on a daily basis with these families, to the families themselves, and to other helping professionals, including teachers, who all form the environment that may best nurture chronically ill children and help them grow to their fullest potential.

Nashville, Tennessee   James M. Perrin, M.D.
August 1985   Henry T. Ireys, Ph.D.

Acknowledgments

The experience and wisdom of many individuals enriched this project. The most valuable help came from parents of children with a chronic illness and from the children themselves. Their willingness to tell us about their lives helped form the basis for this book. Their stories have enabled us to understand, however imperfectly, what it is like to live with or to be a child with a chronic illness. In Nashville, a group of parents of children with various chronic illnesses met with members of the staff on several occasions. Their comments and recommendations inform many sections of this book.

Several professional groups contributed substantially to the project's work. A distinguished National Advisory Committee provided wise counsel in the early conceptualization of the project. Later, collectively and as individuals, the committee members assisted in formulating the project's recommendations. The names of the members of the National Advisory Committee are listed at the end of these acknowledgments.

With the advice of I. Barry Pless, we organized the Research Consortium on Chronic Illness in Children in 1980. This group of research scientists studies the epidemiology of chronic illness, the impact of illness on family life, and the interaction between illness and development. The biennial meetings of the consortium were invaluable, both in keeping project staff abreast of research developments and in helping to relate empirical findings to policy issues.

With the assistance of Robert Haggerty and the William T. Grant Foundation, the consortium continued to meet after the completion of the Vanderbilt project.

A panel of representatives of federal agencies provided an essential understanding of current government programs relating to chronically ill children and of the problems and prospects that these programs face. The staff periodically consulted with representatives from several voluntary associations. Arthur Salisbury of the National Foundation–March of Dimes greatly assisted these efforts. The perspectives of both panels shaped our thinking in important ways, especially in the development of policy options.

Special thanks are owed to Frederick Robbins, for making available resources of the Institute of Medicine and for helping to orchestrate a major conference at the institute to disseminate the project's findings; to C. Arden Miller, for criticizing with precision early formulations of the project's recommendations and for general perceptive counsel; to Lee Schorr, who read the entire manuscript with great care and whose comments never failed to improve our work; to Vince Hutchins and Merle McPherson, of the Office of Maternal and Child Health in the U.S. Department of Health and Human Services, for assistance in contacting representatives of agencies, for access to their enormous wealth of knowledge on all matters governmental, and for their advice freely given and never imposed.

During the first three years of the project, a group at Vanderbilt University collaborated to gather the background material for the project. Samuel C. Ashcroft and Susie M. Baird, experts in the field of special education, contributed substantially to the analysis and issues presented in Chapter Four. Moreover, they gave initial shape to the concepts underlying policies and recommendations for the education of children with chronic illnesses. John Harkey, a sociologist, studied the epidemiology of childhood chronic illness and explored the genetic and environmental influences on illness. His thinking is reflected especially in Chapter Two. Carolyn Burr, a pediatric nurse practitioner, and Mark Merkens, a pediatrician, provided much insight into the nursing and medical issues that arise during the care of children with chronic illnesses. They were also instrumental in identifying problems in the organization of services and were especially sensitive to the struggles of families. Karen Weeks, an expert on tax policy, led the research group through the intricacies of financing health care for children. Chapter Seven reflects much of her thinking and her assistance. Alice Christensen helped to gather information on ethical issues and on family responses to a chronic illness. Her efforts made the writing of Chapters Three and Ten far more manageable than it might have been. Lisa Reichenbach helped with the difficult task of gathering the best information available on the costs of care. Robert Hauck, political scientist, broadened staff understanding of the political framework in which health policy has developed over the past few decades and explored prospects for the implementation of policy recommendations.

It is impossible to measure accurately the contributions of May W. Shayne to this project. From its inception, she assisted with its every phase. She devoted special attention to maintaining liaison with the representatives of federal agencies and voluntary associations, to assuring that Chapter Seven adequately covered its subject, and to planning conferences designed to disseminate the project's findings. Of equal importance, she maintained a firm grasp of the project's importance and its overall mission. Our efforts thrived as a result of her unfaltering commitment.

In the last two years of the project, Linda C. Moynihan, an extraordinarily effective child advocate, played a major role in organizing the state and regional conferences and in overseeing the final preparation of the manuscript. When our energy ran low, she replenished it with her optimistic, ebullient determination.

This project is no exception to the usual pattern of repeated revisions of the text. Over the study's lifetime, Marika Jacknycky Bertolini, Catherine Carroll, Pat Patton, Regina Perry, Diane Shrum, and Lottie Strupp worked with unusual ability and commitment to the project. But it was Dane Wadkins, cheerful even in the face of yet another revision, who saw the study to its completion. We are grateful for her unflagging patience and good will.

Nicholas Hobbs wisely saw the need for this study in the late 1970s. His efforts led to the original grant, which began under his direction in July 1980. Midway through the study, Nick died after a relatively brief illness. But his vision of the project remained alive in the ideas that he had so creatively nurtured among those who were to finish the study. His words continued to inspire, as they had for so many others before us. We hope that Nick's voice remains strong in this work, but we absolve him (and all our many colleagues) from any of our ungracious errors in logic or phrasing.

National Advisory Committee

Elizabeth M. Boggs, Ph.D.

Antoinette Eaton, M.D.
Children's Hospital
Columbus, Ohio

Rashi Fein, Ph.D.
Professor of Health Economics
School of Medicine
Harvard University

Loretta C. Ford, R.N., Ed.D., Dean
School of Nursing
University of Rochester

Frederick Green, M.D.
Department of Pediatrics
Children's Hospital National Medical Center

Robert J. Haggerty, M.D., President
William T. Grant Foundation

The Reverend Robert K. Massie, Jr.

Judith S. Mearig, Ph.D.
Graduate Program in School Psychology
St. Lawrence University

C. Arden Miller, M.D., Chairman
Department of Maternal and Child Health
University of North Carolina

T.M. (Jim) Parham, A.C.S.W.
University of Georgia

I. Barry Pless, M.D.
Montreal Children's Hospital

Frederick C. Robbins, M.D., President
Institute of Medicine

Lisbeth Bamberger Schorr, Co-Director
Child Health Outcome Project
University of North Carolina

Doris Tulcin, Chair
Research Development Council
Cystic Fibrosis Foundation

Note to the Reader

A major source of information upon which this book is based is a collection of works that were commissioned for the project "Public Policies Affecting Chronically Ill Children and their Families." The forty-two contributions are published separately in a volume titled *Issues in the Care of Children with Chronic Illness.* They present a systematic and reasonably comprehensive summary of current knowledge about children with severe chronic illnesses and their families and about the diverse policy issues related to them.

  Issues in the Care of Children with Chronic Illness is a companion to this book. The chapters provide guidance to anyone wishing to explore in depth policy issues and options concerning severe childhood chronic illness. Prepared by experts from many fields (physicians, nurses, social workers, educators, psychologists, and policy scholars), they summarize existing knowledge in a broad range of topical areas. There are chapters that deal with basic concepts about childhood chronic illness, epidemiology and demography, policy implications of eleven selected illnesses, professional activities on behalf of chronically ill children, educational opportunities and programs, organization and financing of services, and other topics.

  The chapters in *Issues in the Care of Children with Chronic Illness* are referenced throughout this volume, using the standard citation format of the author's last name and the year of publication, 1985. We list here, for the reader's convenience, the chapters in the companion volume:

Introduction
James M. Perrin, M.D.

Part I: Basic Concepts

1. The Constant Shadow: Reflections on the Life
   of a Chronically Ill Child
   Robert K. Massie, Jr., M. Div.

2. Impact on the Family of a Chronically Ill Child
   Carolyn Keith Burr, R.N., M.S.

3. Issues Common to a Variety of Illnesses
   I. Barry Pless, M.D., F.R.C.P.[C]
   James M. Perrin, M.D.

4. Paternalism and Autonomy in the Care
   of Chronically Ill Children
   Loretta Kopelman, Ph.D.

5. Genetic Strategies for Preventing
   Chronic Illnesses
   Neil A. Holtzman, M.D., M.P.H.
   Julius B. Richmond, M.D.

6. The State of Research on Chronically Ill Children
   Barbara Starfield, M.D., M.P.H.

**Part II: Chronic Childhood Illnesses:
Epidemiology, Demography, and Representative
Conditions**

7. Demography of Chronic Childhood Diseases
   Steven L. Gortmaker, Ph.D.

8. Juvenile Diabetes
   Allen Lee Drash, M.D.
   Nina Berlin

9. Neuromuscular Diseases
   Irene S. Gilgoff, M.D.
   Shelby L. Dietrich, M.D.

10. Cystic Fibrosis
Norman J. Lewiston, M.D.

11. Spina Bifida
Gary J. Myers, M.D.
Margaret Millsap, R.N., Ed.D.

12. Sickle Cell Anemia
Charles F. Whitten, M.D.
Eleanor N. Nishiura, Ph.D.

13. Congenital Heart Disease
Donald C. Fyler, M.D.

14. Chronic Kidney Diseases
Barbara Korsch, M.D.
Richard Fine, M.D.

15. Thalassemia and Hemophilia
Margaret W. Hilgartner, M.D.
Louis Aledort, M.D.
Patricia J. V. Giardina, M.D.

16. Leukemia
Thomas W. Pendergrass, M.D., M.S.P.H.
Ronald L. Chard, Jr., M.D.
John R. Hartmann, M.D.

17. Craniofacial Birth Defects
Donald W. Day, M.D.

18. Asthma
Fred Leffert, M.D.

Part III: Populations with Special Needs

19. Delivery of Care to Inner-City Children
with Chronic Conditions
Ruth E. K. Stein, M.D.
Dorothy Jones Jessop, Ph.D.

20. Special Problems of Chronic Childhood Illness
in Rural Areas
James M. Perrin, M.D.

**Part IV: Provision of Services
and Professional Training**

21. Interprofessional Issues in Delivering Services
to Chronically Ill Children and Their Families
Lorraine V. Klerman, Dr.P.H.

22. Medical Services
Michael Weitzman, M.D.

23. Training Physicians to Care for
Chronically Ill Children
*C. William Daeschner, Jr., M.D.
Mary C. Cerreto, Ph.D.*

24. Nursing Services
Debra P. Hymovich, Ph.D., R.N., F.A.A.N.

25. Training Nurses to Care for
Chronically Ill Children
Corinne M. Barnes, Ph.D., R.N., F.A.A.N.

26. Mental Health Issues and Services
*Dennis Drotar, Ph.D.
Marcy Bush, M.A.*

27. Training Psychologists to Work with
Chronically Ill Children
*Susan M. Jay, Ph.D.
Logan Wright, Ph.D.*

28. Training Social Workers to Aid
Chronically Ill Children and Their Families
*Claire Rudolph, M.S.W., Ph.D.
Virginia Andrews, M.S.W.
Kathryn Strother Ratcliff, Ph.D.
Dorothy Downes, R.N., M.S.W., M.P.A.*

29. Meeting the Service Needs
of Chronically Impaired Children:
Individual Portraits
*Tom Joe, M.A.
Cheryl Rogers, M.Ed.*

Part V: Educational and Vocational Issues

30. Public School Programs for
Chronically Ill Children
Deborah Klein Walker, Ed.D.
Francine H. Jacobs, Ed.D.

31. Need-Based Educational Policy
for Chronically Ill Children
Susie M. Baird, M.Ed.
Samuel C. Ashcroft, Ed.D.

32. Cognitive Development of
Chronically Ill Children
Judith S. Mearig, Ph.D.

33. Psychosocial Development of
Chronically Ill Children
Phyllis R. Magrab, Ph.D.

34. Employment Opportunities and Services
for Youth with Chronic Illnesses
Paul Hippolitus, M.A.

**Part VI: Programs and Organizations
Serving Chronically Ill Children and Their Families**

35. Public Programs for Crippled Children
Arthur J. Lesser, M.D.

36. Integrating Federal Programs at the State Level
Antoinette Parisi Eaton, M.D.
Kathryn K. Peppe, R.N., M.S.
Kathleen Bajo, M.S.

37. Self-Help and Mutual Aid Groups
Leonard D. Borman, Ph.D.

38. Charitable Associations
Carl Milofsky, Ph.D.
Julie T. Elworth, M.A.

39. Professional Organizations
Morris Green, M.D.

Part VII: Economic Considerations

40. Health Care Expenditures
for Children with Chronic Illnesses
John A. Butler, Ed.D.
Peter Budetti, M.D., J.D.
Margaret A. McManus, M.H.S.
Suzanne Stenmark, M.S.
Paul W. Newacheck, M.P.P.

41. Parental Opportunity Costs and Other Economic
Costs of Children's Disabling Conditions
David S. Salkever, Ph.D.

42. Private Health Insurance and
Chronically Ill Children
Karen Weeks, M.A.

Epilogue
James M. Perrin, M.D.
Henry T. Ireys, Ph.D.
Nicholas Hobbs, Ph.D.
May W. Shayne, A.C.S.W.
Linda C. Moynihan

The Authors

Nicholas Hobbs was professor emeritus of psychology at Vanderbilt University and senior research associate at the Vanderbilt Institute for Public Policy Studies prior to his death in January 1983. He was awarded the B.A. degree from The Citadel, the M.A. and Ph.D. degrees from Ohio State University, and honorary degrees from the University of Louisville, The Citadel, and Université Paul Valéry in Montpellier, France.

Hobbs taught at the Teachers College of Columbia University, Louisiana State University, and George Peabody College for Teachers. At George Peabody College for Teachers, he was the first director of the John F. Kennedy Center for Research on Education and Human Development. He was provost of Vanderbilt University from 1967 to 1975, then joined the Vanderbilt Institute for Public Policy Studies, where he was director of the Center for the Study of Families and Children for five years. He served on a number of regional and national bodies concerned with children, health, and education; was the first director of selection and research for the Peace Corps; was a member of the advisory committee on child development of the National Research Council; and was a member of the Select Panel for the Promotion of Child Health established by Congress in 1979. For the American Psychological Association, Hobbs chaired the committee that first developed the *Ethical Standards of Psychologists* and, in 1966, served as the association's president. In 1980, he received the American Psychological Association's Award for Distinguished Professional Contributions and the

xxxvii

award for Distinguished Contributions to Psychology in the Public Interest.

Hobbs's previously published books include *The Futures of Children* (1975), *Issues in the Classification of Children* (1975), *The Troubled and Troubling Child* (1982), and *Strengthening Families* (1984).

James M. Perrin is senior research associate at the Institute for Public Policy Studies and assistant professor of pediatrics at Vanderbilt University. He received his B.A. degree (1964) from Harvard College in chemistry and his M.D. degree (1968) from Case Western Reserve University. Perrin did his pediatric residency and fellowship training at the University of Rochester. He then became medical director of the Oak Orchard Community Health Center in Brockport, New York, while continuing teaching and research at Rochester. Since coming to Vanderbilt University in 1977, he has headed the Division of General Pediatrics and directed the Vanderbilt Primary Care Center, a multidisciplinary teaching and research program of the School of Medicine.

Perrin's research interests are in child health, behavioral medicine, and health policy. His publications include work on middle ear disease in childhood, problems of lead in the environment, policies relating to high-cost illness in childhood, and distribution of health manpower.

Henry T. Ireys is assistant professor of pediatrics and psychiatry at Albert Einstein College of Medicine in New York City. He received his B.A. degrees from Williams College (1975) in psychology and English and his M.A. (1978) and Ph.D. (1979) degrees from Case Western Reserve University in clinical psychology. In 1979 he was awarded a National Institutes of Mental Health-supported postdoctoral fellowship in public policy at the Institute for Public Policy Studies, Vanderbilt University. He is currently a codirector of the Preventive Intervention Research Center for Child Health at Albert Einstein.

Ireys's primary policy research activities concern state programs for chronically ill and handicapped children. He is also investigating interventions designed to prevent emotional problems in children with a chronic illness and in their families.

Ireys contributed a background paper to the Report of the Select Panel for the Promotion of Child Health (1980) and currently serves on advisory committees to New York State's program in Coordination of Care for Chronically Ill Children and to the project at Albert Einstein entitled Health Financing for Chronically Ill and Disabled Children.

Chronically Ill Children and Their Families

Problems, Prospects, and Proposals
from the Vanderbilt Study

1

Introduction:
Severe and Chronic Illness
in Childhood

Children who suffer from severe chronic illness are a neglected group in our society. Their suffering, the heavy burdens they and their families bear, the human resources lost to us all are matters largely unknown to the general public. Awareness of a particular chronic disease may occasionally be heightened briefly by efforts of a voluntary group to raise money on behalf of children with "its disease." But interest is fleeting. Chronically ill children live out their lives in a twilight zone of public understanding. As a consequence, our nation, often attentive to problems of children and families, has lagged grievously in its response to the urgent needs of children with long-term health conditions. In this book, we attempt to make available to caring citizens and to the shapers and makers of policy the information they need to address effectively one of the nation's least known but most urgent health problems. We believe that an informed people, with a quickened conscience and a heightened sense of community, will insist that continued neglect of chronically ill children and their families is intolerable and that there must be a public response adequate to address the catastrophic consequences of chronic illness in childhood.

1

The Chronic Illnesses of Childhood

The focus of our attention is on chronic and severe illnesses of childhood. The category is wide and diverse, encompassing many rare diseases including juvenile rheumatoid arthritis, phenylketonuria, diabetes, asthma, agammaglobulinemia, sickle cell anemia, thalassemia, and leukemia. More or less arbitrarily, we have selected eleven conditions that are representative of the severe chronic illnesses of childhood: juvenile-onset diabetes, muscular dystrophy, cystic fibrosis, spina bifida, sickle cell anemia, congenital heart disease, chronic kidney diseases, hemophilia, leukemia, cleft palate, and severe asthma. These conditions, which include some of those most prevalent in childhood, are treated as marker diseases; that is, they have characteristics that make them representative of the total range of such illnesses. Although we do not describe the literally hundreds of exotic diseases to which children are susceptible (for example, the rare immunodeficiency diseases that require a child to be isolated from all possible sources of infection), the concern of this book includes this wide array of chronic illnesses in childhood.

From 10 to 15 percent of children in the United States have some chronic health impairment (Gortmaker, 1985; Pless and Roghmann, 1971). Most chronic illness is mild, and children with mild illness are in general reasonably well cared for by family physicians, pediatricians, or public health nurses, with the occasional guidance of other specialists. The inadequacies in their care reflect the inadequacies of the nation's health care system in general. Our concern is with the extreme end of the distribution of chronically ill children—with perhaps 1 percent of the childhood population whose problems are so special that the health system falters and extraordinary efforts are required to make it work even moderately well.

The extent of a child's problem has only a modest relationship to the severity of a child's condition. Some children with severe disease in a physical or physiological sense will have little impairment of their ability to participate in usual activities with healthy children. Other children with only mild physical illness find their lives greatly affected by disease (Pless and Pinkerton, 1975). Overall, chronic illness will interfere with the child's or family's functioning in numerous ways.

Considered separately, each disease is relatively rare and occurs in a small percentage of the childhood population. Taken together, however, at least one million children have severe diseases (no small number), and each child may be ill for a long time. Each afflicted child belongs to a family, and each member of the family inevitably shares in the child's suffering. When we write of children with severe chronic illnesses, we thus refer indirectly to at least three million family members who may face each day heavy of heart, burdened with caring responsibilities, wracked by anxiety and sometimes by guilt, strapped by unpredicted expenses and possible economic ruin, and facing a future that often has only one certainty: the premature death of the child. Thus the emphasis on families in this book.

A systematic review of the needs of children with severe chronic illnesses and of their families is important and timely for several reasons. First, chronically ill children have not received the same measure of public concern that has appropriately been afforded other groups of handicapped children and youth. Second, many chronically ill children who would have died young are living longer, largely as a result of dramatic advances in medical care and in the organization of services. Most children with severe chronic illnesses now survive to adulthood. Third, new technologies, which have done much to improve the lives of many families, also challenge the boundaries of reasonable concern for quality of life, and attention has recently been sharply focused on public and private responsibilities in the prolongation of life or in the withholding of certain medical treatments. Fourth, expenditures for the care of children with chronic illnesses constitute a major portion of the child health dollar (Butler and others, 1985), and little attention has been paid to the options available for the distribution of resources for the health needs of chronically ill children and their families.

There are other important sources of childhood disability, such as severe and catastrophic trauma—from injuries in the home and in sports; from accidents of automobiles, motorcycles, bicycles, or skateboards; or from assault. Many children with traumatic injuries may suffer acutely and require long-term care, thus placing grave emotional and economic burdens on their families. We have excluded this group of children in order to limit a topic already quite broad. Further, childhood trauma raises policy issues of a special character (such as those of prevention of child abuse, gun control, and the design of vehicles and highways) that, again, would too greatly expand our task.

Other children with handicaps offer pressing concerns. These children (for example, those with mental health disorders or developmental disabilities such as cerebral palsy) have benefited a great deal from public concern, and attention to their needs has led to much knowledge applicable as well to the families of chronically ill children. Many of the problems and policy issues are the same.

The experience with Public Law 94-142 (the Education for All Handicapped Children Act) has been instructive. Public attention to improved educational opportunities for children arose from a concern for the civil rights of handicapped persons. This focus has taught the nation much about the potential stigma and isolation of children with special needs (Gliedman and Roth, 1980), about the culture of handicap, and about the effects of an ill child on the whole family. The public effort in support of this law also showed that diverse groups can form coalitions and that parent groups can be effective. The legislation demonstrated that new social arrangements are possible for handicapped children, exemplified by the concepts of the individual educational plan and the least restrictive environment. Moreover, implementation of this educational policy highlighted two problematic issues: that professional concerns rather than family needs often drive programs and that there are limits to what can be achieved through legislation. The best of policies fail to eliminate all the effects of a handicap.

Unlike children with mental retardation and related developmental impairments, children with chronic physical illnesses have been relatively neglected in considerations of public policy. For example, the parents and policy makers who developed the state and federal programs for the education of handicapped children largely overlooked the population of chronically ill children (Walker and Jacobs, 1985). A careful review of pertinent federal and state policies reveals that in the last twenty years chronically ill children have shared in relatively little of the sustained attention given to children with other handicapping conditions, such as mental retardation. Except for the provision of specialized medical care to indigent children with a chronic illness, government programs have largely passed these children by. The reasons for this neglect are unclear. Perhaps few individuals realize how many children and families are involved when the chronic illnesses of children are considered as a whole. Perhaps the public has remained uninformed about the severe consequences of a chronic illness on child development and family life. Few policy makers have taken an accurate measure of the problem.

Chronic Illnesses Described

The chronic conditions of childhood show much variation and can be classified in several ways—age of onset; whether the disease is fatal; whether the course of the disease is stable, downhill, or tending to diminish after a few years; whether it affects mobility or the child's learning abilities to name a few (Pless and Perrin, 1985). Diabetes and asthma, for example, are predominantly medical in their care. Spina bifida, cleft lip and cleft palate, or congenital heart diseases require surgical therapies. Still others, such as end-stage renal disease, sickle cell anemia, or hemophilia, entail long-term care that must meet frequent daily or weekly demands of illness. Others, such as cystic fibrosis and muscular dystrophy, markedly curtail a normal lifespan despite great advances in medical care.

Because the chronic illnesses used here as general markers of chronic illness are so poorly understood by citizens and policy makers alike, we describe certain characteristics of each disease. The sketches are brief. They touch on the most salient aspects of each condition, including both physiological aspects and the consequences of illness for the child and family and for such public institutions as hospitals, schools, and places of employment. They invite consideration of the kinds of responses the larger community should make as a matter of public policy. These brief sketches are supplemented by more detailed descriptions and thorough analyses in Hobbs and Perrin (1985).

Juvenile-Onset Diabetes. Juvenile-onset diabetes results from an insufficient secretion of insulin by the pancreas. Well-known in its adult form, its manifestation in children is unfamiliar and presents special problems (Drash and Berlin, 1985). For example, adults may attain sufficient insulin and sugar control by oral medications and diet; children, however, must meet their total needs for insulin by injections one or more times a day. Control of juvenile-onset diabetes requires a precise balance of diet, exercise, and insulin (hard to achieve with young children and often extremely difficult with adolescents) and urine or blood tests two or three times daily to monitor sugar levels. Failure to maintain this rigorous regimen may have serious consequences requiring hospitalization. The disease has a hereditary component but may require some precipitating event such as a viral illness. Onset and diagnosis can occur soon after birth but usually peak in late childhood and early adolescence. Some children achieve good control and appear quite normal; others have great difficulty and require frequent emergency treatment. In its early stages, diabetes may cause dizziness, weight loss, fatigue, excessive thirst, and even coma.

Even when their diabetes is well controlled, children still need to monitor closely the levels of sugar in their blood and to adjust their diet to different levels of physical activity. Snacks may be needed, often during hours when school authorities discourage the presence of food. In its later stages, diabetes may affect one or more of several major organ systems (kidney, heart, eyes) and lead to death. Although essentially all children with diabetes survive to adulthood, their average life expectancy is markedly reduced. Increasing responsibility for care falls to these children as they grow. During adolescence, issues of dependence and independence may lead to serious problems of compliance and to greater risk of mental health problems. The emotional burdens of diabetes on child and family are heavy, and the cost of treatment is more than many families can manage. Health insurance may be difficult or impossible to obtain, and older adolescents and young adults with diabetes may experience discrimination in seeking employment.

Asthma. Asthma is a chronic lung disease characterized by a high degree of bronchial sensitivity to many different stimuli. It primarily affects children and adolescents, although it can occur or recur throughout life. Although death from asthma is now rare, the disease is one of the major causes of health impairment in childhood. It is the most frequent cause of lost school days due to health (Parcel and others, 1979), and it imposes heavy burdens, including substantial monetary costs, on child and family. Yet it is one of the most treatable of the severe and chronic illnesses of childhood. Asthma and diabetes are similar in that they have few visible manifestations and their treatment is medical rather than surgical.

Asthma is the most common long-term physical disorder of childhood, affecting between 3 and 5 percent of the childhood population (Williams and McNicol, 1975). Most children have mild cases of asthma; episodes occur once or twice a year, require a minimum of medical care, and leave the child and family unhindered by health problems through the rest of the year. Children with mild illness may have only a few episodes during their lifetime. Severe disease afflicts between 5 and 10 percent of children with asthma. These children are subject to frequent hospitalizations, many unpredictable attacks, and impairment of lung capacity between attacks. They frequently must take daily medications, some of which may cause nausea and other uncomfortable symptoms.

Asthma is polygenic in origin. In some patients, there is clear evidence of a genetic origin with a strong family history of the disease. In other patients, environmental factors are important in the origin of the disease and in its management. Asthma has been widely regarded as a psychosomatic disorder or as an allergic disease, but neither view explains all cases. The most promising contemporary concept is that asthma results from an imbalance in autonomic nervous system function that leads to hyperreactivity of lung tissue to a number of stimuli, some of which can be allergic, others psychosomatic and stress related, and still others directly environmental (Leffert, 1985).

Although prevention of asthma itself remains an elusive goal, prevention and treatment of attacks can often be accomplished with knowledgeable and skillful health care. There are three general approaches to treatment: environmental modification to prevent contact with allergens and irritants such as smoke, immunotherapy (allergy shots) to reduce allergic sensitivity, and medications. Evidence for the efficacy of allergy shots is somewhat limited, and the procedure commits a family to the high expense of initial allergy testing and both child and family to frequent office visits (often weekly) for injections. Several new drugs and the improved monitoring of a number of older ones have led to great improvement in the management of asthma.

Because asthma accounts for a large amount of illness-related school absenteeism, affected children may fall behind in their school work. In most school systems, children become eligible for home-based educational services only after having missed a certain number of consecutive school days, usually two or four weeks. The child with asthma characteristically has frequent brief absences and thus is ineligible for compensatory services.

For the child and family, perhaps the most compelling issue of asthma is its unpredictability—not knowing when an episode may interfere with a child's participation in a special event or favorite sport, not knowing when an attack will necessitate an expensive emergency room visit or costly hospitalization.

Spina Bifida (Myelomeningocele). Spina bifida or myelomeningocele results from improper closure of the spinal column during fetal life. Although its cause remains obscure, there is increasing evidence that environmental and nutritional factors play a major role. Prenatally, the condition can be detected, with high but not perfect accuracy, by a combination of blood tests and examination of amniotic fluid. Routine screening has been instituted in some countries especially in Scandinavia.

At the place where normal closure of the spinal column is interrupted, two phenomena occur that affect the growing child. First, certain nervous tissue elements adhere to surrounding bony structures and interfere with the normal growth of nervous tissue and bony spinal column, which develop at different rates. Many afflicted infants develop hydrocephalus, a blockage of the normal drainage of fluids bathing the brain. The second phenomenon at the site of the spinal defect is an interruption in the nervous system elements that allow the brain to control bodily functions below the site of the defect. Thus, children with this condition may have difficulties with movement of their lower extremities; this can vary from poor coordination to complete inability to use their legs. In addition, they may have bowel problems and loss of bladder control that lead to fecal and urinary incontinence.

The condition, although resulting basically from a single problem in intrauterine development, causes major effects in a number of organs (Myers and Millsap, 1985). The child and family are seen by many health care providers, including pediatricians, physical therapists, neurologists, neurosurgeons, social workers, urologists, psychologists, and orthopedists. The child may take several different medications, undergo multiple surgical procedures, and need physical and occupational therapy. Children are often wheelchair-bound or dependent on braces or crutches. Their incontinence leads to the need for diapers well beyond infancy and in some cases for life. To maintain best urinary function, children may need frequent care by others, including parents at home or nurses in school. Finally, children with myelomeningocele are at higher risk of developmental retardation than able-bodied children.

The burdens on family and public institutions can be enormous. The cost of health care can be very high, with many operations (especially in the first few years of life) and the need for appliances and wheelchairs to aid mobility. Children face difficulties with access to appropriate schooling both because of physical barriers and because of limitations of adequate school personnel to deal with the essential daily and hourly nursing services sometimes needed.

The most promising element of care of children with spina bifida is the suggestion that the condition itself may be preventable through improved nutrition of the mother during pregnancy (Smithells and others, 1981; Stein and others, 1982). Once present, there is no way of curing it, although excellent medical and surgical care in collaboration with adequate family support can help families best care for their child.

Cleft Palate and Other Craniofacial Anomalies. The craniofacial anomalies represent a collection of defects in the normal formation of the face and related structures. Some of the conditions that cause craniofacial anomalies are genetic. The degree of problem varies from minimal abnormalities in the formation of the soft palate (roof of the mouth) not visible at birth, to larger openings (clefts) involving palate, jaw, and lip, to even greater abnormalities in the formation of visible bony structures of the face.

The delivery of the child with a significant craniofacial anomaly creates special problems for the family, which must now adapt to the problem of disfigurement of the face, an area of great contact between the child and family. A cleft palate may cause special problems in the interactions between a mother and her infant. Nursing may be especially difficult with a baby who regurgitates milk through the nose or who has trouble sucking because of the opening in the palate. These children are also at high risk of middle-ear infections and of hearing loss.

Some craniofacial anomalies can be easily repaired by surgery; others require many surgical procedures and still leave the child with a face quite different from that of other children. As with spina bifida, a major craniofacial anomaly entails many hospitalizations, especially in the first few years of life. The absence of normal palate function creates great impediments to the development of normal speech, and these children usually need intensive speech therapy.

In some parts of the country, there exist a few exemplary team care programs designed for children with craniofacial anomalies and their families. Although these efforts have greatly aided parents to care for their own children, the vast majority of children with cleft palates and related conditions do not have access to multidisciplinary services (Day, 1985).

Congenital Heart Diseases. Congenital heart diseases include a wide variety of structural anomalies in the development of the heart. Although some of these conditions are uniformly fatal, the large majority of children with congenital heart disease can now undergo successful surgical repair of the heart defect (Fyler, 1985). Some heart problems cause babies to appear blue (cyanotic) because blood that would normally return to the lungs is instead diverted, without adequate oxygen, to the rest of the body. In a normal heart, blood pumped from the body to the lungs is kept separate from oxygen-rich blood that is taken from the lungs and then distributed to the rest of the body. Some congenital heart defects, however, create connections between the two systems allowing oxygen-poor blood to pass to areas from which it is normally excluded. Surgery to repair these conditions is often complex and is best carried out in centers that have frequent experience with heart surgery. Children who are blue at or shortly after birth are at especially high risk, primarily because the blood being sent to their vital organs has insufficient oxygen. Blue babies born in small community hospitals need quick referral to a center that can provide them with either palliative or corrective surgery.

The costs of surgery for many of these heart conditions are extremely high. For some children, available operations make them better but fail to cure them of their basic problem. These children often face restrictions on their growth and activities and an uncertain future because of greater risks of serious infections and long-term heart and lung problems. For many other children, prospects have dramatically improved because operations are now available that essentially restructure their hearts to normal patterns. These families, too, face uncertainties, however, because many corrective operations cannot be performed in infancy but must wait until the child has reached adequate size. Concerns about the child's survival of the operation are a difficult burden for many families. Although many children may have no demonstrable cardiovascular problems after the operation, parents often feel that they must still protect a child from overexertion. Thus, growing children may face restrictions (appropriate or not) placed by parents or caretakers on the child's daily activities.

Most operations appear free of lasting harmful side effects. Yet it is unclear whether the correction is permanent or whether children who survive to middle age will have some new heart disease related to the healed scars from their original surgery. Children who have survived their operation seem in general to be able to lead fully normal lives; yet at this time, information regarding the long-term risk for these children is unavailable. Partly because of this uncertainty, there remain barriers to insurability for these children as they become young adults.

Leukemia. Leukemia is the most common cancer of childhood. In its most typical form, it starts with anemia, weight loss, and at times bleeding. The cause of leukemia remains obscure, although increasing evidence points to a viral cause for at least some forms (Pendergrass, Chard, and Hartmann, 1985). In leukemia, cells that would usually differentiate into normal white cells in the bloodstream multiply instead in excessive amounts. These cells often impair the individual's ability to make other normal blood components and may lead to the growth of the abnormal cells in many different organs in the body, especially the central nervous system and, in boys, the testes.

The care of children with leukemia has improved dramatically in recent years. Where the diagnosis of leukemia in childhood little more than a decade ago almost always meant a fatal outcome, the majority of children now achieve long-term survival without evident signs of still having leukemia. The improvements in long-term outcome have resulted largely from the careful study of new medications, primarily under the auspices of the National Cancer Institute. Well-organized, sophisticated studies involving many medical centers across the country have led to identification and careful testing of new drugs and radiation procedures to treat leukemia. Children with leukemia nevertheless face frequent hospitalizations and need large amounts of medication and radiation therapy that may cause them to feel sick or to lose their hair. The medications are very expensive, although many families receive drugs from research centers supported by the National Cancer Institute and do not pay for them directly. Other costs to families can be enormous, however, and include travel to and from the hospital for twice-weekly injections, frequent hospitalizations, and costly antibiotics necessary to treat or prevent infection, especially when the child's resistance is low because of the illness itself or medications.

Families of children with leukemia face tremendous uncertainty. Will the medications work or will the cancer progress despite them? If the child gets better once, will there be a recurrence or a fatal relapse? What can be expected about the health, as adults, of children who have survived for a number of years without continuing signs of the disease? Will they suffer recurrences or long-term consequences of their early therapy, including the radiation and the very powerful medications that were used to rid them of the leukemia?

Hemophilia. Hemophilia is a genetically transmitted disease in which the absence of an important blood clotting factor leads to episodes of uncontrolled bleeding. The disease occurs almost entirely in males but is genetically transmitted from mothers, who are carriers of the disease. Although some bleeding episodes result from direct injury, the large majority are spontaneous with no apparent preceding injury. Bleeding may be into joints, especially elbows, ankles, and knees, and can cause a painful arthritis of these joints that at times necessitates orthopedic surgery to improve joint function. Pain can be severe and persistent enough to require potent painkillers, and teenagers and young adults are at risk of narcotic addiction. The average child with hemophilia has a bleeding episode approximately twice a month.

Hemophilia, too, is a condition marked by unpredictability. Parents, especially mothers, often face feelings of guilt about their role in causing their child's illness. Even without such feelings, they face the difficult parental task of determining appropriate autonomy versus safeguards against bleeding for their child. As with other genetic diseases transmitted in this way, there is a 50 percent risk of further boys in the family having the disease, and a second pregnancy may occur prior to the diagnosis of the first child.

In the past decade, with the development of a number of blood products that can be used as replacement for the missing clotting factor, treatment of hemophilia has improved dramatically (Hilgartner, Aledort, and Giardina, 1985). Such materials can be administered at home, either by parents or by the child himself, whereas in the past, frequent hospitalizations were necessary for the management of the bleeding episode. With fewer and less severe bleeding episodes, the need for surgical treatment of joint problems has also decreased. Although the total cost of care has decreased greatly as a result of home-based care replacing expensive hospital care, families with children with hemophilia still face high costs that are partly related to the high cost of the replacement materials. Furthermore, there are risks, including hepatitis and AIDS (acquired immunodeficiency syndrome), in the administration of some replacement materials. A few patients develop antibodies to the usual replacement materials and require a much more expensive product to stop a major bleeding episode. For these children, the cost of materials for just one episode may run into thousands of dollars.

Hemophilia, then, is a chronic condition, characterized by unpredictable bleeding and risks of developing joint dysfunction and pain, for which medical care has vastly improved in the past several years. New therapies that allow many people with hemophilia to live relatively normal lives also carry risks of major secondary diseases. The costs of care are high, and the unpredictability and risks of other complications are always present for these children and their families.

End-Stage Renal Disease. End-stage renal disease (ESRD) is an extremely severe complication of a variety of conditions that affect the kidneys. Prior to the introduction of hemodialysis and kidney transplants in the early 1960s, ESRD was invariably fatal. Since that time, survival has improved tremendously, and major kidney centers now report a five-year survival rate of 70 to 95 percent (Korsch and Fine, 1985). There is little apparent overall difference in survival rates between dialysis and transplantation, but there are large variations in survival depending on such factors as age, cause of renal failure, and personality characteristics of the child.

In the United States, the preferred mode of therapy for children is transplantation rather than dialysis. On the average, transplants from cadavers are less successful than living donor transplants, and first-graft survival is lower with cadaver transplants. Approximately one-third of those children who survive the first procedure need an additional transplant. As with hemophilia, the care of children with end-stage renal disease requires careful collaboration between medical and surgical specialists, here pediatric nephrologists and kidney surgeons.

Dialysis is a method of replacing kidney function by using an external filtering system to remove body waste products. In one form (peritoneal dialysis), fluid is injected into the abdominal space and then drawn off as a means of removing body wastes. In hemodialysis, blood is withdrawn from the blood vessels, passed through a filtering mechanism, and then returned. In either case, the child may undergo several treatments per week, sometimes at home and at other times in a hospital outpatient setting. The frequent procedures often cause stress, both psychological and metabolic, at times of sufficient degree to lead the child to commit suicide through stopping treatment.

Transplants present a different series of stresses for the child and family. Immunosuppressive drugs decrease the likelihood of rejection of the transplanted kidney but also create risks of serious infections and may lead to marked changes in body shape and appearance. Transplantation itself is very costly and requires lengthy hospitalization.

There are no known preventions for these chronic kidney diseases. For those children whose disease begins in infancy, there is a great risk of significant growth failure. These children may be tiny and may have major bony abnormalities because their kidneys fail to metabolize bone minerals properly.

The group of chronic kidney diseases represents a situation of great stress for the child and family. Again, uncertainty about the outcome and the risk of early death aggravate the stress. The development of new and effective, albeit very expensive, technologies has meant that a number of children who would have certainly died from their kidney disease are now able to live and to function normally.

Sickle Cell Anemia. Sickle cell anemia results from an abnormality in the structure of the main oxygen-carrying compound in the red blood cell (hemoglobin). When the oxygen available to the red cell is diminished, the abnormal hemoglobin molecule changes shape and makes the red cell change from the usual disk shape to a jagged irregular shape called a sickle cell. Sickled cells pass through veins and smaller blood vessels much less well than do normally shaped cells. Blood vessels may become blocked with collections of abnormally shaped blood cells. Areas of the body supplied by those blood vessels may then be damaged or destroyed by lack of adequate oxygen. Patients with sickle cell anemia are at risk of infarct (destruction by lack of oxygen) of almost any organ in the body. Children with sickle cell anemia are especially susceptible to certain kinds of bacteria that can cause bone infections and meningitis (Whitten and Nishiura, 1985).

Sickle cell anemia is transmitted genetically, with each parent supplying half of the needed gene material. Parents at risk of having a child with sickle cell anemia can be identified because their blood will sickle under laboratory conditions although not in usual life states (sickle cell trait). In addition, sickle cell anemia can be diagnosed in utero. The diagnosis occurs mainly among black populations. There is a risk of recurrence in future children in the family, and diagnosis of the first affected child may have been made after a second pregnancy. During the first several months of life, children with sickle cell anemia are often without symptoms because they continue to have a special fetal hemoglobin that does not have a sickling tendency. When this hemoglobin is replaced by sickle hemoglobin, the child begins to develop symptoms.

In addition to their tendency to block passage to blood vessels, sickle cells have a shorter life span than normal red blood cells. The body attempts to compensate by increasing its production of red cells, but production is usually insufficient to meet the rate of breakdown. Thus children with sickle cell anemia are anemic. There are numerous other complications of the disease, including diminished growth and late onset of puberty.

There is no known cure for sickle cell anemia. Although several treatment methods have been proposed as ways to protect the cell from sickling, none so far have proved successful. Some infections caused by a particular group of organisms can be partly prevented through vaccination against this group. Although sickle cell anemia is compatible with a normal life span and most children survive to adulthood, on the average the life span is significantly shortened. Moreover, children can be severely debilitated from their disease. Children with sickle cell anemia have frequent and unpredictable hospitalizations, which are usually associated with significant pain requiring potent painkillers.

Cystic Fibrosis. Cystic fibrosis is another genetically transmitted condition. It causes major chronic lung disease and recurrent lung infections. Both can be very difficult to treat, although longevity of children with cystic fibrosis has greatly improved in the last ten to twenty years. The usual cause of death is deteriorating lung function with ultimate respiratory failure. Present average life span for a child with cystic fibrosis is about twenty years (Lewiston, 1985).

Lacking the digestive enzymes normally produced by the pancreas, children with cystic fibrosis frequently have problems with absorbing food. Usually the defect can be corrected by replacing the enzyme with medications. Most males with cystic fibrosis are sterile because of blockage of the tube that allows sperm to pass out of the testicle.

Usually the diagnosis of cystic fibrosis is made during the first two years of life and is based on the child's poor weight gain or frequent lung infections. Although there is no cure for the disease, its care has been greatly improved through comprehensive treatment programs that include pancreatic enzyme replacement, frequent use of antibiotics, and physical and respiratory therapy to keep lungs as clear and functional as possible.

As with most other genetic diseases, younger brothers and sisters are at risk of developing the disease, although (as with sickle cell disease) they may have been conceived or born prior to the diagnosis of the disease in an older sibling. Children with cystic fibrosis are frequently hospitalized. Even at home, they need extra equipment, mostly to aid their respiratory care. Parents become intimately involved with the care of the child with cystic fibrosis and usually take responsibility for frequent treatments to aid the child's breathing. Medications, special diets, and respiratory equipment can be expensive, adding to the family's already tremendous burdens of daily care. As with efforts to combat other chronic conditions, a number of exemplary cystic fibrosis centers have developed across the country. Excellent interdisciplinary care is available to children and families fortunate to live near the best centers, and the quality and length of life of children seen in these centers have greatly improved. For children living at great distances from such centers or otherwise lacking access to them, the outlook is less optimistic.

Muscular Dystrophy. Muscular dystrophy occurs in several forms. Of these, the most common is Duchenne's, a sex-linked genetic disease inherited in a pattern similar to that of hemophilia. Duchenne's muscular dystrophy is almost always a disease of boys, although other forms may occur in girls. Duchenne's muscular dystrophy is progressive. Increasing weakness, especially of the large muscles of the lower limbs, extends gradually to involve many other muscles of the body. Patients with muscular dystrophy usually become wheelchair-bound during the second decade of life and die soon after age twenty (Gilgoff and Dietrich, 1985). Thus, children with muscular dystrophy also face the invariable prospect of early death.

Duchenne's is often not diagnosed until the age at which children enter school. As a result, other boys may have been born to the family before the diagnosis of the first child. A carrier state (the likelihood that a woman may pass the condition on to her son) can be identified through blood testing. Girls whose brothers have had Duchenne's can also be tested, and their risk of having a child with this condition can be determined.

Families that have children with Duchenne's face tremendous problems of physical care of their child or children as these boys become increasingly unable to get around by themselves. Toward the end of the child's life, he becomes subject to serious lung infections and requires ever more frequent medical care. Given the genetic nature of the problem, families may have to manage two or three boys at one time with this condition. Death often results from suffocation because the child loses the capacity to control even the musculature of breathing.

At present, medical treatment of this condition is limited. There is no known therapy to reverse the basic underlying process of muscle destruction. At times, orthopedic surgery will help keep the child out of the wheelchair for longer times, but otherwise, surgery is of little benefit. Children with muscular dystrophy have been thought to be at greater risk of mental retardation although most children with this condition are of normal intelligence and can participate adequately in school, assuming that there are no physical barriers (Mearig, 1985).

Chronically Ill Children as a Class

At first glance, one may be struck by the great differences among the severe chronic illnesses of childhood. Physiologically they are about as diverse as one can imagine. Hemophilia is a disease of the blood, muscular dystrophy of the muscles, myelomeningocele of the spinal column, diabetes of the pancreas, and so on. Each disease has its unique pattern of symptoms, and each disease follows a different course, with wide individual differences among children with the disease. Hemophilia results in bleeding in the joints, in intense pain, and in severe arthritis. Cystic fibrosis leads to a buildup of mucus in body cavities, to a general failure to thrive, to a noxious odor, and to painful efforts to remove the excess mucus. Severe asthma results in an excruciating impairment of the ability to breathe. Spina bifida may be associated with mental retardation, and muscular dystrophy with lower scores on intelligence tests. Leukemia and congenital heart defects may lead to early death or, with successful treatment, to varying degrees of health including complete cure. Most of the diseases lead to a shortened life span, although there is great variation among diseases and among different children with the same disease.

Narrowly defined for clinical purposes, the diseases are clearly discrete. They require diverse treatments: surgery, chemotherapy, radiation, renal dialysis, pulmonary assistance, or the administration of insulin or of blood and blood products. Each disease has its corps of specialists, its affiliation with special research or clinical centers, its champions in the Congress and state legislatures, and its own advocacy group, each disease competing with the other for scarce funds.

Yet, many issues faced by chronically ill children and their families are similar regardless of the specific condition, and these issues do much to distinguish chronically ill children from their able-bodied contemporaries (Pless and Perrin, 1985; Stein and Jessop, 1982a, 1982b, 1984). As with any large group of individuals sharing common characteristics, there are common issues and dissimilarities; however, with respect to policy considerations, the common elements among severely and chronically ill children are more weighty than the inevitable distinctions. We here examine some of these similarities and some of their sources and the compelling reasons for treating severe chronic illnesses in childhood as a class for purposes of public policy formulation and implementation.

Not all of the diseases share all of the characteristics described in this section, but they are securely laced together by strands tying disease entities together in varying numbers and patterns. It is necessary to preface each of the following paragraphs with an unvoiced "in general" to allow for exceptions while emphasizing the wholeness of the class of severe chronic illnesses of childhood.

Most of these diseases are very costly to treat, a compelling consideration calling at once for urgency and caution. Direct treatment costs, including hospitalization, can run high. A kidney transplant and follow-up treatment in the first year can cost

$25 thousand (Korsch and Fine, 1985); surgery to correct myelomen-ingocele, $10 thousand (Myers and Millsap, 1985). Long-term care can be costly, too: blood and blood products, insulin, syringes, special diets, drugs, orthopedic devices, transportation, long-distance telephone calls, oxygen, control of environmental temperature, glasses, hearing aids, special schooling, and nursing care provided professionally or by family members and friends. Most of the diseases require care over an extended period of time, for years; thus, costs mount steadily. In acute diseases, costs may be high, but for a short period; by contrast, severe chronic illnesses have brief periods of high costs plus long periods of steady costs. The costs of these diseases may be so great that a family can be made bankrupt, insurance may be impossible to obtain, and employment opportunities for parents may be severely curtailed.

Most of the diseases, at least in their early stages, require intermittent medical care—at the time of diagnosis and establishment of a treatment regimen and at subsequent periods of crisis. But the burden of care, day after day, week after week, year after year, falls on the family. Society is organized to take care of some handicapped people, young and old, but not the chronically ill child. Formal resources for the daily out-of-hospital care of such children are almost nonexistent. The burdens on the child and the family weigh heavily; that they have persisted unrelieved for many years is surprising until one realizes that before a problem can be solved it must first be defined, which is one purpose of this book.

Most of these diseases have a strong genetic component. Some, such as sickle cell anemia, hemophilia, and muscular dystrophy, have distinct hereditary predictability when sufficient information is available. Some, such as juvenile-onset diabetes, show a clear hereditary influence but may require some environmental event to precipitate symptoms of the disease itself. Some of the diseases (a severe cardiac condition, for example) may be congenital but have no clear genetic linkages. And some, such as leukemia, may have a genetic component but may also depend heavily upon environmental or infectious events, many of which are obscure at present.

Many of the diseases entail a slow degeneration and premature death. Furthermore, the future course of all these diseases is highly unpredictable. The uncertainty thus generated creates profound psychological problems for the children themselves as well as for those who care for and about them. Problems of adjustment can be enormous, and they can be exacerbated during normally difficult periods of development, such as the establishment of independence and identity in adolescence.

Most of the diseases are accompanied by pain and discomfort, sometimes beyond appreciation by the healthy individual. Furthermore, most of the diseases—diabetes, cystic fibrosis, hemophilia, sickle cell anemia, muscular dystrophy—require treatments that are arduous, often painful, and sometimes embarrassing, to the point where the afflicted person may wonder whether a prolonged life is worth it after all.

The fact of chronicity itself creates a special problem of coping for the child and family and links families with diverse conditions. The crisis of acute illness passes fairly quickly, at times with the tragic outcome of death but more often with resolution and repair. Chronic illness is constantly there, adding its special shadow to the daily tasks of children and families.

Many providers are involved over an extended period of time, and treatment regimens are often complex and at times conflicting. Medications for one problem may have side effects in another part of the body. One physician may restrict a child's activity to protect a joint; another may encourage exercise to strengthen it. A pediatrician may suggest allergy shots for a child with asthma, but an allergist may recommend another course of treatment. Already faced with the burdens of chronic care and concern, families face great difficulties in making sense of conflicting advice.

The integration of medical care takes on serious proportions when severe and chronic illness of children is involved. Chronically ill children require specialty care at the time of diagnosis and periodically thereafter. They also require excellent general care, as all children do. However, the integration of specialty and general care is essentially nonexistent. Few general physicians ever see a child with hemophilia. During a lifetime of practice, they may see only a half dozen children with diabetes. Confronted with a child at the onset of a chronic condition, they may be unable to recognize it, or if they do, they may have no knowledge of the referral and specialized resources for health care urgently needed by the child. The relative rarity of many of the illnesses contributes to public and professional misunderstanding and to the educational, social, and psychological isolation of children and parents.

From a policy perspective, it is important to know whether chronically ill children can be considered as a class for the purpose of organizing services and allocating resources. Public policy infrequently provides for rare events affecting few individuals; these are best handled as individual variations to which existing policies designed for larger groups can be adapted. It would make little sense to have a separate national policy with respect to each of a dozen (or a hundred) diseases or disorders. A compelling argument for a separate policy emerges only when the numbers of people affected and the resources required for their care are sufficiently great to make it difficult to develop special rules for the group. From our study of the problem, we think it evident that the nature of chronic illness in childhood calls for public policies that treat chronically ill children as a class. The special needs of severely and chronically ill children and their families cannot efficiently and effectively be met by extending to this group policies that are efficient for children with routine illnesses, with acute or even fatal illnesses, or with mild chronic illnesses, such as allergies, transient asthma, and minor gastrointestinal problems.

Policies relevant to the common illnesses of childhood work reasonably well for many children. For others, there are problems of costs, of payment mechanisms, and of distribution of health care providers. Despite public programs, close to half of all poor children are ineligible for Medicaid, and death and hospitalization rates for poor children are much higher than for nonpoor children. The problems generated by the general health needs of infants and children, as well as of pregnant women, have been examined at length. Policies ensuing from attention to the health aspects of getting born and living into adulthood are either well worked out or well identified (Select Panel for the Promotion of Child Health, 1981). Not so with the problems of providing health care to chronically ill children, among whom the lack of sustained public consideration creates a common bond. Furthermore, the expense of caring for a chronically ill child exceeds all boundaries of expectation of what health care should normally cost. Our nation as a whole simply does not provide, at a cost manageable by most parents, the resources it takes to treat a child with a severe chronic illness.

As a further link among these disparate physiological conditions, the variation in policy itself creates ties. By policy, some states provide treatment for sickle cell disease, some do not; some provide treatment for the complications of diabetes, others do not. Parents who are fortunate enough to be informed move to communities where there are specialty centers or to states that have policies providing assistance to children with their particular disease. Perhaps there is no stronger bond among children with severe and chronic illnesses (and their families as well) than the absence of a thoroughly examined and consistent policy pertaining to them.

Policy and Policy Analysis

This book is primarily concerned with public policies that affect large numbers of chronically ill children and their families— that is, with policies of governments (federal, state, and local) and of large organizations, such as professional associations, academic health centers, industries that are large employers, voluntary associations, and insurance companies. Generally speaking, policy pertains to the way governments and other organizations govern the distribution of resources and control access to them. Thus, policy embraces not only legislation and the defined purposes and programs of organizations but also regulations designed to put purposes into practice, plus the habits and styles of management through which purposes find their active expression. What is not done is also reflective of policy. We are concerned with policies of particular hospitals, clinics, and schools as they represent comparable institutions affecting large numbers of chronically ill children and their families.

Policy makers are constantly confronted with the tough problem of how to get the information they need to make intelligent choices about issues of public concern. The problem is especially difficult when they must deal with technical matters with which they may have little cumulative and shared experience rather than with issues that are constantly on the political agenda. Over the years, legislators at the federal and state level as well as the officers of large organizations, both public and private, have developed an impressive understanding of the complexities of the problems involved in some technical matters. But not so with public policies affecting chronically ill children and their families. Here the issues are complex and the terrain unfamiliar, perhaps unknown. Many policy makers have never known a chronically ill child and may have only vague notions of the nature of severe and chronic illness in childhood.

In undertaking this study of public policies affecting children with chronic illness and their families, it has been our central purpose to make available to policy makers, in usable form, the knowledge they need to make intelligent choices among the various policy options worthy of serious consideration. We have made no attempt to develop new knowledge but have limited ourselves to the task of organizing knowledge already available and summarizing it in language that can be readily understood by a lay person. We then proceed to identify criteria that reflect human values and ethical considerations in the distribution of resources. Fundamental principles to guide the analysis and formulation of public policy are then developed. Policy options that grow out of the political history of programs for chronically ill children or that have been advocated by credible authorities are next considered, and these options are analyzed with respect to the set of principles. In the end, we move deliberately from an analytic mode and make specific recommendations.

The process just described falls reasonably well into five steps, and the discussion that follows is organized that way; but the analytic process is only roughly sequential. Much weaving back and forth is required by the task. For example, the identification in step 4 of some ambiguity concerning values served by a particular policy may require a return to step 1 to search for knowledge that could resolve the conflict. But the five-step scheme has its value in ordering thought and organizing work, so we describe it here.

Step 1—Defining the Problem. We start by defining the problem through exploration of its dimensions and of the research that can illuminate its character. We assume that the first definition of the problem will be inadequate and that the process of discovering what is known about it will require its redefinition in a cyclical fashion. We further assume that new knowledge that will emerge will invalidate existing or recommended policies and require different strategies reflecting these new insights. Thus the process is openended, dynamic, and continuous.

What kind of knowledge is relevant to questions of policy? With respect to severe and chronic illnesses of childhood, prudent policy shapers and makers would want answers to such questions as these: What are the etiology, presentation, course, treatment, and outcomes of the disease? How many children are affected? How is the disease distributed in the population? How does the disease affect the normal sequence of development of the child and especially how does it affect transactions within the family? What special services for health care, education, vocational guidance, financial counseling, and jobs are required by chronically ill children and their families? What is the cost of treating any one of the severe chronic illnesses of childhood? What specialized personnel and facilities are required for treatment? What are the possibilities for prevention? What new knowledge is required for treatment and especially for prevention? And so on for myriads of questions, many of which cannot be anticipated or, when specified, answered precisely.

As our group searched for answers to policy-relevant questions, we found a paucity of knowledge; the scholarly and scientific literature on the topic is thin indeed. For many policy issues bearing upon the well-being of the population at large (such as income supports, employment, housing, and health care in general), the policy analyst is faced with the Herculean task of making sense of an enormous body of knowledge, of reducing it to manageable proportions. Just the opposite is true with respect to policy issues involving chronically ill children and their families. We therefore commissioned some forty experts to prepare original papers on topics relevant to the formulation of public policy concerning severely and chronically ill children. The papers, which have been a rich source of information for the preparation of this book, are published separately in another volume (Hobbs and Perrin, 1985). On some issues, the Vanderbilt staff working on the study of public policies affecting chronically ill children and their families has independently reviewed the literature and prepared papers as a foundation for this report.

Step 2—Review of Existing Policies. Before undertaking to approach a problem or to explore some new set of policies or programs, the people who influence, shape, and make policy should have a grasp of existing policies and how well they have worked. The policy slate is seldom clean.

Policy development is nearly always incremental; great leaps forward or radical shifts in direction are unusual. The democratic process coupled with a system of checks and balances tends generally to dampen oscillations in policy. Even when dramatic departures from accustomed ways of doing things are advocated, the advocate must reckon with the hard gneiss of laminated programs and their attendant bureaucracies. Thus, when considering new policy directions (modest or grand), it is first necessary, if the analysis is to be rational, to inventory existing policies and programs and to describe and assess the effectiveness of those judged important.

Especially at a time of a great political sea change, as experienced in the 1980s, a meticulous assessment of extant policies and programs is extraordinarily important in the process of finding new compass bearings. As the states assume more and more responsibility for programs once centrally regulated and monitored, state policy makers must have a full understanding of programs previously operated under direct federal funding and with federal surveillance.

Policies in four broad areas are important to chronically ill children and their families; these areas are organization and financing of health services, schools, training of professionals, and research. Of the many federal policies and programs in these areas, only three affect children with chronic illness directly: Title V of the Social Security Act of 1935, and as subsequently amended, which provides assistance to the group of children of concern through Crippled Children's Services programs in all the states and territories; the Developmentally Disabled Assistance and Bill of Rights Act of 1975, which provided assistance initially to children severely handicapped by mental retardation, cerebral palsy, and epilepsy and was later amended to make it possible to include in the program children who are severely and chronically ill; and the Education for All Handicapped Children Act of 1975, which makes provision for federal subsidies to states to improve educational opportunities for handicapped children including health-impaired children. In addition, funds to pay for services to severely and chronically ill children are channeled through Medicaid, under Title XIX of the Social Security Act, and through the Supplemental Security Income Program, which is also under the Social Security Act. There is also one categorical program within Medicare to provide resources for people (including children) with end-stage renal disease.

Much of health care for chronically ill children is supported (to various degrees of breadth and depth) through private health insurance benefits. The public regulatory and tax policies regarding health insurance and access to insurance coverage thus have great impact on families with chronically ill children (Weeks, 1985). Furthermore, institutional policies and reimbursement mechanisms have led to certain forms of cross-subsidization that occur when the costs of severely ill patients are shared with those of other patients using that health care facility and with insurors and employers who pay insurance benefits.

Children with severe chronic illnesses also benefit from programs that were designed primarily with the health problems of adults in mind, most notably from research done under the auspices of the National Institutes of Health. All of the diseases included in this study are covered by one or more of the health institutes, and most of the institutes support research bearing directly on the health problems of children, although the familiar story of a great imbalance in dollar investments is evident here as elsewhere. One institute, the National Institute of Child Health and Human Development, focuses entirely on the health problems of children but tends to define these problems in biological terms and thus fails to consider the full range of developmental problems faced by the chronically ill child.

Step 3—Identification and Description of Policy Options. At this point, we attempt to identify the various policy options that should be considered by policy makers (in federal, state, and local governments and in private organizations) at levels of policy formation that will influence the well-being of large numbers of chronically ill children and their families. Step 3 is essentially a synthesis of steps 1 and 2 considered from the standpoint of how what is known and how existing policy suggest actions that might appropriately be taken in the interest of chronically ill children and their families.

At this point, identifying policy options relevant to chronically ill children as a class is an exercise in frugality. Except for programs developed under the Crippled Children's Services, relatively few proposals have been advanced for debate. Professional people and voluntary groups concerned with specific disease entities have offered proposals for program development in the service of children with particular diseases. But the consideration of chronically ill children as a class in the context of policy development has only now advanced far enough to influence public debate appreciably.

Options for policy consideration must grow out of political history, out of advocacy efforts, and out of extrapolations to chronically ill children of policies developed with other groups in mind. We think this is the first time there has been a systematic assessment of alternative courses of action that might be embodied in a public response to the heavy burdens of children with chronic illness and their families.

Step 4—Assessing the Relative Merits of Policy Options. Having identified policy options that appear worthy of consideration, we attempt in this step to assess the relative advantages and disadvantages of each of the policy proposals. This process of defining trade-offs assumes the existence of a set of criteria on the basis of which such judgments are made. Policy analysis is inescapably an exercise in specifying what *should* be. The issue is clearly one of values. The process of policy analysis presumes the existence of criteria essential to making value judgments.

Values are concerned with the well-being of people rather than the efficiency of programs. Human values incorporate concerns for broad social purposes of national and local communities; for moral and ethical conduct; for the well-being, dignity, and self-realization of individuals; for the quality of social relationships;

and for the development and utilization of knowledge. Human values are extraordinarily powerful in the shaping of public policy.

In spite of their importance, principles expressing human values are seldom articulated either by policy makers or by policy analysts. They spring from personal intuitions about social purposes and how to achieve them, intuitions that go largely unexamined. They often express the ethos of a time in history, and they tend to be highly contagious, transmitted occasionally by explicit statements of philosophy but more often by implication through debate or through recommended actions. To illustrate, the past two decades have seen three profound shifts in the human-value commitments of the federal government. During the 1960s a commitment to equity, to fair play, to human rights, and to community ran high in the land. The 1970s began a period of muted concern for equality of opportunity, of greater enthusiasm for privatism and personal initiative, and of growing skepticism about the effectiveness of government in promoting the general welfare. Now the nation is wrenched by a concept of the relationship between the federal government, the states, and individuals that rejects the human values, and their attendant structures and procedures, that have been nurtured for the guidance of the nation by both Democrats and Republicans for more than half a century. How such shifts in ideology occur is far beyond the scope of this book. However, ideologies find expression in public policies and programs and are of enormous importance as we examine what should be the public response to chronically ill children and their families.

The principle statements that summarize values that seem important cannot be applied mechanically to the various policy alternatives; the process is far too imprecise to permit that. Instead, the principle serve as guides to the process of determining the relative advantages and disadvantages of proposed policies and programs.

Step 5—Recommendations, Implementation, and Evaluation. To this point, we have attempted to supply the shapers and makers of policy with information and analyses that should enable them to arrive at their own conclusions about the best course of action. The discourse so far intentionally says nothing about our own convictions about how the policy problems can best be resolved. As discussed, our biases inevitably intrude themselves and nowhere more explicitly than in the selection of value criteria. However, our policy study group has probed, immersed itself in the problem for a period of several years, and must in consequence have recommendations worthy of consideration by others who share our concern for chronically ill children and their families. In step 5, we make our own recommendations clear. We also discuss, in general, problems of the implementation of policies and programs considered in the analysis, our own recommendations included.

Summary

Despite the great variations in the physiology, treatment, and expectations associated with varied chronic illnesses, they bring to families similar burdens and challenges. When we have gathered together groups of families with chronically ill children to benefit from their accumulated wisdom, they have usually spent the first half hour trying to understand the names of each other's child's disease. After that time, they have quickly noted the many similarities of the daily problems they face: getting needed complex medical care, the financial burdens of costly illness, coping with the added stress of raising a child with a health problem, facing unpredictability. Perhaps 15 percent of the issues identified by families are specific to the disease; the other 85 percent are common to most families with a child who is chronically ill.

In this book, we explore the policy implications of the burdens and challenges that families face in nurturing their growing child. We move from discussion in Chapter Two of the numbers of affected children and the opportunities for prevention to consideration in Chapters Three, Four, and Five of these children in their families and communities and of their interactions with society's institutions including the worlds of school, work, and health care. The costs of care in childhood illness are broad; they include not only the financial costs but also the social and family costs related to a child with a severe health problem. In Chapters Six and Seven, we describe the financial costs of illnesses and the present system of paying for them. Training of health professionals to work with families of children with chronic illnesses and needed research for the coming decade are discussed in Chapters Eight and Nine. In

Chapter Ten, the book turns to a consideration of underlying values that help clarify issues in public policy formulation for these children and their families. The discussion of values provides the base from which a series of principles to guide policy formation are then offered in Chapter Eleven. Chapter Twelve presents six options for national policy concerning children with chronic illnesses and their families. Delineation of the advantages and disadvantages of each option in light of the principles developed in Chapter Eleven leads to the recommendation for a new policy approach. The book concludes with a detailed discussion of this recommended policy.

2

Changing Patterns of Childhood Illness

During the past few decades, much has been achieved to improve the lives of children with chronic illnesses and their families. Tremendous advances in medical and surgical care have allowed most children with chronic illnesses to survive to adulthood. Indeed, the available evidence indicates that most of the achievable improvement in childhood mortality has already been obtained. The challenge now is to enhance the quality of the lives of the survivors and to help these children function as effectively as possible as they grow into adulthood.

In this chapter, we first examine the epidemiology of childhood illness to provide perspective on the magnitude of the problem. How many children have severe chronic illnesses? And how do certain other characteristics, such as poverty, influence severe illness in childhood? We then describe recent achievements important to children with chronic illnesses. What advances have made chronically ill children healthier, and how have public responses improved access to needed services for these children? Many childhood chronic illnesses have a genetic component, and a discussion of achievements in genetics leads to consideration of opportunities for prevention of childhood chronic illnesses and their consequences. The chapter ends with a discussion of the challenges ahead.

Changing Patterns of Childhood Illness

What number of American children have chronic illnesses? Are chronic conditions increasing, and what are the prospects for changes in this population within the next decades?

Chronicity and Severity. Prior to considering the number of families affected by childhood chronic illness, it is important to understand what is meant by severe and chronic illness. Defining chronicity is a relatively easy matter. A chronic illness is one that lasts for a substantial period of time and has continuing and often debilitating sequelae. Most common illnesses of childhood (for example, ear infections, intestinal viruses, and urinary infections) are self-limited and run their course in a period of hours, days, or weeks. With proper treatment, even the acute and serious illnesses of childhood (for example, pneumonia, appendicitis, severe croup) require only a month or so for complete convalescence. By contrast, the severe chronic illnesses of childhood persist for a number of years after onset and often become progressively worse. For our purposes, a chronic illness may be defined as a health condition that lasts for more than three months in a year or that leads to continuous hospitalization for at least one month in a year (Pless and Pinkerton, 1975). Although this definition incorporates such conditions as mild acne or hay fever, the addition of severity narrows the focus considerably.

The definition of severity is a good deal more problematic than that of chronicity. In physiological terms, severity can more easily be stated for certain conditions than for others. For diabetes, as an example, there is a strong inclination among physicians and others knowledgeable about the disease to refuse to assess severity at all. A child with juvenile diabetes is considered to be sick, no matter how well that child may be getting along at a particular time; a child either does or does not have diabetes. For hemophilia, the definition of severity is easier because the level of clotting factor can be used as an indication of severity. About 55 percent of children with hemophilia have less than 5 percent of the usual levels of the deficient clotting factor and are considered severely affected (Hilgartner, Aledort, and Giardina, 1985). The other 45 percent of affected people have higher levels ranging from mild to moderate.

In general, patients with less factor have more prolonged bleeding and bleed more often. Even here, though, the relationship is less than exact. Some children with low amounts of clotting factor will bleed less frequently than do other children with more factor.

The concept of physiological severity is often confounded by the question of how well the disease is controlled. In diabetes, the levels of blood and urine sugar are more a measure of how well the child's insulin is working in conjunction with the rest of the treatment program than they are a measure of the severity of the diabetes. Most children with asthma have a mild form of the disease; only 5 to 10 percent have severe asthma (McNicol and Williams, 1973). The definition of severe asthma is usually based on the frequency of attacks of asthma, the number of hospitalizations, or the degree of lung impairment between attacks. Yet all of these measures are clearly affected by the quality of the control of the child's disease and may only reflect indirectly some inherent characteristic of severity.

Beyond physical severity, three other considerations help define the severity of impact of illness. First, an illness is severe if it places a large financial burden on the family; for example, if out-of-pocket medical costs exceed 10 percent of the family income after taxes. Second, severity can be measured by the degree to which an illness contributes to emotional or psychological problems for the child. If the presence of a chronic illness increases the risk of significant behavioral or developmental disorder, for example, then the psychological impact affects severity. Third, severity can be measured by the degree to which an illness contributes to disruption in family life, as indicated partly by marital friction or sibling behavior disorders. Important for the consideration of program and policy development is the understanding that these measures of severity—economic, psychological, and familial—may correlate poorly with indicators of physiological severity. In juvenile arthritis, for example, there is evidence that children with milder forms of the disease have more psychological problems than children with more severe arthritis (McAnarney and others, 1974).

Defining severity is thus fraught with difficulty and potential disagreement. For the purposes of this public policy discussion, we intend to focus on those conditions that cause severity in any of the four realms just discussed. We give little attention to children with mild chronic illnesses but focus instead on those chronic conditions that interfere in an important and continuing way with the child's physical growth and abilities or with the functioning of the child or family.

Improved Mortality Rates Among Children. Definitions of several terms used in this chapter may be useful to the reader. *Epidemiology* refers to the distribution of illness in different groups of people, its incidence and prevalence, and characteristics of populations that may change these patterns. *Etiology* refers to the origins and causes of diseases and disorders. *Incidence* of a disease refers to the frequency of its occurrence; *prevalence* refers to the number of children affected by the disease in the population at a specific time. *Functional impairment* is the degree of limitation in performing daily behaviors, such as dressing, toileting, eating, and moving around. *Morbidity* refers to the illness and its consequences, and *mortality* to death.

Severe and chronic illness contributes heavily to childhood mortality and morbidity, and its relative contribution has increased over the last several decades. Although the care of many chronic illnesses has greatly improved, there has been less progress in their prevention and treatment than has been achieved with other types of childhood health conditions, particularly the severe infectious diseases that previously accounted for many childhood deaths.

In comparison with risks for adults, the likelihood of disability and death among children is rather remote after infancy. For example, in 1979, the death rate for children aged five to fourteen years was the lowest of any age group (0.3 deaths per year per hundred thousand population). The figure for adults twenty-five to forty-four was approximately five times greater, and the figure for adults fifty-five to sixty-four was almost fifty times greater (National Center for Health Statistics, 1979a). Similarly, less than 4 percent of children under age seventeen are limited in activity as a result of a chronic health condition; the comparable figure for adults forty-five to sixty-four is 25 percent. Yet the probability of death or disability among children, although remote, is not negligible. Furthermore, because the potential for lost years of meaningful and productive life is much greater for persons afflicted at the beginning of a normal life span than for those afflicted later, even these low rates can have large consequences for both financial costs and quality of life.

Current relatively low mortality rates for children reflect a long trend in this century of decreasing childhood mortality, particularly in infancy and early childhood. Since 1950, the infant mortality rate has been reduced by half. Death rates for children between the ages of one and fifteen have decreased approximately 30 percent. Death rates for persons fifteen to twenty-four years old have remained relatively unchanged, however, because of a sizable increase in deaths from accidents, suicide, and homicide.

The relative contribution of chronic illness to childhood mortality has changed in the past several decades (Figure 1). Congenital anomalies contributed only 6.4 percent of infant deaths in 1915, but they now contribute 17.3 percent. Furthermore, in 1976 the death rate for congenitally malformed infants was about 40 percent of the 1915 rate; however, the rate for those without congenital malformations had declined to 13 percent of the 1915 rate (National Institutes of Health, 1979). Actual death rates from chronic illnesses have declined moderately during the past few decades; the greatest improvement is in infectious diseases, which have been largely replaced by accidents, homicide, and suicide. The control of infectious diseases previously associated with significant mortality and morbidity is striking. Even the decades from 1950 to 1970 have shown a marked decline. Polio in 1950 affected 25 in 100,000 people; by 1970, the rate was less than 1 percent of what it had been twenty years previously. Measles, which accounted for 500 cases in 100,000 people in 1950, had fallen to only 5 percent of that rate in 1970 and has fallen greatly since. Tuberculosis in 1970 had dropped to 35 percent of its rate in 1950 (Pless, 1974).

Improvements in mortality rates from infectious diseases characterized the earlier part of the last half century. The past two decades have seen great improvements as well in mortality rates from serious childhood chronic illnesses. Although many illnesses still have a fatal outcome in childhood, most children now survive into young adulthood or beyond. Gortmaker (1985, p. 136) writes

Figure 1. Contribution of Selected Causes of Death to Total Death Rate,
1950 and 1979, United States.

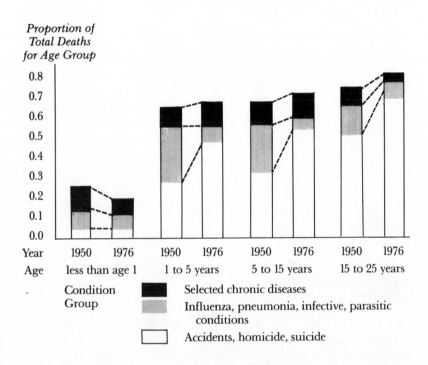

Sources: Graph adapted from Harkey, 1981, Figure 3; based on data
from Table 1-26, *Vital Statistics of the United States, 1979*, and Table 52,
Vital Statistics of the United States, 1950.

that "drastic changes in the numbers of children with these chronic
illnesses are not expected in the United States in the coming
decades." As shown in Table 1, the relative prevalence of the
different childhood chronic illnesses and current rates of survival
of children with each illness indicate that much of the possible
improvement in survival has already been achieved. Survival is
quite high for the severe chronic illnesses that are most common.
Affected children, however, may be left with significant disability
as they become adults. The 1980 prevalence estimate for the eleven

Table 1. Prevalence Estimates for Eleven Childhood Chronic Diseases,
Ages Birth to 20 Years, United States, 1980.

Disease	Estimated Proportion Surviving to Age 20* (percentage)	1980 Prevalence Estimate per 1,000**	Estimated Maximum Prevalence, Assuming 100% Survival to Age 20***
Asthma (moderate and severe)	98	10.00	10.20
Congenital heart disease	65	7.00	9.33
Diabetes mellitus	95	1.80	1.89
Cleft lip/palate	92	1.50	1.62
Spina bifida	50	.40	.67
Sickle cell anemia	90	.28	.29
Cystic fibrosis	60	.20	.26
Hemophilia	90	.15	.16
Acute lymphocytic leukemia	40	.11	.22
Chronic renal failure	25	.08	.19
Muscular dystrophy	25	.06	.14
Estimated Total (assuming no overlap)		21.58	24.97

*Estimate refers to the survival expected of a birth cohort to age 20, given current treatments.

**Estimates are from population prevalence data or are derived from estimates of incidence (or prevalence at birth) and survival data.

***Most of the rates used in our calculations are not true incidence rates; rather they are prevalence estimates at birth.

Source: Gortmaker and Sappenfeld, 1984.

representative childhood illnesses is approximately twenty-two per thousand children under age twenty, using conservative estimates of the proportion surviving to age twenty. The maximum possible prevalence, assuming 100 percent survival with current rates of onset, would achieve not quite twenty-five children per thousand. These eleven representative conditions account for only about 20 percent of all U.S. children with chronic health conditions. Although similar data are unavailable for all childhood chronic illnesses, the eleven conditions likely represent the more severe illnesses. Current mortality rates may therefore be even lower among the 80 percent of children with other chronic health conditions.

Further advances in mortality rates will certainly occur, although their overall impact on these figures will be less than in years past. Yet this statement neglects the fact that many of these children will lead foreshortened lives as adults. The pursuit of improved mortality rates among young adults remains a high priority for several diseases, such as cystic fibrosis and sickle cell anemia.

How Many Children Are Affected? With approximately 62 million children under age eighteen in the nation (Select Panel for the Promotion of Child Health, 1981), the prevalence estimates suggest that 1.5 million have the eleven illnesses defined here as marker conditions. However, because these marker diseases are only 20 percent of children with any chronic illness, we estimate that about 7.5 million children under age eighteen have chronic health conditions. This figure represents approximately 12 percent of the childhood population. We are confident that at least one in every ten children has a chronic health condition. Studies both in the United States and in other industrialized countries have consistently arrived at this rate of chronic illness (Pless and Roghmann, 1971). As we have noted, however, only a portion of this group have physiologically severe conditions. For example, only 5 to 10 percent of all children with asthma are so impaired by the disease that it interferes with their ability to carry out their usual daily tasks. Where physiological severity has been carefully examined, it generally appears that about 10 percent of children with chronic illnesses are severely affected (Pless and Roghmann, 1971; Haggerty, Roghmann, and Pless, 1975). Three quarters of a million children (10 percent of 7.5 million) in the United States, then, have physiologically severe chronic illnesses. When the definition of severity is broadened to include financial, psychological, and family stress factors, the figure of 1 million children reasonably defines the size of the group with which we are concerned.

Similar estimates arise from other studies. For example, the Child Health Supplement to the National Health Interview Survey (begun in the early 1960s) provides estimates of the number of children limited in their major daily activity due to a chronic health condition. In 1980, 2 percent of children were reported as having limitations in major activities as a result of chronic conditions (Table 2). An additional 1.8 percent were reported to have less severe limitations. Assuming approximately 62 million children under age eighteen in the United States, this survey estimates 1.2 million children with major functional limitations caused by chronic health conditions.

Limitations in major activities almost doubled during the past two decades, increasing from approximately 1.1 percent in 1967 to the present 2 percent. Twice as many children have severe health

Table 2. Estimated Number and Percentage Distribution of Persons Aged Birth to 16 with Limitation of Activity due to Chronic Conditions in the United States, 1967–1980.

Year	Estimated Number in Thousands		Percentage Distribution	
	With Activity Limitation	With Limitation in Major Activity	With Activity Limitation	With Limitation in Major Activity
1967	1,418	712	2.1	1.1
1968	1,427	825	2.1	1.2
1969	1,760	810	2.6	1.2
1970	1,820	873	2.7	1.3
1971	1,942	972	2.9	1.5
1972	1,921	1,037	3.0	1.6
1973	2,149	1,191	3.4	1.9
1974	2,305	1,199	3.7	1.9
1975	2,283	1,165	3.7	1.9
1976	2,267	1,179	3.7	1.9
1977	2,012	1,104	3.4	1.8
1978	2,309	1,178	3.9	2.0
1979	2,291	1,232	3.9	2.1
1980	2,223	1,180	3.8	2.0

Source: National Center for Health Statistics, "Current Estimates from the Health Interview Survey, Series 10." In *Annual Reports 1967–1980*, numbers 52, 60, 63, 72, 79, 85, 95, 100, 115, 119, 126, 130, 136, 139.

conditions today as they did two decades ago. Although some of this reported increase may reflect changes in the methodology of the survey during this time (Newacheck, Budetti, and McManus, 1984), a large proportion of it represents the improved survival of chronically ill children, many of whom have some continuing disability from their disease.

The Rochester Child Health Studies (Haggerty, Roghmann, and Pless, 1975) found a slightly higher prevalence (137.5 per thousand children ages six to seventeen), with 10 percent of illnesses rated as severe. Central nervous system, respiratory, and skin diseases represented a large proportion of these children (Table 3). Again, most of these conditions are mild (although chronic) and have little influence on the life of the child. The most common condition here is hay fever, an annoying allergic condition but one that carries little serious morbidity or long-term consequences. The more severe chronic illnesses, such as diabetes or congenital heart disease, are less common. Although only 10 percent of children with chronic illnesses had a severe limitation in activity, 37 percent of parents thought their children were unable to participate in some activities because of illness. Only 10 percent of the children with chronic illnesses received special education services because of their illness; 27 percent of them had missed some school during the previous year because of illness.

Recent studies in Flint, Michigan, found that 1 percent of children had a serious medical condition with functional impairment; 2.7 percent had a less severe medical condition leading to some functional impairment. One third of children with serious medical conditions and functional impairment were in special education. Sizable differences in functional impairment of children, based on different chronic illnesses, were found (Walker, Gortmaker, and Weitzman, 1981). This issue is discussed further in Chapter Four.

Poverty affects the health of children. Parents of children from low-income families judge their child's health as fair or poor 3.5 times more frequently than do parents in middle- or high-income families. Children from poorer families also have significantly more disability days as a result of health conditions and more days missed from school than do children in middle- or high-

Table 3. Prevalence of Chronic Illnesses, Ages 6–17,
Monroe County, New York.

	Rate per 1,000 Children	Percentage of all Cases
Respiratory conditions		38.3
Asthma	8.5	
Hay fever	36.2	
Other	7.9	
Nervous system and sensory organs		26.2
Deafness	9.9	
Refractive error	7.9	
Strabismus	1.3	
Cerebral palsy	2.6	
Epilepsy	2.6	
Migraine	4.0	
Speech disturbance	8.6	
Skin and subcutaneous tissue	18.4	13.4
Genitourinary system	6.6	4.8
Endocrine system		2.9
Diabetes mellitus	2.0	
Other	2.0	
Digestive system	4.1	2.9
Musculoskeletal and connective tissue	4.0	2.9
Congenital anomalies		2.4
Cardiovascular	2.0	
Cleft lip and/or palate	0.7	
Limbs	0.7	
Other	8.0	5.8
	137.5	99.6

Adapted from Haggerty, Roghmann, and Pless, 1975, p. 81.

income families (Kovar and Meny, 1981). Poor children are likely to have more illness and more severe illness than nonpoor children (Starfield, 1982).

Future Trends. For fifteen years after the Second World War, there was a steady rise in the number of children born each year. Since the early 1960s, however, there has been a slow decrease in the number of children born per year, dropping to a level of 3.1 million in 1975 (compared to 4.4 million in 1960) (Gortmaker, 1985). Present census projections suggest that the total number of new births per year will increase slowly in the next several decades, perhaps until the year 2020 (U.S. Bureau of the Census, 1977). This slow rise leads to the prediction that no significant increase in actual numbers of new cases of childhood chronic illness is expected during this period unless there is an important change in frequency of onset. Although advances in genetic treatments have begun to play a role in diminishing the likelihood of certain conditions, the vast array of different childhood chronic illnesses assures that many conditions will continue to exist despite the benefits of genetic research. Thus, the number of children with chronic illnesses should remain stable, at least over the next few decades.

In summary, 10 to 15 percent of U.S. children have a chronic health condition. Only about 10 percent of the group with chronic health problems, however, have severe chronic illnesses. Approximately 1 to 2 percent of all children in the United States (close to one million children) are afflicted with severe chronic illnesses.

Achievements in Combating Childhood Chronic Illness

Faced with a formidable problem, it is easy to overlook progress already made toward its solution. So it is with the problem of severe chronic illness in childhood. Dramatic progress has been made in preventing some diseases, in bringing others under at least a measure of control, and in actually curing some children with diseases that were formerly incapacitating or lethal. Much of the progress has resulted from research leading to new knowledge and from technological developments leading to improved treatment techniques. Progress has also been made in shaping public and private health care programs so that afflicted children and their families can benefit from scientific and clinical advances. Research in genetics and in other areas has vastly expanded opportunities for prevention of some illnesses and of their consequences. The prospects today for the child seriously ill with a chronic disease or disorder are considerably better than they were in years past. We present a few examples of achievements—first in acquiring knowledge and then in putting that knowledge to use through enlightened public policies.

Control and Treatment. In 1922, Banting and Best published their discovery of insulin, a pancreatic hormone regulating the metabolism of glucose, amino acids, and fat—a discovery that revolutionized the treatment of diabetes mellitus. Then a quickly fatal disease for children (who lose their ability to produce insulin), now diabetes can be controlled reasonably well and life expectancy has been extended dramatically. With proper care, including daily administration of insulin, the person with juvenile-onset diabetes can lead a relatively normal life into the adult years.

Within the past two decades, following the development of renal dialysis and kidney transplant technology, "the outlook for treatment of children with irreversible renal insufficiency or end-stage renal disease (ESRD) has changed dramatically from one of frank pessimism to cautious optimism" (Korsch and Fine, 1985, p. 283). Progress has been made in controlling the rejection of a transplanted kidney, and a portable dialysis machine (a "wearable kidney") is being developed. The development of surgical techniques has made it possible to alleviate completely some conditions (such as some congenital heart defects) and to reduce substantially the amount of impairment associated with others (such as neural tube defects).

Next to accidents, cancer is the leading cause of death of children aged one to fifteen years, and leukemia accounts for 30 percent of childhood cancers. Less than two decades ago, a diagnosis of leukemia meant death within months. Now as a result of development of chemical and radiation therapies, 90 to 95 percent of children with leukemia achieve some remission and 50 percent remain in remission for at least five years (Pendergrass, Chard, and Hartmann, 1985).

In hemophilia, spontaneous or stress-related bleeding into muscles, joints, or body cavities results in severe pain, crippling arthritis, and premature death. Until recently, treatment was largely palliative. In 1965, Pool and Shannon described a procedure for isolating the crucial blood-clotting factors, and treatment improved dramatically. Within a few years the life expectancy of the child with hemophilia increased from twenty to thirty years and more. The quality of the child's life markedly improved, and the majority of care is now provided at home rather than in a hospital.

The care of lung disease in children has been improved by the new medications for the treatment of severe asthma (Galant,

1983). In the past, children with severe asthma faced frequent, lengthy periods in bed recuperating from attacks of asthma. Now most attacks can be aborted in a brief period of time, allowing the child to remain in school and to participate in other daily activities.

New techniques for monitoring fetal development (such as amniocentesis and various scanning procedures) have made it possible to identify in utero various anomalies, such as neural tube defects, that can lead to severe and chronic illness in childhood (Myers and Millsap, 1985). Early intervention and prevention of the birth of an affected fetus have become possible.

Research into genetics has expanded the understanding of the causes of certain diseases, their transmission within families, and the possibilities for their prevention. Genetic typing and counseling allow improved family planning and may reduce the incidence of some of the chronic illnesses of childhood. Advances in genetic engineering that permit the replacement of abnormal genetic material have tremendous implications for families at risk of having chronically ill children.

Provision of Health Services. Advances in scientific knowledge and in clinical skill and technology are of limited value unless there is in place some mechanism for their application. The transfer of knowledge and skill into practice often requires new policies and programs. In many instances, the scientific and clinical achievements described in the preceding section have been paralleled by the development of new social arrangements.

Technical advances in the treatment of orthopedic conditions that were so prevalent in the 1920s as a result of polio epidemics led to the development, in 1935, of the Crippled Children's Services within the Children's Bureau (Lesser, 1985). This was the first federal program providing grants-in-aid to the states to encourage the provision of health services. Prior to the institution in 1981 of the Maternal and Child Health Block Grant, every state and territory had a Crippled Children's Services program through which, in 1980, flowed almost $100 million in federal funds supplemented by more than $200 million in state funds. Once the technological capability to immunize was developed, federal support of immunization programs began. Immunization of children against poliomyelitis and other childhood illnesses is now required, and both federal and state funds are available to support immunization programs.

In 1965, with increasing awareness of the benefits of general medical care and of the lack of access of some families to services, the Congress amended the Social Security Act to finance health services to children receiving assistance through the Aid to Families with Dependent Children program. Known as Medicaid, in 1980 it provided more than four billion dollars for health services to poor children. In the early 1980s, changes in Medicaid regulations allowed states to experiment with home-care programs supported with public funds; previously, most funds had been allocated to direct physician or institutional care. Also in 1965, the Congress established the Supplemental Security Income (SSI) program, which provides financial assistance for children with severe handicaps including severe and chronic illnesses. SSI funds are available to disabled individuals into their adult years. In May 1972, the Congress passed legislation entitling all individuals in this country, regardless of age or economic status, to reimbursement under Medicare for end-stage renal disease treatment by dialysis or transplant.

The comprehensive treatment of cystic fibrosis, hemophilia, sickle cell anemia, and juvenile arthritis has developed in centers supported with both public and private funds. Centers provide a broad variety of services to families whose children have these diseases. For cystic fibrosis, this comprehensive care has led to an ever-increasing life span for children afflicted with this condition, such that now, in the mid 1980s, the average life span is more than twenty-two years (Lewiston, 1985).

Through two statutes in the early 1970s, the Congress established the Developmental Disabilities program, which initially provided assistance for children and adults severely incapacitated by mental retardation, epilepsy, and cerebral palsy. In 1978, regulations were modified to define developmental disabilities functionally rather than categorically, making it possible to include in the program some individuals with severe and chronic illnesses.

Public funding for genetic services began with the passage of the National Sickle Cell Anemia Control Act in 1972. In 1976, the act was broadened to include several additional genetic diseases, such as Tay-Sachs disease and thalassemia. The legislation led to a national program to improve screening and diagnostic services for genetic diseases, to encourage areawide efforts improving access to services, and to support the integration of genetic services with other health services. The effort provided an important focus on genetic diseases and established some public responsibility for screening and education about genetic disorders (Holtzman and Richmond, 1985).

Public Law 94-142 (the Education for All Handicapped Children's Act of 1975) encompasses in its definition of the handicapped other health impaired children, which includes some chronically ill children. In the vital tradition of public education in this country, Public Law 94-142 provides educational services to handicapped children without regard to economic status. It has major implications for providing health services to some children with chronic illness (Baird and Ashcroft, 1985).

Prevention of Illness and Its Consequences

In the long struggle for better health and longer life, there is a well-established principle that it is better, more efficient, and more humane to prevent an illness or disorder than to treat it once it has occurred. Great advances in health have occurred largely as a result of preventive measures, of improved sanitation, and of inoculations against ravaging diseases (of which smallpox and poliomyelitis are stunning examples). For the chronic illnesses of childhood, the problem is made more complex by the large number of different diseases and the relative rarity of each individual disease. Prevention remains a goal that demands constant dedication as well as the investment of substantial resources. There are compelling reasons to press to the limit the possibility of preventing severe and chronic illnesses in childhood and the consequences of those conditions once they occur.

Three levels of prevention can be distinguished. All three have substantial importance for families with chronically ill children. Primary prevention avoids the onset or development of disease. For conditions that are predominantly genetic in origin, primary prevention consists of avoiding the conception of an affected fetus—for example through the choice of a high-risk family to avoid pregnancy. For conditions with later onset, in which environment may play a major role (for example, leukemia), primary prevention may be accomplished by avoiding environmental conditions that increase the likelihood of the occurrence of the disease. Where environmental toxins, such as alcohol or lead, affect the developing fetus or young child, disease is prevented through reducing maternal alcohol use or through programs to eradicate lead-based paint from homes.

Secondary prevention takes place after the conception of an affected fetus. Once a pregnant woman has been identified as either at high risk or clearly carrying a fetus with a severe chronic disease, options include termination of the pregnancy or, for some conditions, fetal surgery (for example, for children with hydrocephalus) (Clewell and others, 1982). Research in genetics may soon allow enzyme modifications that will reverse the effects of some conditions.

Tertiary prevention involves avoidance of the untoward or unnecessary consequences of disease. What can be done for children who are born with or who acquire a severe chronic illness to prevent the disease from interfering with physiological, educational, or psychological functioning? Tertiary prevention aims at improving school participation, safeguarding the psychological integrity of the child and family, maximizing the child's functional abilities to carry out usual daily tasks, promoting emotional and physical growth most effectively, and limiting the effects of illness on the child's physical capacities.

Tertiary prevention, that is, diminishing the impact of illness on daily life, is best understood in light of the distinctions among disease, disability, and handicap. *Disease* reflects the underlying interference with physical processes (for example, arthritis). *Disability* is the direct expression of disease (a knee joint functioning poorly because of arthritis, for example). A disability may or may not affect everyday activities of the child. *Handicap* refers to the impact of illness on normal growth and development or on specific tasks (such as the inability to climb stairs because of nonfunctioning knee joints). Some children with severe disease will have little handicap; others with mild disease may be severely handicapped. Tertiary prevention aims to diminish disability and to prevent a disability from becoming a handicap.

Genetics and Environment: Primary and Secondary Prevention. Effective primary prevention generally develops from an understanding of the ways diseases are caused. For many conditions, however, mechanisms of onset may be poorly understood. Some conditions are clearly genetic in origin; others seem to have a clearly environmental basis, even when both genetic and environmental influences interact. Knowledge about etiology, although incomplete, is useful in suggesting where to look for cause-effect relationships that may allow for intervention.

The understanding of genetics and the expansion of genetic principles have developed greatly during the last two or three decades (Holtzman and Richmond, 1985). As a result, relatively few physicians in practice have had formal exposure in medical school to the broad area of medical genetics. A central task in implementing modern findings in genetics will be to provide education and adequate consultation to the many primary physicians working with children and their families.

Familiarity with key concepts of genetics will help with understanding the changing opportunities for prevention. In the appendix to this chapter, we offer a brief, technical description of genetic inheritance, providing a basis for greater awareness of genetic influences and their relationship to the effects of the environment. Several modes of inheritance, including chromosomal and nonchromosomal single-gene inheritance and less well defined genetic predispositions to specific illnesses, are described in the appendix.

The varied modes of genetic inheritance carry different implications for families. For some modes, the lines of inheritance (including males and females) are easily traced within families, and affected families often know their risks of having a child with the condition. In other modes, parents have no other family members with the condition when their child first shows signs of the disease. Because the first child may be diagnosed after a second or third pregnancy, these latter parents frequently bear more than one afflicted child. Sex-linked conditions pose special problems. These illnesses affect males but are transmitted by females. Hence, females in the family may carry a special psychological burden, considering themselves the source of the disease for their children.

There are other patterns of inheritance as well. Some health conditions are thought to be influenced by many genes interacting in a complex fashion; conditions following this pattern are termed *polygenic* in origin. Environmental agents may also contribute, and if so, the causation is termed *multifactorial*. Here, an individual gene contributes only partially to the resultant health condition. Many polygenic conditions are likely a manifestation of a basic underlying phenomenon that is influenced by both genes and environment. Because family members share a much greater proportion of their genes with each other than they do with the general population, possession of the threshold number of genes for a given polygenic condition is much more likely in families with a history of the disorder. Asthma, cleft lip and/or palate, congenital heart defects, diabetes, and spina bifida appear to be polygenic with some influence from the environment.

Environmental factors too have been implicated as causes of chronic illnesses. Although exposure to hazardous environmental factors (especially radiation, toxic drugs, or infections) can occur at any age, exposure to adverse agents during the prenatal period is likely to be most detrimental. Radiation may cause chronic illnesses. Its effects on the human embryo can be substantial and include retardation, malformations, and death (Brent, 1977). In animals, radiation during prenatal life brings on major structural abnormalities, including heart defects and cleft lip or palate. In postnatal life, radiation has been implicated as a cause of leukemia and other malignancies. Among the Japanese children exposed to high levels of radiation in Hiroshima and Nagasaki, there was an approximately tenfold increase in the rate of leukemia (Brent, 1977).

Drugs and related substances ingested during pregnancy are major causes of childhood chronic disability (Wilson, 1977). High alcohol use by mothers has been associated with the fetal alcohol syndrome, a cause of mental retardation as well as abnormal facial features. Anticonvulsant medications taken by women with epilepsy appear to double the risk of having a congenitally malformed infant. Estimates of the rate at which drugs may cause malformations are difficult to make, however. Most medications commonly used to treat illnesses have received only limited study of their safety or their likelihood to cause malformations when taken by pregnant women. Yet most pregnant women do take some prescribed or over-the-counter medication. Further experimentation in this area is unlikely because most researchers are reluctant to take the risk of examining directly whether a particular medicine causes malformation. Much of what has been learned and will continue to be learned about drug effects will come from natural experiments, in which the effects of drugs are noted through observation of different groups of women who differ in their use of medications during pregnancy.

Infections may damage the developing fetus during pregnancy and may affect the onset of certain other chronic illnesses during childhood. Intrauterine infection with several viruses has been associated with developmental retardation, congenital heart defects, and abnormal brain development. The German measles (rubella) virus, for example, creates a number of abnormalities, most importantly structural abnormalities of the heart and developmental retardation. Immunization against rubella has markedly decreased the number of children born with rubella-induced abnormalities in the past decade.

In childhood, infectious agents have been associated with the development or exacerbation of attacks of asthma (Leffert, 1985). Certain viruses, including mumps, have also been associated with the development of sporadic cases of diabetes mellitus in childhood (Gamble, 1980). Viruses may also play a role in the development of other chronic illnesses, such as leukemia and juvenile rheumatoid arthritis.

Most chronic illnesses arise through a combination of both genetic and environmental factors. Chromosomal or single-gene disorders are less likely to be influenced by environmental conditions, and polygenic conditions are more likely to result from synergistic interaction between genetic susceptibility and environmental influences. As an example, leukemia may be more likely in some patients who are genetically susceptible. Children with Down's syndrome, a specific chromosome abnormality, have a much higher risk of contracting leukemia than other children. Similarly, some forms of childhood leukemia are associated with observable abnormalities in chromosomes. Yet environmental agents, especially radiation, may increase the risk of leukemia. And mounting evidence suggests that certain viruses play an important role in the genesis of this disease. This complex interaction of environment and genetic makeup has implications for the prospects of developing effective primary prevention techniques for the chronic illnesses of childhood.

That many of the chronic illnesses have genetic roots leads to both despair and hope. Parents may experience unrelievable guilt in having a child so sick, who suffers so much. Uncertainty and conflict may attend the decision to have additional children. But hope may come from understanding the genetic origins of severe and chronic illness in childhood, for such an understanding leads to their prevention.

Public support for genetic and other preventive services, including amniocentesis and prenatal diagnosis, has been cyclical. The majority of Americans seem to support assuring families access to the basic genetic information needed for family planning. A vocal minority, however, have espoused the view that genetic services should be curtailed because they may encourage termination of pregnancy. That the availability of amniocentesis may also increase the birth rate is often neglected in these debates. Knowing that amniocentesis will allow them better information about the risks of having an affected fetus, families at high risk of certain genetic diseases may be more willing to commence pregnancies (Roghmann and others, 1983; Whitten and Nishiura, 1985). Thus, amniocentesis may actually lead to increased pregnancies. Amniocentesis without pregnancy termination is also important to families in that it helps them prepare for the birth of an affected child. That amniocentesis and its related outcomes are controversial is clear. Yet the issues must enter the public debate in a reasoned fashion if the prevention of chronic illnesses in childhood is to receive the attention it deserves.

Although the history of treatment of these diseases is filled with dramatic achievements (the treatments of diabetes and of leukemia provide good examples), in most instances, that treatment is palliative—adding years to a still-shortened lifespan, opening up opportunities for self-realization (but always within limitations), reducing pain and discomfort (but never completely), improving the quality of a life that remains inevitably flawed in some measure. There can be no slackening of effort to improve the care of those with these diseases, but disease prevention holds the greatest promise.

Tertiary Prevention: Diminishing the Impact of Illness on Daily Life. When a child has a chronic illness, it becomes an inescapable part of that child—a constant shadow. For families with affected children, the goals are to prevent deterioration of the organs involved and to diminish the impact of the illness on the child's development and family life. Although tertiary prevention may be less well defined than primary and secondary prevention, it is concerned with diminishing the interference of disease with the growth of the child and the family.

As we describe in the next two chapters, chronic illness in a child is associated with greater risks of problems of psychological adjustment for the child and greater stresses for the family. Chronic illness may also interfere in fundamental ways with the schooling of the child. An important component of tertiary prevention is to diminish these occurrences. An ecological approach and understanding of ecosystems put this form of tertiary prevention into perspective.

The term *ecosystem* encompasses all the individuals and institutions involved in the life of an individual child. Hence, the child defines the ecosystem, with parents, teachers, friends, and relatives arrayed around the child. When a child is born healthy, a new, comparatively small, and relatively uncomplicated ecosystem develops. Major figures in the ecosystem typically include the parents, at least one grandparent, a physician, perhaps some siblings, and scattered relatives. If the infant is seriously ill, this system can extend itself dramatically to encompass many more physicians, nurses, social workers, the claims manager of the health insurance company or the Medicaid program, and possibly parents of other seriously ill children. When a chronic illness is diagnosed in a previously healthy child or adolescent, similar forces come into play.

Whereas healthy children typically expand their own ecosystems gradually, slowly incorporating a playmate, a relative, several teachers, and so on, a chronic illness can expand the child's environmental group rapidly. Frequent visits to a specialty clinic or repeated hospitalizations may thrust a child into a bewildering number of interactions with individuals who make important decisions about the child's life.

Although the initial diagnosis of a chronic illness may expand the boundaries of the child's ecosystem, its continued presence may over time shrink those same boundaries. A child with muscular dystrophy, for example, becomes less independently mobile as the disease progresses and eventually must depend entirely on someone else to dress him, move him, and feed him. He may go to a school with other health-impaired children with whom he has close and good relationships, and he may be comfortable in the setting of the hospital, where he is familiar with certain nurses, social workers, or child life workers; but unless members of his extended family and community make great efforts to remain closely involved, the boundaries of his life may become limited to parents, other ill children, and a familiar circle of professionals. The normal sources of diversity and growth for other children—new acquaintances, new teachers, a special friend, cousins—all remain unexplored. For many children, the presence of a serious illness over time attenuates the beneficial diversity of the environment defined by that child.

The members of any ecosystem are highly interrelated. Any event that happens between two members affects the others. For example, if a mother of a chronically ill child becomes seriously depressed, her mood and behavior are likely to be felt not only by the child but also by her friends, the child's doctor, and the child's schoolteacher. Like a pebble tossed in a pond, a major event in the life of a child ripples through the child's ecosystem. This interrelatedness is often unacknowledged by service providers. For example, when major decisions about the treatment of a chronically ill child are made, the parents become involved but siblings are frequently left out. When many individuals are involved in the care of the child (for example, someone with spina bifida) the interconnectedness of all members of the system takes on a special complexity. Several types of physicians (a neurosurgeon, an orthopedist, a pediatrician, a urologist) as well as a social worker, a visiting nurse, parents, and grandparents may all be directly involved in this child's care. If the neurosurgeon initiates a new treatment without ensuring that other members of the system are aware of it, much confusion can ensue. The grandmother may see no reason to give the child more medication; the orthopedist might schedule an additional surgical procedure thereby increasing stress for the child and family to an intolerable level; the social worker may be unable to arrange quickly for additional transportation.

A smoothly functioning ecosystem can be made turbulent when any one member acts as if independent of the others. On the other hand, the interrelatedness, when used effectively, can result in extremely positive consequences. For example, if parents and the medical care team work closely together when a child suddenly refuses to take medications, the chance for an adequate understanding of the problem and an effective solution to it is enhanced.

In many health care institutions, in recent decades, the emphasis on the understanding of the whole child has brought to physicians and nurses a greater appreciation of the influence of family life on the health of the child and on the utilization of medical services. The notion of ecosystem has value here because it provides a means of mapping the terrain in which a particular child lives, yielding a picture of where the important persons stand, what the lines of communication must be, what services are needed, and what obstacles may interfere with good care. More than a conceptual tool, the notion of ecosystem provides a starting point for identifying issues of tertiary prevention and defining needed services.

Tertiary prevention is linked to distinguishing between the child and the disease. All too often a child with cystic fibrosis is referred to as a "cystic" or a child with thalassemia as a "thalassemic." This generalization of the disease to characterize the whole child limits, in a profound but subtle fashion, the future one might envision for that child.

This point is crucial because treatments vary in response to the way one thinks of a child and the child's future. One's vantage point will determine even the initial question: Is treatment for the disease or for the child and family? If treatment is for the child and family, then other questions follow: How can the child grow to maximum capacity despite the illness? How can a family meet its own developmental tasks with the least negative impact from the child's illness on its goals and aspirations? What can be done to prevent the social isolation of the child and the family? How can brothers and sisters, at times neglected in favor of care for their ill sibling, gain from the experience and grow into caring adults? And how can the costs to society of caring for children with chronic illness, both in institutions and out, be safely diminished while allowing for optimal participation of the child and the family in society? In essence, these questions and their answers form a large part of what this book is about.

Challenge: The Tasks Ahead

Although much has been accomplished, much remains to be done. Problems that call for more public attention include inequities in access to services, incentives emphasizing high-cost and high-technology services to the neglect of other needed services, insensitivity on the part of many providers, and inattention from schools.

Diversity, fragmentation, and high expense characterize the organization of health services for chronically ill children. Access to nonmedical services is highly variable. The fundamental problem in providing many of them is the lack of reimbursement for the services. In almost all circumstances, payment is skewed to a narrow range of services, mainly medical and surgical.

The typical pattern of a high-cost childhood chronic illness generates many obvious medical costs—for hospitals and physicians, medications, and lab and x-ray services and often for such services as physical therapy or social work. Many costs not easily categorized or assessed are also generated; these include transportation costs, extra telephone costs, costs associated with time lost from work or school, costs for special diets, and emotional costs associated with increased worry and stress within the family. The system for financing health care for chronically ill children in this country is a complex interaction of federal programs, state programs, and private insurance arrangements. Although most chronically ill children have a large portion of their medical care supported by some third-party arrangement, there are major gaps in coverage.

These challenges in the organization and financing of health services for chronically ill children are accompanied by similar issues in other realms. School policies have not kept pace with the greater opportunity for chronically ill children to receive schooling. For example, instructional programs for children who are absent from school are usually available only for those who are absent for long, continuous periods of time. Yet exacerbations of chronic illnesses often cause frequent, brief absences for which schools rarely make provisions.

By increasing understanding of the causes and mechanisms of diseases and potential medical and surgical therapies, basic biomedical research has greatly enhanced the lives of children. Much less attention has been paid to new areas of concern, such as ways of diminishing the developmental, family, or psychological impacts of chronic illness, that arise partly because of the success in keeping many children alive.

Professional training, too, has not kept pace with the changing needs of families with chronically ill children. Although chronicity obviously connotes persistence over long periods of time, professionals in training usually work with children over only brief periods. Physicians in training become knowledgeable about the episodes of illness but not about the illness over time or about the development of the child and family as they grow with the illness. Other professionals may have even less direct exposure during training to the longitudinal care of children with chronic illnesses, and the concepts presented throughout this book are rarely available to most professionals in training.

Summary

In the past few decades, great achievements have occurred to benefit those afflicted with chronic illness in childhood. Many chronically ill children who would have died young are living longer, principally because of tremendous and exciting advances in medical care and in the organization of services. These advances, coupled with birthrates, make it likely that the number of children with severe, chronic illnesses, broadly defined, will remain stable for the next several decades. These children and their families have benefited from the services of comprehensive treatment centers, the development of genetic services, the growing knowledge of the relationship of environmental factors to chronic illnesses, and the thrust to support preventive services.

The challenge now is to relieve the burdens on families by consolidating these many advances, remedying inequities in access to the broad range of needed services, and encouraging fruitful growth in the understanding of these diseases and their treatments. How can children be encouraged to meet their own physical and intellectual capacities most effectively? In what ways can policy help children participate as fully as possible in the varied family, social, athletic, and academic opportunities available to children who do not have serious health or handicapping conditions? This book brings attention to these challenges, to opportunities in the organization and financing of care for families of chronically ill children, to greater integration in school and other community activities, to improved training of professionals, and to continued advances in research. These five main groups of policy issues form the basis of our work: organization of services, financing of care, the needs of chronically ill children in schools, education of varied providers, and support of research. Chapter Three lays the groundwork for meeting this challenge by focusing on children with chronic illness in their families and communities.

Chapter 2 Appendix: A Primer on Genetics

The basic entity in heredity is the gene. Each gene produces a unique effect at the cellular level, and traits observed in individuals (for example, height) result from the aggregated effect of one or more genes as mediated by environmental influences. The nucleus of each cell in the body (except reproductive cells, sperm, and eggs) contains a full complement of genes, organized into structures called chromosomes. Chromosomes occur in pairs, and each cell contains twenty-three pairs, for a total of forty-six chromosomes. One pair of chromosomes determines sex; these are called the sex chromosomes. The other twenty-two paired chromosomes are called autosomes.

Specific genes occur at specific positions along the chromosomes. Within each pair of chromosomes, a gene at a specific position on one chromosome is matched with a gene at the same position on the other chromosome. The exception to this general rule occurs for the sex chromosomes (X and Y) in the male. Here, a number of genes on each sex chromosome have no match on the other. Females have two X chromosomes (XX).

The genes occurring at each position on the chromosome can take one of several forms, and each unique form produces a unique effect. Consequently, the paired genes, those in the same relative position on paired chromosomes, may produce the same effect or may produce a different effect. When the paired genes produce the same effect, they are termed *homozygous*. When they produce different effects, they are termed *heterozygous*. Although each gene produces a unique effect, some genes have more influence than others. The genes with more influence in a pair are referred to as *dominant genes*. Those with less influence are termed *recessive genes*.

Human reproductive cells (germ cells) contain half of the chromosomal content of the individual, that is, one chromosome from each pair of matched chromosomes. Assortment of chromosomes within a germ cell is random, meaning that the division of chromosome pairs to form the germ cells occurs independently among the twenty-three pairs. Offspring resulting from the mating of germ cells thus receive one half of each chromosome pair from the father and the other half from the mother.

Chromosomal defects may include extra chromosomes, missing chromosomes, or damaged chromosomes. Chromosomal disorders are exemplified by Down's syndrome, which causes certain specific facial characteristics, delayed development, and often congenital heart disease, among other problems. For children with Down's syndrome, the most common form includes an additional chromosome, and most such children have forty-seven separate chromosomes. On occasion, a large portion of the equivalent chromosome is attached to another chromosome so that the child has only forty-six chromosomes, but one is abnormally large and contains a sizable amount of extra genetic material.

In addition to chromosome abnormalities, a number of chronic illnesses have been associated with single-gene disorders.

Three main types of single-gene transmission can be described: autosomal recessive, autosomal dominant, and sex-linked recessive.

Autosomal recessive disorders are expressed only in individuals who are homozygous for the disorder. Two individuals who are heterozygous for the disorder mate, and both must then transmit the relevant gene to the child. The heterozygous parents (carriers) show no direct evidence of the disorder, nor do most other members of their family. Here, the dominant gene is the normal one, and the condition is expressed only if both genes are recessive or abnormal. A heterozygous parent has a one-in-two chance of transmitting a defective gene to the child. The disease can occur only if both parents are heterozygous. The mating of two heterozygous parents carries the risk that one-in-four children will have the disease (be homozygous), two of four will be carriers (be heterozygous, without disease), and one will be normal, not having received the defective gene.

Examples of autosomal recessive disorders are sickle cell anemia and cystic fibrosis. Sickle cell anemia in the United States is generally limited to blacks and persons of Mediterranean origin. Among American blacks, the carrier (heterozygote) frequency is approximately 80 to 120 individuals per thousand population. Among carriers, the trait may be partially expressed under certain extreme circumstances of low atmospheric pressure, but in general, the trait carries no direct health hazards. The homozygous state occurs in approximately 2 per thousand children among American blacks. Cystic fibrosis is the most common severe single-gene disorder among whites. The carrier (heterozygote) frequency is approximately 40 per thousand, and the affected (homozygote) population frequency is approximately 0.5 per thousand.

In autosomal dominant disorders, the affected gene is dominant in comparison to the normal, non-disease-producing gene. The heterozygote has the disease, and clear transmission within families from parent to child is usually observed. If a heterozygote mates with a healthy person not carrying the affected gene, each child carries a one-in-two risk of developing the disease. The child receives a normal gene from the healthy parent and an equal chance of a normal or affected gene from the parent with the disorder. Two heterozygous people mating have, in theory, a chance of three in four of their children having the disease (one homozygous, two heterozygous), with the fourth receiving two normal genes, one from each parent. In reality, the homozygous state is often incompatible with life. Furthermore, many autosomal dominant conditions are affected by what is termed incomplete penetrance. Even though the gene is dominant, it may be incompletely expressed in affected individuals, who will demonstrate varying signs of the disease. In osteogenesis imperfecta, for example, children are born with especially brittle and fragile bones, subject to frequent fractures. The whites of their eyes are often blue, and frequently one parent may have blue whites though no bone disease.

Sex-linked recessive disorders are carried by the mother and expressed mainly in the male children. In the reproductive process, the mother supplies an X chromosome and the father an X or Y chromosome to the offspring. The sex is female if two X chromosomes are received (one from each parent) and male when an X and Y chromosome are received. When a defective recessive gene on the X chromosome is transmitted to a male offspring, it is almost always expressed because there is no comparable normal gene on the Y chromosome to suppress the effect. On the other hand, when the defective gene on the X chromosome is transmitted to a female offspring, it becomes paired with the comparable gene on the X chromosome received from the other parent. If the paired gene is normal and the trait is recessive, the girl will not express the trait. She will, however, be a carrier for the trait and can pass it on to her offspring. If the mother is heterozygous (a carrier) and the father normal, one half of male children will be normal and all female children will be carriers. It should be possible to trace sex-linked recessive disorders through the family history, with previous males having been affected with the disorder. Hemophilia and Duchenne's muscular dystrophy both appear almost entirely in males, although rarely a female may be homozygous for these genes and have the disorder.

3

Effects of Chronic Illness on Children, Families, and Communities

A child's chronic illness engraves a family's life with worry. Variable in its daily effects yet ever a threat to the child's survival, a chronic illness is inescapable. For both child and family, it is a perpetual, demanding companion; a lifelong associate; a constant shadow.

The shade of a child's chronic illness extends beyond the family. For the communities in which these children live, a chronic illness is often troublesome and puzzling, sometimes a source of fear. Parents report, for example, that neighborhood children refuse to play with their son or daughter who has a chronic illness out of fear that it is contagious. Yet a chronic illness can also be a wellspring of learning for the larger community. That these children are able to live their lives with any degree of calm and graceful acceptance must surely inspire those who are not so burdened. If these children serve to help others take stock, however momentarily, of what is and is not important, then they have given a great gift to their community. One author, writing about children with cystic fibrosis, speaks well for children with any chronic illness: "Throughout it all—amongst the survivors, the families, the 'victims' themselves—inextricably intertwined with the sadness, the grief, and the anguished projections into the future, in among all these threads of sorrow runs also one deep beauty. It comes from facing with dignity what has been dictated by fate; from persevering in the face of encroaching debilitation; from knowing what the end will bring, yet living each day, and the day after, and the day after that, as if each were of vintage quality" (Shepard, 1981, p. 16).

Many accounts—from parents, siblings, and professionals—document the extraordinary influence of a child's chronic illness on the life of a family (Burton, 1975; Deford, 1983; Lund, 1974; Mikkelsen, Waechter, and Crittenden, 1978; Solnit and Stark, 1961, to name but a few). Collectively, these accounts make clear that, despite recurrent periods of crisis and danger, many families with a chronically ill child are able to sustain themselves in the face of much stress, to rise to the occasion, to live days of vintage quality. Some families find a greater closeness in a mutual commitment to caring for their ill child; siblings have profited by the experiences of having a sister or brother with a chronic illness, becoming by their own accounts more sensitive and caring adults. Past reports have often presented a bleak picture of families with a chronically ill child. This picture is inaccurate. Many families take the illness in stride, doing what needs to be done and living as normally as possible. Nevertheless, even these families endure problems unnecessarily complex, their lives made more burdensome by policies ill suited to their needs and by communities hobbled with myths and prejudices.

For some families, the challenges of raising a chronically ill child are too great. The child brings little hope or pleasure but rather financial ruin, attenuated careers, and despair. Some families have few of the financial, emotional, or social resources a chronically ill child will require. Moreover, high rates of divorce, shifting currents in employment, new roles for women and men, and rapid mobility all influence the ways families respond to a childhood chronic illness and may make a positive response difficult to sustain. In this book, we emphasize the central role of families and prefer a definition of *family* that is sufficiently broad to account for the many configurations of living arrangements that this word currently describes.

One of the most important issues in chronic childhood illness concerns the impact of the illness on the psychological well-being of the child and family. At first glance, the issue seems easy to resolve. Methodologically sound research should yield reliable evidence about the nature and strength of the psychological consequences of childhood chronic illness on child development and family life. After considerable effort over several decades, much has indeed been learned about how children and families respond to illness. Yet, key questions remain unresolved. Their lack of resolution stems from several overlapping problems, best understood from a historical vantage point.

The earliest reports on the effect of illness on the emotional functioning of children were published in the late 1930s (Beverly, 1936; Barraclough, 1937). In the following decade, pediatricians, psychologists, and psychiatrists began actively to investigate the emotional consequences of illness and hospitalization (Edelston, 1943; Greenberg, 1949; Jackson, 1942; Jetter, 1948; Langford, 1948; Richards and Wolff, 1940; Senn, 1945). In large measure, these reports were based on hospitalized children and focused on the responses of children when they were separated from their parents. These reports are generally case studies of children with acute or relatively minor physical problems as well as case studies of children with illnesses that required lengthy hospital stays. Without exception, these reports documented the extreme anxiety, distress, and withdrawal common to children left without access to their parents in a foreign and frightening world. The major differences between children with transitory problems and children requiring lengthy hospitalizations were seen primarily as a function of the length of time of the mother's absence; chronically hospitalized children were portrayed as falling into a depression and withdrawal that became known as hospitalism (Spitz, 1946).

In the 1950s, the crusade for changing hospital visiting rules grew strong, bolstered by a series of films (Robertson, 1952, 1958), a stream of reports on the negative effects of extended parent-child separation (Freud, 1952; Prugh and others, 1953; Vaughan, 1957; Platt Committee, 1959), and the disproval of the notion of cross-infection that had been used to justify keeping parents out of the way of nurses and doctors (Mason, 1965). With few exceptions, the conclusions of these various reports were based on case studies or clinical impressions and again ignored distinctions between the categories of acute and chronically ill children.

As concern about separation from parents diminished in response to improvements in parental visiting rules, professionals turned their attention to the problems of the dying child. In the late 1950s and early 1960s, there began to appear articles and book chapters concerning the special needs of dying children and their families and the proper response to them by physicians and nurses (Alexander and Adelenstein, 1958; Solnit and Green, 1959; Natterson and Knudson, 1960; Plank, 1962; Friedman and others, 1963). Shortly thereafter began the appearance of articles focused on mental health issues generally applicable to the care of children with chronic illnesses and their parents (Tisza, 1962; Garrard and Richmond, 1963; Green, 1967). To a large extent, these articles were again based on case studies and thoughtful impressions of clinicians who looked at their material through psychoanalytically oriented theories rather than through data systematically collected with more objective measures. Partly as a result of their theoretical bias, these authors tended to focus on the more negative outcomes and processes inherent in chronic illness and hospitalization; nevertheless, as Mason (1965) observed, most of these early reports note that lasting psychological problems infrequently resulted from the illness and that some families appeared strengthened as a result of the illness and its treatment demands.

By the end of the 1960s, there had arisen several professional organizations especially interested in hospitalized and chronically ill children (Shore and Goldston, 1978). The Association for the Care of Children's Health (ACCH) began in 1965; both the National Association of Children's Hospitals and Related Institutions (NACHRI) and the Society of Pediatric Psychology (SPP) started in 1968. By the early 1970s, a diverse group of professionals had recognized the special needs of chronically ill children (Mattsson, 1972; Lowit, 1973), a volume of papers had appeared (Debuskey, 1970), and an entire issue of a professional journal had been devoted to them (Steinhauer, Muskin, and Rae-Grant, 1974).

In addition to the more general focus, first on hospitalization, then on dying children, and then on chronic illness, authors have written about the mental health of children with specific diseases. One of the earliest reports concerned children with diabetes (Bruch, 1948). In the 1950s, parallel to the psychoanalytically oriented investigations into the effect of hospitalization and separation from parents, professionals studied illnesses that have a large psychosomatic component; these included asthma (Little and Cohen, 1951; Cutter, 1955; Neuhaus, 1958; Fitzelle, 1959) and diabetes (Kubany, Danowski, and Moses, 1956). During the 1950s, psychological consequences of cancers in children first received attention (Bozeman, Orbach, and Sutherland, 1955; Richmond and Waisman, 1955), and this increased greatly during the following decade (Chodoff, Friedman, and Hamburg, 1964; Toch, 1964; Vernick and Karon, 1965). The early 1960s also saw investigations of children who had hemophilia (Agle, 1964; Browne, Mally, and Kane, 1960), kidney problems (Korsch and Barnett, 1961) and cystic fibrosis (Turk, 1964). To a great extent, these studies document the emotional and social problems of the ill child and the family but fail to provide information on the percentage of families who are seriously troubled. Most of the studies were limited, as well, by the lack of well-researched, objective measures of emotional functioning. By the late 1960s, children with many different chronic illnesses (and in some cases their families) were the target of psychological studies.

From 1970 onward, the number of research studies on these children has increased steadily. In the sense of incorporating appropriate control groups and objective measures of emotional disturbance, the field has become more scientific, and it has moved away from an emphasis on case studies. Several researchers have begun to develop measures to ascertain the impact of a chronic illness on the child and family (Pless and Satterwhite, 1973; Stein and Riessman, 1980). A review of the current status of the methodological sophistication of research indicates that investigations have improved dramatically in respect to design and analysis, although problems persist in the measurement of psychological status and family functioning (Pless and Zvagulis, 1981).

Greater understanding of the psychological consequences of chronic illness for the child and family awaits continued improvement in the basic science in this area. Improvements in measurement, design, and analysis are all needed; this we discuss further in Chapter Nine. Aside from technical matters, other problems also create obstacles.

First, the medical outcome of many childhood chronic illnesses is improving at a rapid rate. Each year, a higher percentage of children with leukemia achieve five-year remissions. In many illnesses, there are improvements in basic physical functioning, despite the continued presence of the illness. Psychological consequences are likely to change in response to these developments. For families with children with leukemia, the earlier emphasis was on adaptation to the prospect of the child's certain death; now it is on adaptation to the uncertainty of achieving and maintaining remission. The psychological consequences of childhood chronic illness are a moving target for researchers; consequences change in response to the rapid developments in medical care.

Second, the locations where research is conducted make a difference in the results of the investigations. For example, research in a sophisticated, multidisciplinary center may show different effects of the illness in comparison with research conducted in other health-care-delivery contexts. Results from academic centers, which tend to have more comprehensive resources available, may not reflect the general state of affairs in the nation as a whole.

Third, traditional families (those in which the husband works, the wife stays home, and the couple remain married until one member dies) are becoming less common. The postponement of marriage, lower birthrates, steady rise in divorce rates since 1960, increasing participation by women in the work force, large number of remarriages, and high rate of children born out of wedlock have all contributed to substantial changes in the American family (Thornton and Freedman, 1983). These changes make a difference in family life for all children, including those with a chronic illness. The changing nature of the family has made it more difficult to study the effects of chronic illness on the family and the effects of family structure on the emotional well-being of chronically ill children.

Despite these limitations, the following conclusions merit a firm endorsement:

1. The presence of a chronic illness is a major and enduring source of stress for a child, but no calculus can yet predict whether this stress will result in enduring emotional scars.

Such factors as family environment, quality of medical care, community support, course of illness, and the child's own psychological resiliency will all shape the child's responses. For a few children, the diagnosis of a chronic illness may be the proverbial straw, ushering in a major psychiatric illness. For most children, however, a chronic illness brings emotional troubles that would be classified as adjustment disorders: a sudden refusal to take medications; an unusual amount of fighting in school; withdrawal, with evidence of loneliness and low self-esteem; refusal to go to school; persistent temper tantrums at home; fighting with siblings; and behaviors immature for the child's age. As Drotar and Bush (1985) note, these problems are more frequent by severalfold among children with chronic illness than among healthy children. A childhood chronic illness may not lead to major psychiatric disturbance, but it is likely to place a child at great risk for emotional distress.

2. The emotional distress that accompanies a child's chronic illness extends to the rest of the family. Mothers, fathers, and siblings of children with a chronic illness are subject to high levels of what would be formally termed adjustment problems. Acute depression, overeating, sleeplessness, irritability, poor school performance, marital tensions, fatigue, and a sense of helplessness and isolation are common problems for members of families with a chronically ill child. Yet, again, a chronic illness alone is unlikely to be the cause of divorce or major psychiatric disturbance. Many families report that meeting the challenges of chronic illness has brought the family closer, although this phenomenon has had little careful attention. Active practice of religious beliefs, a mutually supportive marital relationship, and a supportive community of relatives and friends are some variables important in contributing to this sense of greater closeness. Some siblings of chronically ill children report that the experience with a chronic illness brings greater sensitivity to others; again, little is known about how this sensitivity develops.

3. The way that care is delivered can make a difference in mediating the stress of a chronic illness. Medical care delivered

in the context of a supportive environment and accompanied by services designed to ameliorate the negative effects of the illness can assist the family in shouldering the burdens of care. Support groups for parents and adolescents, home-care services, respite care, relaxation methods for stress reduction, and other services all have the promise of preventing the accumulation of stress that can overwhelm a family's resources or hinder seriously a child's development. Several groups of researchers have committed themselves to careful evaluation of strategies in the prevention of severe emotional distress in children with a chronic illness and in their families (see, for example, Stein, 1982, and Perrin and MacLean, 1982).

What actually happens when a child is born or diagnosed with a chronic illness? What are the varieties of family responses? In what ways is the community likely to respond? How does the illness influence the child's development? What special services are required by chronically ill children and their families for health care, education, vocational guidance, financial counseling, and jobs? What personal and social factors shape the way a family and child incorporate the illness into their lives? As the child grows and the course of the illness becomes apparent over the years, what special community services will help the family sustain its caring?

In this chapter we search for answers to these and related questions. Our first intent is to describe broadly the experiences that characterize the lives of chronically ill children and their families. We examine what it is like for a child to grow up with a chronic illness, for a family to raise a child vulnerable for so long, and for a community to learn that one of its children has an incurable illness. Because childhood chronic illness is poorly understood by the public as a whole, we seek to describe the events that punctuate and give texture to the lives of these children and their families.

In this chapter, we rely heavily on the conversations we have had with parents of chronically ill children; on the books parents have written about their families as their chronically ill child grew up; on conclusions from empirical research, generally completed within the last decade and aimed at understanding the impact of these illnesses on development and on family life; and on relevant chapters in Hobbs and Perrin (1985). In reviewing this material, we were impressed with the apparent importance to these families and children of a community that could extend both practical aid as well as compassion. We were equally impressed with the lack in the professional literature of sustained attention to the relationship between the family of a chronically ill child and the community of which it is a part. Researchers have yet to examine systematically either the consequences to the chronically ill child of a community's often uneasy response or how a supportive response might be fostered. For this reason, we pay special attention to the notion of community in the lives of chronically ill children, seeking to illumine the complex relationship between families with a chronically ill child and their communities.

Becoming a Person with a Chronic Illness

In his sensitive account of growing up with a chronic illness, Massie (1985, p. 14) writes, " 'Having a chronic illness' is sometimes an elusive concept because one's illness becomes melded into one's identity. To ask what I would be like without hemophilia is an impossible question to answer, like asking who Abraham Lincoln would have been if he had been a midget. Clearly there *is* a me distinct from hemophilia, but it is hard to say sometimes where the boundaries to that me are. Who would Helen Keller have been if she had been a sighted and hearing little girl?"

His words underscore the fact that a child with a chronic illness remains always a developing individual, responsive to the world and needful of care and support. Yet, recurrent events and experiences unknown to most other youngsters punctuate the lives of these children. The pain, anticipated and actual, of repeated medical procedures; the boredom of waiting for the doctor or lying in bed until one's body finally heals; the rage against an indifferent nurse or physician; the sense of gratitude for those who care in special ways; the fear of death in the midst of a frightening, unpredictable crisis; the repeated separations from parents and family, sometimes for far too long; the embarassment of being physically different from other children; the relief when symptoms abate; the despair when the pain begins again: these are events that may occasionally touch all children, but they are well known only to those with a chronic illness.

To appreciate the cumulative influence of these events is to recognize the intricate relationship between a child's understanding of illness and a child's emotional development. As several researchers have shown (Bibace and Walsh, 1981; Perrin and Gerrity, 1981, 1984), childhood notions of illness begin from a primitive sense of magic and mystery and differentiate into an accurate appraisal of cause and effect. Simultaneously, a child's sense of self emerges, tied to the accomplishment of the developmental tasks that both Piaget (Piaget and Inhelder, 1969) and Erikson (1964) have detailed well. Several authors have traced the reciprocal interactions between a chronically ill child's understanding of illness and the progressive developmental tasks of infancy, childhood, and adolescence (Magrab, 1985; Perrin and Gerrity, 1984).

The presence of a serious physical illness in an infant compromises the infant's social and physical development in several respects. First, many chronic illnesses interfere directly with basic functions of movement, feeding, and touching. Through these modalities, infants learn about the world and develop a sense of trust that their needs will be met. To the extent that an illness restricts or disrupts this learning, the emotional development of a child is threatened. Second, many seriously ill infants are scrawny creatures, surrounded by the tubes and machines common to intensive care units. Parents have to overcome natural feelings of fear and distance in order to touch and cuddle their child. To the extent that a chronic illness makes attachment difficult, emotional development falters.

As most parents know, toddlers are on the go. A seemingly limitless desire to explore their world, even in the face of stern prohibition, fuels a developing sense of autonomy and self-control. The wise parent balances restriction with appropriate choice. This balance can be elusive under the conditions imposed by a chronic illness. For example, should a parent of a child with hemophilia let him run free at the risk of an accident that under normal conditions might be minor but might in this case be life threatening? The judgment required by the presence of a chronic illness demands a constant calculation of potential risk. To a toddler, illness is only another obstacle in the way of play. Furthermore, as Perrin and Gerrity (1984) note, "Because of their magical and egocentric views of causality and their desire to be in control, they interpret illness and hospitalization as events that they somehow caused to happen" (p. 23).

In preschool children, mastery and success become important. When a chronic illness imposes restraints that make mastery difficult, it can also impose a lasting sense of failure. The thinking of preschool children—still illogical, egocentric, and concrete—is no longer bound by what they can see. As a result, preschoolers can imagine the inside of their body, but in a limited mechanical way. Perrin and Gerrity again note the implications for a chronically ill preschooler: "Their magical and egocentric orientation and tenuous grasp of causal relationships may result in the frequently noted belief that their illness is probably a punishment for some bad action or thought. Children with diabetes often imagine that their illness was caused by eating too much candy" (p. 25).

By the time they are in school, children develop a more workable understanding of cause and effect: Illness results from contamination, and health returns when the doctor's orders are followed. But along with this limited sense of causality comes a deeper appreciation of difference. Children with asthma see that other children do not wheeze; children with diabetes let other children eat their piece of birthday cake; for no apparent reason, boys with muscular dystrophy can no longer stand without crutches. It is at this age, also, that children begin to understand their role in the family—and that everyone contributes to family tasks. Chronically ill children can suffer greatly if their only role is one of taking, with little chance to play an active, contributing role in the family.

Even with an intact, well-functioning body, it is hard enough to negotiate the currents and challenges of adolescence. For teenagers with a chronic illness, the body can be a continual source of embarrassment. Furthermore, limitations of physiological functioning thwart the desire for autonomy and independence. Partly as a statement of independence, most adolescents refuse, at some point, to comply with medical treatments, but they do so without a good sense of the consequences of noncompliance (Coupey and Cohen, 1984).

Regardless of the age of a child, a chronic illness represents a powerful source of stress, similar in consequence to other traumas of life, including divorce, parental alcoholism, or the death of a parent. But a chronic illness for a child must be distinguished from other sources of stress by its constancy, by the likelihood of an early death, by an often unpredictable but usually deteriorating course of illness, and by the demands of the treatment itself, including both hospitalization and routine care. Furthermore, the daily care routines and medical treatments for these children often generate more burdens than the illness and can themselves lead to emotional or social problems. Youngsters with diabetes can be the target of classroom jokes because they have to test their urine; a father's desire to protect his son with hemophilia from unnecessary falls may eventually lead the boy to develop a paralyzing fear of playing sports.

Whether a child has hemophilia, diabetes, sickle cell anemia, or any of the other chronic illnesses, the relentlessness of the disease and the continuing need for treatment necessarily limit activities, impose rigid routines of care, challenge a child's sense of self-worth, and force entry into a frightening world of emergency rooms, hospital corridors, and medical machines. Here we enumerate more specifically the consequences of growing up with a chronic illness.

Separation from Home and Family. Having a chronic illness often means hospitalization and therefore separation from parents and family. These events assume a different meaning for infants, toddlers, children, and adolescents, but long-term or repeated separation from home and family as a result of hospitalization can have profound consequences for the development of any child. With different illnesses, of course, hospitalization comes at different times and in different ways. For disorders diagnosed at birth, such as cleft lip and/or cleft palate, spina bifida, and congenital heart diseases, hospitalization occurs early and may continue intermittently through the first few years of life. With most other illnesses, the child will typically enter the hospital suddenly, often in an acute or painful crisis: in ketoacidosis for a child with diabetes, with severe joint bleeding for a child with hemophilia, in great pain for those with sickle cell disease or with leukemia. For almost every chronically ill child, hospitalization becomes a familiar event—one that brings that child into a world that can be mysterious and frightening.

For an infant born with a chronic illness, hospital care involves treatment in a neonatal intensive care unit. Here the physical vulnerability of the infant is guarded by an imposing array of medical machines including heart rate monitors, respirators, feeding tubes, and special lights. An infant in such an environment is at great risk for delayed emotional development, both because of intrinsic physiological problems and because the parents are frequently unable to develop a special attachment with this child. They report being afraid to look at or touch their infant; some refuse to believe that such a small, scrawny, discolored, or misshapen creature is their long-awaited child (DuHamel and others, 1974). Even when the infant leaves the intensive care unit, continuing problems may hamper the development of a special closeness between a parent and an ill infant. Some parents, for reasons as yet unclear, seem especially vulnerable to the obstacles that impede this attachment—an attachment necessary for subsequent developmental and emotional growth (Klaus and Kennell, 1976).

For other children, anxieties surrounding hospitalization may be quite different, but they become no less potent in effect. To a preschooler, being left in a hospital can bring out a powerful feeling of abandonment. This sense can be aggravated by the normal tendency to believe that they are responsible for all events. Hospitalization can also raise overwhelming anxieties about the loss of one's hands and toes and other body parts or about being taken to the operating room and left there. Unless the staff of the hospital helps the child overcome these fears and helps the parents understand and address them, hospitalization can remain an unnecessarily traumatic event.

With the benefits of further growth in understanding, a school-aged child who is often hospitalized will learn that parents return on a predictable basis but may be convinced that friendships with school chums will suffer irreparably. Massie (1985, p. 17) describes the difficulties associated with hospitalization for a school-aged child for whom friendships are enormously important:

Apart from the worlds of family and friends, chronically ill children must also learn to survive in the world of medicine. This strange land of machinery, white coats, frequent medication, and alternating states of anxiety, boredom, and suffering is a challenge to any person, but for the chronically ill child, it is part of daily life. For those chronically ill children who commute between a normal school and occasional hospitalizations, there is a constant challenge to reconcile the two worlds, to explain to one's friends about medicines and procedures, and to retain in the midst of the medical world an active hope to return to a more normal life. For the chronically ill child who is hospitalized most or all of the time, there is the struggle of learning to live in a world of which most people are not even aware, or, if they are, of which they are afraid.

Hospitalization can be frightening to a chronically ill adolescent as well, regardless of the number of previous hospitalizations. The return to a well-known hospital floor may usher in a depression and a withdrawal that can be hard to reverse. For some chronically ill adolescents, hospitalization reawakens dormant fears of death and ultimate separation from friends and family. Adolescents, after all, can for the first time actually imagine future events in realistic terms. At times of hospitalization, some chronically ill adolescents begin to write their wills—a reasonable, adultlike way of dealing with the fear of an impending death.

Facing Frustration, Boredom, and Pain. Television dramas about doctors and hospitals idealize patient care. Nurses and doctors are shown as efficient professionals working in clean, cheerful settings; patient needs are addressed rapidly and well; and medical technologies generally lead to happy and definitive outcomes. The reality of medical care can be quite different. Nurses and doctors can be tired, inefficient, and callous. Patients can find themselves waiting a great deal, often for intolerably long periods of time. Sophisticated lab tests frequently yield a confusing picture. The right or best decision can rest on an educated guess. What is clear and forceful in fiction is muddied and hesitant in fact.

This observation applies with special force to children who must regularly depend on the medical care system. Because they use hospitals and clinics so often, chronically ill children spend a lot of time waiting. They wait for the nurse to answer their calls, for the doctor to finish rounds, for the operating room to be available, for the x-ray technician to finish lunch, for the social worker to get off the phone, for the special bus to take them to the clinic, for the line at the pharmacy to get shorter, for some attention from those who are busy caring for emergencies, and for their bodies to heal enough so they can return to a normal life. The waiting and the boredom that accompany a chronically ill child's life are neither benign nor neutral. Worry, sadness, impatience, and fear fill hours that would otherwise be spent in play or school.

In addition to the waiting, chronically ill children must cope with repeated painful experiences. Worse yet, they can find themselves in a system whose members fail to appreciate that pain. A father, writing about the life of his daughter, Alex, who had cystic fibrosis, recalls the following:

A particularly officious young doctor brought a bunch of students over to examine Alex. He pointed to the tube in her chest, explaining that the incision of an inch or so had been made while she was under a local anesthetic, and then he declared, "This procedure is not very painful to the patient." Immediately, he proceeded with his lecture.

All the years of hearing these cocky young experts talking at her as if she were a body on display, as if a child—a sick child—could not be a real person, welled up in Alex. "Wait!" she suddenly cried out.

But the doctor ignored her and kept right on with his spiel. "No, wait, you," she said again, louder still, and tugging at his sleeve this time, too.

He stopped. He had to. Alex had made him stop. And, only then, with a condescending look of annoyance, he turned down to her. "Yes, what is it, dear?"

"How do you know?" Alex asked.

"What, dear?"

"How . . . do . . . you . . . know?"

"I'm sorry, but . . . ."

"Have you ever had a big tube stuck in you and then taken out again?"

"Well, no, I, I . . . ."

"Then don't you tell me—or them—it doesn't hurt. Because I don't like being lied to" [Deford, 1983, pp. 140–141].

Other accounts in both the professional and lay literature testify to the fear of painful medical care (Covelli, 1979; Eland and Anderson, 1977; Lund, 1974; Massie and Massie, 1976; Shore and Goldston, 1978). These accounts also pay tribute to physicians, nurses, playroom supervisors, and friends who have provided shelter for these children, who have acknowledged the pain and helped the child endure it through play, talking, or simply holding hands. We draw a simple conclusion from these accounts: Chronically ill children need sustained and sensitive assistance in negotiating the events that define chronic illness care.

Obstacles to Making and Keeping Friends. Most chronically ill children have periods when they are free of symptoms, when they seem indeed just like any other child. For them, as for all other children, their natural inclinations to play with other children and their participation in birthday parties, summer camps, and weddings will lay the foundation for friendships. Most chronically ill children have the opportunity to enjoy these events; most will develop at least part of the cultural foundation on which friendships can be built. But a chronic illness invariably shapes this foundation and limits opportunities for making and keeping friends.

For example, chronic illness can impart a sense of exile, locking a child into loneliness. Covelli (1979, p. 28), writing from the vantage point of an adult looking back on being a child with diabetes, recalls that at age ten, "My single most persistent feeling then was of separation: *Other children do not take a needle. I cannot eat the same foods they do. I do not feel the same as I did before. I am different.*" He tells what it is like to go to school for the first time, knowing that he has something called diabetes and, in his own way, knowing what it means:

On this particular morning the dread was intense. I was going to school; my classmates would know I was different.

At school I sat at the polished wood desk, my head down, my eyes on the childish graffiti etched in the wood. I could not look at the other kids in the face, I could only shoot glances at the blackboard in front of the room. Was everyone staring, or was my shame a product of my imagination?

Doctors often soothe the diabetic by saying that people have no way of knowing he has the disease. Comforting to an adult, perhaps, but to a child, surface appearances mean nothing. I believed that my classmates could see through me. The damage done me was not inflicted by others, but came from within myself: I created the shame that damaged my identity. And, of course, someone came along to reinforce my fears.

He walked over to me during recess. I was standing alone on the rim of the school yard, kicking stones against the fence, when I saw him coming. He stood a few feet away from me, a wide smile splitting his face. "Teacher told us you were in the hospital," he said.

My breath got short. I did not answer. He knows, I thought, he knows.

"She told us what it was," he said.

I wanted to run, to push him aside and find a place where no one would see me, no one would know.

"She said you were real sick and we had to be nice to you when you came back," he said. "You don't look sick to me."

I didn't realize that he couldn't see the illness.

"She explained about diabetes; she said that's what you got." I met his eyes for a moment. "I never heard about that diabetes before, so I asked my mother. She said it was catching and to stay away from you or I'd get it, too."

So that's why he was keeping his distance. I was so terror-stricken I could not reply.

"Why'd you come back to school?" he asked. "You want to make us all sick? You better stay away from *me*."

When I later learned that I could not spread the disease, I didn't feel much comforted. What other children thought of me was more important at that stage of my life than the actual truth. I felt set apart from my own small society. I was deeply, everlastingly lonely [pp. 29–30].

Partly because other children fail to comprehend what having a chronic illness means and fail to understand the odd language of "ketoacidosis," "bone marrows," "factor VIII concentrate," "dialysis," and so on, chronically ill children frequently view the hospital or clinic as a refuge. Despite the pain and discomfort that accompany a hospitalization, hospital floors are at least a place where illness bears no stigma and explanations are unnecessary.

The urge to cloister oneself can be powerful, especially during adolescence. The presence of a chronic illness, regardless of its degree of visibility, can deter socializing with friends and acquaintances. Sexuality, an uncertain domain for most teenagers, raises special problems for a chronically ill adolescent: Does your boyfriend need to know about your cystic fibrosis? Do you tell a girl on the first date that you have sickle cell anemia? What does having sex do to insulin levels? How will my disease affect my sexuality, my attractiveness, and my ability to have babies?

These questions justly claim much attention from adolescents, for in fact, a chronic illness can affect physical development profoundly. Changes in physical appearance, such as loss of hair from chemotherapy treatment for cancer, can decrease physical attractiveness. Some studies report that it is out of embarrassment, fear, and uncertainty that adolescents avoid peers who have cancer. Other illnesses, such as chronic heart conditions or juvenile diabetes, increase the risk of problems for the mother during pregnancy and childbirth. Few research efforts have investigated this area, but one study (Drotar and others, 1981) found that young adults with cystic fibrosis told only very close friends about their disease, a strategy that appeared to be an adaptive way of maintaining some control over the impact of the illness and of coping with realistic social barriers toward finding jobs, continuing school, and developing a circle of acquaintances. Discovering sexuality or learning the skills of dating and having fun with the other sex is only one task of adolescence, but it is an important and vulnerable one. If there is no one with whom an adolescent can discuss these matters, a chronic illness can seriously attenuate the exploration of friendship, dating, and sex (Coupey and Cohen, 1984; Dorner, 1976).

Families of Chronically Ill Children

Chronic illness does not strike individuals; it strikes the whole living unit of the family. The presence of a chronic illness creates such enormous financial and emotional demands that every family member is affected—the parents and brothers and sisters as well. The ability of the family to respond and the manner in which its members choose to do so can be the decisive element in how a child learns to work with and overcome the effects of a chronic illness [Massie, 1985, p. 15].

Families with a chronically ill child confront challenges and bear burdens unknown to other families. The shock of the initial diagnosis and the urgent, compelling need for knowledge; the exhausting nature of constant care unpredictably punctuated by crisis; the many and persistent financial concerns; the continued witnessing of a child's pain; tensions with one's spouse that can be aggravated by the fatiguing chronicity of care; the worries about the well-being of other children; and the multitude of questions involving the fair distribution within the family of time, money, and concern—these are challenges that parents of a chronically ill child must face. By many accounts, most families with chronically ill children resolve these challenges successfully, despite the many obstacles raised by an often perverse health care system, professionals who may be poorly informed, and insensitive communities. That families overcome such obstacles testifies to the resiliency and strength of family ties. Yet many families lack this resilience, and for them, the emotional price of the illness is severe.

Moreover, current changes in American families may threaten the bonds that assist in the care of children with a chronic illness. Note the following from a report written in the early 1980s (Thornton and Freedman, 1983):

- Over a million children are affected by divorce each year in the United States [p. 8].
- In 1980, the proportion of babies born to unmarried mothers was 18 percent of all births. Out-of-wedlock births made up nearly half (48 percent) of total births to nonwhite women and close to one tenth (11 percent) of births to white women [p. 21]. Partly because of out-of-wedlock births and partly because of a high divorce rate, there were 6 million households maintained by single mothers in 1982, a figure that represents 19 percent of all American households with children [p. 33]. If current trends persist, 40 to 50 percent of all children will live in a fatherless family before they turn nineteen [p. 33].
- In 1982, 49 percent of married mothers with children under six were in the labor force [p. 24]. Furthermore, in 1977, 29 percent of children under six whose mothers worked full time were

cared for during the day in their own homes (most frequently by a relative); 47 percent were cared for in the home of others; and 15 percent were taken to group care centers [p. 26].

- Over the last decade, the number of families with three or more children has decreased dramatically; the number of families who have one or two children has increased [p. 14].

- In 1982, 51 percent of married women were employed, up from 22 percent in 1948 [p. 24]. In large measure, the decision for a wife to work hinges on family financial need.

For chronically ill children, the consequences of these figures are likely to be profound. For many, the stress of divorce adds to the stress of the illness itself. Many will live in households with only one parent. Many will question whether their illness contributed to their parent's divorce. Many may never know whether their mother stayed home to care for them instead of starting or continuing a career. Many will find themselves under the care of relatives, parents, or friends who are unfamiliar with or frightened by a chronic illness. Many will live in families burdened by the events associated with poverty: frequent moves, poor housing, chronic disruption. All of these consequences may in turn aggravate the symptoms of the illness or hinder adequate care.

For families with only one or two children, the diagnosis of a chronic illness alters the parents' expectations about having more children. When one's only child is ill, parents may wish to have more children. Yet, the desire to have a healthy child can provoke troubling questions: Will the new infant also be ill? Will we be able to afford to raise another child while taking care of a chronically ill one? Are we having another child because this one has disappointed us? Furthermore, the relative decrease in family size means that there will be fewer aunts, uncles, and cousins to provide emotional solace or from whom practical assistance may be sought.

That families now are so varied in form and composition urges caution in generalizing about the consequences of childhood chronic illness for family life. Yet the testimony of family members, both in published accounts and in direct conversation, has convinced us that almost all families with a chronically ill child struggle with similar issues, crises, and concerns.

Responding to the Diagnosis. Policy matters seem distant from the moment when parents are told that their child has a chronic illness. This news may evoke a wide array of emotions: disbelief, shock, disgust, relief, guilt, despair, hate, rage, confusion. Although such reactions may be inevitable, the way in which the diagnosis is made and communicated can assist the parents in negotiating these emotional currents. In many instances, parents have reported that they knew something was wrong long before the problem was given an accurate diagnosis. One report (Mikkelsen, Waechter, and Crittenden, 1978) about children with cystic fibrosis notes, "Almost all of the families interviewed in our study told us that they knew 'something was wrong' with their child in early infancy, but over half described great difficulty in securing an accurate diagnosis. Some were told that their child had asthma or allergies, and ineffective treatment was prescribed. Some were told that they were just over-concerned, that the child would 'grow out of it' " (p. 23). Other reports, on other chronic illnesses, confirm this finding (Firth and others, 1983).

In addition to delays in reaching an accurate diagnosis, parents report concerns with the way doctors have told them the diagnosis. In some instances, physicians are abrupt. The Massies' account illustrates this:

On the evening of the second day we were still waiting in a stifling, overheated waiting room with hospital green walls and antiseptic furniture of cheap chrome and plastic. I smoked cigarette after cigarette. Bob was exhausted. It had been his first day on the new job. He had just joined us again. Suddenly a man entered. It was at last the long-awaited Eminence, "Doctor" himself. He was wearing a grey suit, and his eyes looked down at the floor as he hurriedly came in. There were no preliminaries. He announced, coldly and matter-of-factly, "The child has classical hemophilia. There will be compensations, you may be sure." And with these enigmatic words, he turned on his heel and walked out [Massie and Massie, 1976, p. 12].

In other instances, physicians overwhelm the parents with information and facts far in excess of what they can initially understand. The physician may emphasize the physiological reasons for treatment, the spectrum of variations in the course of the illness, and the specific long-term physical consequences when the parents only want to know what and how they are going to tell their other children.

Those involved with the care of children with chronic illness and their families frequently misunderstand the difficulty of managing the demanding practicalities of treatment and care while simultaneously coping with the emotional impact of the diagnosis. The timing of communicating basic knowledge to parents must be matched to the parents' emotional readiness to understand its relevance. As an aid in accomplishing this task, several groups have charted the evolution of a family's response to the diagnosis of a chronic illness (Drotar and others, 1975; Solnit and Stark, 1961). Such models typically define stages in a parent's response to the birth of an imperfect infant or the diagnosis of a chronic illness. These stage theories generally postulate an initial period of shock and bewilderment followed by a time of denial or a sense that the situation is unreal or a bad dream. The third stage, according to Drotar and colleagues (1975), includes a time of sadness, anger, and much worry as the demands of care continue unabated and limitations become more apparent. Final stages generally describe some measure of adaptation, defined as a lessening of the intensity of feelings and a time of reorganization, in which parents are able to offer support to each other and to emphasize any positive aspects of the situation.

Parents, as well as many professionals, caution that theories of how parents respond to a traumatic event are limited in their utility. They may help professionals anticipate some of the problems that families might encounter, but they communicate inaccurately the ebb and flow of feeling that accompanies life with a chronically ill child. One father with whom we spoke indicated that stage theories are not so tidy as they seem. He noted that, even if there had been no crisis or problem, he would become angry again and have to start at the beginning. He said he sometimes felt everything at once: discouragement, anger, love, hope, despair, determination. "You know, I don't think I'm ever going to accept the fact that my daughter has a life-long and serious illness. On most days, I have learned to come to terms with it, but I cannot accept it" (Shayne and Cerreto, 1981, p. 5).

Searching for Knowledge. Along with the initial shock and disbelief, parents typically have many questions: What does the disease do? Will my child's life be shortened? Is there a cure? Will there be pain? Can my child be normal? Could I have done something differently to avoid this? What does it really mean? These are often the first of many questions that propel parents into an urgent search for knowledge.

Sometimes this search is fruitful. Parents may find a physician who takes the time and has a special sensitivity, who remains available to answer questions, and who can explain the disease and its implications in a manner neither technical nor condescending. Some parents find useful the brochures or relevant books made available by the local association representing their child's disease. A few parents may discover other parents with children similarly afflicted, who can offer helpful advice unaccompanied by frightening horror stories about potential disasters.

But for many parents the search for knowledge is a frustrating one. Answers to even relatively straightforward questions are elusive, partly because these diseases are uncertain in their prognosis and partly because physicians remain tentative, knowing that the course of an individual's illness can defy accurate prediction. Sometimes, too, physicians are unavailable to answer questions. For example, the physician who makes the diagnosis is usually a subspecialist, unfamiliar to the family, often quite distant from the family's home, and frequently too busy to be readily accessible. Yet the family's general practitioner or pediatrician is rarely well informed about the intricacies of specific chronic illnesses; he or she may be available but inaccurate. Furthermore, in many cities and towns, the local health charities (if they exist) are poorly organized. As a result, parents remain ignorant of potentially helpful newsletters, services, and self-help groups.

Parents of chronically ill children discover that they want knowledge in three areas: the basic physiology, course, and treatment of the illness or condition, including what could prevent problems from developing; the workings of the health care system and related services; and the management of the strong emotions that the illness arouses. Parents who have sought to gain this knowledge assert that without it their children's care would suffer (Shayne and Cerreto, 1981).

Although they base their conclusions primarily on their research with families who have a child with cancer, Chesler and Yoak (1984) stress the importance of information in caring for any chronically ill child. "If parents are to be involved in the long-term care of chronically and seriously ill children, they must have adequate and detailed information about symptoms, disease progress, danger signals, and treatment procedures and options. Gathering and understanding information may be critical to the child's survival as well as to parents' own emotional stability and integrity" (p. 486).

Parents, of course, differ widely in their capacity to search for information, to formulate questions, and to express their worries. They often find themselves in a position of knowing too little to know what questions to ask—or failing to ask questions out of a fear of sounding "dumb" to the doctor. Sometimes they assume the doctor will tell them what they need to know. In many instances, a physician or nurse must help parents formulate questions and find answers if they are to become educated caretakers of their child. The same points apply to adolescents who must learn basics of the physiology of their illness in the growth of their responsibilities for self-care.

Unfortunately, several reports indicate that parents often labor under serious misconceptions about their child's illness—misconceptions that are often brewed by cultural myths about bodily functions or by half-knowledge that leads to faulty conclusions. Whitten, Waugh, and Moore (1974), for example, discovered that even several years after the diagnosis of sickle cell anemia in their children, a large percentage of parents had serious misunderstandings of many aspects of the conditions of the disease—misunderstandings that would interfere with effective care. Whitten found that much basic information either had not been presented to the parents or had been presented in a confusing fashion. Parents also tend to forget facts they once knew and often are reluctant to discuss their questions and uncertainties with their child's doctors. Parents of children with sickle cell anemia are not alone in their misunderstandings. Other reports focused on other illnesses confirm that this predicament is widespread (Chesler and Yoak, 1984; McKeever, 1981; Korsch and Fine, 1985).

Knowledge of basic physiological function is insufficient for parents of a chronically ill child. Because many of these children require frequent hospitalization, visits to different clinics, and involvement with many ancillary agencies (such as the Medicaid office, an insurance company, a social services program, or a rehabilitation center), parents need help in negotiating the service system. It is difficult to appreciate the byzantine quality of the health care and social services bureaucracy in the large hospitals on which these families depend. For example, a clinic card, easily left home in the midst of getting to an appointment, can be the difference between rapid attention to a child and long hours of waiting.

Learning how to negotiate the medical care system comes by way of firsthand experience. Rarely does anyone teach the family about the structure of the hospital, the rotation of interns who will care for the child, or which social workers are most helpful. The complexity of the business of health care in this country may be a nuisance to families who occasionally come in contact with it, but to a family with a chronically ill child, it is a serious obstacle to efficient care. One benefit of support groups for parents of chronically ill children seems to be sharing the tricks to bypassing bureaucratic obstacles (Chesler and Yoak, 1984; Milofsky and Elworth, 1985).

Although parents need to know much about their child's illness and about the health care system, an overwhelming worry for their child can turn askew their search for knowledge. In many instances, for example, parents purchase medical textbooks in an effort to learn about basic biochemical processes underlying their child's disease (Massie and Massie, 1976; Shayne and Cerreto, 1981). Rumors of an herbalist's cure for cystic fibrosis or meditation to cure muscular dystrophy have sent many families on fruitless and expensive journeys (Weisman, 1982). Emotion can cloud the judgment of the most careful and knowledgeable parent. For this reason, most parents need assistance at some point in negotiating the currents of their own emotional responses to their child's illness. They need to know that being angry at the unfairness of the illness is a common feeling and that it is possible to express that anger in ways not hurtful to the ill child or to other members of the family.

Parents need to know that becoming tired of taking care of the child is to be expected rather than an indication of a failure of will or an abandonment of the child. Accounts of parental responses to a chronic illness document the range of strategies parents use to manage their own feelings (Chan and Leff, 1982; Sabbeth, 1984; Chesler and Yoak, 1984; Shayne and Cerreto, 1981; Pediatric Ambulatory Care Division, 1983).

Many parents face this task alone, unnecessarily abandoned to the mystery of coming to terms with their child's chronic illness. For other parents, sustained support in this task is found along with their medical care in the form of organized support groups, knowledgeable nurses and physicians, or experienced mental health professionals.

Watching the Pain and Fear. One of the most difficult burdens for parents is watching their child suffer. A mother of an adolescent with leukemia relates a simple event representative of many others witnessed by parents:

And Eric lost his hair. In one afternoon. The goddess Adriamycin took it as a sacrifice. I was there that day it began to happen. Eric sat with me out in the lobby, which was unusually deserted. His tan had already turned sallow; his eyes were gray-shadowed with drugs. He pulled a tuft from his head, then another, and stared at the reddish-gold clumps in the palm of his hand.

"It's all going," he said. His mouth trembled slightly. He touched it with two fingers to make it stop.

"Maybe not," I said stupidly.

"Of course it is."

He was right. I had seen too many hairless souls walking these halls with their IV hat racks to dispute them. Soon he would be one of them [Lund, 1974, p. 271].

All children at one point or another ask questions that are answered with difficulty, questions about death or sex or growing up. For parents of a chronically ill child these questions can assume an unusually serious character. Let us illustrate by again excerpting a story told by a mother whose eleven-year-old child, Peter, had muscular dystrophy. Peter was in a hospital and on a respirator because he had a serious respiratory infection. His disease had progressed far enough that his chest muscles were too weak to breathe. The respirator had taken over his breathing until the infection cleared. At the time of this event, he was unable to talk because the respirator's long tube sat in his throat. Quite frail, he nevertheless kept in touch with his family and with visitors by writing. His mother recalls the following:

He begins to write. Because I must be standing to support his moving hand properly, I cannot see what he is writing. His hand blocks my view.

I stare at the top of his hand as it moves diagonally, from right to left, in a downward stroke. Then he lifts his hand up ever so slightly off the paper and makes another downward stroke—this one from left to right. I know it's going to be the letter A before he draws the final horizontal line.

The next one is an M. He makes those strokes straight up and down, so I have to wait until the third stroke to make sure it's not an N.

I can't tell if the next one is going to be a T or an I or an L until he draws a horizontal line across the top and bottom, and then I know it's an I.

I'm pretty sure from the spherical way he starts out on the next letter that it's going to be an O, but I'm wrong. He stops in mid-circle and finishes it off as a G.

The next letter is an O. He is writing: "AM I GOING TO DIE?"

I wait until we're finished writing, until the dot is under the question mark, to answer him. I give myself that much time to think. Any more would be suspicious.

"No" [Weisman, 1982, p. 267].

Most persons who have worked with chronically ill children and their parents would agree that the mother's response could have been different. Her desire to protect her child and perhaps her own discomfort led to a false reassurance. At some level, children who are very ill know that death may be quite close. A parent's refusal to acknowledge it simply communicates to the child that it shouldn't be talked about when, in fact, the child's need to do so may be urgent. But such an observation overlooks the difficult nature of the situation. Comforting a gravely ill child when the fear of death arises is only one of the exceptional events that occur in the lives of those who care for chronically ill children.

Financial Concerns. Early in the course of the illness, many parents begin to worry about money. The parents with whom we met insisted that lack of funds had never interfered with their intentions to get the best care for their children, but they testified unanimously that financial worries were a major, constant burden. Their words confirmed the findings from other surveys and studies (McCollum, 1971; Pearson, Stranova, and Thompson, 1976). Regardless of the specific insurance coverage a family might have, it is usually insufficient. Slowly at times, but often quite dramatically, the care of a chronically ill child drains the family's purse. This constant strain can aggravate tensions already high.

The specific financial burdens for parents of a chronically ill child spring from many sources. Hospitalizations, physician visits, special medical procedures, nursing care, and drugs are expensive for a child whose life depends on medical care. The costs generated by these services can be extremely high one year, relatively low the following year, high again the next year, moderate the next, and so on. The pattern of costs varies a great deal among diseases and among different individuals with the same disease. The consequence of this pattern, however, remains the same: health care that is unpredictably expensive in the short run but predictably costly over the long haul.

In addition to these major expenses, families are burdened by many smaller costs related to the care of a chronically ill child, costs that mount because of daily care requirements. There may be expenditures for special foods, transportation to the hospital, fees for a baby-sitter for the other children while parents are at the hospital, time lost from work or school, modifications in the home, a special bed, cosmetic devices to cover unavoidable disfigurements, syringes and Band-Aids, urine testing kits, and extra diapers. Although no child will require all of these extras for care, every chronically ill child will need some of them.

For any expense—major or minor, infrequent or recurrent— the source of payment can be elusive. Some families have insurance plans that cover part of the bills; some families rely on Medicaid or on a special program such as the state Crippled Children's Services or on a clinic whose services may be supported by a research grant. But the patchwork of payment sources rarely covers the full range of costs for any individual family. Leftover costs are either paid by the parents or absorbed by the providers of care.

The constant pressure of unpaid bills, coupled with the great daily care demands of a chronically ill infant or child, added to the lack of daycare or afterschool facilities willing to take such a child can collectively ruin a family's bid for a stable financial future (Meyerowitz and Kaplan, 1967; McKeever, 1981; Tiller, Ekert, and Richards, 1977). Although the specifics may differ among families with different incomes, the costs of care for chronically ill children tangibly influence the quality of family life. For lower- or middle-income families, mothers who might otherwise take a full-time job outside the home or pursue a career often remain at home to care for the child. These families may have extra bills, but they have no second income to help defray them. Reports document that the presence of a chronic illness and the importance of maintaining proximity to a medical center dissuade fathers from pursuing financially more promising jobs (McKeever, 1981; Tiller, Ekert, and Richards, 1977).

There is insufficient information to know precisely the full impact on parents' productivity, but the weight of available evidence points to lowered productivity for two reasons: (1) mothers tend to limit participation in the work force and (2) fathers face incentives to retard career development.

Financial costs are unlikely to impede directly or seriously the delivery of medical care to chronically ill children. But they are likely to shape a family's life by eliminating the family's ability to pay for other services not strictly medical. These include services that address needed emotional relief, such as baby-sitting or respite care, or those designed to ease the daily demands of care, such as special transportation or local access to specialty medical supplies. Many families have foregone vacations because of limited finances (Allan, Townley, and Phelen, 1974; Dorner, 1973).

Maintaining Family Equilibrium. When a chronically ill child can justifiably absorb virtually all of the time and energy of parents, how do parents decide that they must turn their attention away, toward other children or toward themselves? How can a financial balance be achieved when the medical care of the ill child could easily exceed the total family income? Should the parents risk having another child who might also be chronically ill and threaten further the stability of family life? In their search for a balance in family needs, how much community support or financial help are parents entitled to and how far should they go in seeking it? These questions have no clear or easy answers, yet they demand resolution. What is the right choice? Whose beliefs determine what is right? Who is to help the parents in this task of clarifying their values and acting on them courageously?

In our search of the available literature, we found little that spoke directly to these difficulties, although often they lie at the root of many conflicts within families of chronically ill children or between these families and the social institutions that surround them. Because of this lack, we drew up a list of questions related to these problems and asked several parents to answer them. For example, we asked the question, "How do you decide between your ill child's maximal well-being and your own health, energy, and overall well-being?" One mother, who has had two sons with muscular dystrophy, responded in this way:

This "happy medium" between well-being for the child and for the parent is tricky. It takes a whole lot of energy and time to care for a chronically ill child. I find that through the years (it has been thirty-seven years of caring) I have sacrificed my own health to care for my sons, to ensure that their health was as good as possible under the circumstances. Getting up night after night to turn my sons over in bed when they called me—sometimes six and seven times a night—took a toll on my nervous system and several times I had to be hospitalized for exhaustion. I believe that for the child's well-being it is important for the parents to take good care of their own health, also. Try to find people to relieve you from time to time. *This is not easy, finding people to help you out.* But, try to take a few days off, once in awhile; try a change of scenery. Try to relax! When you come back refreshed, you will be able to cope with your problems and to take better care of your child in a more optimistic and cheerful way which will certainly be to your child's advantage and your own as well. *Remember,* who will take care of your child, when you are sick [Roy, personal communication with the authors, 1981].

To care simultaneously for a chronically ill child, for healthy siblings, for one's spouse, and for oneself is an enduring struggle. Compromises must be made, but they are often made with consequences unnecessarily severe: guilt on the parents' part if they take a vacation, exhaustion if parents fail to find time for themselves alone, resentment of a sibling because of lack of attention. A family can work together in solving these problems, especially if they have sustained counsel from someone who is worthy of their trust and who is knowledgeable about the illness itself. The problems are hard to solve, and counsel often hard to find.

Failure to maintain a reasonable balance between competing needs in a family can find expression in marital problems, including marital distress and divorce. Recent reviews of the literature on divorce (Kalnins, 1983; Sabbeth and Leventhal, 1984) have noted that divorce is no more likely in families with a chronically ill child than in families with healthy children. Kalnins notes, however, that systematic investigations have yet to take account of factors that may increase the probability of divorce, including the birth of an ill child within two years of marriage, after an unplanned pregnancy, as a first child, or in the context of a previously stressful marriage. Although divorce is no more likely, tension and stress between spouses—as manifested in arguing, lack of closeness, and difficulties in decision making—do run higher between parents with a chronically ill child than between those who do not have such a child. Marital integration, harmony, distress, agreement, and friction have been assessed through various means, and in each area, spouses with a chronically ill child appear more troubled than their counterparts who have healthy children. Sabbeth and Leventhal (1984, p. 767) conclude: "We are convinced by the research, albeit imperfect, that parents of chronically ill children experience more marital distress—they express more dissatisfaction, and they argue and disagree more—than other parents; yet, the data do not suggest that these parents tend to become divorced."

In addition to marital difficulties, disruptions in family equilibrium resulting from the illness can both contribute to and be aggravated further by a parent's illness or reaction to stress. Among mothers, depression, fatigue, headaches, insomnia, and loss of appetite have all been reported (Allan, Townley, and Phelen,

1974; Kalnins, 1983; McCrae and others, 1973; Lascari and Stehbens, 1976). Complaints of depression, fatigue, ulcers, headaches, and obesity have come from fathers as well (McKeever, 1981; Walker, Thomas, and Russell, 1971; McCarthy, 1975).

A major challenge in maintaining family stability involves the inherent unpredictability of the child's illness. In many instances, a parent is uncertain when the next crisis may strike, whether the illness will be better or worse next week, and what expectations for the future are realistic. This uncertainty can be an omnipresent threat to a family's equilibrium (McKeever, 1981; Jessop and Stein, 1983).

Brothers and Sisters. While parents struggle to help the ill child through periods of crisis or calm, the needs of the child's sisters and brothers can take second place. Siblings are often the target of cruel jokes at school, and the limits on sibling rivalry may be unfairly drawn against the healthy child. Hidden beyond the shadow of their sibling's illness, these children may fall prey to inadvertent neglect.

That children have compelling emotional responses to their sibling's severe illness is incontestable (Cairns, Sussman, and Weil, 1966; Harder and Bowditch, 1982; Lund, 1974; Massie and Massie, 1976; Sourkes, 1981). Guilt that they caused the illness in some magical way, jealousy and anger over the special attention afforded their ill sibling, embarrassment in response to uncontrolled symptoms, and fear of contracting the illness or of being a carrier have been reported in a variety of studies (Azarnoff, 1984; McKeever, 1983). Furthermore, several reports indicate that siblings of children with chronic illness, in comparison with siblings of healthy children, are more likely to have adjustment problems, behavioral difficulties, and academic troubles (Allan, Townley, and Phelen, 1974; Drotar and Bush, 1985; Lavigne and Ryan, 1979; Tew and Laurence, 1975). Some researchers have suggested that extra chores fall disproportionately on older siblings who are female (Breslau, Weitzman, and Messenger, 1981; Burton, 1975) and that younger male siblings are more sensitive to their peers' comments about the illness. In certain circumstances, siblings must play a special but potentially frightening role in treatment. For example, siblings may be asked to donate bone marrow for children who have leukemia.

One girl's account of having an older brother with hemophilia reveals many of these problems. A mother has asked her daughter, now in her midteens, to recall what it was like to grow up with a brother who demanded so much of the family's resources:

"It wasn't until I was seven or eight, I think," she said, "that I began to get a real awareness that something was different about him. But I got it from others. It had never occurred to me before that he was in any way ill. For me he was absolutely normal—at home, everything was natural.

"But from the outside, I began to feel something. I would overhear things in school. I heard kids whispering, 'What's the matter with him?' when he was in a wheelchair or on crutches. You know, kids can be mean. They were always staring at him.

"When he was really sick, I felt bad. I often felt responsible because, although you didn't know, I used to slug him in private. I would taunt him and make him run, and when he was sick I used to think it was my fault. Then I was sad, and when everyone was running around taking care of him, I stood looking on. I felt like a shadowy figure and I couldn't do anything, so I would just go away in my room. I used to wish somebody would come and talk to me and tell me it wasn't my fault, but of course you didn't know I did these things.

"It's true, it was hard for me sometimes. . . . He would get all the attention. I was counted on to be a 'good girl.' I would get bitter and say to myself, 'One of these days I could just die and then they'll see. Then they'll cry.'

"I'm still very touchy about things I hear in school. In science, when they start talking about it, I turn red. There are hemophiliac jokes. Didn't you know? The kids tell them and say things like 'poor twerp hemophiliac,' not knowing about Bobby" [Massie and Massie, 1976, pp. 187–189].

But to emphasize siblings' negative responses is to provide only a partial account of a complex topic. Many brothers and sisters claim that their experience with chronic illness has yielded them more compassion, more sensitivity to the needs of others (Burton, 1975). Harder and Bowditch (1982), in a study of siblings of children with cystic fibrosis, report the following comments from a teenager: "Before my brother was born, I wanted to do whatever I wanted. I was carefree; I didn't care about anybody at all, except myself. But now that Joey has come and we've found out he has cystic fibrosis,

I've become more attracted to doing for him. And the more I think about it, the more I want to do for other people. Because if I can do it for Joey, surely I can do it for someone else" (p. 116).

What factors determine whether a chronic illness brings bitterness or sensitivity to a sibling? Existing evidence provides no clear answer, but age, socioeconomic status, and the parents' own way of responding to the illness are likely to figure predominantly in the final outcome. Whatever that might be, siblings of children with a chronic illness have questions and needs that must be addressed. As McKeever (1983) states, "The fact that many siblings of chronically ill children do not develop symptoms that dictate professional intervention may reflect their capacity to function effectively under stress. This does not, however, absolve health professionals from their clear responsibility to include siblings in both their practice and research endeavors" (p. 217).

Communities: A Neglected Source of Assistance

To be in a community is to become known, to share your life with others, to embrace a common history and anticipate a common future. Sharing defines community: an ethnic neighborhood shares a language and religion; a professional group shares a commitment to a particular identity; an isolated rural town shares a way of life. Like everyone else, chronically ill children and their families need a community.

Travis (1976, p. 1) is especially sensitive to the reasons why chronically ill children need a community:

The chronically ill child spends most of his life in the community, not in a hospital, and thereby comes under the purview of all who work with families and children. Physicians come rarely to the home. Modern hospital practice limits stays to an absolute minimum. Long-term convalescent institutions for children are nearly extinct under the burden of staggering medical costs. Money for the child's food, lodging, medicine, transportation, and supervision come from the parents or community agencies. The administration of medication, preparation of special diet, transportation to the doctor, supervision of school work, and often the performance of physical therapy are provided not by hospital staff but by mother, teacher, baby-sitter, day-care operator, or foster mother.

The chronically ill child, then, is not the concern of doctors and nurses alone. He is the concern of social workers, teachers, psychologists, educational counselors, recreational workers, eligibility clerks, day-care personnel, foster parents, adoptive parents, public and private health agency personnel, clergy, and all of the others who will be working with him or his family in one way or another through the long course of his illness.

Because they come to know well other patients and medical staff, children with chronic illness often make a psychological home in their medical community. Becoming a part of other communities can be a formidable challenge. Sharing can be compromised by embarrassment and by a reluctance to burden others with problems that frighten those unfamiliar with hospitals, pain, and illness. In addition, communities can be wary, intolerant of those who are different, who look funny, and who have "something wrong with them."

Moreover, the myths surrounding many chronic illnesses are powerful deterrents to normal social intercourse between chronically ill children and other families. False beliefs (leukemia is catching, so don't play with Johnny) interfere, but so do basic feelings of uneasiness. Many healthy persons have never had sufficient opportunity to learn how to become comfortable with a chronically ill child.

Two examples illustrate the problem. The first is from a father with a child with cystic fibrosis:

There's a real problem in not losing friends. I guess we don't lose friends; they're the people who end up understanding and caring. I've lost a lot of acquaintances. For example, a family calls you up and wants to come visit. You say you'd love to see them but also ask if any of their kids have a cold. The parents answer, "Oh sure, you know, the ordinary sniffles." Well, ordinary sniffles could kill my kid. So I tell them they can't come over; they don't understand and get angry (Shayne and Cerreto, 1981).

The second is from a mother who has a child with severe asthma:

You can't even count on your own best friends. Even my mother is afraid. I've got to do some shopping and who wants to

lug a screaming five-year-old boy through the lingerie department
at Macy's? So, I call up Esther, my friend for ten years, and ask if
Johnny (my son) can stay with her. *Big* pause on the phone.

"Uhh," she says, "what if something happens? You know,
Lucille, I wouldn't know what to do. You better not leave him with
me."

My mother? Same thing: What if, what if, what if. I can't
stand it. We haven't found a baby-sitter who would come and stay.
We could get a nurse, but we can't afford it (Pediatric Ambulatory
Care Division, 1983).

When a community discovers within its midst a family with
a chronically ill child, what is its responsibility? What services
might community institutions be expected to provide? What can
families justly ask from their neighbors? Should neighbors be
expected to give blood or organs when an ill child requires them?
How can altruism be balanced with respect for privacy?

In considering these questions, we find it useful to distinguish a geographically defined community from a community of
relatives, friends, and acquaintances. The former refers to the
physical place in which a family lives including the surrounding
community institutions, such as churches, schools, local businesses,
and neighborhood centers. The latter notion of community refers
to the invisible but extraordinarily important web of relationships
in which every person is embedded. As a result of moves, professional ties, business meetings, and so on, friendships often develop
between persons who are physically distant. These friendships,
sustained by phone contact and periodic visits, may assume great
importance during periods of crisis.

Childhood Chronic Illness in the Life of a Community.
Chronically ill children now make their presence felt in the life of
a community in several ways. Most communities, for example, have
drugstores or diners in which the cash registers sit next to the
familiar appeals for donations to a charity representing a severe
childhood chronic illness. No one knows how many individuals
actually put money in these cups and cans, but this form of
supplication remains fixed in the American consciousness.

At times, community awareness of childhood chronic illness
is heightened by special appeals on behalf of a stricken child in that

community. Local newspapers often aid these efforts with stories that underscore the sensational side of the problem. Such efforts often collect considerable sums, capitalizing on a community's understandable desire to respond to a tragedy. Yet these efforts may be accompanied by unwarranted intrusion into the family's life. To tell a story that will trigger the impulse to donate money is to disclose much that is usually kept private. Parading a family's problem for the sake of collecting money for needed services can be humiliating (Massie and Massie, 1976).

Furthermore, the generosity that leads to monetary contributions often coexists with a reluctance to reach out on a more personal level. The Massies (p. 96) report a situation familiar to many parents of a child with a chronic illness:

Yes, we worried when Bobby played with other children, but we wanted him to have friends. Yet fewer and fewer mothers permitted their children to play with him. Oh, it wasn't a mean, overt cutting off. Simply, they were "busy" or Tommy had other plans—unfortunately. "So sorry, maybe tomorrow." Occasionally, I would run into one of the neighborhood mothers at the supermarket and she would say, "Oh, you know we'd love to have Bobby, but I would be afraid my little Johnny might hit him or something." I kept hoping they would ask, "Is there a chance he might come? Is there something I should know if he does come over?" But they didn't. It was easier just to cut him out, and then to add, "Really, I think you're so wonderful. I just don't know how you do it."

In other instances, the disease itself or the demands of treatment violate community values and in this way condemn the family to isolation. Although misconceptions are disappearing slowly, many communities still attach the stigma of bad blood, for example, to a family with a child with sickle cell anemia. The special nature of the disease or its treatment can also force families to conflict with prevailing values within their community. Cleveland (1983, p. 17) makes the following observation of Asian families:

There is a high degree of shame associated with receiving charity medicine and welfare. One of the largest social problems confronting the Chinese family, particularly with regard to obtaining health care, is the cultural value of family pride and personal face. This value influences the elderly Chinese and inhibits their ability to reveal their immediate needs to the public agencies of social service and health care. The loss of face is translated as subjecting one to embarrassment and shame but it is more than an individual shame—it reflects not only on the individual but also on the entire family. It is connected with failure, a loss of respect, trust, and a loss of integrity.

For Asian families with a child with a chronic illness, public assistance and the connotations of financial dependency may bring shame to every member of the family. Nor are ethnic or religious minorities the only groups to face the pain of conflicting values; an upper-middle-class father whose son had cystic fibrosis said, "When we finally realized that we were going broke, we had to face the fact that we needed help from someplace, and that someplace was going to be the government. My family? On welfare? *No way.* But eventually I had to do it; I had to accept public monies for my son's hospital costs. It was a long time before I could tell my neighbor about *that*" (Shayne and Cerreto, 1981, p. 13).

The accumulated instances of rejection, however benignly cloaked, assure continued exclusion from the most common of community events. Participating in Little League, helping out with the church fair, an invitation to join the Girl Scouts, these are the events that define community life. In one sense, children with a chronic illness and their families ask only to be included in these ordinary events. To be sure, many of these children and families are included. They find a way to make special arrangements; they are able to ask for help; they gather to themselves the friends they need. But for families who fail to find the needed community resources on their own, responsibility for assistance must lie with their neighbors, friends, and colleagues. These persons must make the special efforts necessary to reach out and include those who hesitate to ask for inclusion. The gift here is an active incorporation of illness into living and into the life of a community. This kind of giving may be far more fair to chronically ill children and their families than a gift of money, although that, too, is important. The active involvement with children who have a chronic illness carries an opportunity for these children to contribute in turn to the community, to become a part of the community's fabric and its future.

That children with a chronic illness can also contribute to their communities is illustrated by an account describing a seventeen-year-old youth with leukemia. During his illness, he spoke to his hospital community: "People ask, 'When is the right time to tell a patient?' In my particular case, it wouldn't have been wise earlier. But you really can't draw general rules about this. There are not really simple answers. . . . It makes it much more difficult on you [the nurses and doctors] because each patient represents unique problems that demand a flexible philosophy and outlook on your part. It requires you to be exceptional people" (Lund, 1974, p. 217). The observation summarizes well why a chronic illness can be important to a community. Just as it requires physicians and nurses to be exceptional people, a chronic illness invites a community to make exceptional efforts in assisting the family.

We have known a neighbor to help two parents by baby-sitting for their eleven-year-old child with muscular dystrophy, asking not "what if something happens" but rather "what special needs does he have"; we have known a neighbor to convince a couple to take a vacation, a needed respite from the care of their child with spina bifida; and we have known friends of a family with a child with leukemia to give a birthday party for the child's older sister when the parents were needed at the hospital. These efforts, accompanied by neither condescension nor pity, represent altruism in the best sense, an acceptance of those who are unfairly burdened and an incorporation of illness into life.

Summary

Many children with a chronic illness face daily tasks of negotiating a world where their peers are unfamiliar with and suspicious of their illness. They must come to terms with a medical environment that pays far more attention to their physiology than to their feelings. And they must incorporate into their identity the fact that they have a chronic illness. Whether this fact compromises the vision of their own futures rests on how it compromises the vision of those who care for them.

In their task of nurturing a child with a chronic illness, parents can face isolation from their own communities, financial pressures, and fatiguing problems of managing their own strengths and emotional resources. Often, they find little or inconsistent help along the way. Siblings, too, face special demands and circumstances as they move through the school years and watch the illness work its course.

If a family can transcend the problems that accompany life with a chronically ill child, if they can find in their community the help and support that they need, then their caring can bring rewards commensurate with the magnitude of the challenge.

A childhood chronic illness, by its extraordinary nature, deeply affects the expressions of concern and caring:

And so I carried Alex into her treatment room. By then she had prepared herself fairly well, but as soon as she saw that stark table where she was to lie and receive her shot and her incision, she stiffened and was the little girl again. "No, not yet! Not yet!" she cried, and she clung to me as tight as ever she had.

In time, when she had composed herself, she said, "All right, I'm ready now." And so she was.

So I started to lay her down where they would cut her open. And in that moment, I could not hold back any longer; one tear fell from all those welling in my eyes. And Alex saw it, saw my face as I bent to put her down. Softer, but urgently, she cried out, "Wait." We all thought she was only delaying the operation again, but instead, so gently, so dearly, she reached up, and with an angel's touch, swept the tear from my face.

I will never know such sweetness again in all my life.

"Oh, my little Daddy, I'm so sorry," is what she said [Deford, 1983, pp. 146–147].

4

Identifying Educational Needs and Employment Opportunities

School is important in the life of every child. In addition to imparting knowledge, school is a proving ground for the exercise of physical abilities, for the development of social skills, and for the display of special talents. For the child with a chronic illness, it can be the place where the limitations of the illness are transcended, where one's identity comes not from a diagnostic label as a diabetic or a hemophiliac but from achievement in schoolwork, in the band, or on the stage. School can also be the place where one's limitations are most acutely felt. The child with asthma who avoids gym, the young adolescent who is physically immature because of an illness, the youngster who never becomes a full member of the class because of frequent absences—all of these children are viewed by their classmates as different, stigmatized in some way. The resulting isolation and sense of rejection can compromise the achievement and self-confidence of even the brightest child.

In the past, children with a chronic illness have been a small part of the school-age population. Many of these children died soon after the onset of the illness; others, who had disfiguring illnesses or orthopedic impairments, went to separate schools; many children were kept at home. Until the early 1960s, regular schools largely overlooked children with chronic health or physical impairments (Walker and Jacobs, 1985).

During the last two decades, three developments have profoundly altered the ways of educating children with chronic illnesses. As a result, schools have assumed a much expanded role in assuring appropriate educational opportunities for every child, and institutions once quite separate must now seek close collaboration.

The first development has been the rapid advance in medical care. As we have documented in Chapter Two, medical advances have dramatically improved the capacity of children with chronic illnesses to participate in the typical activities of childhood, including attendance at school. In large measure, this chapter addresses the educational and vocational services that these children and adolescents need to become full participants in the social and economic life of the nation.

The second development reflects the increased attention to the educational needs of all handicapped youngsters. In the 1960s, many states began reforms in the education of children who were mentally retarded, developmentally delayed, or learning disabled. The passage of Public Law 94-142 (the Education for All Handicapped Children Act) in 1975 signaled a new era in the education of children with various special needs. This law ushered in a range of new ways to assure appropriate placements of these children in settings that least restricted their educational opportunities. In 1978, one year after this legislation went into effect, Palfrey, Mervis, and Butler predicted accurately that "P.L. 42-142 will have wide ranging effects on education, on state and city programs for children in other sectors, and on the ways in which citizens and professionals view handicapped children" (p. 819). In this chapter, we discuss the implications of this law for chronically ill children.

The final development, much less visible than the first two, reflects the changing pattern and potential of school health nursing. Over the last few decades, the number of school nurses has declined in conjunction with the disappearance of serious contagious diseases of childhood. Where there are school nurses, their activities are typically limited to a narrow range of health care and clerical duties (Select Panel for the Promotion of Child Health, 1981; Walker and Jacobs, 1985). Recently, countering these trends, a few school systems have bolstered their health services by adding school nurse practitioners who may assume an active role in overseeing services for children with a chronic illness.

The challenges of educating children with chronic illnesses are varied. Periodic hospitalizations or acute exacerbations of symptoms can interrupt school attendance erratically, fatigue and pain can inhibit concentration, the visible side effects of treatment or the physical manifestations of the underlying illness can be extremely embarrassing and can lead to withdrawal and isolation, and school buildings and programs may be ill-suited to children with physical or physiological limitations but who are academically competent. In many local school systems, there is confusion about the needs of children with a chronic illness. Frequently, school programs and teachers set up obstacles to effective educational plans for these children (Baird and Ashcroft, 1985; Walker and Jacobs, 1985).

Partly because adolescents with a chronic illness are a new population, vocational training programs have yet to develop experience with these youngsters. In addition to acquiring skills, they need assistance in locating jobs with employers who will be tolerant of periodic absences, daily care routines, and variations in energy level. They also need help in finding appropriate health insurance if they are to become independent adults.

In this chapter we examine the education and employment of youngsters with a chronic illness. We start by drawing distinctions among three groups of chronically ill children and the different educational needs that distinguish them. We then consider the ways in which schools currently respond to these needs. We address the issues and opportunities related to placement of these children in either special education or regular education programs. To what extent is Public Law 94-142 (the Education for All Handicapped Children Act of 1975) appropriate for meeting the needs of children with a chronic illness? Do chronically ill children whose intellectual and learning abilities remain intact have trouble finding special services in the context of regular education? How adequate are school health services? The chapter's final section discusses the problem of vocational services for these children, an area that has sadly lacked attention.

Educational Needs

When defining educational needs, it is helpful to separate children with a chronic illness into three groups. The first includes children who have severe cognitive or perceptual deficits in addition to or as a result of the illness. Some children with spina bifida and muscular dystrophy are members of this group. A second group includes children who have physical impairments (either temporary or permanent) without any associated deficits in cognitive or intellectual functioning. Most of these children have difficulty in mobility, which may hinder access to classrooms and other facilities; but they otherwise lack problems that impede participation in a standard curriculum. Children with hemophilia (who need crutches or wheelchairs during severe joint bleeds) and some children with arthritis, spina bifida, or muscular dystrophy would fall into this group.

The third group, by far the largest, includes children who have no intellectual or physical impairment directly attributable to the illness but who may fall behind in school as a consequence of the illness or its treatment. Children with asthma, diabetes, and leukemia typify members of this group. These three groups of children have different educational needs. Moreover, many needed educational services remain unavailable because these children fit poorly into existing educational categories.

Chronically Ill Children with Intellectual or Perceptual Impairment. Healthy children who are mentally retarded, developmentally delayed, or learning disabled are entitled to an educational program tailored to their individual needs. For these children, a wide range of classroom settings, curriculum modifications, and well-trained professionals is required to accommodate the variety of special educational needs. In many instances, other services, such as physical therapy or language instruction, are necessary for these children if they are to participate in and benefit from the classroom instruction.

Children with intellectual or perceptual impairments who also have a chronic illness require a range of both educational and medical services, provided under a coordinated plan. The presence of the illness may affect energy level or attention span in an unpredictable manner; the child's school year may be disrupted with frequent hospitalizations; the treatment of the child's condition may require nursing or medical care during the school day. To address these problems well, close collaboration is essential between the child's health care providers and the child's school. A school's failure to incorporate the medical aspects of a developmentally delayed, chronically ill child's care into the individual education plan for the child may seriously compromise the success of that plan. Similarly, a medical team's failure to explain to the school, in understandable terms, the ramifications of the illness and its treatment may allow the school only a partial grasp of the child's problems.

The number of chronically ill children who are mentally retarded, developmentally delayed, or learning disabled is small. However, because their needs are often complex and the medical and educational services challenging to integrate, these children tend to capture a major portion of the attention. Because of this, many educators assume that these children represent the norm for chronically ill children as a whole when, in reality, they do not. In fact, of the eleven marker diseases, only one (spina bifida) is commonly accompanied by mental retardation. Other very rare chronic illnesses may also have a greater likelihood of retardation, but the total number of children with chronic illnesses who are retarded or who have serious cognitive or sensory problems is small in comparison with chronically ill children who do not have these problems. Chronically ill children are less likely to be in the group of severely developmentally delayed children than in the group with normal intellectual and learning potentials (Pless and Pinkerton, 1975; Rutter, Tizard, and Whitmore, 1970; Walker and Jacobs, 1985).

In comparison with healthy children who have intellectual or cognitive limitations, however, chronically ill children with severe learning problems pose a considerably greater challenge to educational authorities. For example, schools must both integrate the medical treatment demands into the school day and sustain communication with the child's physicians. Because these children are invariably placed in special education programs, the burden of these tasks generally falls on the special education teachers and staff.

Chronically Ill Children Who Have Functional Impairments Without Intellectual Deficits. In Chapter Two, we define functional impairment as a decreased capacity to participate in age-appropriate activities. Children who have serious intellectual limitations may also have functional impairment in the sense that they are unable to participate in a regular school setting. But children may have a functional impairment *without* being cognitively impaired or learning disabled. Intellectually normal children who need braces or a wheelchair typify the group of children who have functional limitations without intellectual deficits.

Table 4, based on a survey of a county in Michigan, illustrates the percentages of children with a variety of chronic illnesses who also have a functional impairment. Approximately one third of children with epilepsy and permanent stiffness have a functional impairment. Only about one in every four with asthma, bronchitis, kidney trouble, heart trouble, or arthritis is likely to have a functional impairment. Other categories reflect even lower rates.

Table 4. Estimated Prevalence Rates (per thousand) of Symptoms
of Chronic Health Problems and Related Functional Impairment
in Children, Ages Birth–17.

Symptom or Condition	Rate with Reported Symptom	Percentage of Children with Reported Symptom Who Have Functional Impairment
Allergy	118	10.5
Diabetes	3	11.1
Hayfever	65	15.6
Heart trouble	24	20.3
Kidney trouble	26	22.2
Arthritis	1	25.0
Asthma	61	25.1
Bronchitis	69	29.4
Other	74	30.4
Epilepsy	11	35.3
Permanent stiffness	14	35.6

Source: Adapted from Walker, Gortmaker, and Weitzman, 1981.

Overall, the number of chronically ill children with functional impairment is somewhat larger than that of chronically ill children with intellectual or perceptual impairment. Many children with spina bifida and other orthopedic conditions, many with muscular dystrophy, some with hemophilia, and those with a variety of other illnesses (for example, osteogenesis imperfecta) would fall into this group. These children often require architectural modifications to assure access to classrooms; many will require special services, such as help with toileting. For these children, needed services are directed toward diminishing physical and health-related barriers to their participation in regular classrooms. With these services, most of these children could handle a regular curriculum.

Hence, children in this group need special services; they do not require special education curricula. Yet, in order to receive essential health-related services, they are often classified as requiring special education because regular education programs lack the resources to provide the special services needed by children with functional impairments. Furthermore, functional impairment appears to be an important factor in the classification process. From a community-based study, Walker and Jacobs (1985) report that children with selected chronic illnesses (asthma, kidney problems, and heart problems) were more likely to be in special classes if they had a functional impairment than if they did not. Regardless of the educational category in which they may find themselves, chronically ill children in this group, like those in the first, require sustained communication between the school and the health care team. In some instances, the health care team is in contact with the special education team; in other instances, with staff from the regular education programs.

Chronically Ill Children Without Intellectual or Physical Impairment. This group includes the majority of children with chronic illness. These children have no intellectual impairments for which special curricula or classes are required and no physical mobility problems for which structural changes are needed. Yet, despite the potential for at least average school achievement, chronically ill children in this group are likely to do less well academically than their healthy peers. Several factors may contribute to lowered academic performance; these include absenteeism, limited alertness and stamina, and psychological difficulties (Pless and Pinkerton, 1975; Rutter, Tizard, and Whitmore, 1970; Sultz and others, 1972; Walker and Jacobs, 1985).

Absenteeism for children with chronic illness may be of two types: (1) prolonged absences for hospitalization and recuperation and (2) brief, episodic absences for treatment of specific symptoms or problems. Even if a child lacks new symptoms, monitoring of care may require frequent physician visits, each of which contributes to the number of days missed from school. Absences can have a cumulative effect and can lead to the pressure of always having to catch up. Asthma is a major cause of absenteeism and accounts for 25 percent of all school days missed for illness in the United States (Parcel and others, 1979; Green and Haggerty, 1975). Children with asthma may receive weekly allergy (hyposensitization) shots. These weekly visits may interfere with school attendance or with participation in after-school activities, such as sports or clubs. Cystic fibrosis, kidney conditions, leukemia, and sickle cell anemia are also associated with excessive absenteeism from school (Walker and Jacobs, 1985).

Limited alertness, stamina, and capacity to concentrate may result from illness or from medications required for treatment. The drugs used to control leukemia, for example, may induce temporary states of confusion that can affect school performance. Children with cystic fibrosis or sickle cell anemia may fatigue easily and thus lack the stamina necessary to complete their daily schoolwork. Some children may gradually become poor students because their illness is no longer well controlled. The child with diabetes whose blood sugar is no longer maintained at acceptable levels or the child with spina bifida and hydrocephalus whose shunt stops functioning may be less well able than others to concentrate on tasks at school. Adding to this misfortune, parents and teachers may misinterpret the child's inability to participate as willful resistance or laziness.

Although children in this group typically need neither special education nor structural accommodations to allow their full participation in school, they may require intermittent special health services or other modifications of the school program because of their illness. Medications may have to be administered at school (for example, antibiotics to treat or prevent infections in children with cystic fibrosis). Other children may need special diets (among them, children with diabetes or with chronic renal disease). Children with diabetes, for example, may require snacks during the day, and schools must have the flexibility to permit this. For other children, it is important to have well-understood plans for ready access to needed health services in an emergency. An attack of asthma may happen at school; a boy with hemophilia may start to have a significant bleeding episode. Through collaboration among health providers, family, and school, the school must have adequate information so the child can obtain appropriate health care when crises arise.

For many children, there is a delicate balance with respect to appropriate restrictions and exercise. School staff should know when a child with cystic fibrosis should be excused from recess or encouraged to play with classmates. They should know when a child with asthma can play on the basketball team or when that child must stay on the bench. To meet the health care needs of children with chronic illnesses and to encourage the most effective participation in daily events, schools must develop effective collaboration with health providers, along with mechanisms for providing medications and other needed health and nutritional services. In many instances, schools may need to develop consistent methods for assuring these services outside of the special education program.

Psychological health, including positive self-esteem and expectations for success, can contribute to school achievement. Failure to develop or sustain emotional well-being can lead to poor academic performance. Although having a childhood chronic illness does not necessarily mean that a child will be psychologically troubled, there are aspects of school life for a chronically ill child that are particularly threatening to self-esteem. Having to take medications, being unable to participate in sports, looking odd or different can all set a child apart from peers and lead to ridicule and isolation. Teachers may also react with discomfort and rejection of the ill child, a reaction possibly prompted by the teachers' own feelings about illness. Lack of information about the child's prognosis or about the disease itself can influence a teacher's sense of what the child can accomplish. The ill child's motivation may be undermined by a "why bother" attitude (Walker and Jacobs, 1985). Here again, it is essential that the child's health providers share information regularly with the school and that the school be prepared to use this information in the best interests of the child.

In most instances, children in this group participate in regular classroom settings although special education placements may be required as a result of extreme behavioral or emotional problems related to the illness. The daily treatment regimen for the illness may require certain modifications—some temporary, some long-lasting—in the school day, but the illness itself typically allows a child to be in regular school classes.

Educational Placements

Regardless of the groups that best characterize their specific educational needs, all chronically ill children have several common needs, including those for sustained contact between the school and the health care team, for school personnel who understand the complex interplay between the illness and class participation, and for continuity in educational efforts when the child is hospitalized or convalescing at home (Baird and Ashcroft, 1985).

In what ways do schools currently address these common needs of their chronically ill students? How adequate are these measures? To a great extent, the answers depend on whether the child is placed in a regular school setting or a special education program. In Table 5, we portray the possible combinations of the three groups of chronically ill children and the two educational categories into which they might fall.

Children with chronic illnesses often depend on health-related services to stay in school. In many school systems, these services are situated in special education departments. Most children with chronic illnesses have no need for direct special education services because they have no unusual academic needs. Yet, to gain access to health-related services, they may need to be identified by the special education system. In many instances, special education programs are neither the best nor the most feasible placements for these children. Regular education programs, buttressed by im-

Table 5. Educational Placement of Three Groups of Children
with a Chronic Illness.

Grouping	Regular Education	Special Education
Chronically ill children with intellectual impairments	Not placed here	Always placed here
Chronically ill children with impairments only in physical mobility	Occasionally placed here	Frequently placed here
Chronically ill children without intellectual or physical impairments	Frequently placed here	Sometimes placed here

proved school health services, may provide more appropriate settings for most children with a chronic illness.

Placement in Special Education. Under the rules of Public Law 94-142, chronically ill children may be placed in special education on the basis of an existing learning disability, developmental delay, perceptual handicap, or some other learning problem. Lacking any of these problems, they may still qualify for special educational services by falling into a category named "other health impaired." Federal regulations that define this category give examples of the range of conditions involved and include "chronic or acute health problems such as heart condition, tuberculosis, rheumatic fever, nephritis, asthma, sickle cell anemia, hemophilia, epilepsy, lead poisoning, leukemia or diabetes, which adversely affect a child's educational performance" (45 CFR 121a5). In discussing this category, Walker and Jacobs (1985, p. 624) note:

Children so designated may receive the full range of evaluation and educational services, including "(specially designed) classroom instruction, instruction in physical education, home instruction, and instruction in hospitals and institutions," as well as the necessary related services (45 CFR 121a14).

However, as with other disabilities covered by the federal and state laws, there is a functioning (or severity) condition applied to the eligibility; this "adverse effect test" means that the handicap has to be serious enough to impede successful progress in a regular education program (Comptroller General of the United States, 1981). A slight limp, a transient behavior problem, or myopia corrected by glasses would not qualify. The application of this measure of functional impairment is appropriate and necessary for chronically ill children. The child who wheezes on rare occasion does not need to involve the schools in the costly, time-consuming special education process; that child should be identified by the school health department but served in the regular education sector. But then what should happen with the child with more severe asthma who at times needs medication and a modified physical education program but otherwise operates well in regular scheduled classes? Do those difficulties related to asthma constitute a functional impairment that hampers schooling? And do the services that child needs belong within special education?

The legislation gives little guidance to schools on how to determine functional impairment. Because the condition is thought of as a medical problem, many states require physician input, not only to describe the illness to the evaluation team but also to assess the extent to which the condition interferes with learning.

Public Law 94-142 has generated enduring problems for many state education agencies and local school districts. Although educators recognize that many children with chronic illnesses require services beyond those traditionally associated with education, the limits of these services are open to debate. To what extent are schools responsible for attending to the full range of developmental tasks of a child with a chronic illness? What are the financial and ethical parameters of education for a child with a serious health condition? How can state and local education authorities establish workable alliances with the interlocking array of health service and financing institutions involved in the care of chronically ill children? The debate on all these questions has been robust (Farrow and Rogers, 1983).

Much of the debate has centered on the section of Public Law 94-142 that outlines the requirement for related services. *Related services* are those services that must be provided to minimize the adverse effect of the health condition on the child's participation in

school. They include "speech pathology and audiology, psychological services, physical and occupational therapy, recreation, early
identification and assessment of disabilities in children, counseling
services, and medical services for diagnostic and evaluation purposes" (Walker and Jacobs, 1985, p. 623). The concept of related
services has attracted enormous attention, partly because of the
potential costs to the school and partly because of severe disputes
over the definition of related services. Children with chronic illnesses, especially those with spina bifida, often find themselves at
the center of the controversy.

Chronically ill children require many related services. To what
extent are schools required to provide them? What are the limits
of school authority? Baird and Ashcroft (1985, pp. 661–662) illustrate some of the problems by describing the case of Amber Tatro, a child
with spina bifida *(Tatro* v. *Texas).* They note, "Because Amber
needs clean, intermittent catheterization at regular intervals during
the day in order to participate in school, and because education
officials in the Dallas suburb where she lives have opposed providing this service, her parents have spent more than three years in a
series of legal battles. The school superintendent has commented
that the sticking point in the case is not cost but practicing
medicine without a license (Covington, 1982). He contends that,
if schools are forced to provide catheterization, they might eventually have to offer dialysis and even more expensive treatments."

One of the most striking features about the problem is the
diversity of policies across the nation. Martin (1984, p. 71) notes,
"As we worked with the Tatro case, we were impressed by the
incredible diversity of policies with regard to such matters. A school
district next to that of the Tatros, for example, catheterizes 400
children daily in their public schools; another school district,
however, has recently threatened to fire a school nurse if she
continued to catheterize a child."

The boundaries of a school's responsibilities are unclear, and
schools are understandably concerned that they will incur sizable
increases in expenses if they become health providers. Public Law
94–142 requires that an individualized education program (IEP) be
set forth for each child identified as needing special services.
Because a school is more likely to be held liable for provision of a

medical service that has been included in the IEP than for one that has not, some schools routinely exclude medical services, even if they are needed by the child to participate in classes. Other schools have recognized that it is less expensive to hire providers, such as physical therapists, than to pay for contracted services. Such practices, however, open schools to the charge that they are practicing medicine without sufficient oversight by a physician. At least one state now regularly employs a physician in order for the school to qualify for Medicaid payments for certain services provided in the school (Farrow and Rogers, 1983). At the state level, the uncertainty regarding the boundaries of responsibility for providing medical services has led to vigorous efforts to work out mutually agreeable relationships between state education and child health authorities (Baird and Ashcroft, 1985; Farrow and Rogers, 1983; Division of Maternal and Child Health, 1981).

Determination of which services are provided through special education is often dictated by the services available in the school system rather than by the specific needs of the child. As is true with most other remedial or special education services, a child is most likely to receive physical therapy if the school system has a therapist working in the system. For smaller school systems, especially in rural areas, special services are often limited, and the services required for a child to attend school may be unavailable.

Walker and Jacobs (1985) also comment on the relationship between the child's physician and the school's evaluation team responsible for developing the individualized education program required under Public Law 94-142. Ideally, a child's physician or nurse would play a role on this team as needed; the school and the health provider would share information in a fashion useful to both and to the child as well. Yet, there are currently few incentives for schools and health providers to collaborate: schools and health providers speak different professional languages and often function with different concepts about child development, all of which complicates communication. Schools, already stressed by the process of developing the IEP, have little additional time to contact health providers. Physicians, under prevalent fee-for-service payment arrangements, go unreimbursed for the sizable amount of time and effort it takes to participate on IEP teams. Public Law

94-142, although requiring care for some medical problems, did not clarify mechanisms for the involvement of health providers in IEP development (Palfrey, Mervis, and Butler, 1978). Issues of status, problems in communication among experts in different professions, and little guidance in the law have all worked against effective communication.

Why do children with chronic illnesses pose problems for special education programs? The 1960s and early 1970s were a period of intense activity to reform educational practices for students with various learning problems; this reform was accomplished through the development of Public Law 94-142 and the state laws that preceded it. Efforts on behalf of chronically ill children, on the other hand, focused far less on educational matters. The separate disease-specific advocacy groups representing the childhood chronic illnesses concerned themselves with support of research and direct medical care services. Moreover, "parents of chronically ill children whose conditions did not usually produce severe cognitive, orthopedic, or communication difficulties (the traditionally considered 'education' problems) were not clear about the extent to which special education legislation should relate to their children" (Walker and Jacobs, 1985, p. 622). Throughout the period of reform, the educational needs of children with chronic illnesses received far less attention than those of children with other handicaps.

As a result, the degree of functional impairment, which is often difficult to define for a chronically ill child, becomes a matter of local judgment. How severe must a child's arthritis or cystic fibrosis be for eligibility? What types of congenital heart conditions might provide sufficient adverse effect? Does a child on home dialysis qualify? The final decision regarding placement may rest on factors indirectly related to the illness—factors such as parental preference, the availability of services within the regular educational program, and the financial status of the local school system's special education program. Consequently, variation among localities is enormous.

Response of Regular Education Programs. In special education, the development of the student's individual plan provides an opportunity to resolve issues in management of the illness and its consequences at school. To be sure, many issues may be ignored or incompletely addressed, but the presence of the special education team assures that the child's special needs receive some attention. No similar opportunity is guaranteed for chronically ill children in regular classroom settings. These children receive adequate attention to their special needs only if the school has a well-informed and active school nurse or if a local pediatrician has taken the time to work closely with the school personnel. From a national perspective, these are rare events.

School health services vary widely in their quality, in the personnel who deliver the services, and in their financial and legislative bases. Many communities lack any formal school health services. In such cases, school health practices may be limited to ensuring that children's immunization levels meet state laws for school entry and requesting that periodic physical examinations be on record at the school. Some schools require that the name of the child's regular health provider be available along with ways of contacting parents in case of emergency. Schools occasionally institute screening programs to identify children with visual or hearing deficits or teenagers with spinal curvature (scoliosis).

Where organized school health services exist, about half come under the jurisdiction of local health authorities (city or county health departments) and about half under the auspices of the school district itself. Typically school health services are not central to the mission of either public health departments or public school systems; therefore, they suffer from inattention from local school and health authorities and are subject to early budget cuts in times of fiscal restraint. The lack of a considered school health policy and of direct school health services creates special burdens for children with chronic illnesses. Many schools lack procedures for allowing children to take medications at school. Responsibility for getting medications to a child may fall on the school principal or the school secretary both of whom have more than enough to do to accomplish their nonmedical tasks. With the exception of immunization policies, mandatory state health codes are the exception rather than the rule in most states, and local school systems must develop their own policies (if any) with little guidance.

School systems may have difficulty enough coping with the common, acute infections of childhood (such as strep throats and ear infections) and with the administration of antibiotics for these infections in school. As an example, many teachers have little understanding of the similarity of scarlet fever and strep throat; they may be unnecessarily anxious when a child is diagnosed as having scarlet fever, a condition that carries no more risk today than strep throat and is treated in a similar fashion. Luckily, the teacher generally has access to a nursing or medical consultant who can explain the implications of common illnesses and infections. When a child has a rare chronic illness, misunderstandings are far more likely. When the child has cystic fibrosis or a seizure disorder or a congenital heart disease, for example, teachers and their consultants will have much less knowledge about the condition. Furthermore, it is difficult to educate teachers satisfactorily about the rare conditions. What should the teacher do when a child with cystic fibrosis seems especially tired? Renal dialysis may affect the metabolic balance of a child and thus affect intellectual performance. What should teachers know about this problem? And how do they find out about it? It is certainly unrealistic to educate teachers to know key aspects of all chronic illnesses. Rather, they should have easy access to the information needed to make appropriate judgments about a child's behavior in class and set appropriate restrictions or offer appropriate encouragement of the child's activities. Where policies regarding medical treatment in schools are limited and where school health services are sparse, teachers have few places to turn for needed advice.

Schools often must test children to determine their optimal class placement. The educational and psychological testing capacity of schools varies widely and is typically stretched thin. Illness, which may affect the functioning of children in specific ways, may affect their performance on commonly used tests. As Mearig (1985) points out, children with muscular dystrophy, for example, are sometimes labeled developmentally delayed based on inappropriate testing. Few schools have personnel who understand the special effects illness may have on children's test scores.

Where school health services exist in an organized fashion, the basic health team includes a physician, nurse, and health assistant. Typically, the physician is either the medical director for the system as a whole or a consultant who is called when needed. Over the years, the health nurse has been slowly disappearing from school buildings, partly as a result of the disappearance of contagious diseases and partly as a result of personnel reductions. For those schools that do have a nurse, her role depends on the approach in the school system as a whole. Two general approaches to school nursing—the health organizer and the nurse practitioner—are described by Walker and Jacobs (1985, pp. 640–641): "In the health organizer model, the school is seen as the organizing link between a child in the school and community health resources. In this case, the role of the nurse is to ensure that the child receives comprehensive care through an adequate system of referral, which necessitates record keeping and follow-up by written notices, calls, or home visits. In the nurse practitioner model, the pediatric nurse practitioner provides comprehensive care to children, using an adequate record-keeping and follow-up system and backed up by local physicians." School nurses may be responsible for administering medical treatments or medications; but most schools lack full-time nurses, and medications are usually administered by other school personnel.

The health assistant has recently claimed a role in facilitating school health services in some districts (Guyer and Walker, 1980; Nader, Emmel, and Charney, 1972). This person has special training in first aid, injury prevention, and community referral. Unlike the physician director, the consultant, or the nurse, any of whom may be at any one school only occasionally, a health assistant is available in each school every day.

School nurses and physicians may be unfamiliar with the basic physiology of the disease, with the specialty center where the child receives care, and with the potential emotional problems of these children. They may also lack experience or skills in educating teachers (or school children) about the chronic illnesses of childhood.

Recent attempts to reform school health services have allowed nurse practitioners to be more active in the coordination and delivery of care. Nurse practitioners are nurses who have additional training in a specialized area of health—in our case, the common and uncommon health problems of school-age children and elements of healthy living and health promotion that can be taught in schools. Nader (1978) and others (Robinson, 1981) have developed innovative school health programs in which school nurse practitioners work closely with community agencies. These efforts have demonstrated that well-trained practitioners can improve school health services and make more satisfactory the attendance of children with chronic illnesses. Most public authorities have yet to be convinced of the benefits of investing in school health services of this quality.

In addition to improved school health services, students with a chronic illness could benefit from more harmonious interactions between schools and local physicians. Several demonstration projects, sponsored by health and education departments, have encouraged collaboration between the two disciplines in the care of handicapped and chronically ill children (Division of Maternal and Child Health, 1981). To a great extent, physicians and school personnel operate with substantially different views about childhood, child development, and the role of physical illness in the life of a child. Physicians are accused of acting in a condescending manner when cooperation is needed and of withholding information out of a concern for the child's privacy (Nader, 1974). As Walker and Jacobs (1985, p. 645) explain, "Some parents of chronically ill children explicitly request that physicians keep information confidential, partly because difficult situations may arise for children whose illnesses become too public. The issue is complex; parental desire for confidentiality in rare instances conflicts with the school's ability to ensure the child's safety. If, for example, a child whose diabetes is not known to the school experiences an insulin reaction, the child's health may be endangered. Physicians are uniquely situated to allay many parental anxieties about the disclosure of such information to school health authorities." Unfortunately, community pediatricians may have little experience with the rare chronic illnesses and may feel uncertain in their consultations with a school. Specialist physicians involved in a child's treatment may be at a distance from the child's home community and may ignore educational aspects of the child's illness.

Home- and Hospital-Bound Instruction

Virtually all chronically ill children require prolonged periods of hospitalization or convalescence at home at some point in the course of their illness. The predictability of this need underscores the importance of planning for continuity in their educational experience. Yet inflexible patterns of home- and hospital-bound instruction typically lead to discontinuity in a child's education.

Policies for homebound instruction are inconsistent across the states, and some policies work at cross purposes to the needs of children with a chronic illness. For example, states vary considerably in the minimum number of days a student must be absent before becoming eligible for home and hospital instruction (Baird, Ashcroft, and Dy, 1984). "Some states (Montana and South Carolina) reported no minimum absence requirement, while others (Indiana, Texas, and Washington) mentioned four weeks as the minimum length of absence necessary. Wisconsin requires that the student's absence from school be 'anticipated over 30 days.' These absence requirements generally refer to consecutive days missed" (Baird and Ashcroft, 1985, p. 659). Yet children with a chronic illness typically have many frequent absences of short duration. Over the course of a school year, they may miss a total of many weeks yet fail to trigger the provision of homebound instruction at any one time.

In some states, eligibility for home and hospital programs depends on physician recommendations. Other states use a special Hospital/Home Instruction category for chronically ill students; to qualify for this, a child must be classified as exceptional on the basis of having a condition that prevents or renders inadvisable attendance at school (Baird, Ashcroft, and Dy, 1984).

Furthermore, under Public Law 94-142, special education is expected "to meet the unique needs of a handicapped child, including classroom instruction, instruction in physical education, home instruction, and instruction in hospitals and in institutions" (45 CFR 121a.14(a) (1)). Some states interpret this definition to mean that a student must be evaluated and classified as handicapped to become eligible for homebound instruction. Presumably, the child goes back to the regular classroom, if appropriate, on return to school. Unless previously qualified for special education, the student is no longer handicapped until the next lengthy absence. In these states, the excessive paperwork involved in shifting chronically ill children into and out of educational categories discourages the provision of home instruction.

Even if a child is eligible for home instruction, the amount of time that child spends with a teacher is often far less than it would be in a regular classroom. Most states require only three hours per week of teacher contact in a home- or hospital-bound program. Such brief services, often available only after long waiting periods, are inadequate for meeting the chronically ill child's needs for continuity of education.

In recognition of this problem, the Baltimore City School system developed the Chronic Health Impaired Project (CHIP) (Case and Matthews, 1983). Because CHIP represents an innovative approach that deserves replication, we print here a summary description from Baird and Ashcroft (1985, p. 660).

Federally funded under the Elementary and Secondary Education Act (ESEA) Title IV-C, the program is open to all students who are attending public, private, and parochial schools within the Baltimore City area and who have chronic illnesses that may interfere with school attendance and performance. Full-time CHIP teachers visit children participating in the program each day they are absent from school; no minimum number of days missed is required. These teachers attempt to cover the same material that would have been studied in school thus allowing these children to be marked present on the school roll. In addition to home and hospital instruction, CHIP offers individual, group, and family counseling; vocational, academic, and career guidance; referral services to social and health agencies; a peer tutoring program; monthly parent meetings; and home visits by a parent liaison worker.

CHIP offers the additional advantage of avoiding stigmatization of students. Its composition of 90 percent regular education students and 10 percent special education students reflects roughly the presumed proportions of regular and special education students in most school systems.

In offering immediate teacher assistance and other supplementary services to the absent student, CHIP provides an important option for meeting the educational needs of students requiring home and hospital instruction.

Vocational Training

For adolescents, finding a job marks a key developmental transition from child to adult. In the wake of Public Law 94-142 and heightened concern for handicapped individuals, the problems of vocational training for handicapped adolescents have received a fair degree of attention (Hippolitus, 1985; Bellamy and others, 1984). Many inequities persist, but as a group, these adolescents face far better prospects than their predecessors of a decade ago.

Much less attention has been directed toward chronically ill children who have no handicap in the usual definition of the term. The Developmentally Disabled Assistance and Bill of Rights Act of 1975 expanded the criteria for services under its jurisdiction to a functional definition that permits the inclusion of chronic physical illnesses. Nonetheless, many programs geared to individuals with an intellectual or a physical handicap remain inappropriate for chronically ill individuals who have none of these impairments, especially for adolescents who fit in the third group defined at the beginning of this chapter. A major problem facing chronically ill adolescents and young adults is the absence of programs knowledgeable about their needs (Goldberg, Isralsky, and Shwachman, 1979).

What type of vocational or long-range educational planning should be available to the child with cystic fibrosis? The youngster with severe arthritis requires planning and education for an adulthood that is based on a realistic estimation of the degree of disability. Yet most vocational training programs are not geared to the special problems the presence of illness brings to the child growing up.

When entering the job market, young adults with chronic illnesses face the additional problem of finding health insurance. For the most part, adolescents with private health insurance are covered under their parents' plans until they reach age twenty-one or finish college. Many small businesses are reluctant to hire people with chronic illnesses, both because of concern for excessive numbers of days missed from work and because their high use of health services will lead to higher health insurance premiums for the employer. Employment-associated insurance, as we discuss further in Chapter Seven, may also have a pre-existing waiver, a condition of the insurance contract that disallows coverage for conditions that existed prior to the person's starting employment with that business. Thus, young adults with chronic illness face a marketplace with disincentives to hire them in the first place, and if hired, their health insurance may not cover their health problems. Does the absence of adequate insurance force chronically ill young adults to depend on public programs and therefore to forego the search for a job?

Like their healthy counterparts, children with a chronic illness plan to work and have a strong commitment to the importance of working (Goldberg, Isralsky, and Shwachman, 1979; Koocher and O'Malley, 1981). Still, little is known about the employment-seeking behavior of adolescents with chronic illness. Do many of them avoid employment out of a belief that no employer would consider them? Or do they seek employment only to be turned down as a result of their condition and its consequences? If so, are chronically ill adolescents refused jobs because of disfiguring characteristics (if they have them) or because of the potential for absences or because of the social myths surrounding these illnesses? Does the potential for shortened life-span dissuade employers from hiring these individuals?

Few studies address these questions, but those available indicate considerable discrimination and consequently much anxiety in the search for employment. Koocher and O'Malley (1981) found that adolescent and young-adult survivors of childhood cancer reported many instances in which potential employers refused them jobs for which they were clearly competent. Services adequately organized to help chronically ill adolescents find jobs are unavailable in most communities. Glaser and others (1980) reported that the quality of vocational adjustment of adolescents with spina bifida was compromised by the quality of supportive services in the arena of vocational planning. These investigators underscore the discrepancy between the needs of adolescents with chronic illnesses and the capacity of social agencies to meet them.

Summary

The educational needs of children with chronic illness are distinct from those of healthy children with learning disabilities, mental retardation, or developmental delay. Current special education legislation for children can assure educational services that are appropriate for only some children with a chronic illness. Disharmony between medical and educational teams around issues of authority, payment for services, and basic priorities remains prevalent in many locations. Continued efforts, supported in some areas by collaboration between University Affiliated Facilities and Crippled Children's Services programs, promise to yield a greater understanding and more harmonious arrangements between education and health professionals. These developments are likely to improve the health care of all children in special education and may have especially beneficial influence on those children in special education settings who also have a chronic illness.

When chronically ill children are in a regular education setting, other problems challenge educational authorities. These children may require some of the related services and in-school medical care that their counterparts in special education receive. Yet children with chronic illnesses are often outside the jurisdiction of special education programs, largely because their illness affects their learning capabilities indirectly and in a manner quite different from the ways of other handicaps (mental retardation, learning disabilities, and various developmental delays). The relative rarity of these illnesses has contributed further to a general oversight of consequent educational needs by school authorities. These children typically need related services available only through special education, but they are (appropriately) ineligible for special education placement.

To extend Public Law 94–142 to cover all chronically ill children may be counter to the best interests of the children and the schools. Many parents and children will resist the designation of needing special education. Furthermore, the development of individual plans, as required by the law, is a time-consuming and expensive procedure. It would make little sense for these resources to be focused on children whose needs could be appropriately met with proper additions or modifications to health services in the regular school setting. The CHIP program provides an excellent example of such a strategy. Here again, closer ties between schools and medical institutions will also be necessary.

Some chronically ill children with impairments only in mobility are excluded from regular school settings because of physical barriers to the building or to classrooms. These children may be inappropriately placed in special education settings. Sustained enforcement of Section 504 of the Vocational Rehabilitation Act will strengthen the educational opportunities for these children.

A greater understanding of the vocational needs of chronically ill adolescents would go far toward assisting their transition to adulthood. Securing adequate health insurance and finding employers willing to be flexible in response to treatment demands are essential for these youngsters. Yet such activities are foreign to most educational personnel responsible for vocational training or career preparation.

Overall, chronically ill children represent new challenges for school authorities at every level. They fit poorly into existing categories. Schoolteachers, principals, and state education authorities must reach beyond the constraints of boundaries too sharply defined toward a renewed flexibility in matching educational services with educational need.

5

Health and Social Services: Problems and Prospects

The chronically ill children of this nation benefit each day from the impressive progress in medical technology that has occurred over the last two decades. Sophisticated diagnostic tools, increasingly efficient machines that assist or replace normal functioning, and better drugs have all contributed to the lengthening of the lives of these children. Furthermore, the medical community contains a wide variety of physicians, nurses, social workers, and mental health professionals who collectively have vast knowledge about children with chronic illness and their families. Yet, health services, individually sophisticated as each one may be, are poorly organized as a whole; in many locations, those who provide services remain uninformed about the ways in which children and families actually manage from one day to the next. Overall, the organization of available health services has failed to keep pace with the technological advances of medical care and is unresponsive to the many needs of the individual child and family.

A particular child, for example, may be better cared for at home than in the hospital, yet appropriate home-care assistance is unavailable. A physician in one clinic may order a series of uncomfortable laboratory tests for a child, having failed to discover that the very same tests have already been completed for another clinic. The findings of assessments completed in the specialty hospital may reach the child's local pediatrician after a long delay and then only incompletely. The medical staff may explain to a newly diagnosed adolescent what is physiologically problematic when the youngster is only wondering what to tell his friends about the illness. A physician may order for a child special foods the child's family cannot afford. A social worker may help the family find monies to pay for a sophisticated medical procedure but not for daily medical supplies. A child health charity may raise a good sum of money in one year, but little of it supports respite care for parents. These and other examples support the contention that children with a chronic illness and their families must struggle with a health care system that lacks many services from which they could benefit. Professionals themselves are often frustrated by services so poorly organized that they aggravate the emotional and social burdens that accompany life with a chronically ill child. In some instances, the lack of appropriate services coupled with improper orchestration of the many aspects of care can seriously jeopardize the physical as well as the psychological health of the child.

From the perspective of many parents of chronically ill children, the service system is irrational, fragmented, rigid, obscure, and intolerant. This view is largely justified. At times, even the word *system* seems an overly optimistic label for the capriciousness that exists in the availability of services. Partly because of the specialization of medical care and partly because of the tangled boundaries of agencies, specialties, and professions, the service system frequently leaves unattended many needs of families and children. In many instances, it imposes medical and bureaucratic procedures with unnecessary repetition.

In recognition of these problems, a few medical institutions have begun to experiment with new modes of service delivery (Bock and others, 1983; Johnson and Steele, 1983; Pierce and Freedman, 1983; Rosenbloom, 1984; Stein, 1983). Comprehensive care clinics focused on specific diseases and including extensive outreach programs have sprung up. Services designed to assist families in the care of their children at home have emerged in several sites. Groups have begun efforts to help parents close the service gaps embedded in the medical care system. All these efforts deserve support, but for now they are exceptions rather than the norm.

In this chapter, we discuss three types of institutions that bear on the lives of children with a chronic illness and on their families: medical care institutions, social service agencies, and community support systems (voluntary associations and self-help groups). Our review encompasses both the current patterns of transactions between these groups and the families of chronically ill children and the difficulties and benefits that ensue from these transactions. The chapter describes as well three innovative programs for chronically ill children, programs that illustrate sound community-based approaches to the care of the chronic illnesses of childhood.

Structure of Medical and Nursing Services

The socioeconomic status of families often determines the community institutions from which children receive their medical care. Upper- or middle-income families tend to have a private physician in their community; if an emergency arises, they are likely to use a local hospital. For low-income families, emergency rooms of city hospitals, pediatric outpatient clinics based at hospital centers, or nearby public health clinics are the primary sources of medical care. The majority of medical care in all of these sites is routine. Postpartum follow-up visits, well-child or developmental screenings, immunizations, checkups for school, dental health care, and care for the occasional acute illness constitute the basic medical services most children receive in this country. Although sizable gaps in service remain for many children and major difficulties persist for many parents in finding access to needed services, these institutions are designed to respond to the majority of children's medical needs.

These same institutions, however, are often poorly equipped to respond adequately to the many, special, complex, and continuing medical needs of chronically ill children and their families. As a result, children with a chronic illness and their parents seek care in medical centers that have sophisticated technology and a wide variety of medical, social service, and mental health specialists. These centers number far fewer than general hospitals, health clinics, private practicing pediatricians, general practitioners, or family doctors. With few exceptions, these medical centers are associated with universities and medical schools; they are teaching hospitals. In large measure, issues in the organization of care for these children relate to the strengths and limitations of academic medical centers (Lewis and Sheps, 1983).

A chronically ill child, simply by virtue of being a child, needs much routine care in addition to specialized medical care. The common colds, checkups, injuries, and dental problems that plague healthy children also strike those with a chronic illness. Yet, a common cold is hardly a simple matter to a child with diabetes, for example; it represents a major threat to the stability of the illness. Those who provide general pediatric services must recognize the special circumstances of chronic illness. Furthermore, medical services are likely to be most effective when intertwined with appropriate supportive or mental health services (Weitzman, 1985; McInerny, 1984).

In an ideal world, families with a chronically ill child would receive all necessary specialty medical and nursing care, general pediatric care, social work services, mental health care, and attention to school matters in a well-integrated fashion. Throughout the nation, actual practice poorly approximates this ideal. For example, chronically ill children may find excellent social work services in their clinics but not in their communities (Travis, 1976). In some hospitals, services are especially attentive to the full range of concerns of a chronically ill adolescent; in other hospitals attention is limited to medical needs alone (Jackson, 1973). Academic medical centers may attend well to the specialty medical needs but overlook general health services (Kanthor and others, 1974). Overall, the current structure of the medical care system for chronically ill children guarantees an emphasis on some services to the neglect of others equally needed; moreover, services that are available often duplicate each other (Pless, Satterwhite, and VanVechten, 1978). To examine these problems in detail, we discuss in turn the challenges that face general health care providers, community hospitals, and academic medical centers. Special populations face special risks, and consequently we examine the difficulties attendant to chronically ill children in rural and impoverished areas.

Routine child health care includes the familiar medical and nursing services that are part of the lives of most children. General pediatricians, pediatric nurse practitioners, school health nurses, public health nurses in neighborhood health clinics, family doctors, and general practitioners are those professionals to whom parents will turn when something first seems wrong with their child. These individuals represent the entry point to the medical system for almost every ill child including those with a chronic illness. In this role as gatekeeper, the primary care provider must make a number of important decisions. Because of the relative rarity of chronic illnesses, these decisions require skills and abilities that are infrequently exercised. For example, a general practitioner in a rural area must be able to identify important aspects in the history of a problem or in the physical examination that will signal an underlying chronic condition. However, when a condition is so uncommon that the general practitioner might see it only once every several years, the task is a difficult one. As a result, chronic illnesses may be diagnosed accurately long after symptoms first appear. The challenge of accurate, early identification of a chronic illness in a child is a formidable one for physicians and nurses who provide routine pediatric services (McInerny, 1984; Perrin, 1985; Stein and Jessop, 1985).

The general practitioner must also be able to make an appropriate and wise referral. For this task, several questions must be answered: What are the referral options? What are the pros and cons of the different options? What are the treatment approaches of different specialists, and how will those biases mesh with the family's needs? If a pediatrician suspects a child to have cystic fibrosis (a suspicion that will arise every year or so in a busy practice), that pediatrician must learn where the family might be referred for care. Is it better to refer the family to the medical center twenty miles away where there is no pediatric lung specialist or to a clinic a hundred and fifty miles away where there is a full range of specialists? What would be best for the family? Which clinic would work more closely with the family's pediatrician? What are the differences in the supportive services the clinics offer? The decision is important because the pediatrician's referral will marry the family and the clinic for many years.

Continuing care for chronically ill children also demands a major shift in normal routines for the general physician. Instead of doing a brief physical examination for a school health form, the doctor must send to school detailed explanations of how the chronic illness might interfere with classroom functioning. Instead of relatively simple follow-up on the child's flu, the pediatrician must monitor the chronically ill child's flu quite closely to prevent a sudden aggravation of the long-term illness. Instead of being counseled only about normal developmental concerns (sibling rivalry and bed-wetting, for example), parents of a chronically ill child must be counseled about the intricacies of development and growth in the context of a chronic illness. Instead of being the only physician in the child's life, there will be many others to work with, and they may be available only infrequently and by telephone. In comparison with care for a healthy child, care for the chronically ill child requires a fundamentally different mental set, a different repertoire of skills, a greater sensitivity to emotional and family factors, and time set aside for extended visits. The problems of integrating these skills into a practice have been thoughtfully considered by several professionals (Battle, 1972; Bruhn, 1977; Harding, Heller, and Kesler, 1979; Hughes, 1976; McInerny, 1984). Long neglected, the skills and techniques for providing care to chronically ill children are now beginning to be included in the training of pediatricians and other general health care providers, yet even with improved education, obstacles to change remain formidable (Stein, Jessop, and Ireys, 1984). The time constraints on primary care providers prohibit them from including many chronically ill children in a practice or from spending as much time as necessary. In traditional fee-for-service settings, lack of payment for extended visits discourages attention to difficult family, developmental, or social problems.

Small community hospitals face many of the same problems as community doctors and nurses. In a typical local hospital (one with a few hundred deliveries per year) the staff will have little experience with conditions such as spina bifida that occur once in every ten thousand live births. Accurate identification of rare illnesses and continued follow-up are not the strength of these hospitals. In fact, with neither the close contact over time that accompanies local care nor the sophisticated technology found in large medical centers, small general hospitals often find themselves at a loss in providing adequate services to a chronically ill child. Children with severe asthma or initial presentations of leukemia, renal disorders, heart problems, or endocrinological disorders may be hospitalized briefly at general hospitals, but when a chronic illness becomes suspected, they are typically transferred to a specialty medical center.

The failure of general community hospitals to serve chronically ill children may be costly. Partly because of higher overhead and partly because high-cost procedures may be used more frequently, daily hospital rates are higher in large centers than in community hospitals. Hospitals in large medical centers also typically hospitalize more patients whose bills go unpaid, and the daily rate charged other patients is partly adjusted in response. Travel to specialty medical centers may also be longer and more expensive. Although at times chronically ill children need sophisticated technology available only in specialty care sites, this technology is unnecessary for many hospitalizations. In the case of a diabetic adolescent, for example, hospitalization may be needed to stabilize fluctuating blood sugar levels and may not require specialized procedures. Yet, general community hospitals rarely treat these problems. Infrequent use of community hospitals stems from the general lack of knowledge about chronic illness in children. Furthermore, the child's records may be elsewhere and difficult to reach. As a result, when hospitalization is needed, community physicians and nurses depend on the large medical centers and associated specialty clinics.

The academic medical center has become a powerful force in shaping patterns of health care in this country. Lewis and Sheps (1983, p. 43) note, "The academic medical center is at the core of our health care system. It feeds it, fuels it, and overtly runs a substantial part of it. Each center is big and complex, employing thousands of people; many centers spend much more than $100 million per year. As the most important and indispensable element in our health care system, the academic medical center has a special relationship to the needs of the public at large and to its community and region."

To speak of *the* academic medical center is somewhat misleading because there are actually several types of centers that can be distinguished by different affiliations with universities and medical schools, various sources of funding, and diverse histories. In matters of children's care, there are generally two types: pediatric departments that operate children's units within larger hospitals and freestanding children's hospitals. There are also a few hospitals that focus on special problems of children, institutions that have grown out of the former polio and rheumatic fever centers for children common in the 1940s and 1950s. Depending on the particular mix of federal, state, and private monies that support it, each center has different problems, resources, and responsibilities to the public and to its community. A major portion of revenues to academic medical centers comes through the federal government by way of research grants and public support of services; during the fiscal year 1976–1977, 32 percent of medical school revenues came from the federal government.

A characteristic of virtually every academic medical center is its major commitment to sophisticated, subspecialty care. Much of the growth of these centers can be traced to their success in fostering basic research and applying new knowledge to improve medical outcome; miracles of medicine are a trademark of academic medical centers (Lewis and Sheps, 1983). All of these efforts require access to many patients with similar biological problems; hence, the growth of departments organized along the lines of medical subspecialties. A large center, for example, will house a pediatric department that has many divisions, such as pediatric nephrology, pediatric hematology, and pediatric endocrinology. Each division operates its own specialty clinic; for example, the pediatric nephrologists treat children with renal disease, and the hematologists take care of children with cancers. Many of these clinics have entirely separate staffs, with different social workers and nurses associated with different diseases. In rare instances, a social worker will participate in several of the clinics, becoming something of a chronic illness specialist. For most physicians, however, the relatively inflexible disease-specific structure of hospital-based care leads to little contact with children outside their own specialty.

Academic medical centers have come to dominate the health care landscape so thoroughly that they are now the locations "where changes in the nature, scope, and cost of care are first implemented, if not originally developed" (Lewis and Sheps, 1983, p. 65). The disease-specific and biological orientation that is part of the fabric of medical centers runs counter to a generic, community-based notion of childhood chronic illness care. If these centers shift their orientation, however slightly, the way will become clear for modifications in the delivery of services.

Within the world of a large medical center, the various divisions and specialty clinics vary in the quality and comprehensiveness of the care they offer. One clinic may have attracted bright, young specialists with grants that provide support for pediatric nurse practitioners, social workers, and other health providers. Another clinic may have a well-known physician yet lack support staff. Still another clinic may be floundering, losing former support, prestige, and patients to a competitor. The quality of medical care may vary from one clinic to another, but variation in the availability and quality of supportive services is likely to be much greater. Some specialty clinics assure a wide range of medical and other health services; others provide effective medical care but little else. Moreover, the specialty clinics that have the most sophisticated medical care are not necessarily those with the best overall care. In some states, for example, clinics in large teaching hospitals supported by fee-for-service payments from a middle- or upper-middle-income group may have access to very modern laboratories or equipment, yet state-supported clinics serving low-income families may have a more comprehensive, multidisciplinary team attending closely to a range of medical, educational, and social needs of both child and family.

Comprehensive health care programs that focus on individual diseases or groups of diseases have developed in a number of health centers, often with the encouragement and support of voluntary groups concerned with that disease. Working both on the local and national level, for example, the Cystic Fibrosis Foundation has been a major force in the development of high-quality research and service programs for children with cystic fibrosis. At times with direct support from the foundation but more commonly with support from governmental agencies, comprehensive cystic fibrosis clinics offer joint pulmonary and nutritional care, usually associated with additional social and psychological services to help involved families. The many local chapters of the National Hemophilia Foundation have worked similarly to organize comprehensive hemophilia centers that integrate hematology services with orthopedic, psychiatric, nursing, social, and developmental services. In many instances, the local voluntary group chapter plays a key role in organizing community outreach from the medical center's comprehensive program. Similar efforts have been made for children with juvenile arthritis and sickle cell anemia. The best of these programs offer comprehensive services that have great positive impact on the quality of life, health status, and longevity of children who attend these centers.

Because of their relative scarcity, large medical centers are quite distant from many communities—and therefore quite distant from many of the local, general health providers. This distance can lead to severe problems in the transfer of information (Kanthor and others, 1974; Kisker and others, 1980; Pless, Satterwhite, and Van Vechten, 1978). Such problems typically arise when chronically ill children receive technologically complex care in a hospital-based specialty clinic and then return home where a local pediatrician or a public health nurse provides follow-up care. If the family lives a considerable distance from the clinic, a smaller, general hospital closer to the child's home may also be required when emergency care is necessary. Transfer of knowledge about the patient's care among these providers is often haphazard. Frequently, the local pediatrician fails to receive results of the summaries of diagnostic or treatment procedures completed in the hospital-based specialty clinic; the same pediatrician may also fail to contact the clinic staff to ensure that they know relevant facts about the history of the child and family. Also, the local pediatrician may be uninformed about new developments in care or may have only partial understanding of the ramifications of common childhood illnesses for the course of a chronic illness. Inappropriate medical care, contradictory advice for parents, duplication of painful and expensive procedures, premature alteration in management strategies, prolongation of symptoms, and unnecessary medical crises can result when information fails to reach those who are involved with the care of the child at the community level.

These problems of communication among levels of care and between providers and families can be highly problematic for families. Families may be unsure to whom to turn when their child has an acute health problem. Should the child with a severe asthma attack be seen by the local pediatrician or be referred to an allergist miles away at the specialty center? Whom should parents call when their child undergoing chemotherapy for leukemia develops a fever—the local physician or the cancer specialist? Most parents lack clear answers to these questions although they must face them frequently. Furthermore, insufficient communication leaves many families without adequate attention to certain basic needs. The specialist may assume that the community pediatrician is involved in communication with the school about the child's health problem while the physician in the community may avoid doing so, certain that the team associated with the specialty clinic has assumed that responsibility. Similar problems arise around issues of vocational planning, genetic counseling, and several other areas of importance to families (Kanthor and others, 1974). Just as community physicians are unlikely to be knowledgeable about the most up-to-date treatments for a given rare health condition, providers in the specialty centers are unlikely to know which community resources can be applied to improve the functioning of children under their care. The staff of a comprehensive arthritis center is unlikely to know about available home-care services in a smaller community sixty miles away, or to be able to refer families to appropriate support groups in their community, or to have satisfactory understanding of the resources school systems in distant communities will have available for educating children with chronic illnesses. Communication, so important to families facing a difficult chronic health problem and a complex health system, receives little attention in the present fragmented health care system.

Even with the best of intentions, knotty interprofessional problems can arise. Klerman (1985, pp. 422–423) describes these problems with clarity:

Because of the nature of chronic illnesses, children with these disorders and their families are particularly likely to be affected adversely when interprofessional issues are not resolved. As noted

earlier, in times of acute crisis, all members of the health team seem
to know their roles and to integrate quickly into a well-functioning
team. But when the medical condition continues over an extended
period of time, includes multiple interventions by indviduals from
a variety of helping professions, is complicated by socioeconomic
factors, and requires the involvement of family members, there is
greater likelihood of more than one person doing the same task and
of no one doing others.

The majority of interprofessional problems arise either
because more than one individual or profession claims the exclusive
right or responsibility to perform a given task or because no
individuals or professions are certain a task is theirs: Whose
responsibility is it to tell families that a diagnosis is a life-
shortening neurological disease—pediatric neurologists, who have
all the facts of the particular case and many others at their disposal?
or family physicians or pediatricians who have more knowledge of
the family's dynamics? Whose task is it to teach the child and the
family how to detect early signs of an asthmatic attack, how to deal
with it, and under what circumstances to seek medical assistance—
the nurse, the primary care physician, or the pulmonary specialist?
Who should adjust the medication for juvenile arthritis, epilepsy,
or diabetes? And—in the area of neglected responsibilities—it is
clear that there are tasks in the care of chronically ill children that
no one wants, or feels capable of, or has the time for, or is paid to
perform. Examples of such functions are primary care, communication with school personnel, and managing the vegetative or dying
patient.

Many chronically ill children and their families may be
victims of unresolved problems among the professionals who
provide care. They may also encounter discontinuities in their care
because of simple scheduling problems, especially for children who
have multiple problems involving several different physiological
areas. Children with hemophilia, for example, require services of a
hematologist as well as an orthopedic specialist, children with
diabetes require both a pediatric endocrinologist and a nutritionist,
and children with spina bifida may require the services of as many
as five specialists (neurosurgery, orthopedics, psychology, urology,
and physical therapy) as well as general pediatric and nursing care.
Most clinics function independently of each other so that the

neurology clinic frequently meets one day and orthopedics another. This schedule, well-suited to the specialization of a medical center, requires parents to make multiple trips for needed services.

Major medical centers are also training sites for physicians and nurses, a situation that increases the risk of discontinuous care still further. In some instances, the child and family see a different physician every time they attend a specialty clinic; the nurse, social worker, and medical director of the clinic may become familiar, but the physician who checks the child and talks to the mother changes from one visit to the next. This lack of continuity of the physician in specialty clinics, coupled with the relative inexperience of trainees, can delay early identification of problem areas and lead to neglect of the social forces that can so powerfully shape a child's and parent's response to a chronic illness.

In some states, the Crippled Children's Services (CCS) takes an active role in organization and provision of services to children with severe chronic illnesses. This program, which we describe in greater detail in Chapter Seven, has long had great state flexibility. In some states, it serves primarily as an insurance program, helping children with chronic illnesses who are of limited means but otherwise ineligible for Medicaid; in these jurisdictions, the CCS program takes little direct role in the organization of health services. Specific CCS-sponsored clinics (for example, for the evaluation and treatment of children with orthopedic disorders) are organized in other states. Still other programs contract with community practitioners or academic health centers for needed specialty medical and surgical services. The degree to which CCS programs influence the organization of health services varies tremendously from state to state (Ireys, Hauck, and Perrin, 1985), but in some states, the CCS program plays a vital role in fostering the better organization of services and advocating the needs of this relatively neglected group of children.

For families in rural areas, geographical access to primary care and specialty care services, as well as to related health services, may be especially difficult. Roads can be inhospitable for travel when emergencies arise; public transportation in rural areas is sparse or nonexistent; costs for gas and car maintenance continue to rise. All of these problems can pose serious threats to adequate care for a child with a chronic illness.

The relative scarcity of health services in many areas of the nation compounds the problems that stem from the relative scarcity of chronic conditions. The child who has a chronic illness and lives in a sparsely populated rural county is in a particularly vulnerable position. For example, in a county of ten thousand persons, one would expect to find perhaps fifteen children with severe asthma, three or four children with diabetes, one child with cystic fibrosis, one child with spina bifida, and perhaps ten children with any one of several hundred exotic and extremely rare physical illnesses. The county will likely have a local public health department and one or two family physicians. It may lack a pediatrician or be far from a large hospital and have few social services agencies. As a result, it may have relatively few of the special services a chronically ill child will need.

Furthermore, for those health providers who practice in this county, the developments and strategies in the care of a childhood chronic illness will be largely unfamiliar. Identification and accurate diagnosis of a particular problem may be as elusive as the knowledge about long-term management of the child's illness. Pediatricians and family physicians who work in rural areas are likely to practice alone, without the benefit of the collegial consultation available within a group practice. Because of the few times a rural practitioner will see a child with a chronic illness, the problems of developing appropriate referral patterns and maintaining close ties to the specialty centers can be especially severe. The chronically ill child living in a rural area may face medical crises of formidable proportions, endure pain longer than necessary, and miss the benefits of new technologies.

Among inhabitants of rural areas, two groups deserve particular attention: American Indians and migrant laborers. In these groups, the incidence of chronic health conditions is high; the severity of the conditions is likely to be harsh, and patterns of living are unlikely to foster the use of specialized health services. Major publicly supported efforts have yielded substantial improvements in general health care services in rural areas, yet remaining deficits have pronounced consequences for those children with a chronic illness (Perrin, 1985).

Problems in the organization of services can weigh heavily on both the rural and urban poor. Coordinating the many needed services, finding transportation, having extra dollars for special foods or clothing—all of these elements of care for a child with a chronic illness can be more difficult to manage when a parent is also burdened with poverty. In some instances, the extra costs or the added stress of caring for a chronically ill child can be the proverbial straw, overwhelming a family with meager resources. If a family is unable to ensure that their child receives required services, the child's condition can become aggravated, leading to additional medical, psychological, and social problems (Perrin, 1985; Stein and Jessop, 1985).

The problems of poor children who live in rural areas must be distinguished from the problems of their counterparts in urban areas. Both groups of children require attention commensurate with the resources that their respective communities lack.

The problems that face chronically ill children who live in impoverished urban areas differ in character but not in consequence from those that face their counterparts in rural regions. Stein and Jessop (1985, p. 387) provide an important reminder of the social and physical context of life in a slum:

It is difficult for summary statistics to convey graphically the complexity of the real-life situations confronting the individual family in the inner city, including the confusion, the irrationality, and the frustration of the system in which care is given, the intermeshed need-on-need of people's everyday lives, and the coping strategies they develop to come to terms with the situations with which they are faced—situations such as no heat, no hot water, and a baby scalded from water heating on the stove; waiting in successive lines at a hospital with one sick child, while another child comes home from school to an empty house; telephone calls to Medicaid offices that go unanswered, being put on hold for long periods, and making all those calls from a pay phone because there is no phone at home; mail applications lost and requiring a fresh start; forms requiring a twelfth grade reading level when the applicant only reads at the eighth-grade level (Peterson, 1981); a fifteen-year-old adolescent mother alone with a sick child who requires tracheostomy care at home.

Sophisticated medical services may be geographically available, and Medicaid will likely cover specialty medical services, yet many medical centers remain unable to address comprehensively the problems of inner-city families who have a chronically ill child. Medical centers seem especially inept at preventing the consequences that result from poor daily management and from inadequate attention to primary care. As Stein and Jessop note, "Physicians are not trained and medical care facilities are not organized to deal in a total fashion with the range of problems faced by the urban poor. Rather, they tend to address each individual medical problem as if it occurs in isolation and is amenable to a traditional medical remedy" (p. 388). The consequences of this failure may include worsening of the child's condition, higher medical bills, and more turmoil for the family.

Most poor children with a chronic illness who live in inner cities receive virtually all of their care from a large medical center; they are likely to go to the same institution for their specialty care, for their dental care, and for their general medical care. Nevertheless, for these families, coordination of care remains imperfect for several reasons: the single-disease orientation of the large specialty care centers, the interprofessional problems inherent in the care of a chronically ill child, and the complex, overburdened social services agencies typical of large urban areas. The problems of low-income urban families with a chronically ill child result from the failures of specialty medical care centers combined with the limitations of poverty.

For both rural and urban poor, access to and quality of some health services are especially problematic. Genetic counseling and testing are one example. Indeed, the implementation of genetic screening programs over the last two decades underscores several of the problems of these populations.

Genetic services are essential to many families with chronically ill children, whether or not they are burdened with poverty. For all people, such services suffer from problems of quality control, from unpredictable funding, and from limited support of services other than direct laboratory testing (Holtzman and Richmond, 1985). Genetic testing refers to methods based on examining the genetic makeup of a parent or of a fetus. One approach is the mass screening of a selected population in order to identify those at high risk of a particular problem. Examples of mass screening include (1) alpha-fetoprotein screening of all pregnant women as a means of identifying women at high risk of having a child with spina bifida or (2) screening for sickle cell trait in the black population to determine couples at risk for having a child with sickle cell anemia. Aside from the ethical questions mass screening might raise, there are also technical problems related to screening for rare conditions. If the prevalence of a particular condition in a population is low, a screening program is likely to identify a high number of individuals who appear to have the condition or the trait but who in fact do not.

A second approach to genetic screening is to test parents or relatives of children with a genetic condition. In this approach a sister of a child with muscular dystrophy is screened to determine whether she is at risk for giving birth to a son who will develop muscular dystrophy. Under these conditions, genetic testing is likely to yield essential information for families.

The rural and urban poor may be less able to benefit from both approaches to genetic services than middle-income groups; in part this is because screening programs are often established with inadequate resources for providing care to those identified as needing further services. The Early Periodic Screening, Diagnosis, and Treatment (EPSDT) program of the Medicaid program is instructive on this matter. The EPSDT program, as implemented in many states, focused public health attention on establishing systems for screening, but then little effort was made to identify sources for follow-up care or to provide adequate reimbursement for it. Counseling (to help families understand the genetic information, examine the choices available to them, and understand the implications for their own families) was especially overlooked. Moreover, counseling, where provided, frequently gains least attention from staff and is most likely to be curtailed at times of limited funding. Screening without arrangement for appropriate follow-up education and treatment is a disservice. To tell a family that one of its members is a carrier for sickle cell or for Tay-Sachs disease provides little basis on which families must make important decisions. Moreover, screening and follow-up resources are concentrated in urban settings, usually in academic health centers. As a result, the rural poor face major problems in gaining access to genetic services.

Social Services Agencies

Regardless of their level of income, chronically ill children and their families often need the assistance of social services agencies to obtain financial coverage, transportation reimbursements, housing improvements required by the illness, daycare, mental health and family counseling, and care for the ill child at home. In addition, some chronically ill children have families who are unable to undertake and sustain care; these children may need care in foster or adoptive families. The fundamental problems that pervade health care organizations are mirrored by similar problems in the arena of social services. Fragmentation, lack of financial coverage, restrictive eligibility criteria, and inexperience with the special problems of severe childhood chronic illness characterize the social services system. Although a broad array of social services is in place under public and private auspices across the nation, families with chronically ill children may find it difficult or impossible to gain access to them.

In many instances, access to social services is available in the context of the child's specialty medical care. Social workers in outpatient clinics, for example, are generally responsible for assisting families in finding needed services. Families' access to social services, however, is often hampered. Some hospitals do not employ social workers. The American Hospital Association reported in 1974 that only about one half of more than six thousand hospitals surveyed had social work departments (*Encyclopedia of Social Work*, 1977). Only one third of cystic fibrosis centers had a social worker on the staff in the early 1970s (Travis, 1976).

Although social workers are increasingly employed in specialized medical settings (Bracht, 1978)—for example, in the comprehensive treatment centers for chronic diseases such as hemophilia, sickle cell disease, muscular dystrophy, and diabetes—the staff is usually spread thin. Many specialty clinics in academic medical centers are large and the social work staff small. A spina bifida clinic that provides medical care for a hundred children may employ only one social worker. Because specialty clinics tend to care for chronically ill children from numerous towns and counties, an additional barrier to families' access to services is the hospital social worker's lack of familiarity with agencies and programs available in the locales in which the families live. Families continually reinvent the wheel in their frustrating search for assistance. Georgia Travis (1976), a social worker with many years of experience in hospitals and community agencies, wrote:

The hospital social worker in a specialty service, with patients from a wide geographic area, cannot know all the social agencies or all their functions and restrictions; the community is too vast and varied. She may have worked closely with a child and his family over several years, when he is hospitalized or attends a clinic, but have no knowledge of local agencies that could be of help. The family may, in fact, be known to one or more local agencies in connection with that child or other children or family problems, but if the mother does not mention the fact, the hospital worker may continue in ignorance of the potential services the agency offers [pp. 108–109].

Services are highly variable from community to community. Families, and the social workers who would guide them, must struggle to sort through the idiosyncratic patterns of services, the eligibility criteria that vary from locale to locale and from time to time, and the instability of funding that has always characterized social services policy in our nation. Again, Travis describes it well:

Communities differ so widely throughout the nation that no two have identical resources. Furthermore, change is the order of the day. New services spring up, seemingly overnight, and others vanish. Purchase of services from a variety of private agencies; varying public resources and philosophies in different states and counties; shifting fads in counseling; diminution of old needs and the emergence of new ones as changes in demography and life-styles occur; the trend toward alternative services and peer organizations; and underlying all, the changing economic and political mood— all these make it impossible to encapsulate the resources for chronically ill children and their families [p. 75].

The social services that could benefit families with chronically ill children fall roughly into three categories: (1) those that
support and reinforce parental care, such as family and mental
health counseling, case management, anticipatory child guidance,
genetic counseling, training in self-care, group discussions, and
financial counseling and assistance; (2) those that supplement
parents' care, such as daycare, homemaker and home health services, respite care, and transportation; and (3) those that substitute for
parental care, including foster care and adoption (*Encyclopedia of
Social Work,* 1977). Services in the three categories are provided
under various auspices and funding sources. Private nonprofit
agencies serve many communities, as do governmental social services, welfare, mental health, and health departments. The local
chapters of voluntary, disease-oriented associations; church organizations; and private, for-profit social agencies also offer services in
some communities. Among the larger private sources of funds are
the United Way, religious groups, and the disease-oriented associations. The major public sources of financial support are state and
local government and federal revenues allocated to the states in the
Social Services Block Grant.

The fragmentation of social services results in uneven coverage from community to community and in poor or nonexistent
coordination among programs serving the same families. Jackson's
(1980) comments about health care programs for mothers and
children apply equally to social services: "These multiple program
areas cannot be said to constitute a systematic group of services.
There are no standards to which all adhere. No common information system exists nor is there a uniform approach to patient
records. The services represent a mixture of public and private
auspices which appear to be oblivious to each other at least as often
as they are complementary" (p. 14). The result, especially for the
family of a child with a serious, life-long illness, can be a multiplication of already heavy burdens: "Families with a chronically ill
child often appeal to various community agencies for help with
their complex social problems. In many communities, services are
compartmentalized and therefore do not deal with the total family
as an integrated unit. Since each agency sees only its part of the
family problem and since communication between agencies is often

inadequate, a family not infrequently receives conflicting, and at times diametrically opposite, advice from different sources. As a consequence, the parents of chronically ill children often become suspicious or completely alienated toward all health and welfare agencies" (Markowitz and Gordis, 1967, p. 25).

In the early 1970s, in an effort to bring rationality into the fragmented, highly uneven, and diversified social services system, federal legislation creating a national program of social services related to public assistance was enacted. Known in 1985 as the Social Services Block Grant (SSBG), the program's forerunners were Titles IV-A and XX of the Social Security Act. The SSBG provides federal funds to the states for social services. The states may either provide services directly, using state agency personnel, or may use the funds to purchase services from other providers including private and governmental agencies.

The SSBG and its precursors put in place the opportunity for states, rather than the federal government, to take the lead in planning social services. It gave the states latitude to fund services to meet their own needs and encouraged citizen participation in the planning and allocation process. The legislation permits federal funds to pay for services both for families on welfare and for those slightly above welfare levels. One goal is to create a continuum of services, including those in the three categories used by families with chronically ill children—services that support, supplement, or substitute for parental care. In theory, the SSBG is an important source of services for families with chronically ill children. It is intended to establish a national comprehensive system of social services and to make those services available to families who cannot pay for them. The data concerning services provided and individuals served by SSBG funds are extremely sketchy, and it is therefore virtually impossible to count services to specific populations, such as chronically ill children. However, an assessment of the SSBG's structure makes it clear that the practice falls short of the theory in several respects.

First, the SSBG and its predecessor programs serve only low-income individuals and families. The original federal social services legislation, Title IV-A of the Social Security Act, was part of the public welfare law. Title IV-A social services were targeted to families who received public financial assistance—that is, Aid for Families with Dependent Children (AFDC) or Supplemental Security Income (SSI)—with emphasis on enabling those families to become economically self-sufficient and on reducing the public welfare rolls. Although Title XX of the Social Security Act, passed in 1975, broadened the target population and permitted the states to use federal funds to pay for services for low-income people who did *not* receive welfare payments as well as those who did, the eligibility levels chosen by the states have been very low (U.S. Department of Health and Human Services, n.d., p. 9). Thus, many low- and middle-income families with chronically ill children, unable to pay for daycare, homemaker services, counseling, transportation for medical care, and other services available with this federal and state subsidy, are not eligible for assistance.

Second, a limit on federal funds constrained the expansion of social services in most states. The federal limit of $2.5 billion has remained virtually constant since 1972; the states, rather than developing programs for new populations, such as chronically ill children, have struggled to keep existing services in place.

Third, the social services provided within the SSBG give little attention to the special needs of families of chronically ill children. Rather, the services are directed to the needs of other families. Homemaker services funded by the SSBG mainly serve the elderly. The few homemakers for children work primarily with those suffering from child abuse and neglect rather than children who need special, complex health care. In addition, the training most social workers receive ill prepares them to address the needs of chronically ill children and their families in the community social services agencies in which they work (Rudolph, Andrews, Ratcliff, and Downes, 1985). A group of services, called "health related services," which was funded in many states in the early days of Title XX to provide support for home care, education in self-care, case management, and other services of particular relevance to families with chronically ill children, has been severely reduced or terminated (U.S. Department of Health and Human Services, n.d.).

Fourth, the process for determining the allocation of SSBG funds in each state has influenced the priorities. In many states, the planning process for allocating funds to various social services is an open one in which citizens and professionals participate. The largest and strongest interest groups, such as senior citizens, are the ones with the greatest influence on setting priorities. The rarity of childhood chronic illnesses and the tendency for parents and professionals to organize along illness lines rather than according to their mutual need for social supports have made families with chronically ill children weak competitors for SSBG funds in most states. In summary, social services supported by the federal block grant meet the needs of chronically ill children and their families to only a minimal degree.

Children with severe chronic illnesses are among the population of children who are at risk of rejection by their biological parents. No data provide a reliable picture of the frequency of the placement of chronically ill children in foster care or adoption. But anecdotal reports from social workers and nurses in pediatric intensive care units and hospital care-by-parent units suggest that children with special health needs, including severe chronic illnesses, are more likely than other children to require placement in substitute families (Carolyn K. Burr, personal communication with the authors, 1981). A survey of children receiving foster care and adoptive services in twenty-five states in 1982 found that about one fifth of the children had disabling conditions, including both mental retardation and physical disability (Tatara, 1983). Some of these twenty-six thousand children have chronic illnesses, but the numbers and types of illnesses are omitted from the survey. If the other twenty-five states have comparable numbers of children in substitute care, about fifty thousand children with disabling conditions, including severe chronic illnesses, received foster care or adoptive services in 1982.

During the same year, about forty-seven hundred children in the twenty-five states were legally freed for adoption; a disproportionate number of these children fall into the special needs category. Two thirds of the children whose parents terminated their rights to them, thereby freeing them for adoption by other families, had special needs of various types, including disability. Special needs are defined broadly in the adoption lexicon and include older children, those in sibling groups, and racial minorities as well as those with physical or mental disabilities. A relatively small number of children freed for adoption likely have special needs as a result of chronic illnesses. Yet, the high proportion of children who are freed for adoption with some type of special need may indicate that their parents more readily release them for adoption than other parents.

In recent years, the trend toward adoptive placement of children with special needs spurred the passage of legislation to provide financial subsidies to the adoptive families. By 1980, all states but one had enacted some form of subsidized adoption legislation, and in the same year, the first federal adoption subsidy program was created (the Adoption Assistance and Child Welfare Act of 1980, Public Law 96-272—also known as Title IV-E of the Social Security Act). The federal law makes available financial subsidies to parents who adopt children eligible for public financial assistance (AFDC or SSI) and whom the state defines as having special needs that make them hard to place (Office of Inspector General, 1984). The federal subsidized adoption program has been implemented gradually and unevenly by the states: some have a means test and others do not, some provide full Medicaid coverage for the children and some do not, and some offer specialized casework services to support the families while others do not (Office of Inspector General, 1984). However, the trend to seek aggressively and to support permanent family placements for children with chronic illnesses and other special problems is a promising one.

Foster care and adoptive families whose children have serious health conditions need the same supportive social services, health care, genetic counseling, and other programs that all families with chronically ill children need. They, like other families, have diffi- culty gaining access to these services. Furthermore, the process of matching children with special needs and their special substitute families is, in the words of a recent report, "clearly an art and not a science. The technologies of promoting children, recruiting parents, and matching children who have particular special needs with families who are willing and able to adopt such children are still in the early stages of development" (Office of Inspector General, 1984, p. 13). Major barriers inhibit these adoptions, including traditional attitudes of caseworkers about the kinds of children who can be adopted successfully and a lack of adequate postadoptive services. The number of infants who are born at very low birth weights and survive and the number of unmarried single mothers who keep and raise their children will probably continue to rise during the next decades. Hence, the children available for adoption may increasingly be those with special needs. The federal and state adoption assistance and subsidy programs can have important benefits for children with severe chronic illnesses who require adoption.

Our review of the social services that can benefit families with chronically ill children and the system that provides the services suggests several conclusions. First, the lack of access to supportive services is the most important problem. Social services that families need are unavailable in many communities; where they do exist, they are beyond financial reach for many families. Respite care, homemakers and home health aides, daycare, and counseling are unavailable to most families today. Most of the social service and mental health agencies are geared to the needs of broad populations rather than to the less visible and relatively rare numbers of families who have chronically ill children. Social services in the United States, which "evolved in the backwater of social policy" (Benton, Feild, and Millar, 1978, p. 1), require new approaches if chronically ill children and their families are to use them fruitfully.

Efforts of Voluntary and Professional Organizations

In addition to the policies of health care and social service institutions, the policies of a diverse group of voluntary organizations shape the care of chronically ill children and their families. These organizations include disease-oriented voluntary associations (such as the March of Dimes, the Juvenile Diabetes Foundation, or the Muscular Dystrophy Association), self-help groups, and various professional organizations. Some of these voluntary efforts have brought extraordinary benefits to chronically ill children across the nation. Some seek actively to influence policy makers and legislatures; with a long record of success, they are forces to be reckoned with. In other instances, voluntary groups make their presence felt in small ways, often unnoticed by large medical centers, busy professionals, or burdened legislators. Unfortunately, voluntary organizations reach only a few of those children and families who might benefit greatly from their attention.

Disease-Oriented Voluntary Health Associations. For many childhood chronic illnesses, there exists at least one national health charity and sometimes two. The National Hemophilia Foundation, the Muscular Dystrophy Association, and the March of Dimes Birth Defects Foundation are examples of the many voluntary associations concerned with this population of children. Through fundraising strategies of many types, these organizations have mustered considerable financial resources. These resources have been spent on research (mostly biomedical in nature), medical services, patient education, public health education, professional training, and community services. Butler and colleagues (1985) estimate that eight of the largest health charities concerned with children spent $224.6 million in 1979. (In comparison, the CCS program, in the same year, spent about $280 million of state and federal monies.) Other health charities function on just several thousand dollars each year.

Many illnesses, especially those that are very rare, lack formal or incorporated organizations that represent their interests in legislatures or that raise money for services or research. Individuals with these diseases are particularly disadvantaged in the competition for resources. One response to this problem has been the development of the National Organization for Rare Disorders (NORD). NORD's primary objectives are to collect and disseminate information about rare disorders and to encourage formation of new voluntary agencies to help affected families contact each other (National Organization for Rare Disorders, personal communication with the authors, 1983).

As a whole, the voluntary associations have made substantial contributions to the care of chronically ill children and their families. As advocates for the needs of these children, they have managed to help sustain or enlarge public programs that might have otherwise languished for lack of support. For example, the Cystic Fibrosis Foundation, with considerable grass roots organizing and tenacious attention to state legislatures, has guided the passage of state laws supporting care for children and young adults with cystic fibrosis. Between 1974 and 1979, the Cystic Fibrosis Foundation guided the passage of such laws in fifteen states (Cystic Fibrosis Foundation, 1979). The successful advocacy of this foundation and of other voluntary organizations has made them effective guardians of certain categories of chronically ill children who, because of their small numbers, could easily be ignored in the stiff competition for public dollars.

In addition to being advocates and guardians, many health charities support direct patient and community services. The larger organizations are able to contribute substantially to clinics by paying the salaries of social workers and other counselors or by purchasing equipment. Smaller organizations tend to provide seed money for service projects that then work to obtain governmental funds. According to Milofsky and Elworth (1985), many of the younger health charities seek to stimulate and nurture parent support groups both to provide a needed service and to generate a critical mass of informed parents who can then aid advocacy efforts.

The third category where health charities have contributed substantially involves research efforts. In their review, Butler and colleagues (1985) note that some foundations contribute more than half of their available funds to research. Some organizations use their allocations for research in a fashion deliberately designed to garner additional research monies. In a particularly successful effort, the Juvenile Diabetes Foundation (JDF) has used its collections to stimulate matching grants from federal agencies and to fund young investigators who subsequently seek additional monies as identified specialists in diabetes research.

Despite their contributions, child health charities have been criticized for promoting paternalism, sensationalizing the problems of the children, ignoring certain groups of children, and supporting the interests of professionals more than families. Milofsky and Elworth, in a personal communication with the authors (1982), discussed these criticisms:

The associations serving children with chronic diseases have been attacked especially because of the symbolism they promote in fund-raising campaigns. Cute poster children not only give a special advantage to associations, like the Muscular Dystrophy

Association, which serve a relatively small portion of the sick population. They also deflect attention from adults who need help and resources. They emphasize helplessness, dependency, and tragedy rather than independence, adaptation, and growth.

On its face, the system of health charities concentrates resources in research on and treatment of a few diseases while others are largely ignored. One inequity in this is that resources are not necessarily distributed according to the prevalence of illness; rather, they are distributed in relation to the marketability of a disease in a funding drive. Children's diseases, capitalizing on the appeal of poster children, have a decided advantage over many adult diseases. A second inequity is that diseases are represented to the extent there is an aggressive, articulate group willing to champion a cause. Poor people's diseases tend not to be addressed. Only recently was a Sickle Cell Anemia Foundation formed, and there is no rickets foundation. There are no associations to address environmental children's diseases like lead poisoning. Finally, a system of disease-specific foundations diverts attention from common needs of the chronically ill.

Partly out of a practical need to maintain close ties with the specialty centers where their constituents are treated, voluntary foundations have generally supported the priorities of these centers. The largest portion of their contributions have supported basic biomedical research and medical care; relatively few dollars support social programs designed to assist in coordination of services or to help families respond to stressful events (Milofsky and Elworth, 1985). As important as their contributions have been, the health charities generally have had little influence over the organization of health services for children.

A close look at the disease-oriented voluntary associations leads to both admiration and dismay. The resources these groups have brought to bear on some chronically ill children are extraordinary. Severely afflicted children and their families who would have otherwise gone neglected and research projects that would have otherwise been postponed or left undone have received much support. But the resources are often disproportionate to the numbers of children in need and allocated with little public debate or awareness. Voluntary associations representing chronically ill children have generally had to be tough political fighters, vocal and persistent. Over the years, the more successful ones have built a strong financial base. Yet, their tenacious orientation to specific illnesses constrains their collective effectiveness. For certain purposes, such as lobbying Congress for increased research funds for specific National Institutes of Health, they may join together, but history and the reality of scarce donations work against sustained collaboration.

Self-Help Groups. Many voluntary health organizations began as a group of parents with children who had similar diseases; these parents joined for mutual support and collective action. Although only a few such groups evolve into self-sustaining organizations, self-help groups are widespread, diverse, growing, and vital. In many instances, they promote new approaches to care and seek to explore the application of new ideas. Borman (1985) estimates that the number of such groups of all kinds (Alcoholics Anonymous among them) may be close to half a million with a total of perhaps fifteen million participants. The number of self-help groups related to chronically ill children is, of course, much smaller. Nevertheless, these groups represent a major source of support for some parents of chronically ill children and for adolescents with a chronic illness. Furthermore, they attract continuing attention, as witnessed by the many articles describing them (Chesler and Yoak, 1984; Johnson, 1982; Kurland, 1981; Lipson, 1982; Martinson and Jorgens, 1976; Minde and others, 1980; Ross, 1978). Most of these articles are subjective descriptions of small groups centered around one particular disease or condition; good empirical research about these groups (what makes them work, who joins, why do they stop, do they improve outcomes) is virtually nonexistent.

In 1978 the President's Commission on Mental Health wrote:

Self-help groups . . . have long played a role in helping people cope with their problems. Similar groups composed of individuals with mental and emotional problems are in existence and being formed all over America. . . .These largely untapped community resources contain a great potential for innovative and creative commitments in maintaining health and providing human services. In spite of the recognized importance of community supports, even those that are working well are too often ignored by human service agencies. Moreover, many professionals are not aware of, or comfortable with, certain elements of community support systems. The nation can ill afford to waste such valuable resources [Borman, 1985, p. 771].

The observations of this commission apply with special force to the population of chronically ill children and their parents. Mental health professionals (for example, Yalom, 1975) would agree with Borman (pp. 774-775):

> The helping mechanisms that exist within groups are impressive. The importance of universality and acceptance, of being part of a group that shares your condition and understands what you are experiencing, seems to be central. . . .Such universality strengthens elements of cohesion, involvement, and belongingness, which are outside the usual kinds of therapies provided by a conventional therapist or professional. Groups foster communication, provide participants with social support, and respond to their many cognitive and emotional needs. They involve the development of ideologies and belief systems, which appear to be very important in sustaining persons who face a great variety of crises in their lives.

With a small number of participants having common experiences and interests, self-help groups are enormously diverse, engaging in different activities depending on their specific *raison d'être*, their community and medical context, their own particular stage of development, and the needs of their members. In a review of self-help groups for parents of children with cancer, Chesler and Yoak (1984) conclude that such groups typically engage in one or more of five different activities: (1) dissemination of information and educational materials about the disease; (2) sharing and mutual expression of feelings about the demands of care, the development of the child, the child's future, and the family's response; (3) provision of social activities for parents and family members, as a means of having normal good times in a group where no apologies or explanations are needed; (4) fund raising, in order to garner resources generally to fill service gaps; and (5) advocacy focused on any of several levels, including the clinic, community, state legislature, or national government. In addition to much anecdotal evidence regarding the utility of self-help groups as a source of assistance to parents of chronically ill children, professionals can play important roles in their development and maintenance. Professionals can help parents through easing access to hospital facilities, referring parents of newly diagnosed children to an ongoing group, legitimizing the group simply by recognizing and supporting it, mediating when necessary between the group and the clinic staff, being available for consultation on medical matters, and aiding the group in linking up with other resources (Chesler and Yoak, 1984).

Of all the families who receive care from a particular specialty clinic, only some will be ready and interested to form a parent group. Unless the clinic is large, the number of interested families may be too small to generate a critical mass of commitment and energy. In some locations, at the urging of pediatricians and nurses, parents of children with diverse chronic illnesses have come together to form a self-help group. Despite the major physiological differences among their children's illnesses, parents have recognized the similarity of their concerns (Pediatric Ambulatory Care Division, 1983; Shayne and Cerreto, 1981). The noncategorical approach in the area of self-help groups promises to assist in expanding the pool of parents from which a self-help group might evolve.

Participation in parent support groups is unevenly distributed across the socioeconomic and racial spectrum. Members of black and Hispanic communities and members of low-income groups are poorly represented in self-help groups (Borman, 1985; Chesler and Yoak, 1984; Lieberman, Borman, and Associates, 1979). Different coping styles, subtle professional biases, and practical obstacles (for example, being unable to find a baby-sitter) have all been suggested as reasons for low participation rates by families with low incomes. More knowledge is urgently needed to understand this phenomenon.

Professional Organizations. Professional organizations play a subtle but potentially powerful role in shaping health care services for chronically ill children. To convey the scope of these organizations, we list here just a few of the many that have taken an interest in the problems of chronically ill children: American Academy of Pediatrics, Society for School Nurse Practitioners,

Association of Special Educators, Association for the Care of Children's Health, Society of Pediatric Psychology, Association of Directors of State Maternal and Child Health/Crippled Children's Programs, Maternal and Child Health Section of the American Public Health Association, and the National Center for Clinical Infant Programs. These organizations serve several important purposes. First, they provide, through newsletters and journals, vehicles for disseminating information in a relatively rapid manner. This can be used to alert their constituents to new developments in the field and to stimulate discussions around emerging issues. The second purpose of professional organizations is to codify rules of practice or to establish guidelines for care. In this sense, the representatives of the larger professional group act to set and enforce standards, including minimal requirements needed for formal entrance into the profession. The third purpose of professional organizations is to advocate with federal and state authorities for various causes relevant to their own interests. Many organizations concerned with child health, for example, were active during the formulation of the Maternal and Child Health Block Grant in 1981.

The diverse professional organizations have acted in various ways on behalf of chronically ill children and their families. For example, in 1983, the Association for the Care of Children's Health held its annual conference around the theme of chronically ill children. Other groups have been instrumental in the development of new service programs and in the dissemination of research findings. The efforts of these groups, often fueled by a small cadre within the larger organization, can shape new directions for care. Some of the programs that reflect these new directions are described here.

Some Innovative Programs

With a determined spirit of innovation, concerned individuals throughout the nation have begun to take heed of the needs of chronically ill children and their families and to act. Many creative approaches to the care of chronically ill children and their families are under way: collaborations among state departments of health, social services, and education; comprehensive clinics for children with one disease, now broadening their services and the types of children served; hospitals, formerly for children with tuberculosis, heart disease, or polio, whose missions have been expanded and refined; and state programs, once focused solely on children with orthopedic impairments and now seeking ways of serving children with other disorders. All of these efforts deserve wide dissemination. We describe three as examples: Project REACH in north Florida; the Pediatric Home Care Program in the Bronx, New York; and the Home Health Care Team in Washington, D.C. Although the three programmatic approaches differ, the projects share certain common elements: a central sensitivity to families, a recognition of the complexity of the needs of families and children, an emphasis on providing community-based care, a belief that individuals from different professions must learn to work together harmoniously, and a sense that children, regardless of their diagnostic label, are indeed more alike than they are different.

REACH Project. REACH (Rural Efforts to Assist Children at Home) is a demonstration service and training project that provides health care and case management services to children in a sixteen-county rural area in north Florida. The one thousand infants, children, and adolescents enrolled in REACH all receive Medicaid and have various chronic illnesses, including leukemia, muscular dystrophy, pulmonary disorders, failure to thrive, and seizure disorders. A research and development initiative of the Children's Medical Services (CMS) program of the Florida Department of Health and Rehabilitative Services, the project is funded by the Robert Wood Johnson Foundation and the Florida Medicaid program.

REACH evolved in 1980 from several observations of professionals in Florida who had had long experience in the care of chronically ill children and their families. First, they believed that chronically ill children and their families require a broad scope of services and that "diagnosing and treating the child's chronic medical condition without also responding to other needs will only produce a limited improvement in functional status" (Pierce and Freedman, 1983, p. 86). Second, they had found that chronically ill children and their families tended to use services inappropriately,

at unnecessary cost to themselves and to society: "Parents, faced
with caring for a chronically ill or multihandicapped child, may
spend years attempting to find and understand information regarding access to and appropriate use of available services. Their
attempts, often prompted by great uncertainty, are sometimes
referred to pejoratively as misutilization. A more appropriate term
to use in conceptualizing this parental dilemma is 'unstructured
utilization' " (p. 86-87). Further, the CMS staff had observed "the
devastating medical, psychological, educational, and economic
consequences of medically dependent children treated at specialty
care centers who, without community level supportive case management: (a) were frequently lost to follow-up, (b) tended not to seek
treatment until an acute episode of their disease occurred, or (c) were
inappropriately utilizing tertiary care providers" (p. 87).

  To remedy the problems of poor functioning of the children
and families, inappropriate use of services, and unnecessarily high
cost, REACH instituted a system of case management and care
coordination. A REACH nurse—called a Health Care Coordinator—lives in each county and provides a wide range of services to
the children and families in that county. The Health Care Coordinators use home visits to coordinate the complex care required by
the children; teach parents appropriate care; help parents improve
their parenting skills; arrange for special services, such as transportation; and provide liaison among physicians, families, schools, and
community social service agencies. An especially important function of the coordinators is to assure smooth collaboration between
the families and the physicians at the University of Florida Health
Center in Gainesville, who provide most of their medical care.

  The coordinators work independently in their home communities. Their activities are laced together by frequent group
meetings and by supervision and support from the small REACH
management team, who had at the outset three additional important roles. First, they initiated linkage among those who affect the
care of the children and families: specialty health care professionals,
community-based public and private health providers, school systems, and social and economic support agencies. They devised
agreements among the agencies to facilitate the day-to-day working
relationships necessary to care for the families. Second, they

developed a comprehensive record-keeping system—the Progress-Oriented Record (POR), a highly efficient method of documenting the activities of the coordinators. The POR is a tool that permits REACH to facilitate coordination of care, tracks the progress of the children and families, and predicts cost efficiencies. Third, they established training and supervision for the coordinators, who receive graduate credits for participation in an intensive, four-course curriculum that covers the pathophysiology of pediatric chronic illness, family dynamics and child development, communication skills for interdisciplinary collaboration, and a practicum in case management.

Formal evaluation of the REACH program is designed to answer a number of questions: Do the children function better? Do the families cope more effectively? How do professionals involved in the program view its workability? Is the program more effective for children with some conditions than for those with others? Are medical services less expensive for children in REACH? Answers will be available when the evaluation is complete in 1985. Meanwhile, there are at least preliminary answers to the last question, the effect of REACH on costs. A retrospective analysis of data indicated that REACH can generate a significant reduction in the costs of care, mainly by reducing the numbers of days the children spend in the hospital and the number of visits to hospital-based, outpatient facilities. Pierce and Freedman (1983, p. 89) report, "After paying for the Health Care Coordinators, a 17 percent reduction in gross health care costs would have accrued. The costs that would have been avoided were strictly costs of inappropriate utilization on the part of patients in the target population. For example, approximately 40 percent of all institutionally based outpatient encounters were avoidable; approximately 9 percent of all inpatient days were avoidable. Based on a total average cost of 104 high-cost patients of $4,700, the avoidable costs in the study year were nearly $800 per patient."

The Florida legislature and executive branch have not waited for the formal evaluation of REACH before moving ahead. Convinced of REACH's positive effects on the lives of children and families and on the financial investment in care, policy makers have plans under way to implement the REACH approach statewide for high-cost, medically dependent, chronically ill children and their families (S. Freedman, personal communication with authors, 1984).

Pediatric Home Care Program. In 1970, the Pediatric Home Care (PHC) program was established at the Bronx (New York) Municipal Hospital Center, a large general hospital affiliated with the Albert Einstein College of Medicine. The PHC is a "special ambulatory care unit for children who are seriously or chronically ill and whose needs were not being met successfully through conventional programming" (Stein, 1983, p. 90). In contrast with REACH, which serves children and families in rural areas, the PHC serves an inner-city population, primarily poor families from minority groups. The children face "any of a series of . . . difficulties, including: especially complex medical problems that cannot be handled well in the customary outpatient settings; unstable family settings; or extended hospitalizations" (p. 91). Some children enrolled in the PHC have relatively common chronic illnesses made especially serious by their difficult family circumstances; many have multisystem diseases that are particularly complicated. Sickle cell anemia, asthma, diabetes, leukemia, juvenile rheumatoid arthritis, spina bifida, and biliary atresia are among the medical diagnoses of enrolled children, who are generally referred by the resident physicians in the department of pediatrics.

Each child receives care from a core team that has an unusual membership: a pediatric nurse practitioner (PNP), a pediatrician, and the child's family. One goal of care is to enable the child and family to be independent of the professionals; inclusion of the family on the care team assures the centrality of the family in the child's care and is a means toward accomplishing the goal of independence. The PNP provides most professional care, which is often delivered in the home. A social worker, consultant psychiatrist, and physical therapist augment the services of the core team, and the referring pediatric resident and subspecialists are included as appropriate (Stein, 1983).

The PHC team provides comprehensive outreach services to each child and family: delivering direct services at home and in the clinic and hospital, monitoring the child's condition and the family's well-being, teaching the child and family to understand

and carry out care, coordinating services, advocating for the child and family, and providing supportive counseling. The home visits are a special feature of the PHC team's activities. Seeing children at home provides the staff an opportunity to adjust care to the individual circumstances of each home and family; to gain a richer understanding of the medical, psychological, and social needs and of the household arrangements than clinic visits allow; and to teach the child and family caretaking skills adapted to the child's unique surroundings.

In their team approach and home visits and in a number of other features as well, PHC services are qualitatively different from services provided in standard pediatric settings. First, care is flexible, individualized, and responsive to the dynamic, changing needs of the child and family. Second, extensive counseling is a central activity of the core team. Moreover, counseling is geared not only to the child's medical care but also to that child's development and to the family members' needs as well. Third, all care, whether delivered at home or at the hospital, is channeled through the core team, which provides continuity and guidance to the family. Fourth, the family is at the center, and services are geared both to meet the child's needs and to enable the family to gain in confidence in managing the child's care and becoming their child's successful advocate. Finally, the PHC "is organized to address issues of concern to families of children with chronic conditions . . . that . . . cross disease categories" (Stein, 1983, p. 92). The functioning of child and family rather than the child's diagnosis is the focal point of care.

Like REACH, the PHC is the subject of formal evaluation. A randomized experiment has compared children treated through the PHC with children who receive standard care at the Bronx Municipal Health Center. The PHC director summarizes findings of the evaluation of the PHC: "Results show that PHC is an effective intervention that has positive mental health outcomes and improves satisfaction with care" (Stein, 1983, p. 92). The PHC's family-focused team approach has enabled many poor, urban, minority families who have children with a variety of severe chronic illnesses to achieve great psychological health and stability and to gain confidence and satisfaction by participating actively in their children's care.

Home Health Care Team. A group of dedicated professionals at Children's Hospital National Medical Center in Washington, D.C., make up the Home Health Care Team (HCT), which was established in 1981. The children served have a variety of diagnoses; the four most common are prematurity, bronchopulmonary dysplasia, developmental delay, and cerebral palsy (Bock and others, 1983). A number of the children require tracheostomy care, home oxygen, or ventilator support, technology that places stress on families and children alike. During its first eighteen months, the HCT served almost one hundred children (predominantly infants and children under age three) from minority families.

The HCT was established on the premise that families whose children have complex medical conditions that require careful and extensive management can be successfully cared for at home rather than in institutions if the families have adequate and appropriate professional support. The HCT provides a broad array of services— therapy, nursing, social, educational, and counseling—coordinated by a case manager from the team, which consists of a nurse, physical therapist, occupational therapist, educational coordinator, and social worker. The backup services of the hospital (emergency room, outpatient clinics, and consultations by hearing, speech, and nutrition specialists) augment the HCT's services. The HCT works with the child's physicians, who may be located at the hospital or in the community.

The team assists the family in making plans to bring the child home from the hospital and provides intensive services in the home to enable the family to achieve success in caring for the child. An important role of the HCT is to enable families to utilize appropriate community services. The team helps families establish links with health care providers, home nursing services, parent support groups, infant stimulation programs, special education programs, and sources of financial aid. In time, families are often able to shift from dependence on the HCT to reliance on community-based services and to carry the major responsibility for their child's care. The demands of caring for a child with multiple needs are enormous, and "on occasion, the HCT has assisted families in facing the reality that they cannot care for their child at home and then supported them in the difficult task of placing their child in a long-term care facility" (Bock and others, 1983, p. 94).

A key to the effectiveness of the HCT is its sensitivity to the individual needs of families. The HCT members write, "Each family has different goals, priorities, and values. One family may view a baby-sitter as necessary and permissible; another may view it as evidence of lack of care for their child. A family may view medical staff as omnipotent and omniscient; another may view God as the ultimate healer. One family may be anxious to use all available community financial assistance; others may strive to support themselves. The HCT must focus and work on goals established with the family while keeping in mind the needs of the child" (Bock and others, 1983, p. 94).

The HCT has demonstrated that coordinated, transdisciplinary home care of chronically ill and handicapped children can have a number of positive effects: improved health, improved medical compliance, decreased hospitalization, decreased inappropriate use of the emergency room, and prevention of medical complications.

Summary

These three programs illustrate that health services can be organized in harmony with the needs of families with a chronically ill child. In a somewhat different fashion, each program has melded local resources into a system for delivering care that recognizes and attends to individual variation among families. Ecological concepts, including an appreciation of the importance of every person involved and of their interrelatedness, characterize these programs. Further development and extension of their approaches and methods define future challenges for the health care system.

Health care for children with chronic illnesses has improved tremendously. Specialized services to treat many rare diseases are now available, mainly in large academic health centers. In some sites, these clinics have evolved into comprehensive centers offering a wide range of services that include medical, nursing, and social services; counseling; and community outreach. Yet, services that are comprehensive remain the exception rather than the rule, and four continuing problems affect the ways in which families whose children have chronic illnesses interact with the health care system.

First, the large majority of health care services for children with chronic illnesses are provided within specialty health centers, primarily in larger cities. Much of the medical care provided is of high quality, although there may be differences from disease to disease. With few exceptions, those providing high quality medical services have little understanding of the communities from which the children and their families come. They attend well to the metabolic and physiological problems associated with the illness but little to the developmental or psychological or educational consequences. Their understanding of the resources available or needed in the child's community and of the ways to integrate children into the lives of their communities is limited. The challenge is to take the commitment to quality that has characterized medical care in the specialty center and extend it to a broader range of services and to the communities in which children live.

Second, the types of services available to a family whose child has a chronic illness are often dependent on the vagaries of the local disease-specific health charity, the interest of the specialist within the medical center, and whether or not the disease is covered by a comprehensive clinic. In other words, the present organization of health services is highly dependent upon specific diseases, and if a child has a condition falling outside the boundaries of a high-quality clinic or comprehensive center, the child and family go lacking. With few exceptions, current services do not treat equally children with different diseases.

Third, communication among providers and coordination of services are essential from the view of families but typically lacking within the health care system. Even medical records may not be transferred from one health provider to another, and when they are, they may go in an incomprehensible or incomplete fashion. Parents are uncertain which provider to call when their child is ill. Services provided by one physician may affect the care of another, yet these services typically are uncoordinated. The very complexity of these serious health conditions and their interrelatedness with so many aspects of the child's life and the family's activities make effective coordination and communication essential.

Fourth, services at the local community level can be sparse, and providing care at this level forces the physician to face certain difficult realities. With rare conditions, problems abound in the appropriate identification and referral of children needing specialty services. With ineffective communication from the specialty center, community providers can become frustrated in trying to meet their obligations to their patients. Resources supporting health services for children with chronic illnesses have typically been applied only to the specialty centers, leaving communities bereft of needed services and unable to meet the special challenges of children with chronic illnesses. A specialty center may suggest that a child who lives sixty miles away receive certain types of physical therapy, yet the community may have no physical therapist experienced in caring for children. Although medical services for families with chronically ill children have improved, families have little to turn to when they seek help in their home communities. Certain groups, particularly people living in rural areas or in poverty, are especially burdened by greater risks of ill health and by greater problems in access to needed specialty services. Professional training, historical trends, and current funding patterns all serve to maintain a relatively narrow, disease-specific focus on the care of childhood chronic illness.

Social services agencies have largely overlooked the class of children with chronic illnesses. Although medical social workers in specialty health centers attend to some of the needs of children with a chronic illness and their families, such social workers are unavailable in many clinics and hospitals. Communities themselves vary widely in the availability of social services, and government-supported social work programs suffer from inconsistent and meager funding in light of the great need. Training for the large majority of social workers omits careful attention to the needs of chronically ill children and their families.

Overall, the efforts of voluntary and professional organizations have led to important services for chronically ill children. Past achievements are small in comparison to the possibilities of the future. A collective and sustained effort that merges professional

and parent groups and that transcends a disease-specific approach
could fuel a stronger thrust toward innovative service programs.

In this chapter we have measured the strengths and weaknesses of the health service system, but we have ignored one of its
most distinctive characteristics: the high cost of services. We turn in
Chapter Six to this topic.

∞⤳⤳∞ 6 ∞⤳⤳∞

Defining the Costs
of Care

Costs are central to policy considerations. Policy decisions typically find expression through the distribution of financial resources. The development of new policy necessarily requires knowledge of the cost of services and of the demographic and social factors that shape patterns of cost. Rarely is this knowledge more important than in a discussion of childhood chronic illness where attention to the costs of sophisticated medical procedures threatens to distract attention from the many other services equally needed by these children and their families.

Costs are also central to family life. In the care of a chronically ill child, cost is a constant issue for almost every parent. The medical services (hospitalization, surgery, medications, and so on) provided to a child to prolong life or to remedy a physiological problem can generate enormously high costs. Although these are likely to be covered in large measure by public or private health insurance, residual costs in the form of higher insurance premiums or copayments are well known to most parents of a chronically ill child. Parents must also face financial decisions that affect the quality of family life. Should the hospital bill be paid or should the family take a needed vacation? Should a home nursing service be ordered to help with the daily care routines or should new clothes be purchased for the family? Beyond the necessary medical care, costs are often shaped by what the family believes it can afford.

When a healthy child is struck with an acute medical condition—appendicitis, for example—the hospitalization, medical care, and associated services can be quite costly. The parents' insurance may cover some of the costs, but it will fail to cover all of them; out-of-pocket expenses can still mount. Eventually, though, the condition passes and services are no longer needed. Not so with a chronically ill child. An acute exacerbation of the illness may come and go, but more medical care and the next emergency always remain ahead. Expenditures for the care of chronically ill children are characterized by persistent accumulation. Repeated trips to the clinic, periodic hospitalizations, continuous refills of medication, regular use of disposable equipment, new appliances for a growing child: all of these costs, relatively small for any one year, can accumulate over time to become major burdens on the family's budget.

A father said to us, "I'm always worrying about money, but I have tried never to let costs interfere with my intention to get the best care for my daughter" (Shayne and Cerreto, 1981, p. 4). But he was speaking of medical care. As other parents have testified, considerations of cost frequently discourage the purchase of services that could dramatically ease the family's burden (Pediatric Ambulatory Care Division, 1983). Extra nursing services at home, special respite care, or a telephone are examples of services that would contribute substantially to a family's ability to care for its ill child yet that parents have foregone because of lack of money. Worry over the costs of care compound the stress inherent in raising a severely ill child.

The costs of care for children with a chronic illness must necessarily concern parents and policy makers alike, for they tower ominously now and loom larger in the decades ahead. These children and their parents require a broad range of services, some of which are extremely expensive because of the technology involved and some of which are expensive because they are needed repeatedly over many years. Although the sophisticated technological services tend to capture the major share of the attention, both types of services contribute significantly to the high cost of care for childhood chronic illnesses. But how high are these costs? From whence do they spring? What are the trends in costs over time? What is the magnitude of costs for childhood chronic illness in comparison with other child health expenditures? How does the source of payment influence costs? What costs are hidden in days parents lose from work or in promotions foregone? Where are potential sources of savings? Policy makers need answers to these questions. Unfortunately, financial information focused on childhood chronic illness is sparse, and available studies have several major faults. Typically, these studies focus on specific diseases and on small samples that represent poorly the larger class of these children. Most studies account for only some of the many services that generate costs, giving only a partial view of the financial vista; and they fail to gather information on both the sources of cost and their payment. Existing data, therefore, allow for only incomplete answers to many questions.

Most of the available financial information is collected in this chapter. We first identify patterns in the costs of care for children with chronic illness and specify factors that influence these costs. For our purposes, we define *cost* as the amount a provider charges for delivering a specific service or piece of equipment. Specific charges are themselves based on many factors, including the provider's overhead, patterns of accounting for the costs of providing the service, the determination of the market value of the service, and the amount of desired profit. Because the economics of pricing involve concepts indirectly related to childhood chronic illness, we limit our discussion to factors that bear directly on cost as defined here.

In addition to discussing general patterns of costs, we present available estimates of the costs of care for seven of the eleven marker diseases. Reliable data are absent on the other four illnesses and on the many other rare chronic conditions of childhood. This chapter also addresses a topic of great importance that is often overlooked: indirect costs incurred by parents through loss of income or loss of financial opportunities. We end the chapter by examining potential sources of savings.

Scope and Nature of Costs

In general, the nation's health care expenditures are unevenly distributed. A few individuals account for a large proportion of the monies spent. For example, one study reports that only 2 percent of the nation's population use more than 60 percent of all inpatient resources each year (Zook and Moore, 1980). A similar skew marks the field of child health. One report (Kovar and Meny, 1981) estimates that average yearly medical expenses for children were $286.07 in 1978. But this figure hides a great discrepancy. For the vast majority of children, medical expenses are modest; for a few children, yearly costs of medical care are quite high. For example, 5.4 percent of the population under seventeen years of age were hospitalized in 1978 at an average cost of $1,920; the remaining 94.6 percent of children under seventeen had no hospital expenditures at all (Kovar and Meny, 1981).

It is unknown exactly how many children under seventeen with chronic illness are included in the 5.4 percent hospitalized in 1978. It is evident, however, that chronically ill children constitute a group of individuals for whom medical care costs are disproportionate to their numbers. Butler and others (1985) report that chronic health conditions among children under age fifteen accounted for 34.8 percent of inpatient discharges and 36.1 percent of days of inpatient care in 1977. Few data are available that reflect specifically on chronically ill children grouped together. Data from the National Health Interview Survey, however, do indicate utilization of health services by children with and without limitations of activity. Many, but certainly not all, limitations are due to chronic health conditions. In the 1979 survey, 2.1 percent of children under age fourteen had severe limitations of activity due to health conditions. These children accounted for 12.9 percent of hospital discharges and almost 25 percent of total hospital days for that year. They also had more than three times the number of physician visits per child than children without limitations of activity. Estimates of expenditures per child for hospitalization in 1980 were $48 for children without limitations of activity and $758 for children with severe limitations of activity. In 1982, approximately $12.2 billion were spent on physician visits and hospitalization for children in the United States. Children with severe limitations of activity, although comprising only 2.1 percent of children, used $1.5 billion or 12 percent of these expenditures (American Academy of Pediatrics, 1984a). Although these estimates vary somewhat, they all support the conclusion that a relatively small number of children utilize a very high proportion of the total child health dollar in this country. The medical care during the first month of life of one child born with spina bifida, for example, will cost about the same as the first month of care for several hundred healthy infants.

The typical pattern of a childhood chronic illness involves a series of outpatient treatments and hospitalizations over many years, together with routine, daily home-care or self-care procedures. This pattern generates obvious medical costs—for hospitals and physicians, medications, lab and x-ray services, physical therapy, or social work. Costs not easily categorized or assessed are also generated. These include transportation costs, extra telephone costs, costs associated with time absent from work or school (often referred to as lost opportunity costs), costs for special diets, and costs for services to help respond to increased worry and stress within the family. Table 6 conveys the scope of costs that arise in the care of a chronically ill child. Rarely will any child or family require all these services, but most chronically ill children and their families will generate several items from each column during the course of a year.

Furthermore, some children with chronic illnesses seem to need and use services more frequently than other children with similar illnesses (Starfield and others, 1984). In this way, the distribution of costs within the population of children with chronic illness reflects a skew similar to the population of children as a whole: a few chronically ill children account for a disproportionate share of the total costs of care for all chronically ill children. The total cost of care depends on the utilization of services. Utilization is influenced by many factors including availability of and access to the service, the perceived need for the service, the source of payment, the economies of scale, the methods by which services are provided, and the diffusion of new technologies.

Availability and Access. Availability generally refers to the presence or absence of a service within a particular geographic area. *Access* refers to the presence or absence of obstacles inhibiting use of an available service. The pattern of costs of care for a particular

Table 6. Sources of Cost in the Care of Chronically Ill Children.

Initial Identification or Evaluation Period	Initial Treatment Period	Continuing Treatment	Special Services Needed for Limited Duration	Daily Care Routine Services
Emergency room services	Hospitalization	Physician or clinic visits	Camp	Medications
Physician visits	Physician visits in hospital	Urine and blood tests	Respite care	Injections
Urine and blood tests	Outpatient physician visits	Physical therapy	Individual or family counseling	Bowel and bladder hygiene
Hospitalization	Urine and blood tests	Home nursing services	Specialty care for complications	Care of personal appearance
Neurological tests	Teaching of parent and family about the disease	Psychological tests	Re-education in management of care	Appliance care
Transportation	Physical therapy	Dental evaluation	Genetic counseling	Home health nurse visits
Phone calls	Dental visits	Orthopedic fittings	Infant stimulation	Special foods
Intensive care unit services	Orthopedic fittings	General pediatric care for common health problems	Parent support group	Physical therapy
Assessment of family's functioning	Financial evaluation	Transportation	Homemaker services	
Psychological or developmental testing	Transportation	Phone calls	Home health nurse	
	Phone calls	Surgery and operating room services	Transportation	
	Intensive care unit services	Insurance premiums, deductibles, or copayments	Special clothes	
	Social work services	Monitoring of family functioning	Remodeling of house	
	Surgery		Child care for siblings during visits to clinic or hospital	
	Room and board during extended hospital stays		Special foods	
			Relocation	
			Home respirators	
			Emergency room care	
			Occupational therapy and vocational training	

child and family necessarily depends on what services are available and where. In rural sections of the country, for example, long distances from the child's medical center result in high transportation costs (Strayer, Kisker, and Fethke, 1980). Regional differences in the diffusion of new technologies further contribute to the variation in the availability of services. A large urban area, for example, may have hospitals with new technologies (such as open-heart surgery for infants born with serious cardiac problems) and a broad array of specialized nursing or other allied health services. Another town, more modest in size, may lack these services. Even within one city, the use of different types of care depends on where families live and on their income level.

Access to care is intimately related to income status (Starfield, 1982; Select Panel for the Promotion of Child Health, 1981; Stein and Jessop, 1985). Children from impoverished families, for example, tend to spend more days in the hospital each year than other children (Egbuonu and Starfield, 1982). Furthermore, many families living in low-income urban or rural areas have little access to private pediatricians for general health care. When care is needed on an emergency basis or after clinic hours, these families tend to use hospital emergency rooms, which are more costly than clinics or private office visits.

Perceived Need for Services. A service is more likely to be utilized and therefore costs are more likely to be generated if the parents or the child's physician deem it an essential service. Some services, such as hospitalization for a child with diabetes whose blood sugar levels are dangerously high, are essential for the preservation of life. But in many instances, the need for a particular service is a matter of judgment. Should the mother take a wheezing child with asthma to the emergency room? Should another set of expensive laboratory procedures be ordered to confirm the first set of findings for the child with renal problems? How necessary is an additional surgical procedure for cosmetic purposes for the child with a cleft lip or cleft palate? Should the family be referred for professional psychological counseling, or can sufficient help be provided in the context of medical care? The final costs of services depend in large measure on the outcome of innumerable questions of judgment such as these.

Source of Payment. The use of health services depends on whether a way exists to pay for them. Parents, for example, may be able to afford that additional surgery for their child with cleft lip and/or cleft palate if the insurance company pays for it as part of the palate repair. The cost of extra speech therapy during the summer, which is excluded under most insurance plans, may exceed the same parents' ability to pay and thus remain unpurchased.

Some services (such as hospitalization) are almost entirely covered by private insurance or Medicaid. Other services (such as transportation) generate costs for which the parents are alone responsible. For the family, therefore, the more salient costs may be those for which they have no coverage and that tend to mount over the years—costs associated with equipment, appliances, transportation, and extra telephone calls.

The relationship between costs and source of payment for care of childhood chronic illness needs investigation. There is clear evidence that the lack of adequate payment for outpatient services often encourages the substitution of expensive inpatient care (for which reimbursement may be available). Less is known about other incentives that stem from payment mechanisms. For example, does the absence of a payment source for the addition of special air-purifying equipment in the house of a child with severe asthma result in a delay of its installation, which in turn results in more emergency room visits or expensive hospitalizations? Better understanding of the ways in which payment sources encourage the use of more or less expensive services would significantly aid policy development.

Economies of Scale. As Enthoven (1980) has shown, costs of care for certain surgical procedures are lower in hospitals that perform many of these procedures than in hospitals that perform a few. The economy of scale is such that the more procedures done in one location, the less expensive each procedure. This reasoning likely applies also to surgical procedures in childhood chronic illness care. Reduction of costs by concentrating skilled practitioners in one site has been a strong argument for regionalization among children's hospitals. Katz (1980) notes that agreements between hospitals can save money for all because services can be shared thus eliminating much duplication. Regionalization as an approach to cost savings has been examined primarily in relation to inpatient care. It is unclear whether and to what extent costs may be reduced with a regionalized approach to outpatient services for complex and expensive chronic conditions.

Organization of Care. The development of relatively few centers for the provision of sophisticated surgical or medical procedures makes good economic sense. However, providing general health care services in specialty centers may be economically unsound for most parts of the country. General health services can usually be found close to the family's community, and it is often less expensive for a community-based practitioner who is knowledgeable about childhood chronic illnesses to provide general health care than for a specialty center to provide it.

Savings result from close coordination between community-based physicians and specialty centers; this is termed the *shared-management approach.* In a study comparing the shared-management approach with the specialist-management approach to the care of children and adolescents with cancer, Strayer, Kisker, and Fethke (1980) report, "The total estimated cost differences between the alternative systems for the delivery of outpatient care ($2,191.34) represents for shared management a mean saving per patient of approximately 29 percent in direct out-of-pocket expenses and a 59 percent savings in the indirect costs of lost income or productivity. A total theoretical mean 41 percent savings per patient was shown to accrue through the use of shared management" (p. 907). This study illustrates well the relationship between the costs of care and the way services are organized.

Development and Diffusion of New Treatments. New treatment procedures can yield relatively sudden alterations in the cost of care for children with a chronic illness. New developments in treatment occasionally lead to decreased overall costs, but more frequently, they result either in increased costs or in different types of costs. Although there has been progress in the treatment of almost all of the eleven marker diseases, advances have led to substantial cost savings only in the instance of hemophilia. Twenty to thirty years ago, virtually all care of children with hemophilia was provided either in emergency rooms or through hospitalization. Treatment relied primarily on the infusion of whole blood available only from blood storage facilities at hospitals. With the development of more concentrated and stable forms of clotting factors, most care for children with hemophilia is now provided at home. Clinic visits and hospitalization are reserved for monitoring of care, for acute crises, and for skilled rehabilitative services (Levine, 1974).

The social and psychological benefits of home care, enormous by all accounts, include substantially improved attendance at school and work. Some mothers who previously stayed at home because of their child's condition can now seek full-time jobs. Direct medical costs have decreased substantially as well (Aledort, 1982; Linney and Lazerson, 1979; Smith, Keyes, and Forman, 1982; Smith and Levine, 1984). One study reports:

In Rhode Island, the yearly medical cost in 1977 for treating bleeding events in a person with severe hemophilia was $2,902 for services and $7,222 for clotting factor, totaling $10,124. In 1980, services amounted to $422 per patient and $7,375 for the product, totaling $7,797. All medical costs amounted to $11,777 per patient in 1977, as compared with an average of $10,238 per year over the next three years. This amounts to a saving of approximately $1,500 per patient per year, or $64,500 for 43 patients. Even subtracting the $55,000 annual grant, a saving of over $10,000 is realized each year. Comprehensive care thus produces better results while costing less. Ensured employment and increased productivity of patients will enhance these savings [Smith, Keyes, and Forman, 1982, p. 578].

Although costs for most children with hemophilia have decreased as a result of technological improvements, there are a few for whom care has become more costly. Because they are unable to use the clotting factor preparations suited to most children with hemophilia, these children require special blood products that have recently been manufactured at a cost many times higher than the blood products normally used. Here again a few individuals, because of the particular form of the disease, require care the cost of which far exceeds that of the more typical child with hemophilia. Furthermore, as a result of improved prognosis and care, many individuals have chosen to have surgical procedures (such as joint replacements) to correct problems caused by bleeds. The cost of these operations has partially offset savings from the improved technology of blood storage.

The pattern of change in the costs of care of children with hemophilia illustrates well the mixed financial consequences of improvements in medical technology. On the one hand, improvements have decreased medical costs for most children, have allowed children and adolescents to participate more productively in school or work, and have freed parents enough for them to work consistently. On the other hand, improvements have brought higher medical expenses for a few children and, for some, have resulted in additional medical procedures that would have otherwise been foregone.

Hemophilia also illustrates the complexity in accounting for patterns of change in costs of care. Here, the financial consequences of technological advances have been relatively well documented and, on balance, are far more positive than negative. For virtually every other childhood chronic illness, the financial picture is more obscure. Improvements in chronic renal care, for example, have led from inpatient renal dialysis to clinic-based dialysis to home dialysis and to transplantation. In 1969, direct medical costs for kidney dialysis provided to inpatients were estimated to be between $20,000 and $25,000 per patient per year. Excluding complications, outpatient dialysis costs about one half of this amount, as does transplantation; home dialysis costs approximately one fourth (figures cited in Pearson, Stranova, and Thompson, 1976). However, most studies of the economic consequences of this disease have been concerned primarily with adults. We could find no information, for example, concerning the differential effect on parental employment or other family expenses for children with different types of dialysis. Home dialysis likely curtails employment opportunities for at least one parent and may lead to other expenses, such as home nursing care. Transplantation promises major, long-term savings in medical costs (Campbell and Campbell, 1978), but little is known about the extent to which costs involved in subsequent medical complications or emotional problems will offset these savings.

Equally uncertain financial consequences have ensued from advances in treatment for most of the other eleven marker diseases.

Improved drugs for control of leukemia may decrease hospital days in the short run, but over the long haul, the number of hospital days together with the high cost of the drugs themselves may result in larger financial outlays. Rapid and increasingly effective surgery early in the lives of infants with spina bifida may prevent complications that would be more expensive to correct in later years, but in turn, improved morbidity has yielded a demand for more patient and family services.

Estimates of the Costs of Care

With few exceptions, each study of the cost of childhood chronic illnesses focuses on one particular condition. Moreover, many of these studies report only portions of the total costs. One study may examine hospital costs but not outpatient costs. Another study may account for costs insurance companies cover but fail to include the parents' out-of-pocket costs. For some diseases, costs for certain items never appear because government-subsidized grants or special programs provide the items. Many drugs for the care of leukemia, for example, are provided free of charge to patients through research protocols, but the drugs nevertheless are produced at some cost, absorbed in this instance by the government. To convey specific dollar amounts for the costs of care for childhood chronic illnesses, we present available financial information on seven marker conditions, emphasizing that in virtually every case these estimates fall below true total costs.

Cystic Fibrosis. In 1980, the Cystic Fibrosis Foundation (1981) surveyed 2,300 individuals with cystic fibrosis who were more than eighteen years of age. Thirty percent of this group (690 persons) responded to questions on costs during the prior year. Overall expenses ranged from $2,487 to $68,637. Hospitalization was the most expensive service (243 of the 690 required hospitalization, which averaged $11,745; the highest hospital bill was $75,000), followed by physical therapy (57 persons used this service at an average cost of $1,610) and prescription drugs (436 persons required these at an average of $1,509). Other sources of cost for this population include outpatient checkups, equipment, and nonprescription drugs.

Kidney Disease. As one of the few studies of its kind, a report by Campbell and Campbell (1978) documents expenditures over four and a half years for one patient who required renal dialysis and eventually transplantation. For the entire period, the breakdown of costs was as follows: $24,524 for hospitalization, $4,205 for physician costs, $8,874 for personal costs related to the illness, $3,000 for leasing of dialysis equipment, and $7,800 for home-dialysis supplies. The total amount was $48,402. That dialysis and transplantation can be very costly is confirmed by Hoffstein, Krueger, and Wineman (1976). They note that dialysis averages approximately $25,000 per year in hospital centers and $12,000 to $15,000 per year in the home. Transplantation costs are $25,000 during the first year, decreasing to between $5,000 and $10,000 in subsequent years.

Leukemia. A study of nonmedical costs of childhood cancer (Lansky and others, 1979) found that expenditures for transportation, food, lodging, clothing, and family care were related to the level of care required by the child, the distance of the family from the treatment center, and family size. Loss of pay was reported by half of the families, for whom the median weekly loss was $68.94. The median weekly out-of-pocket expense was $39.70, mostly for transportation, food, and miscellaneous items. For half of the seventy families, expenses plus loss of pay were more than 25 percent of the weekly family income. A second study (Strayer, Kisker, and Fethke, 1980) compared medical and nonmedical costs for traditional treatment provided by specialists at a tertiary center and for shared management treatment provided largely by local doctors with supervision by specialists. Treatment costs for the two modalities were approximately equal ($1,959 versus $1,889), but there were substantial differences in nonmedical costs ($1,450 versus $502), particularly for transportation and estimated loss of income.

Congenital Heart Disease. According to one study (New England Regional Infant Cardiac Program, 1980), average costs for the first year of life for all infants born with serious heart problems in the New England region were about $5,500 in 1975. Costs were higher for the children who survived, averaging about $13,000. Conservatively, 60 percent of children born with congenital heart diseases survive to age one, and 50 percent survive to age five with correspondingly high total costs. In 1985 dollars, these figures would be far higher.

Spina Bifida. McLaughlin and Shurtleff (1979) estimated that the average medical costs (in the mid 1970s) for children from birth to age six were $13,000 for those with low lesions and $25,000 for those with high lesions. The Spina Bifida Association of the Delaware Valley (1979) reported that average total costs of care (extending beyond strictly medical care) from birth to age two years of age was $70,000 (in 1980 dollars). More recently, Myers and Millsap (1985) estimate that the mean cost of care for the first three weeks of life for an infant born with spina bifida is $6,500.

Asthma. Compared with spina bifida, severe asthma is far more frequent. Yet, available data on the costs of care for children with severe asthma remain equally elusive although average costs are likely to be much less than those associated with spina bifida. Vance and Taylor (1971) showed that costs for twenty families with thirty-five cases of asthma ranged between $800 and $13,407 over a three-year period beginning in 1966 and ending in 1968. In 1985 dollars, these figures would be far higher.

Hemophilia. A survey of children and adults in Tennessee revealed a yearly mean cost of medical care of $8,071 and a median of $5,000. Total yearly medical costs varied substantially, from no cost for a child with a mild case to $56,000 for a young adult with a very severe case (Garr, 1978). Levine (1974) found that the average total yearly cost of medical care in one hemophilia center was $5,220 (in 1973 dollars). In 1980, costs for replacement factor alone ranged between $7,039 and $9,673 per patient (Smith, Keyes, and Forman, 1982).

This review of the expenditures for specific childhood chronic illnesses underscores the wide range of costs within a particular disorder. For one child with a chronic illness, the costs of care in any particular year might be small. For another child— or for the same child in a subsequent year—the costs might be enormous. This wide variation is typical in every diagnostic category and stems (1) from the different levels of severity of an illness and (2) from the varying course of childhood chronic illness over the life of a child. In the first instance, for example, a child with spina bifida involving the upper spine will require care substantially more complex and prolonged than one with spina bifida involving the lower portion of the spine. In the second instance, total costs for any particular child can vary by severalfold from one year to the next in response to the course of the disease. Most children with heart defects, for example, require many costly procedures early in the course of the disorder with decreasing costs over time. A child with diabetes may have widely fluctuating costs depending on many physiological and emotional factors.

Costs for supportive services also vary from year to year, possibly but not necessarily in conjunction with the costs of medical care. For example, a family may need much help for their child's academic difficulties in one year but not in the next. Different children with the same disease can vary widely in the use of health services creating very different total costs in a given year and making accurate predictions difficult.

Indirect Costs

We define indirect costs as monies unearned or financial opportunities unavailable as a result of the demands of care. Examples of indirect costs include loss of income because a mother stays home to care for a child, refusal of a new job offer because the accompanying insurance coverage is inadequate, or loss of interest on savings because all available funds are used to pay outstanding bills. Indirect costs are difficult to measure accurately and are easily overlooked in policy debates. Yet, for families with a chronically ill child, a career foregone may wither hope more effectively than an itemized bill.

Carpenter (1980) and Breslau (1983) have shown that, with few exceptions, the burden of care for a child with serious health problems falls primarily on the mother. Although the available evidence regarding the specific financial consequences of this extra burden emerges from anecdotal reports or studies with small samples, these reports collectively suggest "that the care of severely disabled or chronically ill children restricts mothers' extra-domestic activities, including employment, and increases their burden of daily routines" (Breslau, 1983, p. 621). The actual extent to which the presence of a chronic illness and its associated demands deter a mother from entering the work force on either a part-time or full-time basis remains unknown.

For those families with at least one wage earner, a chronic illness is likely to rob time from the work week. Lansky and colleagues (1979), for example, reported that in a sample of thirty-two families with a child with cancer, sixteen reported some loss of pay associated with the care of the child. For these families, the average weekly loss was about $40 but ranged as high as $163 (in 1977 dollars). Again, this loss is negligible if it occurs occasionally but will be substantial if it occurs with regularity over several years. Another study, conducted in England (Baldwin, Godfrey, and Staden, 1983), documented that women with a disabled child were less likely to be employed than women without a disabled child, and if they were employed, they were likely to work fewer hours. Although these researchers included primarily handicapped children rather than chronically ill children, their conclusions seem especially relevant.

The effect of indirect costs on a family's financial status, coupled with continuing direct costs, increases over time. The English study discovered that severe disability in a child has a detrimental effect on a family's income, a powerful effect that increases as the family ages. Income for all families tends to grow as parents move ahead in their respective careers, but for families with a handicapped child, this growth is slower over time. The child's disablement constrains parents from the full exercise of their earning potential.

Overall, a childhood chronic illness has a different impact on income for different socioeconomic groups. For families in poverty, and especially for single-parent families, the presence of a child with a chronic illness may effectively remove any opportunity to earn sufficient money to climb out of poverty (Breslau, 1983). Real-income loss is small because income is small in total dollars; opportunity for increasing income, however, may vanish under the demands of care. For families in middle- or upper-income brackets, the accumulated costs of care not covered by insurance together with income unearned take an ever-increasing toll. By five to ten years after the diagnosis of a chronic illness in one of their children, a family is likely to be financially far behind its counterparts with healthy children.

Sources of Cost Savings

In the years ahead, chronically ill children and their families are likely to continue their dependence on the public and private funds that currently support their care. The high inflation rate in medical care, their longer life-spans, and the broad range of medical and supportive services needed by them and their families will propel costs ever upward. Yet, innovations both in medical technology and in the organization of services promise to restrain, in some measure, this rapid ascent. These innovations lie in two areas: (1) the prevention of chronic illnesses and their serious medical and social complications and (2) the implementation of new, effective modes of organizing and paying for care, modes that avoid unnecessary reliance on hospitalization or on other high-cost services.

For many children with chronic illnesses, the most efficient way to save money in their care is to stop all treatment and speed their demise. Few services would be needed, and costs would remain low. Every responsible person would immediately reject this course of action, but to reject it is to affirm a continuing commitment to the care of these children. With this commitment comes a financial obligation.

Advances in surgical procedures and in the understanding of the genetic and biochemical processes involved in the chronic illnesses of childhood have increased the possibility of preventing their occurrence. For example, improvements in the identification of fetuses who are severely compromised have made possible the prevention of the birth of infants with spina bifida and other congenital abnormalities. Further advances in this technology are inevitable. The moral issues raised by the termination of a pregnancy that may result in a severely impaired infant deserve long debate. But from an economic vantage point, the discussion is short. The financial savings that accrue from preventing the birth of an infant with spina bifida, for example, are obviously great.

A second promising direction for restraining the increase in costs is through the prevention of serious medical, social, and psychological complications by means of early diagnosis and rapid intervention. For example, surgical intervention in the life of the child with spina bifida avoids medical problems that are more costly to correct later in the child's life; rapid detection and treatment of a bleeding episode in a child with hemophilia decrease joint degeneration and diminish the need for expensive joint-replacement surgery; early support for parents to help them respond to the stress of a chronic illness may avoid a later major breakdown that requires long-term assistance. Despite the promise of these strategies, few data allow careful estimation of the money to be saved. To what extent do the costs of providing these preventive interventions offset the savings? What costs are associated with problems that may be unforeseen at this point, overshadowed by more dominant medical crises? These questions need careful attention to gauge more accurately the financial benefits of preventive strategies.

A final preventive strategy concerns income and opportunity loss. How can parents of a chronically ill child maintain their position in the work force? What special daycare services might be provided, for example, to assist mothers to find and maintain employment? From a strict economic perspective, what are the relative trade-offs between the costs of these services and the parents' level of productivity? Who would pay for these services? Again, these questions deserve far more research attention than they have received to date.

The reduction of indirect costs is closely related to the second major source of potential savings, which is the discovery and implementation of new, effective ways of organizing or paying for care that decrease unnecessary reliance on hospitalization (by far the single most expensive service) or on other high-cost services. One example of this strategy is the increasing attention to home care for children with many of these illnesses. Improvements in medical technology now allow for much care formerly delivered in the hospital or clinic to be provided at home. These improvements have been coupled with a willingness of third-party payors to pay for services (such as nurse visits) to support this home care. More evidence relating to chronically ill children is needed, but early indications suggest that home care can potentially reduce costs by reducing hospital days (Pierce and Freedman, 1983).

Again, several different factors influence potential sources of savings. For example, home care for hemophilia clearly results in savings, although these are partially offset by additional medical procedures. Home care for children who have tracheostomies or who are on respirators promises to save costs of hospital days for the child; however, the impact on the family and direct or indirect costs (such as the need for professional counseling or days lost from work) associated with the stress of home care may partially offset these savings. Furthermore, the burden of paying for the costs may shift from one segment of society to another. In the instance of home care for a respirator-dependent child with muscular dystrophy, for example, the insurance company or a public agency may save money, but the family's costs may increase.

Summary

Costs of care for childhood chronic illnesses are disproportionately high in comparison with the numbers of affected children. Many factors contribute to the cost of caring for these children and their families. Hospitalization, medication, repeated clinic visits, and appliances are some of the more obvious sources of cost. Other less apparent sources can add substantially to the total cost of care. These sources include special diets, modifications in the home, telephone and transportation costs, and time lost from work and school. Overall, the costs of care for children with chronic illness are high because these children and their families require a broad range of services. Some of these services are expensive because they are needed repeatedly over many years; some are expensive because of the extensive or sophisticated medical technology involved.

In addition to variation in the severity of the illness itself, several factors shape national patterns in costs of care. The availability of and access to services can play a major role in a family's expenses. In rural areas of the country, repeated visits to a distant clinic can result in substantial transportation costs. A service is more likely to be used if there is a source of payment for it; hence, total costs of care hinge, in part, on existing patterns of payment. The way services are organized also influences cost. Cooperative arrangements between a specialty center and community physicians are less expensive than if the specialty center alone provides the needed services. The diffusion of new technologies, the perceived need for services, and the economies of scale that derive from concentrated use of an existing service represent additional factors that influence the final costs of care.

Despite the great need for information regarding the costs of care for these children, little specific information is now available. A close examination of the relatively few studies that have focused on specific illnesses reveals a broad range of costs within any one diagnostic category. Different children with the same disease, or even the same child across several years, will vary widely in the use of health services. As a result, accurate prediction of costs for a particular family is difficult.

The size of the direct costs of health care for children with a chronic illness must not deflect attention from another important problem, that of indirect costs. These costs include the loss of parental income or loss of a career opportunity as a result of the illness and its treatment demands. Partly because they are hidden or occasional, indirect costs can erode a family's financial stability with persistent subtlety. The effects vary across socioeconomic groups. For middle- or upper-income groups, indirect costs can effectively constrain the full exercise of earning potential; for lower-income groups, indirect costs may assure continued poverty.

Care for chronically ill children and their families is likely to remain costly in the years ahead. Vigorous efforts at prevention of the illnesses themselves and their serious medical or social complications may restrain, to some extent, the inevitable increase in the costs of care. New modes of organizing, delivering, and financing care can also play important roles in lessening the rapid ascent of health care costs for these children and their families.

The issue of who pays for care is crucial in understanding the policy issues affecting childhood chronic illness. This chapter has striven to capture the scope of the costs, the mixed financial consequences of continued technological progress, and the potential benefits and dangers of new modes of delivering care. In Chapter Seven we address the other side of the coin: the financing of care for chronically ill children.

7

Patterns of Paying
for Care

Who pays for what elements of the care of children with a chronic illness? What problems do children and their families confront in securing coverage for health care? How many of these children lack, altogether, a source of payment for the services they require? What portion of the total costs do parents pay? How do public programs, insurance companies, voluntary organizations, and families participate in payment? In what ways do the patterns of payment influence what services are available? These questions, like estimates of cost, are central to policy making.

This chapter addresses several enduring issues in financing health care for children in general that apply with particular force to the care of children with chronic illness. One core problem is the fragmented and capricious nature of the financing system, which limits access of many citizens to needed health care. Many children have meager coverage, and some lack coverage entirely. Moreover, the extraordinary variation among states in the availability of financial support for health care generates substantial inequities across the nation. A second core difficulty is the poor match between the coverage from most insurance plans and the patterns of cost generated by a chronic illness. Health insurance may protect against the financial burden of expensive health services, especially hospital bills. In so doing, however, it creates incentives to emphasize sophisticated medical technology and to neglect other services (such

189

as counseling, home care, and respite care) needed because of the long-term and unpredictable nature of these illnesses. These incentives may stimulate costs unnecessarily high and limit opportunities to seek less expensive alternatives.

These various problems overlap to a great degree. One report summarizes them in this way:

The way in which health services are financed is the single most important determinant of how the health care system operates, what services are available, which professionals provide those services, and who will receive them. In the Panel's view, existing financing arrangements not only fail to enhance the Nation's efforts to improve the health of all Americans, including mothers and children—they often work at cross purposes to this objective.

The Panel found two fundamental problems with the existing financing of health care. First, public and private third-party payment systems as they now operate provide incentives that result in an allocation of physician time, distribution of physicians by specialty and location, and a manner of providing health services that collectively are unresponsive to a significant part of patient needs, especially those of children and pregnant women, and that unnecessarily drive up health care costs. Second, and equally important, current financing arrangements leave millions of Americans—an estimated 12.6 percent of the population—with no public or private health insurance protection whatsoever, and many millions more with coverage that is so grossly inadequate that insurmountable financial barriers to needed health care remain [Select Panel for the Promotion of Child Health, 1981, p. 319].

In this chapter, we examine how these problems bear on the lives of children with a chronic illness and their families. In the first section, we identify several overarching issues, including the numbers of children with different sources of financial coverage for medical problems, the obstacles inhibiting access to adequate coverage, and the manner in which costs are generally shared by existing sources of payment. Our report in this section is somewhat constrained by a fact that Butler and his colleagues (1985, pp. 828-829) describe well:

Because chronic disability is the high-cost sector of children's health care, one might expect that the financing of services in this realm would have been carefully documented for policy purposes and would have received ample attention in the health services research literature. As it turns out, however, patterns of private and public expenditure on the health care of chronically ill children remain poorly documented and understood—how much is paid, who pays, and for what kinds of services. In particular, no national data base exists that would permit an understanding of specific child illnesses and family background characteristics as these relate to amounts and sources of private and public payment, either at a single point in time or over the life of the child. Instead, there exists a fragmentary and complex assortment of partial data sources, including elements of national interview surveys, Crippled Children's Services program reports, state Medicaid descriptions, hospital records, disease-oriented studies, and anecdotal materials. Such data enable only a partial analysis, even at the level of simple descriptive statistics.

Nonetheless, in the second section of this chapter, we examine closely four major sources of funding: (1) private health insurance, including various prepayment arrangements, (2) public programs, including Medicaid, Crippled Children's Services, state-based categorical programs, and several tangentially related programs, (3) private philanthropic efforts, and (4) the family's out-of-pocket expenditures.

Throughout the chapter, we discuss several trends in cost containment that have emerged over the last few decades and that are now finding expression in new approaches to financing care for children. These approaches hold promise for improved support of children with chronic illness, but the promise will be fulfilled only if their implementation takes account of the special patterns of cost in the care of childhood chronic illnesses.

An Overview

Butler and his associates (1985) present information that illustrates the extent of public and private coverage of varied groups of children, including children with functional disabilities. In Table 7, this material is adapted as a way of framing the problem, although we stress that the number of children with a functional disability only approximates the number with a chronic illness.

Table 7. Insurance Coverage for Children (in thousands).

	Totals	Privately Insured	Public Programs	Uninsured
All children	67,570	50,630	11,340	5,600
		(75%)	(17%)	(8%)
Poverty levels				
Above poverty	55,560	47,460	4,670	3,430
		(85%)	(9%)	(6%)
Below poverty	12,010	3,170	6,670	2,170
		(26%)	(56%)	(18%)
Disability levels				
Without disability	63,810	48,320	10,280	5,210
		(76%)	(16%)	(8%)
With disability	3,760	2,310	1,060	390
		(62%)	(28%)	(10%)
Poverty and disability				
Above poverty				
Without disability	52,820	45,330	4,250	3,240
		(86%)	(8%)	(6%)
With disability	2,740	2,130	420	190
		(78%)	(15%)	(7%)
Below poverty				
Without disability	10,990	2,990	6,030	1,970
		(27%)	(55%)	(18%)
With disability	1,020	180	640	200
		(18%)	(63%)	(19%)

Note: Child counts by state are actuarial projections of 1979 numbers based on the 1970 census adjusted for undercount. Poverty is defined for 1979 according to the 1976 poverty line adjusted for subsequent CPI. The model sets the poverty line at $7,550 for a family of four. Limitation of activity is defined as a positive answer on any of four questions from the Survey of Income and Education regarding the child's ability to do regular school work, play, take part in sports, games, or other play activity, and work around the house or elsewhere.

Source: Data derived from U.S. Department of Health and Human Services health financing model. For details, see R. C. Bonhag, and others, *A Description of the Health Financing Model: A Tool for Cost Estimation.* Department of Health and Human Services, Office of the Assistant Secretary for Planning and Evaluation, Washington, D.C., February 1981. Derived from Butler and others, 1985, Figure 1.

Many of the one million children with severe chronic illnesses have no functional disability, and conversely, many of the four million children with functional disabilities have none of the chronic illnesses with which this book is concerned. Although more specific data are unavailable, we believe that the trends shown in this table apply generally to childhood chronic illness as well.

The table illustrates four important points. First, by a large margin, private insurance covers more children than public programs. About 75 percent of all children (an estimated 50.6 million children) are covered by private insurance, 17 percent (approximately 11.4 million) are covered by public programs, and 8 percent (almost 5.6 million) lack any insurance.

Second, poor children have sources of coverage different from those for families with incomes above the poverty line. Eighty-five percent of children above the poverty line have private insurance coverage; only 26 percent of poor children do. Proportionately, public programs cover more poor children than nonpoor children (56 percent of poor children compared to 8 percent of children above poverty). Six percent of nonpoor children, but 18 percent of poor children, are uninsured. Third, among children with a functional disability, 61 percent (just over 2 million) have private insurance coverage, 28 percent (1.1 million) are covered by public programs, and 10 percent (approximately 0.4 million) have no coverage whatsoever.

Finally, the table shows the difference between children with functional disabilities and those without in the different income groups. Overall, children with a functional impairment are more likely to be on a public program or to be uninsured and less likely to have private insurance than children without disability. But the interaction of poverty and disability makes the discrepancy more striking. For example, approximately 10 percent of all children with disability are uninsured; for poor children with disability, that figure is almost double and reaches 20 percent. Approximately 28 percent of all children with disability are covered under public programs; for poor children with disability, the percentage is more than doubled to 63 percent.

If similar patterns hold true for children with a chronic illness, we conclude (1) that private health insurance is the major source of coverage for many children who have a serious illness, (2) that public programs play an important role in the care of children with a chronic illness, especially for those who live in poverty, and (3) that an alarming percentage of children with a serious illness lack any health insurance whatsoever. Of the approximately one million children with a severe chronic illness, we estimate that between 660,000 and 700,000 have some private health insurance, between 140,000 and 160,000 benefit from public programs, and approximately 90,000 are uninsured at any one time. These numbers, derived from Table 7, must be regarded as estimates, partly because children may receive support from several different sources and partly because accurate data are unavailable.

Defining categories of coverage gives a broad view of children with and without coverage for health services, but the problem for families is typically far more complex. Many families, for example, have private health insurance that is inadequate and leaves them with high bills to pay out of their own pockets. Many families on public assistance become ineligible when they secure a job, yet often the new job offers little or delayed health coverage. Private and public insurance plans are more likely to support specialty care to the relative neglect of supportive or general health services equally needed by these children.

Furthermore, the various sources of payment relate in a complicated fashion, "making the true family economics of chronic disability" a complex problem (Butler and others, 1985, p. 830). In some states, for example, the government-supported Crippled Children's Services program will pay the copayment required by an insurance company but only if the family's medical expenses are above a certain proportion of their income (Ireys, 1980). By way of illustrating these issues, we present here three stories. Each story describes a different financing arrangement: a family with private health insurance; a family on Medicaid; and an uninsured family.

A Family with Private Health Insurance. A fourteen-year-old boy was diagnosed as having diabetes five years ago. He lives with his younger brother and his parents in a suburb of a large city on the eastern seaboard where the father is employed in a factory. The family is covered through the father's health insurance plan, to which he contributes 25 percent of the monthly premium.

After a deductible amount, the insurance plan pays fully for hospitalization and requires a 20 percent copayment for all specialty medical outpatient services and a 50 percent copayment for mental health outpatient care. It will pay none of the charges for general health care, such as a checkup with the pediatrician. The deductible is the amount the family must pay before the insurance company begins its coverage. For this plan, the deductible is $200 for each family member each year. The plan covers 80 percent of the cost of the insulin but none of the expenditures for daily supplies (such as syringes and urine-testing equipment), for phone calls, or for transportation to the physician's office or hospital.

For the first four years following diagnosis, the child did well; the disease remained stable. Within the last year, however, several medical problems have emerged, and the youngster now requires an extensive medical evaluation. In addition, the parents are concerned about the child's deteriorating school performance and wonder whether his own fears may be interfering with school. The medical evaluation could be performed either on an outpatient basis or if the child were hospitalized. What are the financial consequences of these two choices?

From the family's perspective, it is more economical to hospitalize the child for the evaluation; under this circumstance, the father need pay nothing but the $200 deductible. Moreover, as part of the inpatient evaluation, the child would receive all necessary lab tests and could talk with the social worker, psychologist, or psychiatrist as a beginning step to discovering whether his emotional distress could be interfering with school performance.

The total costs of an inpatient evaluation, however, exceed by a large margin the costs of an outpatient evaluation. In an outpatient evaluation, hospitalization and its expense would be avoided, but the boy may need to return several times to the specialty clinic and may require a visit to a mental health clinic for a psychological and educational evaluation. The total costs would be less, but the family's out-of-pocket expenses would be higher. They would, in this instance, have to pay the deductible and then 20 percent of every clinic visit and half the amount for the visit to the mental health clinic. If two additional evaluations were needed over the next two years, the family would likely be required to pay the deductible amounts twice more.

The family's insurance plan provides an incentive for hospitalization and hence for higher costs. Different choices alter the distribution of the financial burden: for an inpatient evaluation, the insurance company assumes the burden almost entirely and the family pays relatively little; for an outpatient evaluation, the insurance company takes care of some costs with the family assuming a larger share.

A Family with Public Insurance. This four-year-old girl with spina bifida lives with her mother and three older siblings in a small southern town about a hundred miles from the multidisciplinary clinic and the hospital where she receives all her care. The family receives AFDC payments and is on Medicaid. Since the child's birth, Medicaid has paid for fourteen days of hospitalization per year and for her many clinic visits. When needed, Crippled Children's Services has paid for an additional twenty days per year of hospital care. At the clinic, the mother and child receive most needed services, including physical therapy, developmental counseling, and speech and hearing services along with medical and surgical evaluations, drugs, and wheelchairs. The clinic social worker also found reimbursement for the cost of transportation (high for a round trip of two hundred miles). The family does pay certain costs, including those for eyeglasses, for food for the mother and her other children during the trip to the clinic, and for lodging when the child is hospitalized. Reimbursement for baby-sitting costs if the mother leaves the other children at home is unavailable. The mother uses some of her welfare payments and her daughter's disability payments (from the SSI program) to cover the costs of daily care requirements (such as diapers). Her funds are insufficient, however, to cover telephone costs, so the family is without one.

At one point the child became ill when the family car was in the shop for repairs. The lack of a telephone delayed the mother's calling the clinic to explain the problem. As a result, an emergency van was sent to the home to take the child to the hospital for three days of treatment for a severe infection that might have been prevented or minimized had the clinic been alerted to the problem earlier.

For this family, the costs for strictly medical care are minimal, but the costs of getting to medical care and for daily maintenance are high in proportion to the family's income. Other problems are present as well. Emergencies are difficult to handle when a telephone is unavailable. In one instance, absence of a telephone led to the high costs involved in emergency transit and hospitalization. According to the social worker, no source will pay for a telephone line to be installed.

A Family Without Insurance. An eleven-year-old with sickle cell anemia lives with his mother, father, and four-year-old sister in a lower-middle-class section of an industrial city in the midwest. The father began a new job about eighteen months ago but was laid off soon after. His employee benefits terminated four months ago, lasting long enough to cover a routine medical evaluation of his son but not a subsequent six-day hospitalization. The mother in this family recently found a full-time secretarial position, after several years of part-time work, but the health insurance will begin to cover her and her family only after six months of employment. Even then, her insurance plan will be of little help because it excludes coverage of illnesses existing prior to employment. The bill for the six days of hospitalization, including inpatient physician visits, remains largely unpaid, and additional costs for further clinic visits loom ahead. The family's available resources at this time fall far short of the amount of existing bills. This family is ineligible for Medicaid because Medicaid covers only single-parent families in their state. However, their state does have a program that will pay some costs of care if the family's medical expenses rise above a certain percentage of the family's yearly income. It is unclear, however, whether they will be eligible for this program because of the mother's full-time employment. The social worker at the clinic did contact a voluntary association in the city in which they reside. This agency agreed to defray the family's transportation and drug expenses but was unwilling to contribute to the hospital bill.

For the hospital and physicians who provide care, this child represents an uninsured individual—a no-pay patient, someone whose family lacks the resources to pay for services. The hospital must absorb the costs of care rendered to this child during the period when the family had no health insurance coverage. From the family's perspective, the only services they will seek are those they perceive to be essential to the child's physical health—for example, those services provided by the specialty clinic. Other cost-generating services, such as visits to a general pediatrician or to a genetic counselor, will be avoided.

Financial Implications. These vignettes illustrate several important points. First, to a great extent, both public and private insurance plans create incentives for the delivery of expensive services. In the first story, insurance coverage led to a costly inpatient evaluation. In the second example, the lack of funds to cover the cost of a telephone line led to the costs of hospitalization for a problem that might have been prevented.

Second, current financing arrangements create major gaps in coverage. In both the family with health insurance and the family on Medicaid, reimbursements for daily care needs were unavailable. Moreover, these plans may exclude coverage of other needed services, such as mental health care, genetic counseling, eyeglasses, or special diets. In turn, families find themselves unable to afford these items.

Third, insurance coverage is unavailable for many families. The family who was uninsured for a period of time found themselves liable for bills of enormous size. The problem of uninsured families fluctuates in response to employment trends and Medicaid cutbacks. If a state with high unemployment elects to trim spending by reducing Medicaid eligibility, the population of families and children without coverage will increase.

Finally, the vignettes illustrate the ways in which costs are distributed. In the first example, the costs are shared by the family and the larger group of individuals and employers who pay premiums to the insurance company. In the second, the costs are shared by the family and the public through public support of Medicaid. And in the third story, costs are essentially shared by the family and the hospital. To an extent, the hospital transfers these costs to other patients by raising overall daily rates in order to protect itself against the loss represented by no-pay patients.

In every instance the public is affected by expenditures for children with chronic illness: With higher expenditures, insurance premium rates increase, more dollars are needed for Medicaid, and hospital charges rise. Policy makers must recognize the extent of current public support for the care of these children, however indirect it may be.

From this examination of the financing system from the perspective of individual families, we turn now to a program-by-program description of the financing system for the care of childhood chronic illnesses.

Private Health Care Insurance

From modest beginnings in the late nineteenth and early twentieth centuries, private health insurance coverage has grown enormously. Today, almost three quarters of all American children are covered by some form of private health insurance (Butler and others, 1985). Private insurance, however, pays for only one third of the total amount of expenditures for the health care of children in this country. This amount is substantially more than any other single source aside from the children's families (Weeks, 1985). Most private health insurance comes as a fringe benefit based on employment, and the employer bears most or all of the cost of the premiums. This fringe benefit is presently exempt from taxation, and estimates are that this exemption diminishes federal revenues by about $24 billion. Although indirect, this subsidy represents the largest single federal investment in health care.

At first glance, it may appear that most of the nation's children are adequately protected. However, a closer look reveals several major shortcomings of private health insurance, shortcomings that have especially severe consequences for chronically ill children and their families. The purpose of most health insurance has been protection against the risk of unpredictable and episodic medical expenses rather than provision of comprehensive health care. Health insurance, which is primarily medical insurance, was never intended to cover the broad range of services often required by chronically ill children and their families because of the complex and continuing demands of care (Weeks, 1985).

Private health insurance derives from two separate historical trends. The first, individually written accident insurance, began in the nineteenth century as a means of insuring against high-cost events, including illness. This insurance, meant to indemnify individuals against unexpected financial calamity, evolved into plans written by private companies (sometimes referred to as commercial insurers) such as Aetna, Connecticut General, and Prudential. The second trend, which began in the late 1920s, had its roots in the voluntary, community-sponsored, fee-for-service hospital and medical care system. Coalitions developed to pay hospital costs for their members in advance, partly in response to increasing hospital costs. Later, programs to pay in a similar fashion for physician services were instituted. This insurance is provided by nonprofit voluntary associations, such as Blue Cross (for hospital care) and Blue Shield (for physician services). In exchange for monthly premiums, both private and nonprofit insurers have traditionally reimbursed patients on a fee-for-service basis, that is, on the basis of medical costs actually incurred.

Initially, the private insurance companies tended to have high coinsurance and deductibles, requiring those insured to participate heavily in payment for covered services. This benefit structure reflected the intention to insure against large financial indebtedness rather than to cover less expensive or more routine medical expenses. In contrast, the nonprofit Blue plans typically paid total hospital and physician fees, insofar as these plans allowed participants to prepay (through monthly premiums) the costs of hospital care and then to draw on the plan's resources when the need for hospital services arose. In recent years, the benefit structures of private and nonprofit insurance plans have become much more similar.

Reimbursement on a fee-for-service basis creates certain incentives. First, because hospitals and physicians are paid more if they provide more services or higher-priced ones, the reimbursement method encourages extensive use of expensive services and offers few incentives to be cautious or to restrain the use of high-cost alternatives. Second, insofar as most plans provide their most generous benefits and coverage for in-hospital care (based partly on the original notion of insuring against major expenses), fee-for-service plans lead both patients and providers to utilize expensive inpatient services so that insurance will reimburse for the entire bill rather than less expensive outpatient services for which the patients will have to pay most of the costs.

Because most coverage is a benefit based on the parents' employment, access of children to private health insurance is extremely uneven (Fullerton, 1982). People employed by large firms usually have reasonably good coverage. Those who are between jobs, who are employed seasonally or by small firms, or who are self-employed typically lack adequate health insurance. In some instances, parents either waive or are denied the opportunity to insure their family members, and hence their children are excluded from coverage. If parents lack adequate family coverage, the onset of a severe chronic illness in a child may represent a catastrophe even though the parents have employment-based health insurance for themselves.

Furthermore, many group policies exclude coverage for pre-existing conditions, illnesses that predate employment with that company. A family may then have health insurance coverage for all of its members, but needed services for the diabetes or sickle cell disease in their ten-year-old may be unreimbursed if the diagnosis was made before the insured parent took that job. Moreover, parents may change jobs for better pay or opportunity. In so doing, they may inadvertently lose insurance coverage for their ill child if the new company's policy excludes pre-existing conditions.

Private health insurance may also be purchased in individual policies, independent of employee groups. Premium rates for individuals, however, are markedly higher than for groups, both because expensive insurance risks can be better shared across a group and because of the higher administrative costs (sales and servicing) for individual contracts.

A critical problem arises for children with chronic illness when they reach the age at which their parents' policies no longer include them (typically nineteen or twenty-one). Family policies may provide for coverage of dependents over the specified age if they are full-time students or are disabled or incapable of supporting themselves. Most young adults with chronic illness are not disabled but may have difficulty obtaining an individual insurance policy because of their chronic condition. Their best hope is to obtain employment in a firm with a large group policy that provides the services required by their condition (Weeks, 1985).

Even when covered by an insurance plan, families are likely to find that payment is unavailable for many services chronically ill children need. As currently structured, fee-for-service private health insurance covers hospital and emergency care quite well. Outpatient and home-based care required for the management of the disease and the prevention of hospitalizations for medical crises are much less well covered. Surgical procedures to treat congenital heart disease or cleft palate are likely to be covered, but the drugs and physician visits required by the child with severe asthma are less likely to be paid. The rationales for excluding coverage of physician office visits, home care, outpatient drugs, and care provided by nonphysicians (such as nurse practitioners and speech therapists) are that such costs are minimal for most of the population and can be included in the family budget and that the costs of processing small claims are high. For the typical child who sees a physician four or five times a year, these rationales make sense.

Families of chronically ill children repeatedly incur health-related expenses that insurance never intended to cover; these include transportation to specialty care facilities, home renovations, special equipment needed at home, childcare, and social services. Historically, insurers, employers, and individuals purchasing insurance have been reluctant to include these nonmedical services, partly because their utilization is unpredictable. Chronically ill children require a benefit structure that takes into account ongoing care and long-term needs. Policies to foster the coverage of other types of services have recently been explored, usually in pursuit of controlling rising health care costs. For example, some insurers have begun to cover home care by specially trained nurses for ill elderly people in the expectation that home-care services will decrease costs by decreasing hospitalization. These efforts will likely benefit families with a chronically ill child.

The characteristic agreement between members and insurer in a fee-for-service plan leaves the family responsible for some medical care expenses. Virtually all plans include provisions for payments by the family, usually including an annual deductible and coinsurance (the payment of a percentage of the cost of certain services). This copayment, designed to discourage frivolous use of services, is based on the assumption that some costs of care can be met by the family budget. With chronic diseases, the cumulative nature of copayments for services used frequently over the course of many years can overwhelm a family's budget.

Private health insurance mechanisms support a large percentage of services in our country. Insurance, mainly as a benefit of employment, assures many families freedom from worry about expensive hospital or medical bills. Yet private health insurance is often inadequate in the context of childhood chronic illness, leaving many children with long-term illness without coverage, leaving many families without financial support for essential nonmedical services, and burdening families with a copayment system better suited for occasional acute problems than for persistent illness.

Prepaid Health Care. Prepaid health care had its origins well over fifty years ago, initially through worker cooperatives in the Southwest and then through collaborative arrangements between industries and physician groups, mainly on the West Coast. Although the exact contractual and organizational arrangements may vary, prepaid programs typically function both as insurers and health service providers, offering comprehensive health care services in exchange for regular fixed payments. They are termed prepaid because payments for services are made to the groups of providers before the services are actually provided. Both outpatient physician services and hospital care are provided under prepaid plans. In most instances, providers share in the insurance risk; that is, if the total system saves money, the provider shares in the additional plan income. If the plan loses money (for example, by long or unexpected hospital stays), the providers receive less income. Thus, providers have incentives to use less expensive services and to diminish hospital use where possible. *Health maintenance organization* (HMO) is a common name applied to prepaid programs. HMOs include both prepaid group practices (PGPs), which typically provide hospital and physician services using salaried physician members of the practice, and individual practice associations (IPAs), which are often sponsored by local medical societies and which contract with physicians for the delivery of services to enrollees. HMO enrollees represent a relatively small but rapidly growing segment of the privately insured population. In 1970, 2.9 million people were enrolled in HMOs; in 1984, 12.5 million (American Academy of Pediatrics, 1984a). As with most private insurance, the access of families to HMOs is based primarily on membership in an employee group. Usually, a child will have access to an HMO only if a parent is employed by an organization offering an HMO option.

Prepayment plans discourage out-of-plan use—that is, the use of physicians or hospitals not participating in the plan—because costs are likely to be higher and unpredictable. A family that has a child with a chronic illness and has developed a trusting relationship with a general or specialty physician may be reluctant to join a prepaid plan to which their physician does not belong. Similarly, because children with chronic illnesses generate high costs of care and may frequently use specialists outside the HMO, prepaid plans may discourage enrollment of children with long-term illnesses. Nevertheless, most prepaid plans are marketed to groups rather than to individuals, and direct exclusion of specific children with chronic illnesses is difficult. Where an HMO option exists, families that report having a chronically ill member (child or adult) are slightly more likely to enroll in an HMO than in a fee-for-service plan (Berki and Ashcraft, 1980).

HMOs may offer a promising alternative for children with chronic illnesses. They include a somewhat different mix of services and are more likely to cover physician office visits and care by nonphysicians (although outpatient drugs are variably covered). HMOs have reduced the rates of hospital admissions for their enrollees (at considerable savings to the plans) and are, as a result, able to cover other services more extensively. Families are less likely to be at risk for large or unpredictable expenses in an HMO because both inpatient and outpatient services are covered and needed specialty care is available on referral. Total costs to families, including out-of-pocket and premium costs, are lower in HMOs than in fee-for-service settings (Luft, 1981).

Recent Reforms Proposed for Health Insurance. During the past few years, several proposals have been advanced to change core elements of private health insurance; most of these proposals have been driven by a desire to control inflation in health costs. Two main forms of cost containment have been proposed: one controls benefits or eligibility; the other provides incentives to replace expensive services with less expensive alternatives.

The first form has been less characteristic of the private health insurance industry than of public insurers, such as Medicaid, and some states have developed stringent criteria for eligibility or have cut out such benefits as dental care or some drugs as a way of decreasing program costs. Along the same lines, many private health insurance plans have raised deductible levels or copayment rates to cut costs and to discourage utilization of benefits.

Typical methods of strengthening incentives to contain cost include expansion of prepayment options, the development of other prospective payment methods, and to some degree, the development of competitive plans. Preferred Provider Organizations (PPOs) are one relatively new form of prospective payment plan. Here, providers, such as group practices or hospitals, contract with an insurer to provide services to an insured population. As an example, a hospital might agree to supply inpatient care at a predetermined rate to patients insured through a certain group plan. In return for lower rates, the group plan assures a steady flow of patients to the hospital. With this system, hospitals can be paid a defined rate in advance rather than necessarily waiting to bill insurance programs on a patient-by-patient basis after discharge. Where different hospitals may bid to be a PPO for a particular insurer, there are incentives to submit a lower bid in order to win the contract. Cost containment is achieved through a competitive bidding process.

Competitive approaches to cost containment work on the assumption that costs will be restrained by forces of the marketplace. An employee is permitted to choose among a few plans for health coverage, including more and less expensive ones, depending on the various benefits available in each plan. Employees choosing a more expensive plan are responsible for the additional cost, with the employer paying the cost only of the least expensive plan offered. To compete in this type of market, plans can cut costs by diminishing benefits or eligibility, increasing copayments, or by providing other incentives to discourage the use of expensive services. Competition theoretically can encourage either a benefit-reducing or a prepayment approach to cost containment.

For families with children with chronic illnesses, competitive approaches may have serious disadvantages. The minimal-cost plans, which are likely to pay for fewer of the services required by families with seriously ill children, would tend to attract healthier populations who could opt for the less expensive version. If those with ongoing chronic health problems choose a more expensive plan, the price gap between the two levels of plans will likely widen over time because heavy use of covered services will increase costs to the insurer and hence lead to rising premium costs. Overall, if mandated minimum benefit standards for competitive plans are low, the plans are likely to be inadequate for children with chronic illnesses.

Protection against catastrophic health expenses has also been proposed as a reform of private health insurance, although not from a cost-containment perspective. Rather, the idea here is to recognize that families occasionally face very high bills, usually associated with a single major illness or accident. Catastrophic health insurance provides coverage for such events through very high deductibles and usually high copayments. A person must generate very high bills before catastrophic health insurance provides benefits. Catastrophic plans could benefit children with severe chronic illnesses, such as congenital heart disease or spina bifida, through insuring coverage of those severe illnesses that depend extensively on high-cost technologies. This would be especially true if the deductible were a one-time-only deductible rather than being reapplied on a yearly basis.

Zook, Moore, and Zeckhauser (1981) observe that most catastrophic health insurance proposals are based on misconceptions about the nature of catastrophic illness. Contrary to popular understanding, high-cost illness "is more often long-term and repetitive than short-term and acute," (p. 67) and few proposals "contain incentives for providers to develop long-term care programs to reduce [hospital] readmissions" (p. 73). Moreover, they argue, a benefit structure based on a one-year deductible presents difficulties for individuals with long-term illness who require a longer-term benefit structure. A child with congenital abnormalities or an ongoing disease might never qualify for catastrophic coverage in a single year but could require an expensive series of treatments and hospital visits over an extended period of time (Weeks, 1985).

Beyond the problem that much financially catastrophic illness is long-term rather than acute, there is concern that catastrophic insurance creates incentives for even greater use of very expensive services. If catastrophic coverage begins, for example, after several thousand dollars of costs have accrued, there is, for many patients, incentive to spend quickly up to that level so that catastrophic benefits may be used.

Several states have developed high-risk pools for people having difficulties obtaining private health insurance. In such states, most or all of the companies writing insurance in the state are required to develop a resource pool of insurance for high-risk patients. These plans usually resemble catastrophic plans in that they have very high deductibles and high copayments. Although high-risk pools and catastrophic approaches carry potential benefit to families whose children have severe chronic illnesses, the very high copayments associated with this form of insurance make these plans too expensive for many people to join.

In summary, private health insurance, mainly through the tax benefits it currently creates, represents the largest federal subsidy to the health care of children with chronic illnesses. Certain aspects of private health insurance limit its effectiveness in assuring adequate care to children with chronic illnesses. Benefit packages are attuned more to acute illnesses than to chronic ones. Problems of access associated with lack of family coverage or exclusion of pre-existing conditions also press heavily on these families. Proposals to reform the private health insurance industry carry varied implications for families with chronically ill children. Some, especially forms of prepayment, carry hope for providing high-quality services at lower cost for children. Others, especially those that limit benefits or restrict eligibility, must be monitored carefully to assure that access to needed services is maintained for these children.

Public Programs

Medicaid. Also known as Title XIX of the Social Security Act, Medicaid is the single largest public program that supports health care for children who live in poverty. It is a major source of financing for the care of chronically ill children who are poor. Extraordinarily important in helping to ensure good medical care for many of these children, its limitations are nonetheless severe.

Medicaid is designed to pay for medical services delivered primarily to individuals who are enrolled in two welfare programs: Aid to Families with Dependent Children (AFDC) or Supplemental Security Income (SSI). Most children who receive Medicaid benefits are eligible on the basis of enrollment in AFDC, although a small number of disabled or blind children qualify through enrollment in the SSI program. In 1980, Medicaid paid for services delivered to an estimated eleven million children. It is not known how many of these were chronically ill. In 1980, the program spent $24 billion, of which $4.2 billion was spent on children. Fifty-five percent of the total amount was contributed by the federal government; most of the rest, by state governments (Health Care Financing Administration, 1983a). Although the federal Medicaid law provides general guidance to the states and establishes specific regulations, the program is primarily administered by state authorities.

An adequate understanding of Medicaid, and especially of its implications for chronically ill children, requires an appreciation of (1) the historical role that federal and state governments have played in supporting health care for recipients of welfare payments and (2) the extent and cause of variations in Medicaid benefits from one state to another.

When it was passed in 1965, Medicaid was seen simply as an extension of the role of the federal government in providing medical care benefits within the context of welfare programs. This role had started in 1935 when passage of the original Social Security Act established federal programs of cash assistance for several categories of individuals: the aged, the blind, and children in families in which one parent (usually the father) was absent or disabled. Cash assistance for disabled persons was added in 1950. Especially important for children was the Aid for Dependent Children (ADC) program, the forerunner of the AFDC program. It authorized federal funds to match state appropriations for direct support of children living in impoverished, single-parent families. There were no direct payments for medical care, but the recipients' medical expenses were taken into account in determining monthly welfare payments. Because many states did not elect to operate the optional ADC program, the financial support of medical services was both indirect and quite negligible until 1950.

In 1950, the various welfare programs began to provide physicians, hospitals, and other health care providers with direct reimbursements (termed vendor payments) for their services to welfare recipients. The federal government encouraged state participation in the vendor-payment system, and by 1960, forty states were participating. During that year, payments to medical care providers totalled $500 million.

The next major extension of medical care benefits within the welfare program came with the Social Security Amendments of 1960, known as the Kerr-Mills Act. This act provided more generous, open-ended federal funds to match state dollars for vendor payments, and coverage was extended (at the states' discretion) to a new group: medically indigent elderly individuals, defined as those whose incomes were too high to make them eligible for cash assistance from a public program but too low to pay their medical bills. Within five years, all fifty states were operating medical-vendor-payment programs within the state welfare system, and all but three provided coverage to the elderly who were medically indigent. In 1965, state and federal expenditures for medical services through welfare programs were $1.4 billion, and expenditures for elderly recipients far eclipsed those for children (Stevens and Stevens, 1974).

Through the early 1960s, the Kerr-Mills program was regarded by many people as a temporary means of addressing the provision of medical care for the elderly. Various proposals for a more permanent program were offered: subsidized insurance for physicians' services for the aged, hospital insurance for the aged under the Social Security Act, and increased federal grants to the states for health services for the poor. Medicare, enacted in July 1965, was the outgrowth of these proposals. Medicaid, passed at the same time, was written quickly, had many of the characteristics of the Kerr-Mills Act, and received little attention during the congressional debate on Medicare (Stevens and Stevens, 1974).

Thus, prior to the passage of Medicaid, certain policies were already in place: a focus on recipients of welfare, direct payments to medical providers, considerable state discretion, and the notion of the medically indigent, later called the medically needy. These policies are Medicaid's heritage. Each has implications for chronically ill children.

1. Medicaid was never intended to be a health insurance plan for all children who live in or close to poverty; it was designed only for those who live in poverty *and* who are also eligible for welfare payments. With a few exceptions, eligibility for Medicaid still depends on enrollment in AFDC or SSI. Gaining access to the Medicaid program can therefore be a major problem for poor children, and it is much worse in some states than in others. The U.S. Department of Health and Human Services estimates that 40 percent of all the nation's disabled children in poverty are ineligible for Medicaid (Butler and others, 1985). Because of state options within the AFDC program as well as within the Medicaid program, the percentage of disabled or handicapped children *not* eligible within each state varies from 79 in Nevada to 14 in New York. Twenty-two states have Medicaid programs that cover at least half of the low-income handicapped children; twenty-seven state Medicaid programs do not cover even half of this population; and one state, Arizona, only recently established a Medicaid program at all (Butler and others, 1985). Thus in many states, for each chronically ill child living in poverty who receives Medicaid, there is another similar child who does not. Equally unfortunate are those families for whom Medicaid benefits are uncertain. Thirty percent of families on Medicaid lose their eligibility each year; this loss, often accompanied by an interruption in care, can have particularly drastic consequences for a chronically ill child.

    The Deficit Reduction Act of 1984 extended Medicaid eligibility to two new groups: (1) children from two-parent families whose financial status is comparable to that of families on AFDC and (2) single and married pregnant women who have AFDC-level incomes but are not enrolled in the cash welfare program. The extension of Medicaid to these children and pregnant women had been sought since the mid 1970s by advocates of improved health care for poor mothers and children. The manner in which the law is implemented will affect both the well-being of many chronically ill children in poor two-parent families and the access to prenatal care of poor pregnant women, which plays an important role in the health of newborns.

2.   Medicaid continued the policy of direct vendor payments without also implementing a way of coordinating services. Because it remains essentially a bank out of which providers draw reimbursements for the services they render, Medicaid lacks the ability to decrease any duplication and fragmentation in the medical care system. In a sense, it is a program that primarily reacts to demands for payment from physicians or hospitals by either issuing a check or refusing payment. It was not designed originally to play an active role in fostering innovative financing arrangements or new types of services. In particular, Medicaid was not intended to foster the service coordination role that is desirable for children with multiple or chronic medical needs.

3.   Medicaid gives considerable freedom to states in deciding what services to cover within its program. The federal law requires states to cover a core set of services (including inpatient care; lab services; Early and Periodic Screening, Diagnosis, and Treatment—EPSDT—services for children; and others) and permits the states to elect coverage of any of twenty-seven optional services (for example, home nursing services or dental services). The choices the states have made result in extreme variation from one state to another. For example, Butler and colleagues (1985) note that most state Medicaid programs pay for care in a skilled nursing facility and for prosthetic devices. They add, "A significant number, however, do not provide eyeglasses (no coverage in seventeen states); physical therapy (no coverage in eighteen states); speech, hearing, and language disorder services (no coverage in twenty-two states); occupational therapy (no coverage in twenty-six states); and dental services (no coverage in twenty-six states). On average, states offer approximately seven out of ten major optional services relevant to chronically disabled children, but state variation is wide. Thus, Medicaid eligibility may mean that a large or small proportion of a disabled child's needs are met, depending on the characteristics of the state program" (p. 848).

From a national vantage point, the states' freedom in selecting services to provide in the Medicaid program ensures extensive variation in coverage of services needed by chronically ill children. Furthermore, many of the services chronically ill children and their families will need—especially services that are not strictly medical—are excluded from both the required and optional sets of services. As with private health care insurance, Medicaid often fails to cover general health services (such as respite care, special foods or appliances, or transportation) needed by chronically ill children and their families.

4.   Medicaid offers the states one option most pertinent to chronically ill children: the provision of services to children defined as medically needy. This option permits a family with one absent or incapacitated parent to qualify for Medicaid even if the family's income is above the Medicaid cutoff point. In some states, children in two-parent families in which the parents are unemployed are also eligible. In essence, the medically needy provision attempts to ensure that the near-poor are not devastated by medical expenses that a chronic illness can generate. In 1980, twenty-eight states had elected this option. Unfortunately, economic pressures have since forced many states to reduce or eliminate their medically needy programs (National Health Policy Forum, 1981). The medically needy program is marred further by the requirement that families qualify through an administratively complex spend-down system— that is, families must document medical care expenditures that reduce their incomes to a level slightly above the amount that would qualify them for cash assistance. The spend-down is so difficult to administer that only one third of those potentially eligible to benefit actually qualify for Medicaid, and most who do qualify are in nursing homes and other residential care facilities (Congressional Budget Office, 1979).

Partly due to the lack of careful consideration during its drafting, Medicaid has been poorly managed from its inception (Stevens and Stevens, 1974). In the early days of Medicaid, federal management was hampered by a small staff and by lack of clarity as to whether Medicaid was a welfare or health program. Federal authority lagged until the debate about administrative control between two federal agencies—the Public Health Service and the Welfare Administration—was finally resolved in favor of welfare. Medicaid's architects especially failed to anticipate the effects of pumping large amounts of public funds into the existing, largely private, fee-for-service medical system. The result was a rapid and steady increase in federal, state, and local government expenditures, from $1.5 billion in 1966 to more than $29 billion in 1981; estimated expenditures for fiscal year 1982 were $32 billion (Health Care Financing Administration, 1983b).

Medical care constitutes the fastest growing sector of governmental human welfare expenditures—a fact that is pressuring federal and state officials to reduce expenditures. At the federal level, the spending on health programs has grown at a rate 40 percent higher than the growth rate in the overall human welfare arena (Shayne, 1981). At the state level, expenditures for human welfare programs grew from 10 to 21 percent of state budgets between 1965 and 1978; 44 percent of that growth was for medical care. Half the states had fiscal problems in the early 1980s as a result of Medicaid's growth (Spitz, 1981b).

Congressional attempts to contain costs and improve management control began early. Amendments in 1967, 1968, and 1972, for example, established procedures for quality and utilization review, set limits on the coverage of the medically needy, permitted the states to reduce optional services, and gave the states the option of charging nominal fees for services. Partially in an effort to constrain the growth of expenditures, the Omnibus Budget Reconciliation Act of 1981 and the Tax Equity and Fiscal Responsibility Act of 1982 increased the states' latitude in administering their Medicaid programs. States have greater authority to define medically needy eligibility and benefits, set rates of reimbursement to institutional providers, reimburse home- and community-based care, purchase laboratory services and supplies through competitive bidding, and restrict recipients' choice in selecting providers of care.

Federal and state actions to slow the rate of increase in Medicaid expenditures fall into the same two strategies available to private insurors. The first strategy, reducing access to services, is accomplished with relative ease. Actions to reduce access include cutting eligibility and benefits, charging fees to patients, and reducing reimbursement to physicians, which tends to discourage physicians from accepting Medicaid patients (Sloan, Cromwell, and Mitchell, 1978). The second strategy, restructuring the organization and payment for services, is administratively more difficult. Methods include prepaid programs, restricting Medicaid patients to certain providers, and providing home- and community-based services as a substitute for institution-based care. Rogers, Blendon, and Moloney (1982) note that strategies to reduce costs that are easiest from an administrative and political perspective are likely to cause the greatest damage to the poor. Conversely, strategies that may benefit recipients involve restructuring the fee-for-service system on which Medicaid reimbursement has been based and pose difficult administrative and political problems. Both strategies have implications for chronically ill children enrolled in Medicaid.

Reducing access by cutting eligibility and benefits has been the dominant cost-containment approach in Medicaid. Federal and state changes in Medicaid and AFDC policy produced a marked decline in enrollment in the late 1970s and early 1980s (Rowland and Gaus, 1981; Budetti, Butler, and McManus, 1981). A recent study found that poor, chronically ill people who lose Medicaid eligibility suffer deterioration in access to care, satisfaction with care, and health status (Lurie and others, 1984). Similarly, narrowing the range of benefits for which Medicaid will pay has the effect of denying access to needed services. Chronically ill children, who rely heavily on a broad range of services, including the optional services covered by Medicaid, and who require more hospital days and physician visits than required by other children, are affected sharply by cuts in eligibility and benefits.

In contrast, the second strategy—structural change in the way services are organized and financed—appears to be less damaging to Medicaid recipients including chronically ill children and their families. Some structural change is likely to be beneficial. Among the approaches to restructuring Medicaid are prepaid plans, primary care case management, home- and community-based care, and prospective payment to hospitals. These strategies are common to the private health insurance arena as well, although they may be cast in a somewhat different fashion.

One approach to restructuring Medicaid is to provide payments for people to enroll in prepaid medical care plans. Several states have used prepaid medical plans for Medicaid recipients since the early 1970s, and federal Medicaid policy changes in 1981 greatly stimulated experimentation with these approaches. The 1981 policy changes permit states to develop Medicaid contracts with prepaid plans that do not meet federal HMO requirements, permit states to implement programs for selected populations and in selected parts of the state, and modify the long-standing requirement that Medicaid enrollees have access to care from any qualified provider—the freedom-of-choice provision. By 1984, twenty-eight states had undertaken programs that shifted from fee-for-service to prepaid contracts of various kinds (Iglehart, 1984).

Spitz (1981a) calls HMOs the "elusive promise" to contain Medicaid costs while maintaining access to services. As with privately supported HMOs, the presumed benefits for Medicaid recipients, including chronically ill children, are several. HMOs provide care at lower cost. Services are more comprehensive and accessible than the care provided in the settings used most by the poor: hospital emergency rooms and outpatient clinics. However, prepaid plans may have features that make them undesirable for the care of chronically ill children.

Another approach to restructuring Medicaid is to lock Medicaid recipients—especially those who are high users of services—into primary care case management systems (Spitz, 1981b; Fox and Bartlett, 1984b). Primary care case management aims at increasing the primary care physician's overall role in patient care. Case managers are responsible for locating, coordinating, and monitoring the medical care and related services of Medicaid recipients enrolled in the system. Except in emergencies, patients are prohibited from using care without consultation with the primary care provider. The case manager is paid a capitation fee or may share in the financial savings resulting from reductions in inpatient hospital use. Since the Medicaid policy changes in 1981, fourteen states have received approval to establish primary care networks (Fox and Bartlett, 1984b). Although no system is planned specifically to serve children with special medical problems, the concept is readily applicable to them. Cost containment and coordinated, managed care could be dual benefits of such a system.

Restructuring Medicaid to substitute home- and community-based care for institutional (nursing home and hospital) care is another approach to cost containment that may improve the care of chronically ill children. The 1981 Medicaid changes permit states to obtain waivers of federal Medicaid program regulations in order to provide reimbursement to providers of home- and community-based services. Under the waiver programs, states may offer a number of services important for chronically ill children, including case management, homemaker services, home health aides, personal care services, habilitation services, respite care, nursing care, medical equipment and supplies, and minor modifications to the home (Fox and Bartlett, 1984a). The waiver program also allows the states to change the SSI eligibility rules regarding transfer (deeming) of parents' income to children on SSI who live at home, enabling these children to receive Medicaid coverage for care given at home rather than only for care they receive in hospitals or other institutions. Although most waiver applications have focused on elderly patients, they are directed increasingly to physically disabled children (Fox and Bartlett, 1984a). The experience of many states in providing home- and community-based services, paid by Medicaid, for children with special health needs will offer the opportunity to accumulate answers to important questions about this new approach to services: How can services be provided to the children who need them without unintentionally opening a Pandora's box of new demand? Does home care really contain costs? What are the possibilities for collaboration between Medicaid agencies, which have financial resources, and other state child health agencies, especially the CCS programs, which have responsibility for chronically ill children? Can the CCS agencies fill the roles some have suggested for them by, for example, assisting Medicaid agencies to define target populations, identifying the home-based services needed, estimating and documenting the comparative costs of home and institutional care, developing standards for providers, and delivering case management services (Fox and Bartlett, 1984a)?

Still another change in Medicaid policy that will affect the care of chronically ill children is the pending shift to prospective payment of hospitals. In 1983, Medicare began using Diagnosis Related Groups (DRGs) as the basis for prospective reimbursement for hospital services. Under the DRG system, hospitals receive a fixed payment per discharge based on the patient's diagnosis, regardless of the length of stay or the services provided. Thus hospitals save money by keeping the stay as short as possible. Although federal law does not require states to use the DRG system for Medicaid, several state Medicaid agencies have adopted the system, and it is likely that the Medicaid program will soon employ the DRG system nationwide (American Academy of Pediatrics, 1984b).

To date, in recognition of the fact that the DRG classifications were developed primarily for adults, children's hospitals have been exempted from the DRG system. A DRG system that will attempt to take into account the particular nature of pediatric hospitalizations is currently being developed (American Academy of Pediatrics, 1984b). For example, children with chronic illnesses and high-risk newborns stay in the hospital longer than older patients. Because children require a more extensive array of support services than most adult patients, they are costly for hospitals to treat. Design of a prospective payment system for hospitals caring for children must take into account the special needs of chronically ill children so that access to care is balanced with the goal of containing costs.

Although Medicaid has limitations in eligibility and benefits, has administrative problems, and is undergoing rapid change, it continues to be an important source of support for the care of poor, chronically ill children. One fourth of the nation's children who have limitations in their activities receive medical services paid by Medicaid (Butler and others, 1985). For poor children covered by Medicaid, the coverage of medical care comes close to that received by children who have private health insurance and far exceeds the care received by chronically ill children living in poverty but who are ineligible for Medicaid.

The Medicaid program has also served to buttress the child health delivery system in the nation. One survey of children's hospitals found that Medicaid is a large source of revenues, averaging about 25 percent of total patient revenues and reaching 80 percent in one facility (National Association of Children's Hospitals and Related Institutions, 1981). Furthermore, in some states, Medicaid payments for hospital and physician services have allowed other programs, such as the Crippled Children's Services, to focus more on social and supportive services. Reforms prompted by a concern with costs have brought the issues of financing into closer proximity with issues of health care organization. In the past, the child health field has been marked by a division between the major public funding program (Medicaid) and the agency (the Office of Maternal and Child Health) with responsibility for overseeing child health programs in the states, including the CCS program (Yordy, 1981). Efforts to improve ties between these public agencies may bring further benefits to children with chronic illnesses and their families.

Despite its achievements, Medicaid is insufficient for chronically ill children and their families. Many children who live in poverty are ineligible for the program. Two chronically ill children who live in adjacent towns but separate states might receive services substantially different, and both are unlikely to receive through Medicaid many of the services from which they could greatly benefit.

Furthermore, even though poor children have gained through Medicaid in terms of the quality of services available, the quality of care tends to differ greatly from that available to higher-income children. With the exception of well-organized specialty clinics that offer comprehensive care and are found in major tertiary centers, poor children's outpatient medical care is likely to occur in hospitals and emergency rooms rather than in private offices and to be characterized by long waits, lack of continuity of caregiver, and lack of access to telephone consultations. Although the care given poor children may be technically adequate, the settings in which the care is given are likely to be deficient in interpersonal aspects of care. And the interpersonal qualities important in the care of all children—continuity, accessibility, communication, and accountability—are of special importance in the long-term, complex care of children with severe chronic illnesses. Financing programs such as Medicaid, effective though they may be in facilitating utilization of medical care for poor chronically ill children, fall short of providing access to high-quality care and to many of the special services needed by chronically ill children and their families.

Crippled Children's Services (CCS). The CCS represents the nation's most direct and sustained support for children with chronic health problems. In comparison with Medicaid, CCS is older by thirty years, involves far fewer dollars, and serves fewer children. But the CCS is more than a financing program. The original legislation gave the CCS the task of "extending and improving services for children with crippling conditions or conditions that lead to crippling" (Title V of the Social Security Act of 1935). With this mandate, the CCS has the potential both to shape the form of the health care delivery system and to pay for needed services. It is one of the few programs with some influence over both the organization *and* the financing of care for children.

In 1943, CCS programs in fifty-three states and territories served approximately 175,000 children, about 0.3 percent of the nation's population under twenty-one (Children's Bureau, 1951). Virtually all of these children were poor or near poor, and most had various orthopedic problems. In 1958, about 325,000 children received services through state CCS programs, and the range of conditions covered had broadened (Lesser, 1960). Children with heart problems, for example, had been enrolled because of the recent developments in cardiac surgery. By 1979, according to the best estimates available, the state CCS programs had grown to serve about 650,000 children (Ireys, Hauck, and Perrin, 1985; National Public Health Program Reporting Service, 1981). The range of conditions covered by the state programs has continued to expand (although along different paths in different states) to include leukemia, asthma, diabetes, and renal disorders. The state-by-state variation in coverage of conditions is enormous. To a large extent, however, the original emphasis on orthopedic problems and on conditions requiring surgical procedures continues. Consequently, many states concentrate their resources on orthopedic problems or conditions such as spina bifida while conditions requiring medical treatment (asthma, diabetes) are less emphasized or, in some states, altogether overlooked (Ireys, Hauck, and Perrin, 1985).

When it was created in 1935, the CCS program broke new ground in financial arrangements for the support of child health.

The program was funded jointly by the federal and state governments; the federal appropriation ($1,187,000 in 1936) was given to states according to a formula based on the number of individuals under age twenty-one in the state, the size of the rural population, and per capita income. The states were required to match a portion of this amount, so that the monies available to the program were at least double the federal appropriation. Because many states actually contributed more than was strictly required, federal monies have always amounted to less than half of the total expenditures by state CCS programs; in some states, they have been less than 10 percent. Overall, in 1978, the federal appropriation to state CCS agencies totalled $97 million, 38 percent of the $255 million that the state agencies actually spent (National Public Health Program Reporting Service, 1979).

What do the state CCS agencies do with this money? Like Medicaid, the state CCS programs vary widely in the services they support. In fact, state variations in services provided by CCS programs exceed those of Medicaid, partly because required services were never defined and partly because the state CCS agencies have considerable discretion in organizing their programs.

At one end of the spectrum, some state CCS programs support only a narrow range of specialty services, such as hospitalization and surgical procedures. In these states, the program functions much as Medicaid does, primarily reimbursing physicians and hospitals for services rendered to enrolled children; however, CCS programs generally have higher income cutoff points than Medicaid. At the other end of the spectrum, a few CCS programs have organized and supported clinics and special health teams that address the wide range of medical, emotional, and social needs of enrolled children. In these states, program funds tend to support efforts that make the existing resources work well for these children rather than simply paying for additional care. Funds may be used to fill lapses in the availability of services by directly paying a provider to deliver a certain service; more typically, the program's monies support the structure within which comprehensive care clinics or teams can operate effectively. Under these arrangements, payments for specific services come from other sources, such as Medicaid or private health insurance. Regardless of its particular structure, virtually every CCS program is closely related to specialty medical centers.

Another important feature of the CCS effort involves a long-standing concern with improving care for children and families regardless of income. At no point was there a federal rule regarding the financial eligibility for the CCS program. In fact, the original legislation required CCS programs to provide free diagnostic and evaluation services to anyone who asked for them. Treatment services could also be provided to any child who was medically eligible; because all CCS programs have limited funds, however, virtually all have established financial cutoff points above which they will not pay for care. In a few states, the CCS program functions as a government-subsidized insurance program for all children with a chronic illness or handicapping condition, enrolling children from all economic levels, providing oversight and needed services, and requiring full or partial reimbursement from parents depending on their economic status. These programs largely avoid the problems of a two-tiered system in which one tier includes the poor and the other includes the middle- and upper-middle income groups (Ireys, 1980).

Evidence of the CCS program's concern with quality of care comes from its historical emphasis on standard setting. States have expressed this concern in ways that range from establishing a list of CCS-approved physicians to threatening to withhold reimbursements from clinics that did not meet specified staffing or procedural requirements. Aside from anecdotal reports, it is unclear to what extent these standard-setting mechanisms have shaped delivery of care.

If the CCS has taught the nation any lesson at all, it has showed that public programs and the private sector can work together harmoniously. The state programs that have been most successful and innovative are those programs that are most supported by private physicians. Across the country, the CCS has met many of the needs of private physicians, often serving as a payment source for high-technology care when no other was available. Yet, without support from the private sector, a CCS program is unlikely to make major inroads into the health care system for children who have complex medical problems and who require much specialty care.

Many state CCS programs are mired in agencies that discourage innovation and hobbled by old allegiances to orthopedic and surgical subspecialties. Health care is a far more complex business than it was in 1935, requiring knowledge about eligibility criteria for many other programs, reimbursement strategies, and effective advocacy techniques. Additionally, rapid technological advances for a variety of illnesses have overtaken many of these programs, forcing them to stretch their severely limited resources thinly. Those who have given the CCS program much attention believe that state CCS programs now find themselves unprepared for the last decade's many changes in the care of handicapped and chronically ill children (Altenstetter and Bjorkman, 1978; Ireys, Hauck, and Perrin, 1985; MacQueen, 1974).

But the future holds much promise for state CCS programs. Despite the uncertainty that accompanied the Maternal and Child Health (MCH) Block Grant in 1981, many state programs are maintaining and, to some extent, even increasing their available monies, partly through increased state appropriations (U.S. General Accounting Office, 1984). Several innovative projects have arisen in the context of state CCS programs (Pierce and Freedman, 1983).

In sum, a variety of problems attend the state CCS programs: extreme variability from state to state, such that one child may be enrolled in a state CCS program but another child with the same condition who lives in another state will be excluded; extremely uneven support of comprehensive services among states coupled with a continuing emphasis on surgical and orthopedic care; a focus on the poor or near-poor despite the potential for supporting a system inclusive of all economic levels; and a history that discourages innovation. Yet the pluralism within the CCS program, its traditional concern with standards and quality of care, and its experience in melding state-based public support with the expertise of community-based private practitioners all work jointly to provide the nation with a fortuitous opportunity. CCS programs are located in state bureaucracies, most of them in public health departments. With a return to increased state control of health care programs, the CCS program is in a position to assume more authority. If state CCS programs can let loose of old anchorages, they will have the chance to chart a course for substantial improvements in the care of chronically ill children and their families.

Other Public Programs. In addition to CCS and Medicaid, the federal government and to a lesser extent state governments have supported a variety of other programs directly relevant to the health care of chronically ill children and their families. These programs include: the Supplemental Security Income Program, established in 1972; the Supplemental Security Income/Disabled Children's Program, passed in 1976; the Genetic Disease Act of 1976; the Hemophilia Diagnostic and Treatment Center Act of 1976; and state-based categorical programs, primarily for children with cystic fibrosis. Collectively, in 1979, these programs served roughly between 60,000 and 75,000 chronically ill children, many of whom were also enrolled in Medicaid or CCS. We estimate the total expenditures in 1979 for these programs to be close to $50 million, slightly more than 1 percent of the total Medicaid expenditure on children in 1980.

Although this money represents a tiny amount of the public monies supporting health care for these children, there are two reasons for which we include a brief discussion of these programs: first, the programs incorporate several sound ideas pertinent to chronically ill children as a whole; second, the programs illustrate the relative strengths and drawbacks of previous attempts to finance care for chronically ill children and their families.

In 1972, Congress established the Supplemental Security Income (SSI) program. Designed to replace and expand three existing federal-state welfare programs (Aid to the Aged, Aid to the Permanently and Totally Disabled, and Aid to the Blind), SSI provides direct payments to individuals over age sixty-five who are poor and to individuals of any age who are blind or disabled and who are poor.

Largely as a result of the earlier programs' emphasis on adults and the lack of explicit reference to children in the legislation, only a small percentage of SSI beneficiaries are children. In 1979, children were only 5 percent of all recipients of SSI payments. This figure (approximately 200,000) represents a small fraction of the children theoretically eligible for the program. In addition, the percent of potentially eligible children who are actually enrolled in

SSI varies widely across the states, ranging from 7.4 in Wyoming to 57.8 in Illinois (Butler and others, 1985; Rymer and others, 1980). The available information is not precise, but perhaps 30 percent of the children on SSI have the sorts of chronic illnesses with which we are concerned here. Thus, the SSI program serves, at best, an estimated 60,000 chronically ill children.

For the children it does serve, the SSI program is not generous. In 1979, 67 percent of the children on SSI received a federal grant averaging $158 per month; the other 33 percent received both federal and state support, which together average less than $225 per month per child (Butler and others, 1985). As it exists now, the SSI program contributes little to financing care for chronically ill children. Although it provides direct payments to families and makes some recipients eligible for Medicaid, the SSI program touches only a few children with a chronic illness.

Before it was embedded in the MCH Block Grant in 1981, the Supplemental Security Income/Disabled Children's Program (SSI/ DCP) had existed for four years. Federally funded and administered through the state CCS agencies in all but five states, the SSI/DCP provided federal funds ($30 million per year) to ensure the provision of comprehensive care to those children receiving SSI benefits. We estimate that in 1979 the SSI program itself had only 60,000 chronically ill children enrolled; only some of these 60,000 children were enrolled in the SSI/DCP. Hence, the program brought benefits to a relatively small number of chronically ill children (Ireys and Merkens, 1981). Yet, the program's history is useful because it illustrates an attempt to provide coordinated care to children with chronic handicaps or physical illnesses. Moreover, it represents an attempt to modernize the CCS program through the introduction of requirements for case managing and planning of services on a patient-by-patient basis. The legislation required the state agencies (1) to develop individual service plans (ISPs) for children referred from SSI rolls, (2) to counsel the children as necessary, (3) to refer them to appropriate agencies, and (4) to monitor the services they receive.

The SSI/DCP had many problems, including inconsistent and diminutive federal funding, extensive and complex regulations, unwarranted assumptions that CCS agencies would easily integrate new requirements into ongoing programs, inadequate political clout at the state level, and ethical concerns around the transfer of records between agencies. To a great extent, it became an irritant to most state CCS agencies, and because of this, most state agencies have abandoned it under the block grant. However misguided it was, the SSI/DCP did introduce important concepts into the world of some state CCS programs. The notions of developing a reasonable strategy for planning a child's care, of working actively with other state agencies, and of monitoring the services delivered to a child have prompted or assisted broader reforms in a few state CCS programs.

Although passed in 1976, the Genetic Disease Act was based on earlier legislation that focused primarily on sickle cell anemia. The original legislation led to the allocation of about $3.5 million for the purpose of establishing community clinics to screen individuals and educate communities about sickle cell anemia. Most of these funds were awarded on a competitive basis directly to state and local health departments, which then contracted with pediatric departments of medical schools to provide the services. About twenty-two sickle cell clinics were established on the basis of this legislation (Battle, 1981).

As a result of extensive lobbying by groups representing other genetically based chronic illnesses that afflict children (including Tay-Sachs disease, cystic fibrosis, dysautonomia, and hemophilia), new legislation was passed, creating the Comprehensive Genetics Program. This program supported community-based clinics to provide screening, diagnostic services, genetic counseling, and transportation services as well as materials for the education of professionals and the public. The clinics were discouraged from providing direct treatment services, inpatient care, research, or formal training activities.

One of the most important criteria by which awards were made under the Comprehensive Genetics Program was the extent of community participation. In large measure, clinics were required to have advisory boards with community representatives on them and to operate educational programs in conjunction with community institutions. Over the course of its lifetime, from 1976 to 1981, the program appropriated about $4 million per year to support about forty-five clinics.

Unlike the Comprehensive Genetics Program, the legislation establishing the Hemophilia Diagnostic and Treatment Centers permitted funds to be spent on treatment services as well as on screening and evaluation. The purpose of the Hemophilia Centers Program was to create centers to provide comprehensive care, including medical, social, and psychological services, to children with hemophilia and their families regardless of income. The legislation establishing the hemophilia centers began in 1976 and continued until the passage of the MCH Block Grant in 1981. Federal funding has decreased since 1981, but many centers continue to function with support from a variety of sources. In 1981, the twenty-four centers and their network of sixty satellite facilities served approximately 6,000 patients with hemophilia. Federal appropriations averaged about $4 million per year until 1981 and generally provided only a portion of the centers' actual costs. Estimates of the percentage of federal monies to total expenditures ranged from 6 to 21 percent. Thus, federal funds often acted as mortar, holding the other financial bricks in place and filling in the gaps. By all accounts, these centers have been remarkably successful in implementing comprehensive care and developing materials for multidisciplinary team care.

Overall, the experience with disease-specific programs has been beneficial. These programs, at both the federal and state levels, have demonstrated the success of innovative concepts, including community involvement, community-based care, multidisciplinary teams, the effective delivery of necessary supportive services, and attention to chronically ill young adults. Furthermore, these programs have testified to the success of sustained advocacy on behalf of selected groups of chronically ill children. The relatively small funds generated by advocacy efforts have often been the stimulus for increased attention and, in some cases, for sustained government support (Milofsky and Elworth, 1985).

Experience with the various disease-specific programs underscores the strengths and weaknesses of narrowly focused policy making. On the one hand, the success of these advocacy groups in gaining support for their constituents represents the best of the democratic process. On the other hand, those chronically ill children who lack representation by an organized advocacy group may be ignored. Moreover, the possibility of special legislation for each of the more than one hundred rare chronic illnesses seems remote, politically untenable, and wasteful. A more reasoned stance takes a generic or noncategorical view of childhood chronic illness, incorporating the concepts that have already been tried in disease-specific programs.

Disease-Oriented Voluntary Associations

In addition to private health insurance and public programs, disease-oriented voluntary associations contribute to the health care of chronically ill children and their families. In terms of actual dollars, the support from these associations is small but important. Butler and colleagues (1985) estimate that during one year eight of the largest foundations representing children spent approximately $187 million on medical services, education efforts, and advocacy (excluding monies for research), which is larger by about 80 percent than the federal appropriation to the state CCS programs in 1980.

In addition to their direct support of a variety of services, these organizations play three important roles in the financing of care. First, some of the organizations have worked consistently with state CCS programs, providing special services for particular children and lobbying in state legislatures for support of the CCS program.

Advocacy groups have worked to develop special state programs focused on specific diseases. The most successful efforts have come from the Cystic Fibrosis Foundation. In 1980, as a result of their advocacy, twenty-two states had special programs supporting the health care of young adults with cystic fibrosis. Moreover, advocacy organizations (primarily the disease-oriented voluntary associations) played fundamental roles in the creation and implementation of both the Comprehensive Genetics Program and the hemophilia centers. Without sustained efforts by these groups, the programs might have withered quickly.

Second, the services that the associations provide are often otherwise unavailable to individual children and families. Transportation, educational and recreational activities, physical and occupational therapy, special equipment, and to a small extent, medical care are provided. Unfortunately, the small size of most foundations and their unevenness from one location to another mean that only a relatively few families actually see these benefits.

Third, many of these associations are willing to experiment with new service arrangements. Thus, foundation monies often fuel the start and initial dissemination of innovative methods of care (Milofsky and Elworth, 1985).

Family Support

Aside from private insurance, public programs, and disease-oriented foundations, individual families pay for the care of their own child. From a national perspective, how much do they pay? What percentage of costs come out of the parents' pockets? Again, the available information permits only partial answers, even at the level of individual families. Studies have failed to address the many types of costs a childhood chronic illness can generate for parents.

Available data underscore the wide range of parental contributions within disease categories. For example, in a study of children with thalassemia (U.S. Department of Health, Education, and Welfare, 1979), out-of-pocket expenses ranged from $50 to $5,650 for families with insurance coverage and from $265 to $10,495 for families without coverage. A study of hemophilia patients receiving home therapy indicated that eleven individuals had unpaid bills ranging from $1,000 to $13,500 (Levine, 1974).

Out-of-pocket expenses for the care of a very ill child can consume varying portions of the family's income. Vance and Taylor (1971), for example, found that medical costs took an average of 14 percent of family income. In a 1980 survey, the Cystic Fibrosis Foundation found that one fifth of respondents said out-of-pocket costs were greater than 30 percent of family income; more than half said these expenses were more than 10 percent of family income. For families of children with spina bifida, the average out-of-pocket expenses for medical care were 12 percent of the family income. A study of seventy families with children under treatment for cancer found that for more than half the families combined income loss and nonmedical costs were greater than 25 percent of family income; this study did not consider medical costs (Lansky and others, 1979).

Estimates of the total contribution of families to the support of childhood chronic illness must await additional studies. Even if each family of the one million children with a severe chronic illness contributes $500 to their child's care, the resulting sum far exceeds that which the state CCS agencies spent in any recent year—and not all CCS monies are directed to the population of children with the severe illnesses with which this book is concerned. By any measure, the contributions of families to the care of their own ill children are sizable.

Summary

In this chapter we have attempted to make available information relevant to the general question: Who pays for the services needed by chronically ill children and their families? The issues are complex, in part because of the patterns of cost that accompany childhood chronic illness and in part because of the problems that mark the health financing system in general. In summary, we note the following conclusions:

First, the financing system is inadequate on several counts in providing support for the care of children with chronic illnesses. Almost 100,000 of the one million children with chronic illness lack any coverage whatsoever for their medical expenses. Broader definitions of chronic illness than the one we employ here would include even more uninsured children. Furthermore, chronically ill children who do have a source of support often find the source inadequate. It fails to cover many services from which they or their families could benefit. Current financing arrangements often lead to a disproportionate emphasis on high-cost technology with a corresponding neglect of services that may be substantially less costly and more consonant with the needs of the family and child.

Second, under current arrangements, the distribution of costs is unclear and often unfair. In almost every instance, the public assumes a portion of the costs for these children; in many instances, the portion of costs shouldered by parents is unacceptably high.

When parents face financial obstacles in the use of medical or other supportive services, they tend to use only services that are medically necessary. Under these circumstances, parents avoid services that might substantially improve the quality of the child's or family's life or that might prevent subsequent problems (medical or otherwise).

Third, from a national perspective, the variation among states in eligibility for public programs, the differences in what these programs offer, and the variation in the comprehensiveness of private insurance plans cause inequity in the availability of services. As a result, some families suffer financially far more than others with comparable income. Help from nongovernmental sources is meager. Philanthropic agencies play a relatively minor role in direct financial support of the care of these children. Their importance emerges in the realm of advocacy for improved financing, which again is highly variable among states and among specific illnesses.

Finally, reforms in the health care system, fueled by a concern with rising costs, may bring benefits to children with a chronic illness. To improve care to these children, policy makers must be sufficiently deliberate to assure that reforms balance an emphasis on cost containment with an emphasis on access to a comprehensive array of services.

~~c~~ *8* ~~c~~

Preparing Professionals
for New Roles

A family may need the support and advice of a wide variety of professionals when their child has a chronic health condition. To participate effectively in the care of children with chronic illnesses, professionals must be well educated in several important areas. They must know basic physiology and treatment; human growth and development; emotional factors in health and illness; the beliefs, values, and traditions of communities; types of resources available in communities; and the ways in which children learn and schools function. Each professional must be technically proficient in the special skills of his or her own discipline and must have effective means to maintain and upgrade these skills. How well do professionals learn these concepts? What barriers exist to the effective education of professionals to understand childhood chronic illness? What opportunities may help prepare professionals to meet the changing nature of illness in children and the increasing numbers of families with a child suffering from long-term illness?

New professional roles reflect the changing character of childhood chronic illness. Professionals become responsible for delivering services in a continuous fashion over time and must conceptualize their patients' or clients' needs in a long-term way. In years past, the focus could be on acute crises and on preparing for death. Now, for most children, the preparation is for a life of growth and personal development that may be deeply affected by the constant presence of an illness. Professionals must help families cope with long-term problems and with planning for realistic futures for themselves and for their children. Where schools might have neglected children with chronic illnesses because of limited life spans, they now must seek ways of educating children who bring special health needs with them. The complex problems that families face when a child has a chronic illness typically require the attention of more than one professional. A new role, then, for professionals who aspire to work with these families is to participate as a member of a team and to coordinate efforts with other team members. An ecological perspective aids the understanding of one professional's actions in the larger context of the family and community. Professional responsibilities include assuring access of families to the broad range of services they need.

Just as certain tasks involved in working with families can be carried out equally effectively by nurses, social workers, psychologists, nutritionists, or physicians, educators in each profession, struggling to define curricular concepts and methods, frequently deal with a core of similar issues. Although optimally educating in each of these areas, each profession characteristically emphasizes certain knowledge or technical skills. Social workers excel in bringing families together with public and community resources (Rudolph, Andrews, Ratcliff, and Downes, 1985). Physicians especially learn pathophysiology and medical therapeutics. Nurses excel in understanding the child and family context of illness and in teaching families to meet their own caretaking needs (Norris, 1982). Teachers and school nurses know most about the settings in and methods by which children learn. And psychologists are expected to be expert in understanding the developmental and behavioral implications of chronic illness and in assessing the ways in which families and children cope and grow (Drotar and Bush, 1985).

During their education, the experience of social workers, physicians, nurses, and other professionals with important aspects of the care of chronically ill children may be highly circumscribed. Chronicity means that care is needed over a long period of time, yet educational experiences are typically brief, giving a young physician, for example, little opportunity to observe how a child develops over time in the context of illness or how a family copes with a difficult problem (Daeschner and Cerreto, 1985). To help families best, professionals with varied talents must collaborate. Yet people with different backgrounds rarely train together, nor are they taught concepts of teamwork and partnership (Osterweis and others, 1980). Training programs usually emphasize activities for which reimbursement is likely. Education therefore stresses curing and the performance of specific medical, surgical, and nursing procedures. The time-consuming, difficult, and complex issues of caring receive less attention. To apply their knowledge effectively and to help families care for their child when cure may not be possible, professionals must be skilled in teamwork, in communicating with families, in conceptualizing problems in family and environmental terms, and in dealing sensitively with ethical issues.

Programs to educate providers have been slow to recognize the special needs of families with chronically ill children. There is optimism in the observation that educators in the key professions increasingly acknowledge the complexity of childhood chronic illness and the importance of exposing students to the family, developmental, and multisystem impact of childhood chronic illness. Although debate continues on how to achieve better educational programs, changing awareness provides the opportunity and the will necessary to strengthen the education of professionals who will work regularly with children who have complex, continuing health problems.

Most professional training programs have responded to increasing specialization in health care, although in differing ways. In medicine, the response has been to prepare relatively fewer general physicians in the last thirty years. Physicians who are specialists in one or another group of diseases direct most educational activities. Nursing, on the other hand, has reversed a trend toward specialization by developing integrated curricula that limit the opportunity for specialization prior to master's degree training in that profession (Barnes, 1985). Families with children with chronic illnesses require very specialized services as well as a broad range of more general services. In response, the helping professions must train both specialists and generalists able to work closely with families over time.

In this chapter we explore the areas of knowledge and the types of skills different health professionals must be able to employ to meet the challenge of childhood chronic illness. Directions that educational programs should take to meet the needs of families are outlined. Lay counselors may take greater responsibility for helping families with chronically ill children (Pless and Satterwhite, 1972). The preparation of lay people, although less extensive than that for professionals, will necessarily focus on the same issues. The education of medical professionals is described in some detail to illustrate the issues and opportunities that apply equally to all helping professions.

Areas of Knowledge

The areas of knowledge important to caring for children with complex chronic illnesses reflect the varied needs and concerns raised by families. Professionals should have a basic understanding of child development, of the physiology of illness and its treatment, of the influences of cultural and ethnic differences on illness, of schools and the use of community resources, and of child advocacy. None of these areas are unique to the needs of children with chronic illnesses, but all play some role in the lives of these children. Most professionals will become expert in one or two areas, although acquaintance with each area provides a foundation for coordinated and comprehensive care for families. Can a nurse teach self-care to a family without understanding the physiology of the child's disease and its treatment? Can a physician who lacks understanding of the family and social milieu in which the child eats hope for compliance with a prescribed diet? Each area is discussed briefly to provide an introduction to the knowledge professionals must use in their work.

Childhood is a dynamic and growing time, and providers need a firm grasp of the principles of child development to understand the impact of illness on a child's developmental progress. Illnesses have different manifestations at different ages. The response and understanding of a three-year-old child with leukemia are substantially different from those of a ten-year-old. Only psychologists who choose to get a specialized degree in developmental psychology are likely to have formal instruction in child development. Pediatricians and other physicians learn only the rudiments of development, focusing on physical and motor development and having little exposure to the cognitive or social development of children. Nurses may have more formal education in developmental concepts, although in most curricula, the exposure is brief, even at the graduate level. Nurses are more likely than physicians to have read the works of important developmentalists, such as Piaget, although nursing training in child development may also lack depth and breadth.

All children should have the opportunity to excel in some area. Chronic illness may limit a child in one developmental realm. For the health worker to offer support for efforts to progress in other realms, an understanding of the breadth and varieties of developmental capacity is essential (Gliedman and Roth, 1980). Understanding families—how they cope, interact, develop, meet their needs, come together, and fall apart—underlies the ways in which providers help families utilize their own talents in raising their children. Professional understanding of child development and of families determines how well professionals understand the impact of illness. Is the child developing appropriately despite illness? Are there alternative routes of development or types of developmental stimulation that should be suggested to the family? What are the strengths of the family in meeting a new crisis? How have they fared in coping with a serious illness? Knowledge of family and child development are the specialties of mental health and social services professionals; yet basic principles must be understood by other health providers as well.

Knowledge of the physiology of the body and the mechanisms of disease, coupled with an understanding of pharmacology and therapeutics, is at the heart of medical education (Daeschner and Cerreto, 1985). Similarly, nurses must understand the mechanisms of illness to provide better care for their patients and to help patients comply with medications, diet, exercise, and other prescriptions related to an illness. Although nurses and physicians become expert in pathophysiology, other professionals working with families also depend on a basic understanding of the conditions affecting children. A psychologist counseling a teenager with diabetes who has become recalcitrant about following a diet or taking insulin properly must understand the interaction of diet, exercise, and insulin in order to work out proper contingencies for the teenager's behavior. The social worker involved with the family of a three-year-old boy with hemophilia must understand some of the mechanisms of bleeding in this disease in order to be able to help the family find appropriate daycare or to counsel the mother on appropriate limits for the child's behavior. The schoolteacher whose class includes a child with cystic fibrosis is better able to provide realistic limitations on the child's physical activities, with some understanding of the basic signs and symptoms of diminished lung function in cystic fibrosis (Walker and Jacobs, 1985).

Families in different cultural and ethnic groups respond differently to illness. Certain illnesses vary greatly in their frequency from group to group. Sickle cell anemia is more common among black children, cystic fibrosis among white. Certain rare degenerative diseases of the nervous system are more common in Jewish families; thalassemia is more common among families of Mediterranean descent. Some families believe that disease and its consequences are all a matter of fate, that they can do little to prevent disease, and that it will have the same consequences regardless of how it is treated. Other families have faith that what they do may alter the course of disease or make their families less vulnerable to it. The treatment of disease must often be tailored to the cultural context of the family. A diet appropriate for a Chicano family in Texas may be inappropriate for a Japanese family in California or a Basque family in Colorado. All of these cultural and family factors influence the expression of disease, its treatment, and its outcomes. Professionals are typically educated that disease is an aberration in some body function. In reality, disease represents a variation both in body mechanisms and in a broader family and cultural context. To understand disease, why it came about, and what can be done about it, health professionals must understand the community values, beliefs, and traditions. Often lay coordinators or counselors and social workers are most knowledgeable about these areas, yet a physician, too, must understand how therapeutic recommendations fit into the cultural context of the family.

All providers must have knowledge of community agencies and how to work with them. Most important are schools, although a wide variety of other public and private agencies provide helpful care to families with special needs. Social workers have the most training in the mobilization of community agencies, but physicians and nurses should know the types of resources communities can offer to families. Effective preventive mental health services may depend on a psychologist's knowledge of community support systems for a child or family.

Advocacy for children, a common and essential part of work with families sorely pressed with the burden of illness, requires understanding of public resources as well as the ways in which public policy can be improved (Schorr, 1978). For example, all of the helping professions should understand the ways in which resources like Medicaid, the Crippled Children's Services, or the Education for All Handicapped Children Act can benefit the families with whom they are working. Where inadequacies in policy exist, advocacy through legislative activities or through the efforts of private groups and professional associations are meaningful ways in which providers can help families.

How children fare in school is, of course, the main responsibility of teachers and principals and, at times, school nurses. Yet some understanding of how schools work and how children are taught is essential to other professionals working with children with chronic illnesses. Illness and its treatments may interfere with school attendance and performance. Learning how school programs or treatments may be altered to maximize a child's intellectual attainments is important for physicians and nurses. Children who are doing well in school often also do better with their illness. Physicians and nurses working with families whose children have spina bifida can understand the special issues of schooling these children face and can work with the school to improve the learning environment. A nutritionist planning a special diet for a child with cystic fibrosis or snacks for a teenager with diabetes does so more effectively with an understanding of school routines and schedules.

There are other areas, too; the nutritional needs characteristic of children with chronic illnesses and the special aspects of sexuality for adolescents with disabilities are two examples. None of these areas are unique to children with chronic illnesses and their families. Many apply equally to other children with special needs, including those without major medical problems. Yet all of these areas influence the lives of most children with chronic illnesses, and the broad variety of issues reflects the complex needs resulting from a chronic illness. To use this information wisely and effectively, professionals must learn certain skills, described in the next section.

Skills for Care

Five skills—the ability to provide technically competent services, to communicate with families, to participate as an effective team member, to be sensitive to ethical issues, and to conceptualize problems in ecological terms—are basic to the education of professionals for work with children and families with chronic illnesses.

Each profession has its own collection of technical skills, and the educational process necessarily focuses on assuring technical competence. Physical therapists develop skills in exercises that will help children use their muscles more effectively. Nutritionists become competent in developing diets appropriate for varied conditions and family settings. Physicians seek to become experts in the physiology and biochemistry of disease and in the sciences of medical and surgical therapeutics. The skills of psychologists are focused on an understanding of human behavior and its variations and on means of changing behavior. The best educational programs offer excellent opportunities to learn these skills, which are applicable to professionals whether or not they work with children with chronic illnesses and their families. Other skills, not central to any specific discipline, are key to the capacity of professionals to work with families over time. The ability to communicate effectively with children and families and to collaborate in a meaningful way with other professionals is essential to providing care of high quality. Further necessary skills for all health providers include the capacity to conceptualize problems in terms of their family and community impact and an ability to frame the ethical questions raised by difficult decisions and by the trade-offs in care.

The ability to listen, to find time, to interview sensitively, and to provide advice effectively are central skills that are frequently neglected in the training of professionals (President's Commission for the Study of Ethical Problems in Medicine and Biomedical and

Behavioral Research, 1982). This neglect is reflected in parents' statements about the insensitivity of physicians and other health professionals they encounter (Carlton, 1978). Although at times difficult, communication with families and children provides the foundation from which families can increasingly take responsibility for their own needs. For children to participate in their own care, they must understand basic elements of their disease, the options available for treatment, and the ways in which they can make their condition better or worse. Pantell and others (1982), however, have documented that physicians only rarely talk directly to children, and Perrin and Perrin (1983) report that nurses and pediatricians often mistake the developmental age at which children can understand certain concepts about illness.

Broadly, professionals must refine their abilities to work with families. Nursing educators call for teaching how to "appraise behavior objectively without reacting personally" (Barnes, 1985). Social work educators encourge students to accompany families as they interact with various public agencies (Rudolph, Andrews, Ratcliff, and Downes, 1985). Educators of physicians increasingly call for direct attention to teaching interviewing and providing supervision to people in training to strengthen interviewing skills (Green and Hoekelman, 1982).

Teamwork is essential to the care of children with chronic illnesses, but the mode of practice in the United States is unidisciplinary. Trainees from different professions rarely work together, leaving rudiments of teamwork and collaboration to be learned after the completion of formal education. An important task for each profession is attention to interdisciplinary training. Collaboration will be learned better if considered an integral part of the educational process.

How does a nutritionist participate actively in dietary counseling as a member of an interdisciplinary team? How can mental health services, especially preventive ones, be integrated with the other services provided to families? How can nurses, physical therapists, parents, and physicians collaborate to work out a home-care program for a child with a complex chronic illness? A number of excellent interdisciplinary programs have developed in certain parts of the country, mainly to provide services to children with specific groups of diseases, such as cystic fibrosis or hemophilia or juvenile arthritis. University affiliated facilities for children with developmental disabilities are other excellent training and service models of interdisciplinary care (Daeschner and Cerreto, 1985; Magrab, 1985). Increasingly, centers also educate new professionals in disciplines such as pediatrics, nursing, orthopedics, and psychology. Yet a large majority of professionals have little opportunity to be educated in fundamentals of teamwork and typically lack basic understanding of the skills brought by other professionals to the care of children and families (Mauksch, 1981; National Joint Practice Commission, 1981). How can respect for each other's skills be encouraged? How do teams work through issues of allocating responsibility? How do teams handle conflict? How are decisions made by teams, and how do families participate in the decision making? These are all issues young professionals must be taught to confront.

The ethical aspects of the relationship between providers and families are covered in greater detail in Chapter Ten. Suffice it to say here that professionals face many daily ethical decisions involving the children with whom they work. Skill in identifying the ethical nature of decisions and in learning to deal with decisions in a responsible and professional manner must be taught to nurses, physicians, teachers, and other professionals. Efforts to expand the teaching of ethics in medical, nursing, and other curricula have begun to improve the development of these skills. Both a sensitivity to the definition of ethical issues and an ability to understand the processes of decision making are needed skills (President's Commission for the Study of Ethical Problems in Medicine and Biomedical and Behavioral Research, 1982).

As a fifth skill, professionals need the capacity to conceptualize problems in ecological terms. Some of this skill comes from understanding in the areas of knowledge discussed previously, especially the impact of chronic illness on child and family. However, professionals must be experienced in defining problems and clinical issues in terms of the dynamic system in which children and families live. When helping the patient or family choose between a wheelchair and a walker, a sense of the living environment and the capacity of the family will aid in decision making.

Compliance with medical therapy is more likely when environmental barriers to taking medicine are diminished. This educational process requires structured and supervised learning experiences in which students are challenged to conceptualize the ecology of patients and illnesses.

How are professionals educated to work with families with children with chronic illnesses? An exhaustive description of the training of any professional group is beyond the scope of this chapter although more detailed descriptions are found in the chapters in Hobbs and Perrin (1985). The focus here is mainly on the ways in which training programs do and do not now meet the needs of families whose children are chronically ill and on a review of opportunities facing educators of professionals.

The Education of Professionals

Professional education in most instances allows clear attention to content materials in specific fields and assures that program graduates are trained in the skills defined as part of their profession. Yet all professionals appear to face similar barriers to adequate education about childhood chronic illness: lack of experience on a longitudinal or continuing basis with families, inadequate role models, insufficient definition and pursuit of a broad research agenda affecting childhood chronic illness, and a focus on narrow definitions of outcome.

Entry to the varied professions that work with children with chronic illnesses and their families typically comes at the college or graduate level. As people advance through these levels, they become increasingly specialized. Nurses, social workers, and nutritionists may get their main education at the undergraduate level and then either practice their profession or continue on for further, more specialized training. A nurse might seek further training as a cardiovascular specialist or in psychiatric nursing (Vaughn, 1980). Physicians and psychologists typically begin their professional activities after receiving degrees at the graduate level, although they may have undergraduate degrees in areas related to their long-term careers, such as psychology or biochemistry.

Education of professionals is always progressive, with continued differentiation and continuous specialization. Professionals begin with general principles and then move to more specific understanding. Physicians, as an example, begin with biological principles, move to pathology, and then to the understanding of diseases of specific organ systems. In the clinical interaction with patients and families, professionals function best with a balanced perspective on general and specific principles, although at times the specialization overshadows attention to broader questions.

Initial Education of Professionals. The training of physicians emphasizes the understanding of diseases—their identification, causation, and treatment. Clear comprehension of biological and physiological concepts is important to the understanding of diseases. Generally, students accepted to medical school are well grounded in biological and physical sciences, less so in behavioral and social sciences. During the first two years of medical school, students learn the processes by which disease may occur (such as infections or abnormal metabolism), with an early introduction to pathology or disease as the prime focus. Teaching comes almost entirely from faculty physicians or from scientists with backgrounds in fields such as biochemistry or physiology. Social and behavioral scientists rarely teach these students. The second half of medical school training takes place in hospitals and clinics. Students spend periods of a month or six weeks working with different specialists, such as obstetricians, kidney disease specialists, psychiatrists, cardiologists, or cancer experts. Although most medical care occurs outside of hospitals, most medical school training takes place in hospitals (Cluff, 1982; Green and Hoekelman, 1982).

With an educational emphasis on the identification, diagnosis, and treatment of disease, physicians focus on curing diseases. Yet, by definition, patients with chronic diseases are not cured, and their continuing problems frustrate physicians trained to expect that their treatments will effect a cure. Small wonder then that the care of chronic disease in adults has only recently attracted bright young physicians seeking careers in geriatrics. Specialties such as cardiology, which identify and treat diseases of specific organ systems, are more attractive than the long-term problems of older people, who may have maladies of a number of different organ systems all at once.

During their time on hospital wards, students encounter many patients with chronic diseases, but they miss the opportunity to observe the patient or the disease over a long time. A student may meet a patient with diabetes, learn about the exacerbation that brought the patient to the hospital this time, and then move to another hospital ward in a week or so. On the ward, teamwork is usually limited to collaboration among medical specialists. The surgeon may ask a cardiologist to evaluate the cardiovascular status of a patient. A very ill patient suffering from a combination of heart, lung, and kidney problems is likely to have specialists in all these fields working together. Students come to understand and to value the ways in which specialists work through complex diagnostic problems, and they learn how treatment in one organ system can affect the response of the body or disease in another. Teamwork with professionals from other disciplines, however, is rarely modeled on hospital wards. Students learn that the reward system emphasizes procedures, that the performance of a biopsy or a surgical procedure or the placement of a tube are all rewarded more (or reimbursed better) than less well-defined although equally time-consuming aspects of total care, such as teaching the patient about diabetes, working with the family so they can better care for a person with diabetes at home, or arranging access to community resources (Blendon, 1982).

Uncertainty and unpredictability are among the most difficult problems faced by families that have a child with chronic illness. A youngster with diabetes writes of medical uncertainty:

Doctors have argued that good control is the key in handling diabetes. Others say that control really doesn't make a difference. Some researchers have even gone so far as to say that insulin is the cause of diabetic complications. No one really knows the answers.

I do know that I feel better when my sugar is under control. That, for me, is reason enough for control. The struggle to survive is difficult; a good day is a blessing.

I have to live with unanswered questions. While doctors argue at medical conclaves, my own view is very limited. Do I take insulin, and perhaps go blind? Or do I stop the injections, and die? Some choice. Research is valuable when results are obtained. Suspicions complicate my life [Covelli, 1979, p. 75].

Uncertainty and unpredictability are difficult for physicians to acknowledge (Fox, 1974, 1980; Coser, 1979). Medical students want precise answers; they find it hard to believe that different patients with the same disease may respond differently to the same treatment. They are most comfortable with knowing that a certain infection is treated with a given dose of an antibiotic. A medical student writes of the science of therapeutics:

When Charles was over for dinner last week, I remarked at the time that I was coming to the conclusion that medicine was certainly no precise science, but rather, it is simply a matter of probabilities. Even these drugs today, for example, were noted as to their wide range of action. One dose will be too small to elicit a response in one individual; the same dose will be sufficient to get just the right response in another; and in yet another individual, the same dose will produce hypersensitive toxic results. So, there is nothing exact in this, I guess. It's a matter of conjuring the possibilities and probabilities and then drawing conclusions as to the most likely response and the proper thing to do. And Charles last week agreed that a doctor is just an artist who has learned to derive these probabilities and then prescribe a treatment (quoted in Fox, 1979, p. 24).

Whether a child with leukemia will improve with a certain drug regimen or whether an older person's heart will respond to prescribed stimulants is fraught with uncertainty, and for many medical students, the uncertainty creates anxiety.

At the entry level to nursing, there are three main training programs: associate degree programs (usually based at community colleges and lasting two years), diploma programs (usually in hospital schools of nursing and lasting about three years), and baccalaureate programs (based in colleges of nursing and lasting four years) (Barnes, 1985). Programs vary in content as well as length. In recent years, rather than offering courses in specific nursing specialty areas, nursing training has emphasized the development of integrated curricula based on broad concepts of nursing. Nursing educators note that the integrated curricula have led to decreased attention in specialized areas, such as maternal and child health, public health nursing, and nursing care of children. Little specialization is available during the early phase of nursing training, and exposure to the problems of children, especially those with chronic illness, is sparse in entry level training programs. Nurses who take hospital positions after graduation typically require a lengthy orientation followed by active supervision from more senior nurses (almost in the form of an apprenticeship). The special preparation for the nursing care of children has become a hospital task rather than the responsibility of entry level training programs.

Pediatric psychology, the discipline of psychologists working in child health settings, has developed partly because pediatricians look to psychologists for information about the development and behavior of the families with whom they work (Jay and Wright, 1985; Drotar and Bush, 1985). With larger numbers of chronically ill children surviving, the issues of how children and families cope are gaining more attention from the pediatric community. In general, pediatric psychology differs from child psychology by the settings in which these professionals work. Child psychologists frequently participate in psychiatric settings or in community practice settings, where they provide psychotherapy on a client-by-client basis. Pediatric psychologists work in child health settings, especially in large children's hospitals or outpatient clinics.

The special training of pediatric psychologists comes primarily at the postdoctoral level; no current doctoral level programs train pediatric psychologists. Jay and Wright (1985) list content and skills important in the education of pediatric psychologists; these include understanding the impact of chronic illness, adjustment to illness and its care, and the interaction of concepts from biological, social, and psychological realms. Further, students must become expert in issues of child development, in psychopathology, in assessment, in a variety of psychological interventions, and in consultation. Jay and Wright especially note the need for more neuropsychology training for pediatric psychologists and stress the importance of learning the consultation role.

Differentiation into Child Health Specialists. Physicians who choose to be pediatricians enter a period of training of three or more years following medical school. This training, too, is predominantly in hospitals, although increasingly pediatricians are exposed to other places in which children spend time: daycare programs, schools, and community agencies for children with developmental disabilities (Green and Hoekelman, 1982). Financial support for the postgraduate education of pediatricians comes mainly from the hospitals in which they work, where it is part of the negotiated hospital day rate charged to patients or to insurors. With support mainly from in-hospital services, there is little incentive to allocate the time of pediatricians in training to services outside hospitals.

At this level of education, experience in treating children with chronic illnesses can be extensive although it is markedly skewed to the acute problems that bring the child to the hospital rather than to the long-term care of the child at home. Interns and residents invest great effort and energy in intensive care nurseries that typically take up a fifth or more of the three years of pediatric training. Trainees work under great pressure to treat the problems of very small and often premature infants. The pediatrician in training rarely learns what happens to the children who survive and are discharged. Hospital ward responsibilities change every month or so, and because many children stay in intensive care nurseries for several weeks, the pediatrician in training lacks even the opportunity to follow the entire course of hospitalization. Yet for the physician to practice quality medicine in the future, should he know the progress of the child over the months and years following the initial contact? Should training address how the family adjusts to a child who may have developmental problems? Has the adjustment been comfortable, or has the family been unable to allow the child to grow effectively, erecting unnecessary barriers around the child whom they consider vulnerable to new health problems unless protected?

Pediatricians are taught well the intricacies of fluid management and insulin treatment for children with diabetes who become sick enough to be in the hospital. They learn quickly the exact dosage of insulin for different levels of blood sugar, the ways to calculate the amount of fluids, and the types of minerals that should be given to the child. They are less well trained to understand what to do on Saturday morning about the insulin for a child with an upset stomach or what to do with the teenager whose exercise pattern will change because basketball season is beginning. When a child who has been told to take midafternoon snacks to improve sugar metabolism is in a school that has rules against eating outside of lunch hour and the lunchroom, the pediatrician in training rarely learns whom to call or how schools can adjust to allow the child to have snacks as needed. The educational emphasis, even in the context of many pediatric patients with chronic illnesses, is on acute care and the acute crisis.

At the master's degree level, nursing training permits specialization in areas such as the care of children (Barnes, 1985). Several opportunities exist including training as nurse specialists in general pediatric care and as specialists in the nursing care of children who have specific health conditions, such as malignancies or kidney disease. Few programs offer training for nurses who wish to become proficient in the general problems of chronically ill children and their families. And experience with children and families over time are limited. Most nurses need on-the-job training to improve their clinical skills in working with problems of chronicity (Barnes, 1985; Hymovich, 1985).

Professionals in each discipline solve problems in sophisticated ways. Typically, they define a problem in the child or family, analyze it, synthesize the available data, and define their plans in a way that reflects the emphases of their discipline. The narrow focus of professions often leads to inflexibility in the definition of problems and early foreclosure in information gathering. A child with arthritis may be viewed by a rheumatologist as a problem in the control of inflammatory processes, by an orthopedist as an issue in maintaining flexible joints, by the physical therapist as a challenge in the management of splints and the teaching of effective exercises, by the social worker as a member of a family with limited resources, and by the school as a child whose wheelchair creates physical barriers. The intense concentration of each discipline in its area of expertise typically provides important solutions to problems although the complexity of the family speaks to the need for teamwork in effective problem solving.

In recent years, greater awareness of the problems of education has led to major improvements. Most pediatric training programs now have what are called continuity programs or clinics (Task Force on Pediatric Education, 1978; Daeschner and Cerreto, 1985). Here, for about half a day once a week, a pediatric trainee follows a group of patients, many with chronic illnesses, seeing them consistently over the two or three years of residency training. These settings offer the opportunity to learn about the growth and crises of a child with cystic fibrosis or how families accommodate to the burdens of long-term diseases. In some programs, behavioral scientists help pediatricians understand more about child development and family interactions and their impact on chronic illness. Nurse practitioners may teach pediatricians in continuity programs, and nurses pursuing master's degrees may train in these programs as well. Trainees can learn how to improve their interviewing skills, to develop a capacity in counseling, and to interact with community agencies in advocating for their patients. Most continuity programs, though, are chronically underfunded, making little faculty time available for teaching and supervision and providing little encouragement for the development of multidisciplinary professional efforts.

Through continuity experiences, and from exposure to pediatricians practicing in the community as well, trainees learn that the incentives for pediatricians are badly skewed, discouraging the kinds of complex caring that families with chronically ill children need. Students learn that general pediatricians see forty or more patients quickly through the working day and are often exhausted at the day's end. There is little time for lengthy discussion with patients who have complex problems. Trainees learn that general pediatricians often avoid caring for children with chronic illnesses (who require much more time than do able-bodied children) and that no one reimburses pediatricians for extra time and effort.

Specialist teachers are rewarded more for procedure-oriented activities than for teaching the process of explaining disease to a family, answering their questions, helping them understand long-term implications, or arranging family support services. Certainly, exceptions to this experience exist in every hospital and institution. Yet those in training learn that these exceptions, both general pediatricians providing excellent care to children with chronic illnesses and specialists taking the time to explain and to involve families, face great disincentives. Busy physicians are encouraged to spend their time on other tasks, and they generally do so (Daeschner and Cerreto, 1985).

A recent conference on the education of pediatricians to care for children with chronic illnesses proposed five main areas of responsibility for pediatricians: coordination of care, education, advocacy, provision of continuous care, and counseling (Stein, Jessop, and Ireys, 1984). Yet these are all activities that are typically unreimbursed. It is difficult to imagine that pediatricians in training will be encouraged to take on these tasks unless the ways of paying for them are improved.

Other efforts have helped improve the education of professionals. Some training centers have effective interdisciplinary teams that focus on the special problems of children with developmental disabilities in university affiliated facilities. Here students observe models of effective multidisciplinary efforts on behalf of families: pediatricians collaborating with psychologists, nurses, social workers, and other professionals including nutritionists, speech and language therapists, and physical therapists. Care-by-parent units in hospitals allow parents, with the help of nursing staff, to take partial responsibility for the nursing care of their own ill child. Yet the experience of students with these efforts is brief (lasting only a month or six weeks) and offers little sense of how effective teamwork is over time or how families improve as a result of multidisciplinary activities.

Similar concerns affect the teachers of social workers. Although the social work role is of great importance, few programs train social workers specifically to work with children with chronic illnesses and their families (Rudolph, Andrews, Ratcliff, and Downes, 1985). Any review of families with chronically ill children reveals needs varying from specialized medical care (and its explanation), to respite care for parents, to financial aid for health services. Learning to find and coordinate these complex services over time are among the tasks facing social workers, yet social work training allows little longitudinal experience with families.

Baird and Ashcroft (1985) note the scarcity of training for schoolteachers around the issues of children with chronic illness in school. Almost no courses related to the problems of chronic illness in schools are offered at the undergraduate level, and the picture is but a little better at the graduate level. The University of Arkansas offers a course on medical problems in child development, an exception to the general absence of this topic from the education of teachers. A survey of state education commissioners (Baird, Ashcroft, and Dy, 1984) also emphasizes the lack of inservice training for teachers.

Walker and Jacobs (1985) stress the social and emotional benefits of mainstreaming children with disabilities, especially those with chronic illnesses. To support mainstreaming, teachers must be able to explore their feelings about children who are ill, some terminally. Several curricula are now available, such as the Understanding Handicaps Program in the Newton, Massachusetts, schools. These efforts provide education both to teachers (to improve their skills in meeting the needs of children with chronic illness in the classrooms) and to other children, focusing on the impact of disability on the child and exploring a realistic understanding of handicaps.

Educators, too, need interdisciplinary training. Baird and Ashcroft suggest that there be personnel within the schools who can find information needed because of the presence of a child with a specific condition. They recommend a consultant, much like the professional education consultant, perhaps a physician or a nurse practitioner, who can provide consultation as needed about specific illnesses. Because each individual condition is relatively rare, training about specific conditions is appropriate only when teachers come in contact with that condition. Little is gained from trying to prepare all teachers to know about most childhood chronic illnesses. Baird and Ashcroft also observe that most educational systems have resource libraries that could incorporate a section on childhood chronic illness and offer teachers easy access to information as the need arises.

Further Specialization and Faculty Development. After three years of general pediatric training, most pediatricians enter practice, although some decide to specialize further—in pediatric heart diseases, for example, or childhood kidney diseases. Two or more years of additional training allow for the intensive study of patients with conditions that usually affect one organ system. Sizable efforts in research during the two fellowship years are usually essential to start an academic career. Until recently, all pediatricians who wished to pursue ongoing clinical care of children with specialty needs sought positions in academic health centers. During the past few years, pediatric specialists have also found positions in community settings, often in larger group practices.

Specialty training (fellowship) finally allows a pediatrician to have experience with children with chronic diseases and their families over an extended period of time. The care of a child diagnosed with leukemia may be initiated by the fellow under the supervision of a faculty person specializing in childhood malignancies. The fellow then takes an active role in the care of similar children over time and becomes an expert in the variations of physiological response to illness and treatment. Occasionally, fellows receive training in the family, social, and developmental aspects of illnesses, but most of their time is spent on the study of disease and its variations and treatments. To complete a project within a few years, fellows must focus their research efforts on highly specific questions. A fellow might, for example, study the site of action of a drug—whether it works on the outer edge of a cell membrane or why it works on only some cells and not others. Although they may be highly motivated to help families cope with what may be extremely serious, complex, and unfamiliar diseases, fellows find little support of their endeavors in counseling, patient education, or long-term planning for patients. The emotional drain of caring for these patients and the overwhelming numbers of patients in most settings leave fellows little time for coping with their own feelings or for learning ways of helping families cope with theirs.

Nurses play an essential role in many specialty centers for children with cancers, heart diseases, cystic fibrosis, and hemophilia. A few programs help nurses pursue careers as nurse specialists working with children with diseases of certain organ systems. The rule, though, is for most specialized and longitudinal training for nurses to take place on the job.

Jay and Wright (1985) note the need for more trained clinical child psychologists to work in pediatric settings. Although there has been an increase in numbers trained, the demand far outstrips the supply. Psychologists, too, need greater opportunities for interdisciplinary training (pediatricians in training rarely have the chance to collaborate with psychologists in training) and for longitudinal experiences with families with chronically ill children. Of great importance is the need to educate psychologists in those settings where children receive health care.

The settings in which education occurs affect the quality of the experience. For some professions, such as law or engineering, the educational mission is central to the efforts of the training institution. For others (and commonly the health professions), educational missions must compete with other agendas. In hospitals, where nursing and medical students train, patient care responsibilities and research interests may interfere with educational activities.

Faculties of pediatric departments are made up mainly of people trained as specialists. Few departments of pediatrics or training programs in psychology or nursing have faculty who have focused on the broad, generic problems faced by families with children with chronic illnesses. No fellowship programs train pediatricians in chronic disease in general. Faculty role models are specialists expert in teaching about their diseases. Role models who can teach about how families cope and adjust, what their broad needs are, how to meet these needs more effectively, and how to support families are absent. If role models who educate professionals lack understanding of the broader issues facing families with chronically ill children, students are unlikely to assume a broad approach to defining and solving the problems of children.

Some health professionals seek training for leadership positions with maternal and child health programs, usually in governmental agencies. Most leadership education is in schools of public health, where exposure to clinical problems of children and families is limited. Although exceptions exist, schools of public health are typically far removed from the sites where professionals are trained for practice and where most children with chronic illnesses receive care. Yet professionals educated in maternal and child health programs may have great sensitivity to the general problems of families and experience in finding needed resources. If these varied professionals were trained more closely together, those in public health training could serve as important role models for those in clinical education programs.

Opportunities in Education. What, then, might be done? Several options and opportunities could benefit families greatly. First, greater attention to social and behavioral sciences at all levels in the training of health professionals will benefit children with chronic illnesses as well as the many other families with whom clinicians have contact. Areas that merit particular attention include clinical epidemiology, patterns of human adaptation, ethical decision making in long-term care, and principles of patient management, as distinguished from disease cure. There is greater likelihood of interdisciplinary activities if people of different disciplines are trained together and if people skilled in behavioral and social sciences are active in the training of physicians and nurses. Such training should help physicians, as an example, extend their understanding beyond the biological and physiological aspects of illness to the influences of genetic, familial, environmental, and social factors on disease prevention, cause, and outcome.

At more advanced educational levels, opportunity for professionals in training to provide continuing care to children with chronic illness over a period of months and years should be fostered and expanded. Trainee participation on interdisciplinary teams and the greater presence of social and behavioral scientists within training settings will be helpful. Promising team models have developed within child health training programs such as the care-by-parent units and the Pediatric Home Care Program (Chapter Five). Institutions and community organizations have begun to develop other forms of home-based care for children with chronic illnesses, and opportunities for health professionals in training to work in these model programs could be expanded. There is great need for the development of new models and for development of sites of excellence for the family- and community-based care of children with chronic illnesses. Trainees should participate actively in these new models.

At the level of faculty development, training for research careers, both in disease-specific areas and in chronic illness in general, remains a high priority. There is increasing need for researchers who are well grounded in quantitative skills and methodological principles and who have strong backgrounds in theory applicable to the varied problems of sick children. Yet opportunities now for research training in chronic illnesses of childhood are limited to specialty fellowships for pediatricians who intend to focus on specific disease groups. These important training programs have faced a decrease in funding in the past few years, a situation that needs redress along with the development of opportunities for other types of professionals to become expert in research in the chronic illnesses of childhood. Barnes (1985) notes especially the need, well identified in certain institutions, to expand nursing research and to broaden the group of nurses with doctoral preparation. She notes that important questions in nursing research are likely to be answered only with greater investment in people trained to carry out the research.

Furthermore, a few exemplary training programs in childhood chronic illness should be developed. These should be interdisciplinary in faculty and in trainees and should have the goals of producing both new researchers in the broad area of childhood chronic illness and other graduates to provide leadership for public programs for children with handicaps. The graduates of these programs should become role models within training programs and bring attention to the broad principles and problems that underlie this book.

Training Lay Workers

Independent of efforts to train professionals for new responsibilities in the care of chronically ill children, several projects have trained lay persons to assist these children and their families (Preventive Intervention Research Center, 1985; Pless and Satterwhite, 1972). The arguments supporting these efforts are strong Pless and Satterwhite (1975, pp. 288-290) note them in this way:

In spite of the heavy emphasis that has been placed on the upgrading and retraining of health professionals, many nontechnical health needs can be met adequately by relying chiefly on the personality attributes of the workers. Such qualities are as plentiful among nonprofessionals—lay persons—as they are among physicians, nurses, and social workers. The potential manpower resource that exists outside the professional world, therefore, must be examined carefully. . . . The kinds of help needed vary greatly: in one case it is simply a matter of providing a mother with a compassionate listener; in another it is the more mundane challenge of getting a wheelchair ramp built. There are times when advice is needed, others when the family requires more detailed explanations of the child's condition, and still others when the child himself needs counseling to help him identify and develop his special strengths and abilities. Few of these are tasks that the busy doctor can do, or would be inclined to undertake even if he had the time. Nevertheless, they are an integral part of what comprehensive health care must include, and can be as important in the life of the child and his family as in the medical treatment itself.

Problems like those mentioned exist in abundance, but because they are not central to medical care they are rarely dealt with by physicians. When help is provided, it is usually given by social workers who may be attached to specialty clinics or, if the problem is severe, by referral to psychologists and psychiatrists. But good health care must respond to problems as early as possible, and to meet this requirement, assistance must be available to primary care physicians. With few exceptions, neither general practitioners, family doctors, nor pediatricians have social workers or public health nurses available who can deal with these aspects of care in the home. These considerations led to the development of a program designed to provide assistance for such problems by nonprofessional women who receive a minimum of training and guidance.

Both projects cited here aimed to identify women who were judged through interviews to have certain characteristics, including warmth, a capacity to express empathy and support, common sense, emotional stability, friendliness, appropriate assertiveness, and general wisdom in dealing with agencies and systems. The initial training programs were generally modest in length and size: eighteen hours for about thirty women in one program, twenty hours for about twenty-five women in the other. Follow-up or refresher sessions at regular intervals provided further education. In large measure, the training focused on practical matters.

This training has been shown to be successful in preparing women for their roles (Pless and Satterwhite, 1972, 1975). But more careful study is needed. What elements of training are most effective? What curricula work best? How many individuals are available to fill these roles? How should the programs be supported? Could there be fruitful relationships between these training programs and those for professionals? Do the programs have beneficial effects?

256 Chronically Ill Children and Their Families

An attractive feature of lay workers is their indigenous quality. Those selected can come from the communities in which chronically ill children and their families live and thus may be aware of community myths and traditions, resources and limitations. They may be able to work with families in ways that professionals find difficult or impossible.

To this point, the training of lay workers to assist children with chronic illness has been meager. A recent program of the National Council on the Aging trains older volunteers to work with children who have long-term disabilities. Further experimentation with lay workers may lead to more effective services for families.

Summary

Three basic issues arise from consideration of the education of health professionals to work with families of chronically ill children. First, most training experiences are episodic, yet the needs of children and their families, especially with chronic conditions, are ongoing. Greater opportunity for allowing trainees to work with people over time is sorely needed. Second, interdisciplinary efforts merit vigorous expansion. Effective teamwork in real-world clinical settings is more likely if it begins early in training and if the concept of the interreliance of professionals with different backgrounds is taught early in the educational process. Third, there is great need for research in all of these fields and for people trained to carry out that research. In each discipline, important questions arise that merit careful investigation to determine the best social work interventions, to examine the process by which nursing supports the health care activities of families, or to clarify the ways in which physicians can affect the behavioral consequences of chronic illness in childhood. Yet, few people are trained to study these questions. Preparation for research careers is a high priority.

Recent progress has been made and indicates the directions that should characterize professional education built on interdisciplinary efforts, opportunity for long-term care by trainees, and an expanding research framework to support better care.

∞∞∞ 9 ∞∞∞

Directions for Research:
Areas of Promise
and Guiding Principles

A firm commitment to research has been a cornerstone of progress in recent years, and this has lead to greatly improved treatment and survival for children afflicted with chronic illnesses. In this chapter, we provide examples to illustrate important research advances. Areas of promise are described and underlying characteristics of recent research efforts are explored: What research inquiries may be most effective in improving the lives of families with chronically ill children? What efforts must be made to strengthen the ways of supporting research in this country? Recommendations to guide future research complete the chapter.

Recent History of Research in Childhood Chronic Illness

The dramatic improvements in the health care of many childhood chronic illnesses have, in large part, come from sizable public and private support of basic research. Most research takes place in universities or special research institutes and is funded largely by the federal government (through the National Institutes of Health) or by the private disease-oriented voluntary associations (such as the Cystic Fibrosis or Arthritis Foundations). A few

257

examples will serve to highlight recent advances achieved by research.

Children with asthma benefit from a wide array of new medications that are more effective than earlier ones and cause fewer side effects (Leffert, 1985; Galant, 1983; Becker, Nelson, and Simons, 1983). In past years, many children with severe asthma took daily steroid medications, which carry the risks of interfering with normal growth or diminishing defenses against infection. New and improved treatments have freed most children from regular steroid treatment. Severely affected children who still need daily steroids receive them by inhalation, a route that appears to carry little risk of limiting growth or response to infection (Shapiro, 1983). Increasingly, children are learning ways to manage their own asthma and to diminish the likelihood of attacks (Fireman and others, 1981; Lewis and others, 1984).

Interinstitutional studies of childhood cancers have reversed the prospects for many children with leukemia and other malignancies that were uniformly fatal in earlier years. Less than two decades ago, the most common form of childhood leukemia would have been almost 100 percent fatal; now, more than 50 percent of children who develop this form of leukemia survive without further evidence of the disease (Pendergrass, Chard, and Hartmann, 1985; Selvin and others, 1983). Advances are the result of improved drugs and better understanding of their timing and method of administration. In addition, improvements in supportive medical therapy—especially the use of antibiotics to fight infections and new blood products to manage acute bleeding problems—have aided survival. Bone marrow transplantation, until recently an experimental procedure available in very few settings, is now an accepted and effective therapy for several forms of leukemia (Santos, 1982). Kisker and colleagues (1980) have demonstrated that new methods of organizing health services for children with leukemia can improve both quality of care and satisfaction of families with service received, while also diminishing the total cost of care. Research from genetic, epidemiological, psychosocial, and virological areas is helping to elucidate risk factors for the development of leukemia and to determine the mechanisms by which disease develops (Miller, 1980).

For children with juvenile-onset diabetes mellitus, basic research has increased understanding of the development of long-term complications, especially the kidney disease and blindness that commonly afflict people who have had the disease for many years (Drash and Berlin, 1985). Although they now live for many years after diagnosis, adults with diabetes are at high risk of developing complications related to their high blood sugar levels. The insulin pump and other biofeedback mechanisms offer the hope that children with diabetes can attain normal levels of blood sugar while reducing the likelihood of long-term complications (Tamborlane and others, 1981; Tamborlane and Sherwin, 1983). For the future, transplants of pancreatic elements (islet cells) carry the potential to reverse the effects of diabetes completely (Sutherland and others, 1984).

The development of effective blood-clotting replacement factors has dramatically improved the lives of children with hemophilia. Currently available replacement factors carry risks of infection, especially hepatitis and AIDS. Through recombinant DNA techniques, highly purified, low-risk materials should soon be available (Abildgaard, 1984).

Surgical techniques have changed the outlook for children with congenital heart diseases (Fyler, 1985; Bove and others, 1983). Some heart defects slow the growth and development of children, yet until recently, most surgical procedures could be performed only when the child had gained sufficient size. Technical improvements now allow the repair of many conditions in infancy. Furthermore, the early identification and confirmation of many specific heart defects are now possible through special x-ray and ultrasound techniques that avoid the more dangerous procedure of cardiac catheterization (Nadas, 1984).

Much progress has been made in understanding the developmental and family impact of childhood chronic illness. Two decades ago, it was thought that each disease was associated with a specific personality type. It is now clear that no such disease-specific personalities exist (Pless and Pinkerton, 1975). Rather, the development of psychosocial maladjustment and the crucial role of the family in supporting the effective growth and adjustment of the child have become better understood. Recent work provides evidence that, with respect to the impact of illness on the family, the psychological adjustment of the child, and the financial and service demands created by chronic illness, there is great similarity among children with varied chronic illnesses (Stein and Jessop, 1982a, 1982b). The fact that greater variation in these factors is found within specific disease categories than between diseases documents the notion that chronic illness, regardless of the type, has significant general impacts on child and family functioning.

Similar examples of research advances affecting children with chronic illnesses and their families abound in such areas as chronic kidney diseases, the prevention of birth defects, and the treatment of cystic fibrosis. Starfield and colleagues (1984) have clarified the chronic pattern of certain types of illnesses and their impact on the utilization of health services. During the past few years, research into ethics, much of it with a focus on consent and decision making, has clarified aspects of parental responsibility and the limits of professional authority. Certain areas of research are especially promising, and we discuss them before outlining key characteristics of current research efforts and developing recommendations for future research in childhood chronic illness.

Areas of Promise

Although prediction of areas in which research is likely to be beneficial during the next several years is fraught with risks, some opportunities are especially promising. Ground-breaking research developments often appear in unexpected areas and result from research programs that are basic rather than focused on specific applications. We present the following areas as an approximation of the reality of the next decade.

Six overlapping areas of research can be defined for the chronic illnesses of childhood: basic biomedical research into disease mechanisms, clinical research, epidemiological research, psychological and developmental research, health services research, and research into medical ethics. The boundaries between these areas are always indistinct; for example, studies of a new therapy may require elements from basic research in physiology and pharmacology, clinical research into the application of therapeutics, and epidemiological research to help define populations at risk for developing a disease.

Biomedical Research. Research into mechanisms of disease is perhaps most basic. If understanding of underlying mechanisms leads to the prevention or cure of chronic illnesses of childhood, there will be little need for research in other areas. Yet, the vast number of childhood chronic illnesses, and their physiological variety, make unlikely the eradication of all childhood chronic illnesses in the near future. What, then, are the shorter-term prospects?

An explosion in the understanding of basic genetic principles and their application to the diagnosis and management of disease seems imminent. The technology may soon be developed to replace defective genes, which will free an affected individual from further disease (Nyhan, 1983). Applications of new understanding of genetic control (based on recombinant DNA techniques and on sequencing methods) help determine the pattern of gene segments in both diseased and healthy states. As a result, prenatal diagnosis of many conditions has become available during the last few years and is likely to become available for more conditions as a result of techniques that allow distinction between the DNA of healthy and diseased fetuses. Similarly, detection of the disease state long before its clinical manifestations appear may soon be possible with these techniques. Many conditions now go undetected until a family has had all of its children. Families may be able to have better information about the risk of conceiving a child with a given condition if they have had a previous affected child. For example, Huntington's chorea is a degenerative disease of the central nervous system that is typically asymptomatic until the third decade of life. Because Huntington's is an autosomal recessive disease, any person whose parent had this disease has a 25 percent risk of contracting it as well. Yet that person may live for many years without knowing if the disease will ever develop. New techniques will allow early diagnosis and (probably) prenatal identification of affected individuals.

Because of their use in producing important drugs, recombinant DNA techniques are already having impact on the treatment of chronic illnesses (Caskey and White, 1983). These medications include human growth hormone for the treatment of certain endocrine disorders and new forms of insulin that lack some of the side effects of current insulins. Here, gene fragments are manipulated in such a way that bacteria incorporate new genes for the production of these compounds. These medications are then produced by the bacteria, which can reproduce to form many more colonies and therefore make much more of the compound.

Other areas may carry less fundamental excitement than genetic engineering, but they, too, have potential for improving the lives of chronically ill children and their families. Recent progress allowing the maintenance of more normal blood sugar levels in individuals with diabetes may diminish the serious long-term consequences of this disease. When the technology has been refined, biologically based feedback mechanisms are likely to replace conventional insulin injection therapy for many people with diabetes (Tamborlane and Sherwin, 1983). In the longer run, a cure for diabetes may be found, either through gene replacement or through direct replacement of the cells necessary to produce insulin in the human pancreas.

The treatments for childhood cancers have advanced tremendously. In the search for causes of cancers, breakthroughs may also result from the study of viruses, careful studies of families who appear to be at high risk of developing cancer, and epidemiological research (Pendergrass, Chard, and Hartmann, 1985). For some cancers currently unresponsive to medical therapies, bone marrow transplantation is an effective method of replacing diseased blood-forming cells with healthy cells and apparently eradicating the disease. Much remains to be learned about bone marrow transplantation, including the specific conditions and the stages of disease for which it is most beneficial. However, this procedure has already progressed from one that was highly experimental just a few years ago to an accepted therapy for some forms of leukemia (Santos, 1982).

The growing possibility of early diagnosis of cystic fibrosis should stimulate research in mechanisms of the disease and in clarifying the basic defect (Ad Hoc Committee Task Force on Neonatal Screening, 1983; Holtzman, 1984). For spina bifida, research linking types of malnutrition with greater risk of having a child with this condition carries potential for primary prevention of the disease. Early efforts with vitamin supplementation to mothers are promising and may decrease the number of new cases of spina bifida (Windham and Edmonds, 1982; Laurence, 1982).

The coming decade is likely to bring a number of new technologies to treat the chronic conditions of childhood. Careful and timely assessment of new technology is critical to the care of these children. Federal efforts in assessment have included the establishment of the Office of Technology Assessment and the National Center for Health Care Technology. The former has paid little attention to the needs of children, and the latter was dismantled shortly after its creation. Swift determination of the risks and benefits of new technology will be very helpful. It will also be important to know the levels of care at which various technologies are appropriate. Where, for example, should sophisticated rehabilitation services be made available? Such information is essential for policy decisions and the organization of programs.

Clinical Research. Clinical research is the arena in which most developments in biomedical research are implemented. Clinical observations of the physiological, developmental, and social components of disease allow the development of new hypotheses that form the basis for additional basic research in biomedical and other realms. Here, too, questions develop around issues of the effectiveness of new therapies, their potential side effects (expected and not), and patient and family compliance with therapy.

New therapeutic concepts can be tried in the clinical area, where the interactions of medications and environmental factors can be examined. What are the types of patients for whom new treatments work? What characteristics of individuals or families interact with medications or diet or exercise to improve health status? Insights from clinical care and from the careful observation of groups of patients and families may guide further research into basic mechanisms of disease. Clinical research is the final testing ground for all endeavors to improve the identification, treatment, or outcome of childhood chronic illness.

Epidemiology. Epidemiological research can address the question of whether the chronic illnesses of childhood are increasing in incidence (the development of new cases) or in prevalence (the total number of cases in the population). Gortmaker (1985) finds little evidence of changing incidence of most conditions. Markedly improved survival in most of the more common conditions means that most children with chronic illnesses currently survive at least to adulthood. He documents the increasing prevalence of childhood chronic illness over the past two decades but predicts that prevalence will remain relatively stable well into the next century. Confirmation of this hypothesis and further specifications of variations by type of disorder or by sociodemographic variables require new research. Other epidemiological areas merit attention. Social class differences in the onset or severity of illness and the mechanisms by which these factors influence disease should be specified. Population-based studies of the relationship of functional status to illness would increase understanding of the impact of illness on the child's and the family's functioning.

Work in the study of the distribution of health services is beginning to increase understanding of where children actually receive services and of the impact of these services. Which children with chronic illnesses are served in special education programs and which in regular programs? Who provides the majority of general and specialty health services to chronically ill children and their families? The Harvard Community Child Health Studies (Walker, Gortmaker and Weitzman, 1981) have pioneered in examining service patterns in several communities including Flint, Michigan; Cleveland, Ohio; and some in western Massachusetts. A study in progress at Harvard examines educational programming for handicapped children in five communities around the nation (Walker and others, 1984). This research will identify representative patterns and will clarify the relationship of the organization and distribution of services to child and family functioning. Population-based studies of the long-term outcome of childhood chronic illnesses are also needed. What happens to these children as they grow up? How do their service needs change? Do children with the most severe disease become less affected, or do patterns of severity remain relatively stable over time? By necessity, most studies are cross-sectional; that is, they examine and compare groups of children at a single point in time rather than following them over a period of months or years. Yet much understanding of child development and human behavior can come only from examining these phenomena over time.

Health Services Research. Two main areas in health services research can be identified: the organization and the financing of services. Organizational questions include studies of the comprehensiveness of services, of continuity of care, and of who should provide services, where, and to whom (Starfield, 1985; Perrin and Ireys, 1984). Although evidence to date supports comprehensive services as leading to better functional outcomes for children and families (Aledort, 1982; Levine, 1974), clarification of the actual boundaries of comprehensive services is needed. What are the potential risks of providing too many services to families? At what point does broadening services bring little additional benefit? To what extent does comprehensiveness facilitate diagnosis and treatment? Many families with children with chronic illnesses need comprehensive services. Yet, partly because there has been little development of a theory of vulnerability, it is not known which families need comprehensive services and which cope well and need little help.

Improved continuity of providers encourages compliance with prescribed regimens (Starfield and others, 1976; Breslau and Mortimer, 1981). Here, clearer understanding of the elements of continuity and their relationship to coordination of services is needed. Can continuity be based on institutions, or must it be based on individual providers? Does continuity increase the recognition and treatment of patients' problems? What personnel are best at recognizing problems, and how can the varied skills of different professionals be integrated to improve the recognition of problems and their treatment (Starfield, 1985)? Should services be provided close to home, reducing the interference of medical care in the child's usual daily activities; or should care be provided in academic centers, where the child has greater access to new technologies (McInerny, 1984)? Problems in the current organization of services have been documented well. For example, most children with diabetes mellitus lack regular care by pediatric endocrinologists (Drash and Berlin, 1985). Studies in a number of specialty clinics in academic medical centers indicate that children with chronic illnesses receive the basic elements of immunizations, health maintenance, and developmental supervision less frequently than able-bodied children (Palfrey, Levy, and Gilbert, 1980). Recent efforts to decentralize the care of children with leukemia in Iowa and to evaluate the effects of this decentralization are a commendable start (Kisker and others, 1980; Strayer, Kisker, and Fethke, 1980). How can the role of patients in their own care be maximized; what patient-provider relationships enable children and families to care for themselves?

Similar questions arise in the implementation of programs for children and families. Little is known about the ways in which communities come to understand and accept childhood chronic illness, although in recent years efforts to improve the rights and access of people with handicaps have shed some light on the response of communities. What characteristics of communities make them more amenable to supporting and developing local services? What types of communities are more or less likely to come to the aid of a chronically ill child in their midst?

Several research questions concerning costs and financing of services for chronically ill children and their families were outlined in Chapters Six and Seven. A few issues can be restated here. Children with chronic illnesses account for a sizable proportion of the total child health dollar. What are the effects of various types of payment mechanisms (fee-for-service, prepaid, managed care) on costs? Information on costs of care (both direct and indirect) examined longitudinally and across illnesses is sadly lacking, although it is essential for the development of programs and policies. Who are the main payors, and what are effective ways to limit their costs while maintaining quality? How can the continued effects of poverty and ill health be diminished? What are the effects of regionalized systems of managed care on costs, outcomes, or satisfaction? In several European countries, financial payments are made to families who have the added economic burden of a child with a chronic illness. With the exception of the Supplemental Security Income program, no similar support exists in the United States. Chronically ill children in Europe rarely meet financial barriers to access to health services. The effects of financial payments to families and of free access to health services on health status could be understood through comparison of the American and European experiences.

What are the direct and indirect incentives to substitute low-cost, outpatient services for high-cost, inpatient services? Home care provides one example. Research must define the boundaries of home care—both who may provide it and what services may be provided. Will provision of a new service, such as home care, increase demand for it beyond present estimates of need? Will increased financial coverage of home care empty hospital beds that will then be filled with more children, thereby increasing the total cost of services? How much does a change in benefits increase the demand for services not now covered?

Psychology and Development. Several lines of psychological and developmental research are especially promising (Pless and Zvagulis, 1981). Most studies support the conclusion that chronic illness in childhood carries special risks of psychological maladjustment. The extent of the risk is unclear, and the mechanisms by which risk is induced have been the subject of many hypotheses but relatively little careful research. Prevention of unwanted psychological and developmental consequences of childhood chronic illness is a high priority. Exploration of theories of coping and adjustment in childhood chronic illness and determination of social, family, and economic risk factors are fruitful topics for research. A better definition of vulnerability (that is, of who is really at risk of developmental or psychological problems) and the determination of elements that are protective (that is, that make the child invulnerable) will be helpful.

The relationship of stress to exacerbations of certain chronic illnesses has had limited exploration. Yet stress is often associated with attacks of asthma or with spontaneous bleeding among boys with hemophilia (Mattsson, Gross, and Hall, 1971). Research is needed to define, characterize, and measure stress. Are major life stresses (such as death or separation) most important, or are minor stresses of daily life more likely to be associated with exacerbations? What is the temporal relationship, if any, between stress and worsening of disease (Heisel, 1972)? Does stress play a role in the onset of disease? Stress management techniques, such as self-hypnosis and deep relaxation, may benefit children with certain conditions and should undergo careful, controlled trials. Self-hypnosis may also help management of pain in some chronic conditions, such as sickle cell anemia or leukemia. It, too, merits more careful investigation.

Research at the interface between psychology and biology holds promise of explaining aspects of the etiology of illness, its course, and its response to treatment (Hamburg, Elliott, and Parron, 1982). For example, the new field of psychoneuroimmunology explores the relation between psychological stress and the immune response (Solomon and Amkraut, 1981). Experiments have conditioned laboratory animals to change their immune systems, an essential part of the body's reaction to infection (Ader and Cohen, 1975). In medical students, the stress of examinations lowers the number of certain cells that protect against infection. Studies in neuroendocrinology (the interaction between psychological phenomena and the release of hormones) also merit attention. Certain hormones released during stressful situations are associated with the development of some diseases—for example, hypertension. Recent studies indicate that different types of stress cause elevations in different hormones (Dimsdale and Moss, 1980). Elucidation of these intricate relationships will help clarify the pathways by which stress causes illness. These research areas, where two or more disciplines focus on the same questions, hold exciting potential and merit much greater attention than they have had.

Further study of mechanisms of social support for families is important (Sabbeth and Leventhal, 1984). The presence of adequate support seems highly predictive of improved family coping (Borman, 1985). What can be done to aid families with inadequate support systems? A number of behavioral interventions for children and families have been proposed or are being explored. Randomized controlled trials of counseling, of group support programs, and of community support projects are needed.

Gliedman and Roth (1980) note that much of the understanding of the social and psychological development of handicapped children comes from studying how handicapped children develop differently from able-bodied children. Yet handicapped children may learn alternative developmental pathways of value in the search for variations in the ways growing children develop. Blind children, for example, learn to explore their environment through the early stimulation of hand-to-mouth coordination and the use of the mouth as the main exploratory organ (Fraiberg, 1977). There is an acute need for a developmental psychology of children with chronic illnesses. What are the different developmental consequences of conditions or handicaps present at birth as compared with those that appear at age three or ten or during adolescence? Chronic conditions that affect cognitive functioning have great impact on the development of the child (Perrin and Gerrity, 1984). What other characteristics, such as the visibility, impact on mobility, or natural course of the disease, are also important? Recent work has begun to elucidate developmental aspects of how children come to understand illness and its causation (Bibace and Walsh, 1980; Perrin and Gerrity, 1981). Does better understanding of illness improve psychological adjustment? Better understanding of how to communicate information about disease to children will come from this research. These studies also have implications for improving informed consent for children and for designing for them self-care programs based on developmental status (Leikin, 1983).

Ethics. Research in medical ethics, too, should focus on problems of informed consent. Chapter Ten describes ethical problems of both the provider-family relationship and resource allocation. When may children take a role in agreeing to participate in research efforts? What will encourage professionals to inform families truthfully? How can confidentiality be assured? Recent efforts to clarify ethical considerations in research on children outline an area of fruitful investigation. The proper boundary between the ethical pursuit of new knowledge and the preservation of the rights of children will be difficult to define, but inattention to this problem may lead to potentially dangerous and unproven therapies being applied haphazardly to children. Furthermore, research is needed in such areas as who should make decisions for children and what are the elements of optimal education of families about illness.

Characteristics of the Research Effort

Theories Underlying Research. Much research in childhood chronic illness has lacked a theoretical base. Where a theoretical model exists, it usually has a biomedical base. The advantages of a biomedical model are clear: It provides focus on the physiological aspects of illness and the response of the organism to disease. Yet emphasis on the biomedical model has influenced the choice of research questions and has limited, in important ways, understanding of the etiology, natural history, and choice of treatments for disease. Emphasis on biological and pathological causes of disease limits attention to other causes that may explain why certain people or groups of people are most likely to develop illness. Why is it that some who are genetically susceptible to particular conditions acquire the diseases and others do not? Among the more obvious phenomena related to individual susceptibility are poverty, stress, environmental hazards, and social isolation (Starfield, 1985).

Studies of the natural history of disease are hampered by narrow concepts regarding possible influences on the progress of disease. How an illness worsens or improves may be greatly affected by environmental, nutritional, or social factors (Mishler and others, 1981). Yet, treatments are frequently entirely medical or surgical, and alternative therapies are neglected. For example, the predominant mode of therapy for enuresis (prolonged bed-wetting in children) in the United States is the use of medications. In Britain, therapies that use behavioral or conditioning techniques are far more common (Starfield, 1985). Pain, a concomitant of many chronic illnesses, can be treated in several ways including use of pain medications (varying from aspirin to narcotic analgesics), surgery to decrease sensation in particularly painful areas, biofeedback mechanisms, or self-hypnosis techniques. Treatments that are medical or surgical in nature are most likely to receive careful evaluation or to be subject to thoughtful research.

Theories of vulnerability may benefit research on chronic illness by enriching the examination of the causes of disease and of factors that protect against disease or limit its severity. Why is it that one identical twin develops leukemia and the other, with the same genetic material and similar environmental exposures, does not? Why does asthma appear to be more severe among poor people while other economic groups are relatively spared? The psychological equivalent of vulnerability theories are concepts such as coping and adjustment. Intuitively, one might expect that the more severe the illness the greater the risk of psychological maladjustment. Yet few studies have been able to demonstrate a direct relationship between objective measures of severity of illness and greater psychological handicap. Indeed, some studies provide evidence that children with less severe disease have greater problems in psychological adaptation. Better theories to underpin research in coping will increase understanding in this area (Pless and Zvagulis, 1981).

The work of Lazarus and colleagues (Roskies and Lazarus, 1980; Cohen and Lazarus, 1979) may help in understanding the process of coping with stress, including the stress of chronic illness. Other theoretical frameworks that may elucidate mechanisms of disease and opportunities for treatment include developmental frameworks based on the theories of Piaget (Bibace and Walsh, 1980; Perrin and Gerrity, 1981), which contribute to knowledge of the interaction between the development of the child and the impact and manifestations of illness. Ecological conceptualizations based on the works of Bronfenbrenner (1977) and Hobbs (1975) help clarify the interactions of child, disease, and family and their interactions with the broader community. Minuchin (1978) has examined the dynamics of families involved with chronic illnesses, the impacts of illness on those families, and the ways in which families can hinder or aid the child's ability to cope with illness. Others, including Breslau (Breslau, Weitzman, and Messenger, 1981) and Cerreto (1981), have looked at the impact of childhood chronic illness on siblings.

All of these approaches provide new theoretical frameworks to increase understanding of chronic illness and its causes and impacts. Yet theoretical research, perhaps because it may have little immediate direct application, suffers from inadequate financial support. Progress will occur as the base of support of theoretical research is broadened.

Characteristics of Populations Studied. Most research in childhood chronic illness is carried out with children who go to individual academic health centers. Yet these populations rarely reflect the full spectrum of the disease studied. Children who make their way to academic health centers frequently have the more severe cases of illness, and because these children may appear relatively late in the course of their disease, studies of the natural history of disease that are done in academic health centers often provide limited information about important aspects of the early stages of the condition. Certain medications may be effective among patients with more severe forms of disease in a university hospital. Yet effectiveness among severely affected individuals does not ensure that a drug will be effective in milder cases. Unless effectiveness among patients with less severe illness is examined by careful research, a drug may be used indiscriminately and have harmful results (Starfield, 1981).

Epidemiologically sound, community- or population-based studies will rectify the present biases in research programs. Community studies, which identify all patients with a given disease, provide a different picture of the natural history of disease and allow the most realistic appraisal of prospects for a child and family when chronic illness appears.

Much research in chronic illness has focused, by necessity, on the children seen within only one academic institution. Yet the relative infrequency of most childhood chronic illnesses means that, in any single center, the number of children with a given disease may be inadequate for research. Interinstitutional studies that allow the pooling of larger numbers of children with given diseases improve understanding of the intricacies and predictive factors in disease prognosis, expand recognition of important although potentially rare complications of disease and treatments, and most importantly, allow careful experimentation with new therapies to demonstrate their efficacy and effectiveness. Examples of collaborative study groups include those for childhood cancers and for chronic renal disease in childhood.

The Single-Disease Character of Research. Most studies in childhood chronic illness focus on individual diseases and emphasize the special character of that particular disease and its causes, treatments, and effects. Through emphasizing funding of research to study specific organ systems, the structure of the major public program supporting health research in the United States—the National Institutes of Health (NIH)—encourages researchers to focus on groups of closely related conditions (Frederickson and others, 1981). Research involving groups of children with a variety of diseases, especially those that involve several organ systems (for example, congenital heart disease and hemophilia), is hard to support with present funding mechanisms.

Academic health centers receive a large portion of their financial support from public research funds, particularly from the National Institutes of Health. Compartmentalization of this granting agency is reflected in the organization of research, services, and populations of children and families within the university health centers. Researchers wishing to pursue studies involving multiple diseases may find it difficult to amass groups of children with varied diseases because the children generally receive services in practice settings organized around individual diseases or organ systems.

By stimulating improvements in the understanding and treatment of the rare diseases of childhood, the focus on individual diseases and their pathophysiological mechanisms has been of great benefit to children and families. Yet the commonalities among the physiologically diverse chronic illnesses of childhood call for a sizable research effort that looks across diseases as well as within specific disease categories. The work of Pless and his colleagues, described initially in epidemiological studies of the children of the Isle of Wight (Rutter, Tizard and Whitmore, 1970) and more recently in the Rochester Child Health Studies (Haggerty, Roghmann, and Pless, 1975), has broadened understanding of the impact on family and children of a wide variety of chronic illnesses and has demonstrated their similarity. This work has important implications in the search for improved theoretical formulations, especially in research on health services and on coping with and adjustment to childhood chronic illness. The studies of Pless and colleagues imply that issues in health services research can be studied by using diverse populations of children. For example, continuity of care encourages better compliance with prescribed medications on the part of children and families. Yet here research is needed to clarify whether effective continuity must be based on individual providers, or whether continuity based on institutions or systems of patient records could improve compliance. It is unlikely that the answers to these questions will be influenced by the specific disease, and the research can be carried out through studies that consider chronically ill children together.

The recent work of Stein and Jessop (1982a, 1982b) demonstrates the similar nature of physiologically diverse conditions, in their impact on the family, on the psychological adjustment of the child, and on the financial and service demands created by the illness. If barriers to multidisease research can be removed, basic questions in epidemiology, health services research, and psychological research will be answered more quickly.

Problems in Measurement. Lack of standard criteria for the definition of a number of basic concepts has affected much research in child health. Researchers may apply different criteria for the definition of specific diseases, such as the various forms of arthritis in childhood (Starfield, 1985). Where one study may show that a certain treatment helps childhood arthritis, another may have an opposite finding. This discrepancy may be partly based on differences in the criteria used to diagnose arthritis. The wide variety of childhood chronic illnesses makes the development of diagnostic criteria for each a formidable task. Nonetheless, diagnostic criteria are important for the comparability of studies from different institutions and for support of collaborative studies among institutions.

Criteria for the definition of severity are even more difficult to specify than diagnostic criteria. For a few conditions, such as hemophilia, determination of severity is relatively simple (through measurement of blood-clotting factor levels in the bloodstream). For most conditions, it is far more difficult. Few criteria help distinguish more from less physiologically severe cases of diabetes. The level of blood sugar is more a factor of the adequacy of diabetic control than it is of the severity of the disease. Several schemes for defining severity of asthma have been developed. Most are based on the frequency of attacks of asthma and the amount and type of medication used, all of which reflect the adequacy of medical control or compliance more than an inherent variation in severity.

Similar problems abound in the definition of functional status or disability. Functional status reflects the ability of the child to carry out activities appropriate for age. No single measure in childhood has been applied consistently, and no fully adequate measure of this concept yet exists (Stein and Jessop, 1984). If the goal of services for the families of chronically ill children is to encourage the best functional outcomes for children, then the development of an adequate measure of functional status is crucial.

The conceptual problem for families is much the same. How can family functioning be measured (Stein and Riessman, 1980)? The tasks are complex and may be illustrated by a few questions. In measuring disability, how does one compare being wheelchair-bound with being unable to carry out usual toileting functions? Which is indicative of greater disability? Do families who communicate effectively about problems function better than those who spend leisure time together?

How can psychological adjustment of the child best be determined? Although related to functional status, psychological adjustment reflects such ideas as how a child feels about self, how well the child interacts with family and peers, and other aspects of the child's behavior (Pless, 1984). Earlier work focused on the presence or absence of psychopathology; that is, whether a child has a psychiatric disorder (Rutter, Tizard and Whitmore, 1970). More recent concepts of adjustment examine positive coping skills to determine whether the child has the ability to respond effectively to challenges at school and at home or whether illness has diminished that capacity (Ellsworth and Ellsworth, 1982; Gesten, 1976). Is the child resilient in the face of adversity, or is new stress met with withdrawal?

There is also limited agreement on definitions of such key concepts as comprehensiveness and continuity in health services. Does continuity of care mean for a month, for an episode of an illness, for a year, or for a lifetime? Does it mean that just one provider is involved in most services, or can teams of providers offer continuity?

Finally, research is hampered by measures that narrowly define outcome or health status. To some degree, narrow definitions have been expedient; that is, they allow measurement of that which is easy to measure, whether or not it reflects what may be important for the child or family. A broad-based outcome measure that will examine a wide spectrum of important characteristics is needed. Several approaches have been proposed, including one by Starfield (1974). Her scheme proposes developing measurements across seven dimensions: resilience, activity, disease, satisfaction, comfort, achievement, and longevity. A specific measure would be developed for each dimension, and the dimensions as a group would reflect a profile of the child's status. Examination of this profile would allow consideration of trade-offs in outcome of a given treatment. In asthma, disease (wheezing) may be improved by frequent visits to a health facility, but achievement (in school) may be diminished by frequent absence from school and after-school activities. The development of such a complex measure or profile represents a priority in furthering research of all types in chronic illnesses of childhood.

Public Support of Research

The National Institutes of Health (NIH) provide the largest percentage of support for research in childhood chronic illnesses. Estimates of NIH and other federal agency support of research on childhood chronic illnesses are indicated in Table 8. The growth of NIH over the past few decades has paralleled the increasing attention to biomedical problems in chronic illnesses. The institutes have developed mechanisms for evaluating research proposals, for defining new research thrusts and incentives, for managing ongoing research, and for encouraging new researchers to enter the research community. To a degree, support for basic biomedical research has plateaued in the past few years, and the rapid growth in new knowledge characteristic of the previous two decades may be weakening. In addition, limitations on funding for research and for training have made research careers less attractive to young investigators, and the infusion of new talent to many areas of basic research has been sharply limited.

Federal support for basic research in other disciplines critical to the needs of families with chronically ill children has been far less generous than the support of biomedical research. Investment in behavioral sciences research represents a minimal percentage of the NIH effort in chronic illness. Even less support has been available for health services or nursing science research. Despite the pressing need to understand the psychological consequences of chronic illness, the processes of coping, and the interaction of psychological matters and physiological response to illness, psychologists in academic health centers find it difficult to obtain research support. Support of behavioral scientists involved with

Table 8. Research on Children with Chronic Illnesses: Public Support.

Agency	Childhood Chronic Illness Research Support	Total Research Budget
National Institutes of Health (NIH)	$203,440,000	$2,731,300,000
National Institute of Handicapped Research (NIHR)	NA[a]	36,000,000
National Institute of Mental Health (NIMH) [b]	33,887,000	188,289,000
Office of Maternal and Child Health (OMCH)	557,682	3,855,935
Office of Human Development Services (OHDS)	NA	29,500,000

Note: All figures represent agency estimates. Generally, program statistics do not distinguish child-related research from other agency-sponsored research. Estimates for FY 1984.

[a]NA: not available.

[b]NIMH figures represent *total* expenditures; that is, research, training, and service. Child expenditures represent *all* children and youth activities. Expenditures on research regarding childhood chronic illness will be a very small percentage of these figures.

childhood chronic illness derives mainly from direct service activities rather than from research grants.

Several federal agencies other than the NIH have supported research in childhood chronic illness; these include the Office of Maternal and Child Health, the National Institute of Mental Health, the National Center for Health Services Research and Development, and the National Institute for Handicapped Research. Funding for these efforts has been markedly curtailed in recent years, and agencies have had to redefine and limit their research missions.

Recruitment of excellent scientists to research careers should continue. Research training must again achieve vigorous public support. New groups of scientists, especially in clinical disciplines, will require quantitative and data management skills and understanding of the expanding field of clinical epidemiology. Scientists trained to carry out both basic studies of behavioral aspects of chronic illness and research that considers chronic illnesses of childhood together are especially needed. At present, few institutions can conduct research into the generic issues of chronic illness despite the importance of these problems to families and the promise research in this area holds for families. A high priority should be the development and support of such scientists.

To meet changing priorities in research and especially to broaden the scope of interdisciplinary studies of childhood chronic illness, it is important to recruit and train serious scholars from a number of disciplines. These include members of the key professions—such as physicians, nurses, social workers, and nutritionists—as well as related social and behavioral sciences. Although some of the most creative efforts in research occur where two disciplines interface (Coser, 1965), multidisciplinary training in research is uncommon. The physician intending a research career may never work with a sociologist, although these two scientists may approach the same problem from different viewpoints. Just as multidisciplinary experience is essential for effective training in the provision of services to families with chronically ill children, so too, training for research careers should be interdisciplinary.

Support for basic biomedical research, through the NIH, should remain a high priority. The investment in basic biomedical research should be balanced with an equally vigorous commitment to basic research in other critical areas, including behavioral sciences and health services. Such efforts are unlikely through the activities of the NIH, structured as it is along categorical lines. Only one health institute, the National Institute of Child Health and Human Development (NICHD), has a broad mandate without a focus on a specific disease or diseases. This institute has fostered research efforts in developmental biology, in perinatal medicine, in population studies of mothers and children, and in biological and behavioral aspects of mental retardation among other areas. The institute has demonstrated interest, too, in the interface between biological and behavioral issues as they relate to mothers and children. Although the NICHD may increase its support of research in childhood chronic illness, the categorical structure of the NIH makes it unlikely that either major research programs working across diseases or new biobehavioral or biosocial research will occur under these auspices.

Some have called for formation of a new institute (possibly a National Institute of Chronic Diseases) within the NIH: "These [research] areas are neglected because they are extremely difficult, far from glamorous, not rewarding in academia, and for a host of other reasons of a similar kind. But the most mundane and salient reason for neglect is, in my view, the fact that they relate little if at all to any of the better endowed of the existing structures. The new imperatives to which we must respond if we are to complete the research agenda which lies before us—one that cuts across diseases and categorical agencies—are such that serious thought must be given to the creation of a new National Institute of Chronic Diseases" (Pless, 1983, p. 14).

Alternatively, a new division in the NICHD could fulfill these functions. Such an institute might be similar to the National Institute for Aging, which addresses a wide spectrum of physiological, psychological, and social problems, all of which affect older people. The aging have needs for long-term care, family support, and access to technological services that are similar to those faced by children with chronic illnesses. In France, the Centre Technique des Etudes et Recherches National sur les Handicaps et les Inadaptations is a semiautonomous research institute that receives the bulk of its funds from the central government. It is governed, however, by a body composed of governmental representatives, providers, and consumers. The research agenda for this center is established partly by regional boards, on which representatives of disease-specific voluntary associations sit. The variety of research supported by the center includes epidemiological studies of handicapping conditions, basic research in mechanisms of handicapping, and psychological and educational adaptations of children and adults with handicapping conditions (M. Bauer, personal communication with the authors, 1984). A National Institute of Chronic Diseases might be patterned partly on the French experience.

Summary: Principles for Research

An understanding of the issues in research on childhood chronic illness and of the areas that hold promise suggests principles to guide future research activities. First, there is a need for the development of theoretical frameworks beyond the basic biomedical model in all areas of research endeavor. The work of Lazarus and colleagues in promoting consideration of illness as a stress with which children and families must cope (Roskies and Lazarus, 1980; Cohen and Lazarus, 1979) may increase understanding of the psychological response of child and family to illness. Theories of vulnerability and invulnerability should help explain both the pathological and protective mechanisms in disease. Starfield's (1973) model of structure, process, and outcome provides a framework in the area of health services research. Ecological concepts aid understanding of the interaction of child, illness, family, and community. Research that supports the broadening and deepening of theory is often the most difficult to finance; yet it may carry the greatest long-term benefit.

Second, population-based and interinstitutional research should be fostered. Much of current knowledge comes from studies of children who appear in academic health centers. Yet, these children do not reflect all children with a given condition, nor do they reflect all children with chronic illnesses in general. Population- and community-based studies will expand the understanding of the causes and consequences of illness. Interinstitutional research will enable data collection on larger numbers of children with rare conditions and will expedite resolution of research questions.

Third, the consideration of chronically ill children as an identifiable class will allow diverse health conditions to be grouped together for the purposes of many investigations (Pless and Perrin, 1985). This approach is applied best to questions in areas other than the biomedical and promises to improve understanding of the complex mechanisms in psychosocial and health services research paradigms concerning chronic illness in childhood.

Childhood chronic illness has changed during the past few decades. With improvements in survival (in the context of changes in the social environment of children and families) come new problems and opportunities that can be partly met through renewed vigor in research. The nation's commitment to research in the past has helped immeasurably. A commitment to solving new problems, to including a broad range of disciplines, and to promoting interdisciplinary activities is fundamental to the well-being of families with chronically ill children. The new research questions merit the nation's attention in terms of training scientists and helping them resolve pressing problems afflicting families.

10

Role of Values in Shaping Professional Ethics and Public Policy

Issues of value infuse every purposeful effort to help children with chronic illnesses. Yet those who would help seldom make clear the value assumptions that guide their efforts. Indeed, they are themselves often unaware of the values implicit in their actions. Legislators, government officials, health care providers, school administrators and teachers, and members of voluntary organizations and self-help groups may all be involved in efforts to enhance the well-being of sick children and their families, their actions guided by unexamined intuitions. Nor are commissions, panels, study committees, and policy analysts exempt from the deficiency; they commonly arrive at conclusions and recommendations without ever making clear the values that inform their thinking.

In this chapter, we examine the role of values in decision making by professionals and by those responsible for the allocation of resources. The exploration of values is preliminary to developing criteria that will allow a value-explicit review of present and proposed policies concerning chronically ill children and their families. What are important characteristics of the relationship between physicians and families? What are key decisions for chronically ill children, and who has responsibility for making these decisions? When resources are scarce, how can choices be made

282

among conflicting demands on behalf of one group of children or another or for certain treatments rather than others?

A *value* is a principle, standard, or quality considered worthwhile or desirable. Ordinarily, values are not sought as goals or objectives, but they influence the choice of goals, guide the investment of effort, and limit choices among alternative courses of action. Personal values tend to be absorbed from the culture as experienced by an individual; they change throughout the life-span and are much affected by the changing circumstances of life; they are seldom examined systematically when deciding on a course of action, although they are often addressed directly in essays, political oratory, or sermons; and they may be symbolized indirectly in works of art, novels, poetry, and other representations of human aspirations.

Although culturally shared, values are idiosyncratic, unique to the individual but seldom wholly consistent in the individual at any one period or over time. Social scientists differentiate between public and private values. Public values are expressed when the individual acts in conformity with institutional expectations; private values are expressed when an individual acts unconstrained by formal expectations. A health care provider may espouse one standard in formal settings and act on a contrary standard in practice. Values, both public and private, determine in substantial measure how children with chronic illnesses and their families are treated by friends and neighbors, by professional people, and by service providers of all sorts, including providers of health care or educational services. Equally important, values profoundly influence the allocation of public resources.

Values influence what happens to chronically ill children and their families in two main ways: through the ethical standards governing professional relationships and responsibilities and through underlying assumptions that guide the development and administration of public policies. Usually, professional ethics and the ethics of allocating resources through policy are considered separately, although at times they overlap or conflict with each other. Physicians struggle with wanting to provide the best possible care for their patients (at whatever cost) in the context of limited resources. How to provide rare or costly resources to one patient recognizing that the next may be deprived is but one example of the conflict. Moreover, the professional-patient relationship is often a driving force in the allocation of resources. In this chapter, professional responsibilities and resource policies are discussed separately, with an occasional emphasis on their fundamental inter-relationship.

Values and Professional Relationships

Professional people relate to one another and to their patients or clients in ways that vary greatly in quality and style and represent varying points of view on what is considered worthwhile and desirable. Professionals in health service programs, schools, and social agencies vary widely in their ability and willingness to share responsibility with each other and with the families with whom they work. At times, issues of professional autonomy conflict with the interdependent nature of client-professional relations. Although values associated with professional relationships are less applicable to public policy than values associated with social issues, professional ethics have considerable consequence for children and families and deserve our full attention. Essential issues include confidentiality and respect for the privacy of the family, truth-telling, informed consent, and locus of responsibility for decisions. The catalogue, far from complete, is suggestive of the issues encountered in examining values in professional practice.

Ethical Standards in Professional Practice. One might reasonably expect the code of ethics of a professional group to be a clear window on the values its members espouse and on the ethical choices they make in actual practice. Alas, the hundreds of codes of ethics of professional and trade associations have little or no impact on the behavior of association members. There are exceptions. When a professional group's code of ethics is founded in well-established custom, and when it is accompanied by sanctions against violations of the code, it can make a difference in choices made. *The Principles of Medical Ethics* (American Medical Association, Judicial Council, 1977) is one such reasonably effective code. But even this venerable code has several limitations. Sanctions are seldom applied for its violation, and it is adhered to variably by members of the profession. Veatch (1976, 1981) notes the controversy between the principles as a guide to the profession and as a basis for rule making. Some would like the principles to have the force of law; others seek to have individuals outside the profession actively involved in formulating rules of conduct. Codes of medical ethics address important questions of confidentiality and propriety, yet they are limited by their neglect of other key areas, such as resource allocation or clinical decision making.

Guidelines for ethical conduct are established when there is conflict over what constitutes an appropriate course of action, usually regarding a specific case. Ethical issues are clarified when competent people disagree on what *should* be done. Otherwise, professional caregivers, as well as scientific investigators, follow conventional standards unperturbed, protected from doubt by custom. Escaping public scrutiny and debate, many professional practices are allowed to continue even though they may be demonstrably hurtful to chronically ill children and their families. The recent addition of ethics to several medical school curricula is heartening. Medical programs in ethics and human values grew from eleven in 1972 to sixty-five in 1981 (President's Commission for the Study of Ethical Problems in Medicine and Biomedical and Behavioral Research, 1982). Most physicians, nevertheless, have had little direct exposure to the study of ethics, and other professionals—nurses, nutritionists, teachers—may have even less. Only 5 percent of students graduating from medical school in 1981 reported having had a course in medical ethics (Association of American Medical Colleges, 1981). Yet the ethics of clinical care, of research, and of resource allocation are constant companions of the chronically ill.

In the past, the relationship between physician and patient was largely a private transaction exempt from public concern except when violations of the civil or criminal code were charged. Today, the physician and other health care workers have a fiduciary relationship with both the patient or client and the larger society as well (Stevens, 1971). Public resources are heavily invested in the training of health care workers; in the construction of health care facilities; in paying for services for special groups, such as the indigent and the aged; in underwriting, directly or indirectly, health insurance programs for those who can afford them; and in the development and dissemination of knowledge. The health care provider clearly depends on the public institutions of society and has a clear obligation to serve the public good. Medicine in the United States has a tradition of conservatism, emphasizing private initiative and self-determination for physicians (Stevens, 1971). There is a fundamental and yet at times very creative conflict between the conservative and private character of American medicine and the demands of American society for equity and quality in health services. Nevertheless, medicine is inextricably involved with the public purpose and with ethical principles involving the common good.

There is a certain consistency between the maintenance of respect for the intrinsic value of children with chronic illnesses and the privatism that characterizes American medicine. Both approaches place emphasis on the primacy of the individual. Yet is it ethical to consider the physician's task as a private matter without public consequence? Medicine is no longer simply a private, personal relationship; it is now a public institution.

Children, Families, and Professional People. Most children grow up with relatively little experience with professional people, even in our complex society. Teachers they will know well, and possibly childcare workers; but unless something goes wrong, they only occasionally see a physician, a dentist, or a social worker. Of the things that can go wrong for a child and family, few so greatly involve professional people as the discovery that a child has a chronic and severe illness. Then child and family may become intensely involved with professional people of many kinds and for a long time: physicians, nurses, social workers, psychologists, therapists of one type or another, special educators, as well as sundry agency officials. The well-being of child and family will be affected by the value commitments of these various professional people as expressed in their daily relationships with those dependent on their professional understanding, skill, diligence, and sensitivity as well as on their control over needed resources.

Complex postindustrial societies are characterized by the expansion of human services and the professionalization of much of the caring function, formerly the almost exclusive responsibility of families and communities. The explosive growth of knowledge has inevitably led to professional specialization, which has radically altered the relationship between the helper and the helped. Professionalization of caring imposes a distance between them. Strangers treat and are treated by strangers; understanding and trust, once nurtured slowly, must now be produced instantly and may be formal and insufficient. Specialization leads inexorably to the fractionation of care, so that the child with chronic illness is treated by dozens of different strangers who may, according to their specialty, regard the child as a malfunctioning organ rather than a whole person, as a sickly school child rather than someone desiring to learn, as a third-party payment problem rather than a child and family struggling to cope with the unexplained and the inexplicable. Distance and the alienation of helper and helped have led to professional values that conflict with the helping function by creating dependency rather than collaboration, distrust rather than the mutual respect that would be based on a long-term relationship.

The Ethics of Extreme Situations and Daily Decisions

During the past decade, there has been an important debate of moral and ethical issues affecting the well-being of chronically ill children and their families. In certain circumstances, this debate has been intense, constructive, and useful, but its general applicability to chronically ill children is severely limited by its preoccupation with *in extremis* situations. The debate has concentrated on the circumstances under which heroic measures to keep alive a profoundly handicapped child may justly be stopped and the child allowed to die (Duff, 1981; Fost, 1981). For example, what should be done in the case of a child born without the cortex of the brain? Or what should be done in the case of a child with very severe or high myelomeningocele who can be kept alive only at great expense, who may be mentally retarded, and who will live a short life, much of it in hospitals (Shurtleff and others, 1974)? In the mid 1980s, the widespread development of Baby Doe boards to review the care of severely handicapped infants recognized the extreme situation but offered little attention to daily decision making (Stroup, 1983; Strain, 1983; Fost, 1982). The debate has been worthwhile, yet its applicability is severely limited because there are relatively few occasions when such profound issues must be faced. Of far more consequence to greater numbers of children and families, as well as to professional people, are hundreds of circumstances requiring moral and ethical decisions in daily life and practice. The choices of daily decision making are less dramatic than the rare death-and-dying decisions but of greater import in the total scheme of things (Kopelman, 1985).

Indeed, ethical questions involving the well-being of children and families are a daily challenge. For example, should a child be operated on when there is professional difference of opinion about probable outcomes? Who should make the decision, the physician or the parents, or both? At what age or level of competence should a child be consulted, and when should the child's decision be governing (Leikin, 1983)? Under what circumstances should the activities of a child be limited when the limitations may be as damaging to the child's normal development as the condition they are designed to ameliorate? Complex technical and ethical issues arise regarding children with renal disease: Should they receive dialysis or a kidney transplant (Korsch and Fine, 1985)? Again, who shall decide? What should parents be told about the illness of their child? About the child's prospects for the future? Are there circumstances under which it is ethically legitimate to withhold or distort information essential to an informed choice (Kopelman, 1985; President's Commission for the Study of Ethical Problems in Medicine and Biomedical and Behavioral Research, 1982)? Under what circumstances is there an ethical obligation for a health care provider to seek additional professional consultation? How and by whom should decisions on school placement and special education be made? Are there choices involving chronically ill children where a public presence (possibly effected through the courts) is required to protect the best interest of the child? These and hundreds of similar questions arise in providing care to chronically ill children and their families. It is of great importance that they be debated and that discussion of values and ethics not be confined to *in extremis* issues.

"Every medical decision has a value component" (Veatch, 1977, p. 17). When value principles are applied to specific cases and problems, the complexity of the issues becomes clear. This complexity is illustrated by a discussion of two issues encountered daily in providing health care to chronically ill children and their families: truth-telling and decision making.

On Disclosure and Truth-Telling. In the abstract, most health care providers would likely agree that a patient has a right to all information required to make an intelligent choice regarding personal health. The courts have given formal sanction to this commonsense view: "A doctor may well believe that an operation or form of treatment is desirable or necessary but the law doesn't permit him to substitute his own judgment for that of the patient by any form of artifice or deception" (*Natanson* v. *Kline,* 1960, p. 1104). The statement is carefully crafted. It does not say that a patient is entitled to all available or possible information, only to that relevant to the decision at hand. The expert having the information has an obligation to make it available to the patient in usable form, in other words, in terms that can be understood. The statement calls for telling the truth and for full disclosure. The issue seems simple, but it turns out otherwise. What if experts disagree on what the facts are? Even disagreement can provide useful information, however difficult it may be for experts to admit uncertainty to people dependent on them. What if the information is frightening, demoralizing, a possible cause of despair? If polio vaccine carries a risk of 1:1,000,000 or less of causing paralytic polio, should that information be shared with parents when their children get the vaccine? What if information newly gained impeaches information formerly given by the expert or by a colleague?

Truth-telling and full disclosure are difficult enough in the best of circumstances, but the uncertain conditions of medical practice compound the difficulty (Fox, 1979, 1980). Patients usually expect clear, definitive answers from physicians, yet most medical questions lack clear answers. The great variations among children with the same conditions make it impossible to know if an infant born with a large spina bifida will ever walk or (at diagnosis) if a child with leukemia will live or die. Grave consequences—an exacerbation of an illness, for example—may ensue from a wrong judgment; it may seem safer to be cautious and offer less rather than more information.

Trust in the caretaker is generally believed to be essential to therapeutic effectiveness. What if full disclosure should diminish trust? Are the long-term gains in trust that result from truth-telling likely to be greater than short-term gains derived from dissembling or withholding information? Are there times when distrust is of benefit—when asking a second opinion or challenging a physician's plan may better the lives of the child and family? Physicians often work under great time pressures, and disclosure takes time; are the benefits of disclosure worth the cost? Disclosure to children takes special skills—to recognize the developmental difference that must be considered when explaining diabetes to a five-year-old and a fifteen-year-old or lung mechanics to a three-year-old with asthma or a twelve-year-old similarly afflicted (Perrin and Gerrity, 1981). Health providers are rarely skilled in the developmental aspects of disclosure.

The President's Commission for the Study of Ethical Problems in Medicine and Biomedical and Behavioral Research (1982) supported a survey of physicians and the general public (conducted by Louis Harris and Associates) that demonstrated lack of agreement on proper standards for informed consent. Among public respondents, 44 percent felt that time spent discussing the disease could be better spent taking care of patients; only 21 percent of physicians responded in a similar fashion. Seventy-three percent of physicians felt that the requirements of informed consent put too much emphasis on disclosure of remote risks; only 44 percent of public respondents agreed.

Work with chronically ill children and their families has special difficulties. Physicians are human and need to be liked and appreciated as much as anyone else; they know well that people rarely feel good about the bearer of bad news. Patients or parents may easily confuse the messenger with the message. Further, physicians like to be successful, as do other people. There is a strong tendency for both physicians and patients to define success in terms of cure; by definition, the cure of most chronically ill children is impossible. For these reasons and more, it seems unfair to be overly critical of physicians for their reluctance to share information completely.

But health care workers have been criticized for withholding or distorting information, whatever the reason. Mothers complain that physicians are often too busy and seem anxious to avoid discussing problems. They are often condescending and resort quickly to reassurance that seldom reassures (Carlton, 1978). Parents themselves may deceive a child, most often in a misguided effort to protect the youngster from worry or fear; and they may need the help of a professional person to work through the issues involved. From the parents of a child with cancer (Ipswitch, 1979):

Since [we] had decided not to tell Scott that he had cancer, we lived in fear that someone else would tell him [p. 48]. . . .

All these years, my greatest fear—apart from the overriding fear that Scott would not recover from Hodgkin's—was that somehow he would find out that Hodgkin's was cancer. I worried myself sick about the effect this would have on him and his will to fight the disease [p. 135]. . . .

One afternoon I walked into the living room where Scott was lying on the sofa watching television. There were slides of magnified cells on the screen.

"That's what I have," Scott said, without taking his eyes away from the television.

"What?"

"That's what I have. Cancer," Scott said.

"How long have you known that Hodgkin's was cancer?" I asked in amazement.

His answer was matter-of-fact. There was no hint of emotion. "Ever since I was in the hospital."

"Who told you?" I wanted to know.

"No one," he said. "I just figured it out from what the doctors said."

How I could have thought that Scott would not make the connection between Hodgkin's and cancer is beyond me today [p. 135]. . . . How could I have so underestimated my son? In retrospect I suspect that our not telling him he had cancer was as much to protect ourselves as to protect him. But I don't know. I really don't know [p. 136]. . . .

I had something more on my mind. "Dr. Williams, it just made me sick when you told me in front of Scott that his blood tests were showing leukemic properties. Do we have to tell Scott that he has leukemia?"

"Yes," he said bluntly.

"Why?"

"We can't keep this from him. He will know without our telling him."

I thought about how careful I had been not to tell Scott that Hodgkin's disease was cancer—and how he had known it all the time. I did not want to agree with Dr. Williams, but I knew he was right [p. 185].

Physicians and patients may have very different views of deception. From a scholar studying lying:

I first came to look closely at problems of professional truthtelling and deception in preparing to write about the giving of placebos. And I grew more and more puzzled by a discrepancy in perspectives: many physicians talked about deception in a cavalier, often condescending and joking way, whereas patients often have an acute sense of injury and of loss of trust at learning that they have been duped. . . . for them, to be given false information about important choices in their lives is to be rendered powerless. For them, their very autonomy may be at stake. . . . honesty from health professionals matters more to patients than almost everything else they experience when ill. Yet the requirement to be honest with patients has been left out altogether from medical oaths and codes of ethics, and is often ignored, if not actually disparaged, in the teaching of medicine [Bok, 1979, pp. xvi and xvii].

Professionals, too, must be aware of their limitations and especially must avoid making unwarranted promises or creating false expectations. The same scholar (Bok, 1979), addressing the difficult problems of truth-telling when children are involved, presents guidelines to govern situations in which the physician judges deception to be necessary:

Children are often deceived with the fewest qualms. They, more than all others, need care, support, protection. To shield them, not only from brutal speech and frightening news, but from apprehension and pain—to soften and embellish and disguise—is as natural as to shelter them from harsh weather [p. 206]. . . . Concealment, evasion, withholding of information may at times be necessary. But if someone contemplates lying to a patient or concealing the truth, the burden of proof must shift. It must rest, here, as with all deceptions, on those who advocate it in any one instance. They must show why they feel a patient may be harmed or how they know that another cannot cope with the truthful knowledge. A decision to deceive must be seen as a very unusual step, to be talked over with colleagues and others who participate in the care of the patient. Reasons must be set forth and debated, alternatives weighed carefully. At all times, the correct information must go to *someone* closely related to the patient [p. 252].

Truth-telling in matters of clinical care is highly complex. Should parents similarly be expected to be truthful in their encounters with physicians or teachers? At times, they withhold information through fear of authority or a desire to maintain some privacy. Parents may fear that their child will be unduly restricted if the school is aware of a severe chronic illness. When is this form of parental deception acceptable?

Kopelman (1985) notes the importance of respecting the desire *not* to know—that some families and patients prefer to be spared information and not be told all the truth. Truth-telling, like most other fundamental aspects of the professional-patient relationship, is not described by simple rules. The elements of truth-telling vary with each relationship and can be achieved only with sizable amounts of time and wisdom applied to the process.

On Decision Making. Physicians and other health care providers who make decisions concerning chronically ill children and their families face ethical dilemmas daily. Occasionally, the decisions can be recognized immediately as having profound consequences, as for example, when a life-risking procedure is initiated in an effort to alleviate some life-limiting condition. More often, however, decisions are less dramatic and appear to be less consequential, when in fact, it is an accumulation of seemingly minor ethical decisions that defines the character of the caregiving relationship. These decisions often determine the course of the child's and family's lives in the long run. There are several issues involved in determining who should make these decisions.

Experts in any field are naturally disposed to the exercise of their competence—to make judgments in difficult situations, to move with dispatch to solve problems. In matters of health and disease, patients (or the parents of young children) are inclined, out of uncertainty or deference, to leave decisions to the physician, who is the expert in such matters. And physicians are usually willing to assume the responsibility. Indeed, there are physicians who assert that this is the way it should be, that obtaining informed consent is a meaningless exercise. They argue that the patient cannot be sufficiently informed to make an intelligent choice, that a patient can be easily persuaded to make the choice the caregiver believes is right, and that the physician cannot avoid the decision making that goes along with professional responsibility (Freidson, 1970).

For the professional person—whether physician, psychologist, social worker, or nurse—to take responsibility works well in technical matters but falters when there are conflicting options involving the well-being of individuals and where personal choice is of paramount importance. Pragmatically, an expert's recommended treatment depends on the individual's compliance, which cannot be forced. Thus, the question of who will be responsible for decisions is ever present. In making decisions involving the well-being of a chronically ill child, it is often possible to achieve ready concurrence among physicians, parents, and the child when deciding on a course of action. Difficulties ensue when accord cannot be reached or when the expert falsely assumes that the process of obtaining consent can be short-circuited.

Decisions involving the well-being of a child are complicated by uncertainty regarding the child's competence to decide (Leikin, 1983). When the child is very young, it is clear that parents or other responsible parties must participate in the decision. When the child is older, although still legally a minor, it is obvious that the child should have a voice in deciding what should be done. But determining when a particular child has reached an age of discretion is difficult. Historically, individuals have been considered to be either legally competent or incompetent, with no gradations between these extremes. Arbitrary age limits have been set (usually at eighteen or twenty-one) when individuals can be held legally responsible for their actions. These arbitrary dates have little relationship to a young person's ability to make a sound decision. In recent decades, the courts, on grounds of privacy, have supported the right of adolescents to obtain information about birth control, treatment for venereal disease, and abortion without parental consent and without the requirement that parents be informed (Kopelman, 1985). Research has begun to identify ages at which children and adolescents are capable of understanding illnesses and making certain decisions. Yet there is a pervasive professional bias toward underestimating the ability of children to make mature choices. Children are generally far more competent in such matters than professional people are wont to believe or act upon, often to the detriment of therapeutic purposes.

Therapeutic purpose suffers especially when chronically ill children feel decisions have been arbitrarily imposed on them or when they have not been helped, with respect and patience, to understand and accept a regimen that may be arduous and sometimes painful. Although an adult may decide what is best for a youngster, the decision is meaningless unless the child, too, makes the decision. A physician can ascertain for a child with diabetes a proper balance of insulin, food, and exercise; but the physician cannot day after day, month after month, test the blood, monitor food intake, and regulate the child's activity. No measure of professional responsibility or parental authority can circumvent an older child's ultimate responsibility for self.

As a general rule, decisions about treatment of a child with a chronic illness are made on the recommendation of the physician and with the full concurrence of parents and child. Sometimes a consultation is sought to confirm or modify the physician's recommendation, and sometimes the parents or the child need the help of the physician, a nurse-educator, a chaplain, or a counselor to arrive at a decision they can live with and carry out. Occasionally, this round of events does not lead to a supportable decision. Members of the medical team may disagree with one another, parents may disagree with the physicians or with each other, or there may be reluctant concurrence with a course of action that could lead to guilt, discord, and even punitive legal action. Parents may refuse on religious grounds to allow a blood transfusion necessary to save a child's life. Patients may unwittingly compete with each other for scarce resources, such as a kidney transplant. In such circumstances of conflict and uncertainty, the wise course may be to seek an external judgment, to bring a public presence into the decision-making process. Frequently, medical centers have standing committees to assist decision making in such circumstances, and it is sometimes necessary to turn to the courts for a judgment.

Committees and courts, although sometimes a necessary adjunct to the normal processes of decision making, have distinct limitations, including relieving professional people of responsibility for their own professional values and standards. Duff (1981), a pediatrician and ethicist, states the problem this way: "Passing responsibility for deciding care more and more to committees or the courts would give away or destroy a central ethos of the profession [of medicine] along with that of the family. I refer to the profession's responsibility, in working with individual patients and their families, to establish a standard of conduct for itself and to assert the freedom to do what it considers best. Without this ethos, medicine could no longer be called a profession and might be impotent precisely when strength is most needed to help people in those tragic predicaments which most likely can be only aggravated by societal intrusion" (p. 318).

Research involving children carries its own special questions, especially when the illness is rare. Many treatments are experimental and carry real promise of improved outcomes, although with unknown risks. Much essential research involves children with rare conditions. For the individual child, there may be no foreseeable benefit. Rather, the benefit is for others who will have the condition in the future. There is little problem in justifying research that is neither harmful nor distasteful to the child. But when the research carries risk, how much risk can be justified? When it is painful, who should consent to the pain, the child or the parents (Korsch, 1973)? Most research institutions have committees to review research proposals, to examine the risks for those involved in the studies, and to weigh the potential benefits and risks. Although these boards may impose burdens upon researchers, they provide a degree of careful scrutiny by individuals without a direct interest in the pursuit of the specific research project. The President's Commission for the Study of Ethical Problems in Medicine and Biomedical and Behavioral Research (1982) provides important guidelines on the management of research for children. Maintaining the rights of the child and the family in the face of the desire to know more about a disease requires a delicate balance and continued careful examination both by the public and by the academic community.

The ethics of treatment are just as problematic as the ethics of research. Much of medical therapeutics for both common and rare conditions is based on dogma or belief, and often there is little research to support the benefit of the therapy to patients. The temptation is great to try (because it *might* work) a new therapy for a rare or severe condition without subjecting the therapy to the careful evaluation that comes from research. Both the complexity of mounting a research program and the difficulties of obtaining informed consent and the support of institutional research review committees have heightened the temptation to apply untried therapies without examining carefully their risks and benefits. Often, however, society learns too late that a therapy is useless or dangerous. For children, examples include the thalidomide case (in which sleep medications used during pregnancy created significant arm and leg deformities in children) and the use of high-dose oxygen in very small babies (which led to the development of retrolental fibroplasia, a major form of blindness).

Professional ethics cannot always be distinguished from the ethics of resource allocation, although vigilant attention to the large number of issues of professional ethics is essential to the well-being of children with chronic illness and their families. In broad terms, respect and trust between professionals and family are basic to the implementation of professional responsibilities. We have here focused on truth-telling, respect for the dignity of the child and family, consideration of their wishes in decision making, and informed consent. Other issues, such as confidentiality or professional autonomy, merit equal review. There is no more compelling situation calling for attention to professional ethics than the treatment of a child with a severe chronic illness.

Values and Public Policy

Although individual clinicians and families may commit themselves to an all-out investment to help a specific child, society as a whole avoids this intensive commitment to all children. It could do so by curtailing commitments to the health of older people or to the well-being of all people (including resources for health and security, shelter, education, and recreation, and other valued benefits).

The larger social and political debate concerning how much of the nation's resources should be devoted to child health is beyond the scope of this book. The point, however, is that resources will always be limited. To believe otherwise is to invite individuals less competent and less informed to make the tough choices of allocating scarce resources.

Clinical decisions are influenced by scarcity of resources. Values that guide professional-family relationships and decisions might be viewed as distinct from those of the policy maker because the policy maker is concerned with allocation of limited resources and the family and professional with maximal investment in the affected individual (Veatch, 1981). Yet the value problems overlap. The clinician working with a family may know that resources made available to that family (an intensive care unit bed, a kidney for transplant, financial support from the Crippled Children's Services) may be unavailable to the next patient. A family, too, allocates its resources among conflicting demands—those of a sick child compared with those of an able-bodied child, parents' needs for support or respite against those of the child. The value concepts affecting decisions in the allocation of resources are mainly reflected in the arena of public policy although at times they guide the decisions of helping professionals and families as well.

Value Conflicts in the Allocation of Resources. How should resources be allocated among children? According to varying potentials for a useful, satisfying, and relatively pain-free life or by reference to other criteria that might be deemed important? The essence of policy analysis is to clarify the advantages and disadvantages of alternative courses of political action and to highlight options that are most harmonious with overarching and shared social goals. Issues involving the health of children bear directly on the well-being of individuals, even on their existence, and thus raise questions of deepest moral import.

Public policies are perhaps most directly responsive to conceptions of what constitutes a good society. Narrowly defined political interests play an important role in the short run, but over time, political interests are influenced by ideals of liberty, justice, equality, fraternity, excellence, individuality, and community. These values often conflict one with the other, and the conflict is nowhere more in evidence than in the area of child health. Excellence in the exercise of specialty medical care may be achieved at the expense of equity in the distribution of community and preventive health care. The privacy and autonomy of the family are prized social values that are intruded upon when immunizations are required by the state or when protective services remove children from families judged incompetent to care for them. Values of freedom and of community come into conflict in the practice of medicine as a private enterprise or as a cooperative social effort. Fee-for-service concepts conflict with prepaid, shared-risk plans along the dimension of individualism and community.

Allocation of Resources by States. Values in resource allocation are expressed through choices actually made. Indeed, some theorists maintain that the only valid indicator of values is behavior, that actions speak louder than words. To make the issues more concrete, some of the decisions faced by policy makers administering state CCS programs are described. Although little systematic data exist, we can present some information on the methods of decision making and on the criteria that have been variably applied.

We are unaware of any systematic study of criteria employed by states in allocating resources; however, Ireys (1981) asked state directors of CCS programs to indicate with whom they would consult to determine reductions in services, if necessary. The consultation process itself is revealing of values. For the most part, directors turned for guidance to other state administrators and then to advisory groups made up largely of physicians. Of the forty-nine states that replied, only thirteen state directors reported that they occasionally consulted with parents, community groups, or voluntary organizations; no state reported frequent or regular consultation with such groups.

Regardless of the groups who consult in the policy-making process, the decisions faced by administrators are complex, and the criteria upon which decisions can be made are often confusing and conflicting. Should resources be limited to children for whom there is a good prognosis? Is curability or reparability a reasonable criterion; that is, should services go first to those children who can be restored to complete or near complete functioning? This policy places lower priority on children for whom treatment may improve functioning but who have no likelihood of restoration to full capacity. Or should potential improvement in the functioning of the whole family be emphasized? If resources will allow parents of children with certain diseases to remain employed, should those families receive priority?

Other criteria may apply to the choice of children or conditions. Rather than a criterion of prognosis, the availability of specific procedures to treat a condition might be a driving force in deciding the conditions covered. The early history of the CCS reflected the availability first of orthopedic procedures; later as the prevention of rheumatic fever and the surgical treatment of congenital heart disease became possible, the programs expanded by covering cardiovascular treatments (Lesser, 1985; Ireys, Hauck, and Perrin, 1985). Yet the fact that a condition is treatable (that is, that it has a procedure that can be applied to it) fails to assure that the procedure will improve the health or functioning of a child. A related criterion might be whether treatment is efficacious, whether it has been clearly demonstrated to benefit the children who receive it.

The criteria of curability and treatability result in heavy emphasis on conditions requiring surgery or time-limited, intensive medical interventions—conditions such as cleft palate, spina bifida, heart defects, orthopedic conditions, and some childhood cancers. Children with conditions such as diabetes or cystic fibrosis and others that require long-term and careful management fall outside these criteria and may have lower priority for service.

Still other criteria can define the conditions to be covered. In recognition of the catastrophic financial impact of chronic illness, should services be limited to high-cost conditions, thereby allocating resources where the need is greatest? Children with more limited, less intensive, or less expensive problems could rely on their own resources, with special public support reserved mainly for catastrophic conditions. This policy would select high-cost conditions, such as spina bifida or heart disease, and neglect other medical conditions, such as diabetes and asthma. The catastrophic criterion may conflict with the criterion of good prognosis, although likely not with a criterion based on the availability of treatment. The catastrophic criterion may also conflict with a policy attempting to maximize the improvement in functional outcome among children with chronic conditions for the number of dollars spent (the utilitarian precept). Allocating resources to many children with low-cost conditions might lead to greater overall benefit than focusing resources on relatively few children with catastrophic conditions.

Policy makers can make these decisions in more pragmatic fashion, thereby avoiding the substantive issue of choosing among conditions. Pragmatic decisions may arise from assessment of the relative political strength of interest groups supporting one group of conditions or another. The preservation of political support for a program might dictate that, if the local diabetes association and support groups are stronger than those for muscular dystrophy or sickle cell anemia, diabetes would receive a higher priority in that state's allocation.

Finally, policy makers may choose to increase or decrease benefits according to procedural criteria unrelated to conditions. The age cutoff for services can be decreased; eligibility according to family income can be changed. Or the scope or quantity of services can be varied, diminishing the number of outreach clinics in smaller communities or adding or withdrawing such services as ambulatory medical care, nutrition programs, transportation, drugs, and appliances. Some states have faced the problem of cutbacks simply by removing from the category of eligible conditions those most recently added or by diminishing services (for example, genetic counseling) that had been recently covered.

The Crippled Children's Services has historically given priority to conditions correctable by surgery, such as club foot, craniofacial anomalies, and cardiac anomalies. With the elimination of some conditions, such as poliomyelitis, and with modest increases in program funding, services have been extended to include other diseases, such as hemophilia. Although the CCS program has shifted toward general medical problems, surgeons and orthopedic specialists continue to have heavy representation on medical advisory boards. The recommendation is often heard to cut out the diseases and disorders added most recently and to give priority to the conditions originally covered. Appeals to precedent can be powerful, especially when they coincide with strongly represented, vested interests.

One further value pervasively evident in choices made in many CCS programs is an intuitive commitment to expediency. If it works, if it ruffles few feathers, if it avoids major reorganizational problems, it if avoids an examination of fundamental purposes, do it. As in most human situations, the self-interest of decision makers has its influence, and this would be true no matter how the decision-making process is organized.

These decisions are never easily made. They reflect complex and conflicting choices, and yet we judge that they will be made best when the choices are made explicit and are open to public scrutiny. But why should resources be allocated to chronically ill children at all? What are criteria for a just distribution?

Why Allocate Resources to Chronically Ill Children? Allocation of public resources in the interest of chronically ill children and their families assumes that a prior question has been satisfactorily answered: Why should public resources go to chronically ill children at all? Why should these children and their families receive help beyond some minimum assistance that is available to all children?

Many reasons have been advanced to explain why it is in the public interest to make resources available to chronically ill children. Among them are compassion, community, prudence, economics, and knowledge (Kopelman, 1985). Most are predicated on a sense of the intrinsic value of the individual. By *intrinsic* we mean that children are valued more for their own sake rather than for what they might do for others. Utility and the extrinsic products of the individual are also important in policy considerations, but the reasons listed here place primacy on the individual, with the main goal to foster and aid the individual's self-determination. Competence is genuine when it incorporates both technical knowledge and a critical, caring concern for the fuller dimensions of child and family life in personal, social, and community aspects. The underlying theme of respect is directed toward enabling chronically ill children and their families to live at the most productive levels for themselves, thus minimizing the unasked-for inequities that arise from accidents of birth and illness.

The emphasis on intrinsic human value and on the primacy of the individual is at times supported and at other times diametrically opposed by concerns for the common good. Although often implemented in the very personal relationship between a provider and a family, the theory of the common good is concerned with the ethical responsibilities of human institutions and communities. Some of the more compelling reasons that have been advanced for the allocation of resources to the families of chronically ill children are elaborated here.

1. *For Reasons of Compassion and Community.* A good society is compassionate. People care about and help one another. Compassion is a legitimate basis for providing special resources to those who are handicapped for any reason.

    In his discussion of what it is like to be a chronically ill child, Robert Massie (1985, pp. 22-23) writes:

> Our goal should be a society made up of people who are both individually and collectively compassionate. The United States has far to go along these lines. For one thing, we have fallen into the trap of professionalizing compassion, making it a job for the few rather than a responsibility for all. . . . Although chronic illness touches every family in America in some way, we still prefer the idols of health, youth, and omnipotence nurtured by . . . our own fears. Indeed, fear is what most keeps us from compassion. Illness reminds us of our limitations, of our own inability to affect much of what happens in life. Ultimately, illness reminds us of our own death. Illness in children is somehow even more frightening because we look to children to bring us new life, purer life, and not the tragedy and disfiguration of disease. . . .
>
> So when we ask how we can help chronically ill children and launch into an examination of policies and programs, medical and educational techniques, institutional and financial resources, we must not forget to explore the one place that is often overlooked: our own hearts. The greatest burden for a chronically ill child is not the pain, the anguish, or the disappointments; it is the wall of emotional isolation with which we have encircled that child because of our own fears. We must look inside ourselves, face those fears, and despite them, reach out. Only the power of a warm heart can alleviate the deep chill of a child's constant shadow.

This concept of society's compassion derives from the Schweitzer notion that good fortune obliges, just as bad fortune demands rectification. Our births are unchosen and undeserved; each of us is born with relative advantages and disadvantages. Those with relative good fortune and advantage have obligations to help those less fortunate (Spiegelberg, 1975).

Communities are made strong by the annealing power of mutual assistance among community members, especially when no direct return to the giver can reasonably be expected. In England, it is unlawful to buy and sell blood. As a consequence of this commitment to community, uncontaminated blood and blood products are in abundant supply. This regulation was inspired by a larger vision than merely assuring the availability of blood. It reflects the giving of blood as a metaphorical expression of commitment by individual donors to a caring society. With this highly symbolic expectation established and accepted, it would be easier to encourage other gift relationships (Titmuss, 1972) that are essential to the building of a strong community:

No money values can be attached to the presence or absence of a spirit of altruism in a society. Altruism in giving to a stranger does not begin and end with blood donations. It may touch every aspect of life and affect the whole fabric of values. . . . Moreover, it is likely that a decline in the spirit of altruism in one sphere of human activities will be accompanied by similar changes in attitudes, motives, and relationships in other spheres. . . . If the bonds of community giving are broken the result is not a state of value neutralism. The vacuum is likely to be filled by hostility and social conflict. . . . We are thus concerned—as much of social policy is—with "stranger" relationships, with processes, institutions and structures which encourage the intensity and extensiveness of anonymous helpfulness in society; with "ultra obligations" which derive from our own characters and are not contractual in nature. In the ultimate analysis it is these concerns and their expression which distinguish social policy from economic policy [pp. 198 and 212].

Compassion, however, is a complex emotion and one that can easily turn to pity, which can be demeaning to the person pitied. Public fund-raising efforts sometimes tilt from compassion to pity and may betray their worthy cause.

2. *For Reasons of Prudence.* The argument here runs as follows: I should support a policy providing special assistance to chronically ill children, even strangers, because I may someday have a child or a grandchild or a family member who will need such assistance. The reasoning involved applies with special force to legislators and citizen advocates who do in fact have a chronically ill child in their families. Much health legislation of the past two decades has been championed by people motivated to assure the availability of resources in the event of their own or their family's needs.

The prudential argument from the view of childhood chronic illness rests on the potential occurrence of a rare but severe and unpredictable event. Any one family may have little likelihood of a severe catastrophic childhood illness. Yet to protect itself against a rare and severe event, society may allocate resources to ease a family's burden when the event does occur. Phenylketonuria (PKU) is a rare metabolic problem affecting about one in thirty thousand newborn infants and causing severe mental retardation if not identified early and treated appropriately. Sizable public resources have gone to the early identification of this condition, partly justified by the concern that PKU can occur unpredictably in any family and by the belief that it is prudent to have public programs for these matters of chance.

3. *For Reasons of Economics.* It can be argued that economic benefits to the society as a whole can accrue from the provision of early assistance to chronically ill children and their families. Such help can be seen as an investment that will yield economic returns if the child can be helped to become a productive member of society. The soundness of this argument has already been demonstrated with respect to some diseases, including juvenile-onset diabetes, leukemia, and hemophilia. To the benefit of everyone, children with these formerly lethal diseases may now live well into their productive years. Furthermore, early intervention with still fatal diseases may keep children out of wheelchairs longer or enable them to be less dependent

on public institutions. Early services of high quality to children with cystic fibrosis have enabled many children who would have been home- or hospital-bound to pursue active and reasonably normal lives in school or at work. Early assistance seems both to increase the economic productivity of children with chronic illnesses and to decrease their long-term dependence on public institutions and resources. Similarly, appropriate support may allow family members to stay employed and to be more economically productive members of society. Prevention of the personal and family disability associated with chronic illness is a main component of containing costs.

4. *For Reasons of Knowledge.* Reasons for the advancement of knowledge about chronic illness extend beyond concern for the chronically ill alone. The study of pathological conditions often yields knowledge that is widely applicable, especially in the understanding of normal processes of development. For example, much of the understanding of the ways in which the body fights infection has come from studying people who have defects in their immune system, the system that indicates whether something inside the body belongs to it or is foreign. This understanding has been crucial to the development of the technology of kidney and other organ transplantation. Similarly, much understanding of the processes of clotting of blood has come from study of patients with hemophilia and other inherited disorders of clotting. The knowledge arising from these investigations has vastly improved the blood products available to aid many people with acquired clotting disorders.

   Children with disorders of development or physical handicaps that prevent development through usual pathways may achieve goals through entirely different methods. Their success may enrich our understanding of the complexities and options in the process of human development. The efforts of families may improve understanding of the mechanisms of coping with stress, and study of programs to meet their needs may broaden knowledge of health services.

5. *For Reasons of Moral Discovery.* The fact of a chronically and catastrophically ill child is a compelling invitation to every one of us to rediscover and enrich our understanding of the moral

order, of what it means to be truly human. The child with any one of the chronic disorders may be wracked with pain, burdened with a rigorous and sometimes painful treatment regimen, and threatened by an early death. Children so grievously afflicted do society a service by freshening memories of dependency and illness; of pain, however transient it may have been; and of the finite existence and fragile hold on life. Zaner (1982, p. 36) quotes Schweitzer on the fraternity of all those who suffer or have suffered pain: "All through the world, there is a special league of those who have known anxiety and physical suffering. A mysterious bond connects those marked by pain. They know the terrible things man can undergo; they know the longing to be free of pain. Those who have been liberated from pain must not think they are now completely free again and can calmly return to life as it was before."

The handicapped serve quite as much as those who would serve them, if not more so. They serve by quickening their helpers' moral sensibilities and making them more human through identification with humankind in the particulars of a suffering person. English writer Paul Hunt (1966), who is chronically ill, puts the issue this way:

Obviously we who are disabled are deeply affected by the assumptions of our uselessness that surround us. But, it is vital that we should not accept this devaluation of ourselves, yearning only to be able to earn our living and thus prove our worth. We do not have to prove anything. By our being we cannot help pose questions about values, about what a person is, what he is for, about whether his work is the ultimate criterion of his worth, whether work in the everyday sense of the word is the most important or the only contribution anyone can make to society. At the ultimate point, we may only be able to suffer, to be passive through complete physical disability. Just here we have a special insight to offer, because our position gives us an extra experience of life in the passive aspect that is one-half of the human reality. Those who lead active lives are perhaps especially inclined to ignore man's need to accept passivity in relation to the many forces beyond his control [p. 51].

If these observations have a persuasive validity, then the helping relationship itself is inextricably a moral undertaking. The treatment of a severe chronic illness, which so often embraces the child's whole being, requires mutual dependence of the therapist and child and the recognition that both grow through the interaction.

Justice in Resource Allocation

How can the just allocation of public resources be assured? What are the boundaries of public and private responsibilities in the provision of health services, especially those for chronically ill children and their families? Health care is a *good* that is inseparable from other benefits more or less planfully sought in the construction of a social order. Some theorists claim that health is so important that it has an absolute and prior claim on resources and commitments. Health care, then, could be claimed as a right. Worthy as such expressions of ideals may be, the fact is that health care is not so regarded in most societies and must compete with other benefits widely regarded as good, such as food, clothing, shelter, education, recreation, and security. This competition always proceeds under the restraints of limited resources. If a people choose more of one, they must choose less of another. Yet certain choices have been made in this country. Education is considered a universal right, as is access to a minimum level of shelter. Recreation, on the other hand, commands less public support. Health seems closer to education and housing than to recreation, although controversy continues over access to health services as a publicly mandated right in the United States. Justice is an important principle in deciding among competing options as much for the distribution of care as for the distribution of costs. Thus, one further reason to make resources available to chronically ill children is the need to ensure that justice is done.

Veatch (1976, p. 128) asserts, "Many of the crucial contemporary questions in health policy planning are distributive. How do we allocate health care? Who gets the scarce intensive-care-unit beds or dialysis machines? Why should hemodialysis care be paid for by the federal government, but not cancer care? . . . And which diseases ought to be covered?"

How are funds to be allocated when the dollars available fall far short of those required, when there are insufficient hospital resources for chronically ill children clearly in need of specialized care, or when there are too few dialysis machines to go around? Considerations unrelated to the achievement of justice (such as historical precedent, the exercise of technical skill, and the social, economic, or professional status of the people involved) will inevitably play a role in decision making, but their influence can be attenuated and a greater justice served if there are available some examined criteria for choosing among competing opinions. The following criteria may aid in defining priorities for resource distribution (Outka, 1975).

To Each According to Merit. The notion of awarding goods on the basis of merit is familiar in daily life and could provide the basis for a rough justice in our society. To the extent that the possession of money is an indicator of merit, however imperfect, merit plays an important part in determining who gets what services and what kinds of services they get. Although there is a wide acceptance of this principle in general, no one seems to be completely happy with such an imperfect calculus in matters of health. Unlike fine cars, luxury vacations, and servants, health intuitively appears to have a prior claim on resources, to *feel* like a human right—a right that can be and often is abridged, as are other rights, but always with some pangs of conscience.

The criterion of merit is complicated by the problem of personal effort and responsibility. For example, it may seem reasonable to withhold or reduce services to individuals who make little effort to maintain their own health, who smoke, drink excessively, overeat, or refuse to exercise. However, this distributive policy does not take into account differences in personal circumstances and the ability to influence and change behavior. On the whole, society is remarkably indulgent in such matters and provides services, especially if the person can pay for them. The criterion of responsibility carries even greater problems in childhood. Although there may be occasional occurrence of chronic illness in children where parents can be faulted for the lack of prudence, to place responsibility for the presence of disease on the child seems particularly unfounded. Severe and chronic illness in childhood has all the attributes of a natural catastrophe: it is unpredictable, unavoidable, and grievously burdensome where chance crowds out merit in determining compensation. Responsibility does not provide a just ground for withholding resources from children.

Some have distinguished two kinds of goods (those earned by effort and those demanded by need) and have placed health services in the latter (Outka, 1974), thereby removing the criterion of merit from options for allocation. But if merit remains a consideration, how is it defined for children? Is it based on family merit or some estimate of the value of a child to that child's family? Application of the concept of merit, hard enough among adults, is even more difficult among children.

To Each According to Societal Contribution. There is a certain appeal to the notion that those who contribute most to society have the most cogent claim upon the resources of society. Sometimes such privilege is attendant upon membership in a group, sometimes on individual social worth as judged in some way. For example, it is well established that elderly people and disabled veterans have an uncontested claim to health resources by virtue of their service to society as a group. This line of thought has led to efforts to judge an individual's social worth in establishing priorities for scarce health resources. Thus, when kidney machines first came into use and were in exceedingly short supply, with death a sure consequence of lack of access to a machine, some medical centers set up committees to judge the societal contributions of candidates for dialysis.

Quite apart from the unworkability of this notion and its intrinsic affront to the dignity of the person, the effort generally unraveled in contradiction and confusion and was widely criticized. Who is to judge the worth of another human being? Ramsey (1970) describes the fundamental issues inherent in deciding which adults to dialyze and concludes that "the equal right of every human being to live, and not relative personal or social worth, should be the ruling principle" (p. 256). The criterion of societal worth is especially inappropriate when applied to children who have had no opportunity to demonstrate their worth. Nonetheless, the criterion of societal worth is ubiquitously present in planning for the allocation of health resources both to chronically ill children as a group and to classes of children within that group. For children, the exercise entails a trading in futures.

The principle of allocating resources on the basis of societal worth is expressed partly in efforts to establish future economic benefits from providing services to chronically ill children and their families. The argument is that a present investment in care for chronically ill children will result in their living longer and more productive lives than they could lead without assistance and that society will be the beneficiary of the investment. The criterion of worth is pressed further in the argument that treatment of some diseases should take precedence over treatment of others because of the differential promise of children in one category over another. Thus, it may be asserted, children with diabetes are more worthy of health services than children with myelomeningocele because of the differential prognoses for intellectual development. In spite of their surface reasonableness, such predictions of the future worth of children are as complex as attempts to assess past contributions of adults. Although distinctions might be made among children based on intelligence or function or developmental capacity, no criteria capture the complexity of the child or that child's long-term outcome. This approach, too, falters in implementation.

To Each According to Need. If health is considered to have the characteristics of a fundamental right (such as freedom) limited only by natural circumstance and the rights of others, then it would make sense to distribute health services on the basis of need. The potential conflict with individual liberties must be recognized; health services may not ordinarily be imposed against an individual's will. It is necessary to differentiate among need, want, and utilization (which are not the same) and to guard against the unnecessary, frivolous, or dangerous use of health resources, especially those that are scarce and those supported, directly or indirectly, by public funds. As a general goal, individuals should have access to health services to help them achieve, insofar as possible, a level of health roughly equivalent to that of most other people.

Yet the criterion of need breaks down in the normal circumstance of scarce resources. There will never be enough resources to meet all health needs. Even in countries that have a strong commitment to equity in the distribution of health resources, not all needs are met. To fix priorities for the distribution of health care, it remains necessary to achieve agreement on which is the greater and which the lesser need.

Furthermore, the criterion of need clashes with considerations of equity. Within a population of chronically ill children, there may be a level of health, a threshold, that represents a reasonable level for the population. The resources required to bring one child above that threshold may be equivalent to the resources required to bring nine other less impaired children above the same threshold. Even within defined populations, it is not always possible to maximize both justice and equity.

To Each on a Random Basis. Scarce resources could be made available to chronically ill children and their families on a random basis. On first hearing, this proposal seems irrational, but further examination reveals its merit.

The proposal is most persuasive when resources are sharply limited, when they cannot be made available on piecemeal basis with the hope that withheld treatment can be provided by others or that partial care will have some beneficial effect.

Allocation of resources on a first come, first served basis is a variant of random selection. One may be rueful at arriving too late, but random allocation does not appear unjust. No one would think of taking a child off a kidney machine in order to make the machine available to another child judged more worthy. The allocation of scarce resources on a first come, first served basis does have two clear limitations: (1) people already advantaged know how to take advantage of limited opportunities and have the confidence to do so and (2) there is always the possibility of breaking the queue, being put at the head of the line on the basis of presumed privilege. If randomness of arrival can be assured by the distributors of health resources, it may be a reasonable and readily acceptable basis for choice.

The Fifth Option: Compromise. A fifth choice for the just allocation of resources is a compromise of the previous four. Each of these criteria is an imperfect guide in the practical world, although consideration of them contributes to the level of understanding by which society can approach a more just allocation. To many, the criterion of need is most compelling, but it too is impractical as a specific and sole means of allocating resources.

Summary

We have presented in this chapter a series of problems in professional and public ethics, largely as they relate to the needs experienced by the families of chronically ill children. Policy makers are unlikely to make explicit the values that inform their decisions. Policy analysis, on the other hand, requires close consideration of the underlying values of policy, even where policy making must minimize discussion of values so as to build a policy consensus.

The ethics of decision making and informed consent create hard choices yet demand vigilant attention. The reasons for allocating resources to families whose children have chronic health conditions are varied and compelling. In resource allocation and other matters of public policy, the choices are always difficult. We recognize full well the complex and at times conflicting nature of these issues. Yet we judge that greater recognition of the conflicts will allow more thoughtful attention to value issues in the difficult areas of clinical care, schools and illness, and the allocation of scarce resources. The discussion takes us from a presentation of value issues to lay out in the next chapter principles to guide development of national public policy for chronically ill children and their families.

11

Principles for Assessing Public Policy Options

To this point, we have been concerned with exploring the many issues raised by chronic illness in childhood and with reviewing public responses to the needs of affected families. That government and communities have a responsibility to children with special health needs is incontestable, but the extent of the responsibility, the proper organization of services, and the levels of financial support of the public response are matters of ongoing debate. Based on our review of the tasks families encounter and of the strengths and weaknesses of the public response so far, we have developed a set of principles to inform the debate and to guide national policy for chronically ill children and their families.

Our objective in this chapter is to present criteria by which the merits of public policy options can be assessed. Present programs and new proposals can then be examined for their relative adherence to the principles, which also provide a template against which new policies can be compared. The principles serve as well to inform ethical standards governing the relationship between caregivers and the children and families needing their assistance.

The principles are intended to underlie policies for children with special needs, regardless of the specific condition. Although we have focused some on the eleven marker conditions, the principles allow examination of programs and policies for all childhood chronic conditions and are applicable as well to policy for families

314

whose children have other handicapping or disabling conditions. Policy is implemented at federal, state, and local levels and through many mechanisms, among which are direct financial support of programs or services, incentives for certain services or behaviors, regulation of reimbursement policies or of licensure, support for the training or deployment of professionals, and support of research endeavors. Policy for families with chronically ill children develops in the context of other health and social programs, which receive fluctuating levels of attention. Activities in all of these arenas are important in improving the lives of families, and we view the principles as a guide to policy regardless of where it develops or the forms it takes. In the final chapter, we address options for policy and evaluate them in light of the principles.

The Central Nature of the Family

Families are the primary caretakers of their own children. A goal of policy should be to help the family of a child become competent in meeting the demands of the illness. How can the family's ability to cope well and sensitively with the stress of chronic illness in a child be enhanced? Policy can support families by ensuring that services are provided as close to home as possible in order to strengthen the family's capacity to assume the main responsibility and to encourage care at home rather than in institutions. Facilitating the family's central role often requires providing family services and financial support. Intellectual and financial resources should be allocated toward activities that will enable the family to carry out its own tasks rather than diminish their responsibility or central role in the care of their own child.

Policy can encourage the education of families to be informed consumers and can provide incentives for family involvement in decision making about the health care and education of their child with a chronic illness. We have described the critical and complex nature of the family's participation in decisions (Chapter Ten). Recognition that parents are the primary caretakers of their own children is at times difficult for professionals. Physicians and others often assume that they are the main caretakers of their clients and relegate parents to a peripheral role. Policy can support families by training professionals to be sensitive to family issues. Family rights and responsibilities should be clearly defined, with professionals providing supportive consultation to parents and child.

A perspective incorporating an understanding of child and family development fosters better education of child and family about illness and its consequences. How a five-year-old conceives of asthma differs qualitatively from the ideas of a fifteen-year-old. Families just learning of a new serious diagnosis have needs and resources different from those of families who have wrestled with the illness over several years.

Growing up with a chronic illness provides especially complex developmental issues for adolescents. A key task for the able-bodied adolescent is to become physiologically and emotionally independent of the family, but a chronically ill child often must maintain a moderate degree of dependence. Teenagers should be encouraged to develop as much independence as possible, and support should be provided to help the family understand the prospects for independence of their child. Yet here, there are real limits to our knowledge. Many children with handicaps can exceed parental or professional expectations. Other children, despite minimal physiological disability, may be markedly impaired in their ability to carry out usual daily tasks. The prediction of what can be done by the individual child is fraught with error, and in general, families can best support the optimal development of their child through continuing discussion and reconsideration of their child's needs for both dependence and independence. Policy can encourage the education of families about typical patterns of development and can foster services to help youth with illness and disabilities make the transition to adulthood.

Chronic illness in a child affects the parents and siblings as well and influences the relationships within the family. Parents face special strains from having a child with chronic health problems— strains that may affect the functioning of the family unit, their social ties, or their efforts in the workplace. Adjustment to the birth of a child with a health impairment or to the diagnosis of a long-term serious illness creates special burdens and opportunities for the family. Siblings may have greater caretaking responsibilities and receive less attention from their parents, who are absorbed in the care of the sick child. Conflict may arise through the competing demands of the ill child and those of the rest of the family. There are family needs beyond those of the affected child, and a family-centered policy will address the needs of other family members along with those of the child with illness.

Responsibilities of Communities

Members of the larger community should be encouraged to contribute to the well-being of chronically ill children and their families and to do so without intrusion or obligation. We define community as the shared commitment of a group of people to mutual assistance and the achievement of common purposes. There are levels of community ranging from neighborhoods and other small groups of individuals to villages, towns, and cities with interacting dependencies and loosely shared objectives, to the national community that embraces culturally diverse and widely scattered groups with many separate purposes but with ties of history and tradition, mutually supportive commitments, and generally shared objectives. The concept of community implies mutuality, reciprocal obligations, and common benefits. It has long been recognized that the health and welfare of children are matters of public and community concern. The vitality, the productivity, and the quality of life for all people are dependent upon rearing new generations of children strong in body, quick in mind, and generous in spirit. Community acceptance for a child with a rare, severe chronic illness means that the child has access to community activities and resources and that the community nurtures that child's participation as it does the participation of any other child. Although individual differences may influence any child's activity, policy can help children through encouraging the community to focus on the child rather than on the illness. The commitment and responsibility of communities involve the sharing of burdens and generous support of family needs through the mobilization of community concern. Although some commitment may be financial, much of it involves organization and provision of direct support services. Families will carry out their tasks more effectively if they can rely on their community of neighbors and the public community for support.

The mobilization of community resources is always a creative and demanding task. How can community voluntarism benefit the lives of chronically ill children? How are the special strengths of individual communities best organized to foster families' capabilities to raise their children who have chronic illnesses? Programs and services may be more easily implemented in a centralized fashion, yet it is at the local community level that children live and grow. Policy can help families by encouraging both knowledge of local resources on the part of professionals and education about childhood chronic illness at the community level. The transfer of resources and the development of services at the community level can be emphasized. And professionals can be encouraged to be sensitive to the charàcteristics of communities, especially to the ways in which communities of different ethnic and cultural backgrounds understand illness and care for community members. Fostering community concern through the establishment of basic services in communities and through an alliance of providers and community is a crucial element of a public policy that is effective in meeting the needs of families with chronically ill children.

Commonalities in the Special Needs of Chronically Ill Children

Despite individual differences among the various chronic illnesses of childhood, children with these illnesses should be considered together as a single class for purposes of policy and program development. Policy should reflect the differences and similarities among children with varied chronic illnesses. There are important differences among the conditions and their treatments, yet the majority of concerns raised by parents—perhaps as much as 85 percent—are common to all families with chronically ill children, and only 15 percent pertain to the specific disease. The fact of chronicity, the continuing demands of illness, and the attendant stress are faced by all families with chronically ill children regardless of the specific health condition.

Furthermore, chronically ill children and their families are burdened in ways that distinguish them from able-bodied children.

These distinctive burdens require specific and special services generally not required by most other children. Chronically ill children need easy and assured access to high-quality specialty services. Healthy children should receive the vast majority of their health services from nonspecialty providers near their communities. Most families do well without genetic services. Yet many chronic illnesses have a major genetic component, and affected families should know the implications for themselves and for their children both with and without disease. Families with chronically ill children may need transportation services, financial support to deal with the costly illness, or special help with access to appropriate schooling. A few services (for example, occupational or physical therapy) may be required by other children with handicapping conditions, and other services (such as nutritional counseling) may be of benefit to all children and their families. Policy can help families by addressing the special burdens shared by most families with chronically ill children and by responding to common needs in a coordinated fashion.

The report of the Select Panel for the Promotion of Child Health (1981) documented and clarified the many successes of recent decades in improving health services to children and mothers in the United States. It also proposed an agenda to ensure continued progress. Policy development for childhood chronic illness should be integrated with other initiatives in child health policy. Improvements in general child health services will improve the lot of chronically ill children and their families. Yet no matter what national child health policy develops, the families of chronically ill children will still have special needs that are not met through organized health services for all children. The special burdens attending childhood chronic illness, although best addressed in the context of improved health care for all children, will continue to need direct public attention.

The commonalities of need arising among families whose children have very diverse health conditions allow special opportunities in policy and program formulation. Although the disease-specific needs of children demand careful attention, the great similarity of family concerns encourages the consideration of diseases together in program and policy development rather than in a fragmented or disease-by-disease fashion.

Participation in School

School-age children should be in school to the maximum extent feasible. How can policy encourage these children's participation in schools? Chronically ill children will learn best in the least restrictive setting possible. Efforts to help children with chronic health conditions can assure that plans developed for them emphasize maximum time on-task in school and minimize the interference of the condition or its treatment. For cases in which illness and its exacerbations or treatment do interfere with school attendance, homebound and hospital-based instruction should be available to continue the child's educational advancement. Such services should be provided with the recognition that many conditions (asthma, for example) have brief but frequent exacerbations and that the cumulative effect of a large number of brief school absences may be significant. Physical infirmity is different from cognitive or intellectual impairment, and policy should allow different placement for different needs. Special services to improve cognitive or developmental function are best reserved for children who need special help in the area of intellectual achievement. Chronically ill children who have physical handicaps or who need special access or health treatments within schools are best served if barriers to their participation in regular classroom activities are diminished.

Issues of professional ethics are basic to teachers as well as other professionals working with chronically ill children and their families. Teachers can help by interpreting the child's illness to others and by providing education to children regarding the problems and contributions of people with chronic illnesses. Schools can develop enough knowledge about the conditions they encounter to assure that children are not unnecessarily excluded from classrooms. Further, flexibility in school policies will aid children to receive needed services, such as special diets, medications, and illness monitoring. These special services should be provided with due respect and privacy assured their recipient. Provisions for rest and restrictions on some physical activities may be necessary, although restrictions not required by the disease may inappropriately limit the child's physical and social development.

Range and Quality of Services

Public efforts for chronically ill children and their families should assure that an appropriately broad range of services is available to families. A focus on medical and surgical services alone leaves unattended many of the needs of the child and family and often diminishes the benefits of the medical or surgical procedure. Insufficient physical therapy following an orthopedic procedure, for example, may lessen the long-term functional improvement from the operation. If the goal of therapy is to enable the child to function as well as possible in usual daily activities appropriate for age, a surgical procedure may need to be coordinated with effective home care and homebound teaching in combination with efforts to return the child to school as early as possible.

Services needed by families with chronically ill children can be many in number. Families vary widely in their needs, and the specific concerns of each family should direct the services offered. Yet certain patterns of preventive and treatment services emerge as families with chronically ill children identify their needs.

Preventive services, to prevent the illness if possible or otherwise to prevent or diminish disability, must be available. A high prevalence of certain diseases, such as yellow fever, smallpox, and tuberculosis, kept them in high public awareness and fostered a sense of urgency that something be done to eliminate them. The Panama Canal could be built only when substantial progress had been made in controlling yellow fever and malaria. But the severe chronic illnesses of childhood are relatively rare and seldom intrude into the public consciousness. Economic progress is seldom impeded by the presence of a chronic illness in childhood, and most people know little or nothing of cystic fibrosis or thalassemia. Consequently, efforts to improve prevention must fall on professional people, on enlightened legislators, on citizens who have directly experienced the devastation of childhood chronic illness, or on citizens who can be moved to action by a broad and humane view of community. The rare, serious, and chronic illnesses of childhood exact an enormous toll in physical suffering, in psychological distress, and in the cost of care. On these grounds, they call for determined efforts, with prevention a foremost concern.

Opportunities for prenatal diagnosis of a number of chronic illnesses have expanded tremendously during the past decade. In the next decade or so, it is likely that genetic engineering will influence the molecular basis of disease in utero, thus allowing for prevention of illness in a child before birth. Families should be advised of the availability of preventive diagnostic and treatment services and should be made aware of their options in planned or present pregnancies.

There are economic and social benefits to the prevention of the consequences of childhood chronic illness. Early treatment of chronically ill children may diminish their later dependence on public institutions. High-quality preventive services can both diminish acute exacerbations of disease that lead to hospitalizations and improve long-term physiological and functional outcomes. Maintenance of good glucose control in diabetes, for example, seems likely to diminish the long-term consequences of blindness and severe kidney disease. Cure is rarely available for a chronic illness. Rather, policy and health services must aim to prevent the physiological and psychosocial consequences of chronic illness. Treatment services, too, have a preventive focus in that they can reduce the likelihood that a disease will become a disability.

All children need quality general health care. Chronically ill children often need general health care services even more than their able-bodied peers; they may be especially susceptible to other physical illnesses or developmental problems. Yet they frequently lack basic immunizations and screening for common health problems not directly related to their main chronic condition. The tendency to characterize chronically ill children by their disease ("asthmatics," "cystics") rather than as children who have a chronic condition ("a child with asthma") is reflected in the tendency to provide excellent specialty services while neglecting basic immunizations and other preventive health and family services.

Access to high-quality specialty care offers chronically ill children the benefit of the most recent technological advances for their specific condition. With their greater experience with the condition, specialists are knowledgeable about both frequent and uncommon complications of a specific disorder. Preventing complications and encouraging the best possible physiological outcome are goals of specialty care.

The provision of high-quality general and specialized health services must be balanced with the provision of services to address other family needs. Through emphasizing a broad array of family concerns, policy can enable families to meet their own needs more effectively and encourage the best functioning of their child with a chronic health problem. Recent progress in providing care at or near home highlights this issue. The advances in home management of hemophilia and the decentralization of care for children with leukemia are two dramatic advances of the past decade. New portable equipment has allowed home-based care for many children who previously had to depend on expensive hospital resources. Yet many insurance programs, both private and public, have not kept pace with these advances and have lagged in their support of home-care services.

Home care is but one example of the varied services that may benefit a family. Provision of such services is merited both by humanitarian concern to alleviate the burdens of many families with chronic illnesses and by pragmatic concern to maximize the benefits of medical and surgical care. Furthermore, there is good evidence that the judicious provision of many of these services will lessen the dependence of families on very expensive hospital-based and technological services. For example, among children with asthma, relatively inexpensive activities—the addition of a skilled nurse educator to an allergy practice, the development of parent support groups, improved education about asthma—are all associated with decreased use of emergency services and fewer hospitalizations of children with attacks. The range of family services includes financial support, genetic counseling, support for communication between specialists and other health providers, homemaker services, nutrition services, education for children and families about illness, respite care for family members, and psychological counseling for children and their families to prevent associated psychological handicaps.

How can high standards of quality be ensured for those providing a broad range of services? There is a strong disposition, particularly among medical personnel, to define quality of care in terms of high-technology care; yet these are not synonymous. The exercise of technical competence makes sense in order to relieve suffering but is never justifiable for its own sake. It is reasonable and ethical only in the context of either a comprehensive assessment of the needs of a chronically ill child and that child's family or a convincing need for new knowledge that can then be used to the benefit of the child and other children. The best care may not be the most expensive or most extensive care. The application of high-technology care often carries risks for the child, many of which are neither known nor even imagined at the time the technology is developed. Excessive use of technology has characterized the care of many health problems, perhaps more among adults than among children. Yet the uncontrolled use of high technology, in addition to its obvious financial costs, may run counter to the best interest of the child and family. And where resources are limited, the investment in high-technology services may mean that other needed services are unavailable.

The tasks faced by families of chronically ill children go well beyond the concerns of the medical system, and the medical system alone is neither likely nor able to deal with these concerns adequately. The range of services needed is necessarily much broader than just medical services, and policy can help families by ensuring availability of a full range.

Justice and Equity

Health resources should be distributed in a just and equitable fashion. At the level of public policy, equity requires that health resources be made available to chronically ill children and their families without regard to nonfunctional criteria, such as race, sex, religion, social status, and place of residence. Characteristically, the public sector serves one part of the population and the private another; the main driving force between them is the source of reimbursement. Benefits of separate health services for people according to their differing insurance coverage cannot be demonstrated. Whether separate but equal services benefit the well or able-bodied child, the scarcity of high-quality and comprehensive specialty services for the rare chronic conditions of childhood argues against developing separate systems for chronically ill children based on source of payment. The development of coordinated quality services for rare chronic illnesses requires imagination and great effort, and to duplicate services in the public and private sectors in the many areas of the country where resources are scarce is illogical and inequitable.

Children in rural areas should have equal access to quality specialty services, even though the services are often centralized in larger cities. Policy can help rural families by providing access to specialty care and by encouraging the provision of some services in rural areas. Equity of access is compatible with a system of shared costs. Forms of cost-sharing may influence access of different groups to services. Similarly, equity does not require identical treatment of all persons; some individuals may need to be treated differently in order to be treated equitably.

Justice in the distribution of health resources assumes a manner that would be generally regarded as fair and in accordance with examined and accepted procedures. At the level of program operation (in a state Crippled Children's Services, a medical center resource utilization committee, or a community health resources board), considerations of justice make their most exacting demands. Here especially, considerations of due process come into play. Procedures for the allocation of resources should be formally established after open discussions that include all affected individuals and groups, especially chronically ill children and their families. Affected individuals and families should have responsibilities in overseeing programs, in policy formulation, and in effecting new legislation. Procedures should be open to public scrutiny and should undergo periodic review and revision in accordance with established procedure. This ethical position is best achieved by avoiding eligibility requirements that are intrinsically demeaning to individuals or groups, by encouraging the sharing of information needed by individuals and families to make mature choices, and by assuring both access to programmatic information and its easy distribution through appropriate media so the program can benefit from public scrutiny and criticism.

Attention to issues of justice and equity will help families, although as we observed in the previous chapter, each proposed criterion for just allocation of resources is partly flawed. Family needs and the public concern will be best met if resource allocation is considered carefully and in a public fashion.

Professional Ethics and Responsibilities

Policies should encourage an ethical relationship between providers and family. Respect and trust should characterize the personal relationship among health care providers and both the patient and those important in the patient's life. Similarly, children and families should be able to interact with schools and other important agencies in ways that encourage mutual trust and respect. Careful exchange of information (with an emphasis on truth-telling) and the clear management of issues of choice seem fundamental to ethical relationships.

Truth-telling and the participation of families in decision making are key elements of ethical care. Professonals should carefully explain the disease and its treatment to the family and should outline the options of care in understandable ways. Families expect clear and exact answers to questions whose answers are uncertain and imprecise, and the tremendous biological variation among individuals creates a wide variety of questions lacking exact answers. One cannot know the long-term consequences of a new therapy that has been available for only a year or two. Great uncertainty characterizes medicine in general and especially the idiosyncratic response of an individual to long-term illness and its treatment. Therefore, truth-telling becomes even more difficult. Professionals must provide information, knowing that answers are frequently unavailable regarding the likely prognosis for an individual child, the efficacy of a given treatment, or the degree of worry that should be attached to a new symptom. Information should be shared in a way that informs families accurately and clearly of what is and is not known about their child's condition. Truth-telling should encourage health providers to recognize the limits of their effectiveness. Realistic appraisal of what can be done rather than promises of results unlikely to be achieved are in the family's best interest. Information that is provided should be treated with appropriate confidentiality, respecting the dignity and integrity of families and children.

For children with chronic illnesses, there are many choices, and most reflect decisions other than those of life and death in an acute hospital setting. There is a wide range of daily choices: when to start and stop specific medications, whether to undergo treatments that will interfere with the child's participation in school or club activities, when and how much exercise to recommend for a child with an orthopedic handicap. When does a treatment or a diet become so distasteful that its psychological effects outweigh its physiological benefits? What limitations should be placed on a child's activities because of the illness? These questions are qualitatively different from those usually considered in informed consent, which would include the performance of an appendectomy or some other acute diagnostic or therapeutic procedure. For chronic care, informed consent should also apply to planning of ongoing health and educational programs for the child and family. Choices in the application of technology should also involve families. Policy should ensure that children and families participate in these frequent, daily choices.

Conflicts may arise in decision making. When the conflict is between the desires of the family and what is best for the child, professional responsibilities can become very difficult, although in such cases the services of those working with the family are often most needed. Where the preferences of health providers and those of families conflict, providers should accede to informed family preferences, even when the family requests discontinuation of medical care.

The limitations of any one professional provide a compelling argument for collaboration with other professionals in organizing services; this would be in addition to collaboration with families. Teamwork in the provision of services requires that responsibilities for each team member and each consultant be clearly defined. One team member (or family member) should have a stated responsibility for the coordination of services and for ensuring adequate communication among team members and between teams and family. Many different types of people, including family members, can carry out coordination functions. That provision for coordination be made is more important than who does the coordination.

Policy can help through fostering the education of professionals about teamwork and ethical relationships. And it can encourage research to strengthen understanding of decision making.

The Quest for New Knowledge

Knowledge is a transcendent value in long-term planning for chronically ill children and their families. How can the continued growth of new knowledge be assured? For our purposes, knowledge embraces the understanding of the epidemiology, etiology, manifestations, treatment, course with and without treatment, prognosis, and outcome for chronic illness. We prefer a functional and family-oriented definition of outcome, one that incorporates the physiological course of the illness, individual development, family relationships, and community involvement. As here implied, knowledge places high value on research and scholarly analysis; it includes, as well, the training of investigators along with the wide array of service providers.

The dramatic advances of the past few decades affecting the causes of death of children and improving the care of children with chronic illnesses have come about primarily through investment in basic research. Basic biomedical research should be a keystone of national policy. Yet attention to other areas of promise is needed— to strengthen understanding of the multiple causes of illness or handicap, to explore the processes of coping and adjustment, and to define the mechanisms by which families best receive services. Policy can help families by developing an equal commitment to conducting vital, quality research in basic developmental, biosocial, and health services designed to improve the knowledge base on which services are provided and programs are developed. Policy can also help ensure renewal of the research community by vigorous support of research and training activities.

Summary

The eight principles discussed here should guide policy development for families who have chronically ill children or other children with special needs. The principles may be taken as criteria by which to plan or examine programs and policies. They are applicable, regardless of the means of financing or organizing services for chronically ill children in specific or for children in general. We rephrase them here as specifications for national policy, again recognizing that national policy can be implemented at any level of government.

1. Families have the central role in caring for their own members. The goal of public policy is to enable families to carry out as competently as possible their responsibilities in nurturing their children and encouraging their development.

2. Policy should encourage members of the larger community to contribute to the well-being of children with chronic illnesses and their families. The development of community-based services is a central goal for national policy for families with children with special health needs.

3. Children with chronic illnesses and their families have special needs that require specific attention, regardless of the means of financing and providing health services for all children. With few exceptions, these special needs are common to all children with chronic health impairment. The extent of these similarities encourages consideration of all chronically ill children together as a single class for policy development.

4. Chronically ill children should stay on task in school to the greatest degree possible. Insofar as schooling is the main occupation of young people, the interference of illness with educational activities should be diminished.

5. A broad array of high-quality preventive and treatment services should be available to families with chronically ill children. The provision of medical-surgical or health services to the exclusion of services for the many other family needs diminishes the likelihood of best functional outcome for the child and limits the effectiveness of the medical treatment itself.

6. Services that are provided should be distributed in an equitable and just fashion, specifically excluding from the distribution formula such nonfunctional items as race, sex, religion, and socioeconomic class.

7. Policy should encourage professional services of a high ethical nature. Truth-telling, confidentiality, maintenance of dignity and respect for family preferences, recognition of limits of professional effectiveness, and an emphasis on collaboration are key elements of the ethical provision of services.

8. That many of the tremendous advances in the health of chronically ill children in the United States have resulted from a commitment to sound basic research should be recognized in public policy by continued and expanded investment in basic research. Vigorous support of biomedical research should be accompanied by equal efforts in psychological, biosocial, and health services research as they relate to chronic illness in childhood.

We have enumerated principles that form the basis for a considered public response to the needs of children with chronic illnesses and their families. Yet principles are reflected in large degree through the choices exercised in developing services or training or in financing programs. In the final chapter, we define a series of policy options and explore how they embody the eight principles.

❧ 12 ❧

Chronically Ill Children in Families: Policy Choices and Recommendations

Throughout the previous chapters, we have defined the problems and issues in the care of children with chronic illness, identified the strengths and weaknesses of existing programs, and provided a means for judging the merits of these efforts and of new policy proposals. Our work leads us to outline here specific policy options worthy of consideration. In this chapter, we describe and analyze six policy directions along which this nation might chart its course in providing care to children with a chronic illness.

The options vary widely in the degree of restructuring and changed financing required. Two minimalist options demand the least change in current financial and organizational mechanisms. The first of these directs attention to the health needs of all children and families without addressing the special needs of children with chronic illnesses. The second maximizes investment in research on methods to treat and especially to prevent childhood chronic illnesses. A third option proposes to develop national service or insurance programs for children with chronic illnesses. Additional funding to the present system of care is the fourth option. In the fifth option, we present a number of opportunities for incremental

331

reform in the organization and financing of services and in the ways children with chronic illness are educated. The sixth option calls for development of a national community-based program for chronically ill children and their families; this option incorporates many elements of the reform option.

To each option we apply with broad strokes the value criteria embodied in the principles of Chapter Eleven. We also consider briefly such factors as cost and feasibility of implementation. Estimating costs is fraught with uncertainty. When estimates have been made even for existing programs, prospective calculations have been notoriously inaccurate; such calculations often fail to address adequately both the complex interactions of direct and indirect costs and the potential for benefits and savings. To provide a vision of the opportunities available to help families, the options are purposely presented at a relatively abstract level. Implementation of any of the options will rest on an educated citizenry and on those who assume the difficult task of balancing constrained resources with the pressing needs of these children and their families. Regardless of the direction traveled, difficult choices will always be present.

Progress in improving care for families with chronically ill children will likely occur through adoption of a variety of new policies that incorporate several elements of the options described here. Current service delivery arrangements for these children reflect a pluralism based on the use of both public and private resources. Progress will depend on the vision of those in leadership positions, who may see the range of opportunities within this system. Policies must also interface with activities that support the health and education of all children. Most of the options described here apply equally to the prospects of improving the lives of all children in the United States.

Some of the options we describe entail fundamental reform of the health care system; others represent an incremental approach. Several of the options could be pursued simultaneously in the development of a coordinated and well-reasoned national policy. A fundamental question for each option is how well it strives to improve the developmental capacity of children with illnesses and how it structures the environment to allow children and families to function better.

Minimalist Options

Two options can be defined as minimalist in the sense that they would allocate few resources directly to children with a chronic illness. The first of these embraces the notion of the greatest good for the greatest number; for convenience, we term it the greatest-good option. The second rests on a commitment of all available resources to research alone; we call this the research-only option.

Greatest Good. The greatest-good option is straightforward. The nation would devote its child health resources to improving care for all children. The relatively few children with long-term health problems would receive no overt attention, although they would benefit indirectly from improvements in services geared to all children.

Several powerful arguments support this option. First, in 1981, the Select Panel for the Promotion of Child Health issued a report documenting the serious problems involved in providing health care to mothers and children and focusing especially on those not well served by the current system. These problems remain and deserve continued attention. With limited resources, is it wise to invest more in services for children with chronic illness— especially in light of the fact that these children presently command a portion of the child health dollar well out of keeping with their prevalence? Greater investment in health services for all children might be more equitable and assure a fairer distribution of re- sources. Moreover, the prevention of illness among all children may yield a greater return on investment than the treatment of chronic disorders.

A second argument for this option rests on the belief that economic incentives stemming from public demand for services will assure the provision of services that are truly needed. The assump- tion is that, if sufficient numbers of individuals want a service, providers will offer it—and that if the service is truly needed, sufficient numbers of people will want it. To the extent that parents of children with chronic illness can raise their voices in unison, improvements may emerge. This argument reflects assumptions about the salutary consequences for minority groups of unfettered competition in the marketplace.

A third argument for the greatest-good option involves a traditional view of public responsibilities in health. From that vantage point, public responsibilities would emphasize services, such as preventive and environmental services, that will benefit the population as a whole. Curative and treatment services that benefit relatively few people would be the responsibility of the private sector. This argument assumes that the private sector can respond adequately without public assistance to the needs of children with a chronic illness.

A fourth argument for this option reflects concern that knowledge about chronic illness in childhood is too limited to justify widespread programs. What medical interventions really work? What are the optimal services to prevent both disease and its complications? How are services best organized and distributed? Even such data as the number of children with severe chronic illnesses are hard to find. With tremendous gaps in knowledge, is there wisdom in doing less until more is known?

Although the arguments supporting this option are strong, the ones against it are stronger. First, there is no assurance that the economic incentives that predominate in the private sector will lead to services that are specifically needed by children with a chronic illness and their families. In fact, the relatively small numbers of these children and the complex services they require are unlikely to convince the private sector of the economic benefits of providing these services. There are few, if any, incentives for the private sector to provide many services needed by chronically ill children. That private health insurance plans discourage a wide range of services illustrates this point.

Furthermore, the belief that public monies should be spent on prevention services for all children ignores the special nature of preventive services for the population of chronically ill children. Genetic counseling for families with an afflicted child (which would assist the planning for future children) demands quite different skills and knowledge from those for counseling around family planning in general. Moreover, the prevention of unnecessary functional impairment and disability is an important goal for these children. Services to prevent unwanted conceptions of children at risk for a chronic illness and services to prevent unnecessary dependency will, over time, yield financial benefits to the society as a whole. These services are distinct from the general prevention services typically supported by public health monies and must be so recognized. Although the greatest-good option is the least costly in the short term, its long-term impact may be more expensive.

Most importantly, the greatest-good option fails in the application of the principles outlined in Chapter Eleven. It continues neglect of families and communities with chronically ill children (and their integration into the community), and problems persist in integrating health and educational services for children with special health needs. It offers neither a generic approach to policy making nor an assurance of a broad array of services. Although the option may be equally (un)just, it lends support to a marketplace where those able to purchase services will have them; other less-advantaged children will go unattended. And to the degree that the market is driven mainly by those who pay the bills (private and public insurers), families who need services (and particularly special services) will have limited impact on the market.

Research Only. The second minimalist option reflects a point made repeatedly in this book: The need for new knowledge is great because little is known about these children and their families—from basic disease processes, to child and family development, to effective services. The research-only option calls for investing all new dollars in scientific study rather than in service or program development. This option is based on assumptions similar to those for the greatest-good approach: first, there is far too little basic knowledge about childhood chronic illness to support sizable expansion in programs and, second, maximum long-term benefit may result from investing resources in research on prevention of chronic illness in childhood. On the basis of principles of equity and the generation of knowledge, this option is attractive, provided that research findings have broad applicability across classes and categories of children. Research investment, however, has generally been greater for certain diseases (based often on the skills of their

fund raisers or advocates), and other diseases have been greatly
neglected.

The research-only option is seriously flawed. First, the
assumptions on which it rests are inaccurate and myopic. Much
remains unknown about these children, but enough is known to get
started. To wait until all is certain is to remain passive forever. The
needs of these children are far too urgent for us to refrain from
initiating improvements in their care.

Moreover, the research-only option fails to address the problems in the health care system itself, including a financing system
that discourages access to a broad array of services. It provides no
assurance that families will be strengthened or that communities
will be encouraged to reach out to these children. Important as
research is, committing all monies in this direction is insufficient.

National Health Care

Some argue that radical restructuring of health care delivery
as a whole is a necessary precursor to assuring that chronically ill
children receive needed services. The assumption is that present
incentives encourage the use of costly technological, physician- and
hospital-based services and discourage the application of less expensive and equally effective therapies. Present insurance mechanisms
leave many people without coverage, and even insured persons
often lack access to important services. Restructuring of the health
care system could take several forms, varying from nationalization
of health services to any of the many forms of national health
insurance plans that have been proposed. Restructuring would be
built on both universal eligibility and reordered incentives to make
care more cost-effective. Incentives to diminish unnecessary use of
expensive services would be put in place. On the other hand, some
observers are concerned that the diversity of the American health
care system will diminish under a national program; they point to
the benefits of entrepreneurism, which in this view has been a
prerequisite for many major advances in health care in our country.

National health insurance and nationalized health services
are two related but distinct proposals. The former represents
national support for some or all costs of health care. The latter

consists of health services provided directly by the federal government. Medicare is a national public health insurance program for the elderly. The Veterans' Administration offers direct health services by federal employees (physicians, nurses, and others) to groups of beneficiaries (veterans).

Varied incentives, built into national health insurance programs, can affect costs of care, determination of which services will be supported, and the organization of services. All national health insurance programs are predicated on the concept of universal eligibility (at least of all individuals meeting some demographic criterion—for example, the elderly), although different copayments may be required from different participants. A national health insurance program for families with chronically ill children might be devised by extending Medicare to cover children with chronic health conditions.

Nationalized health services provide all (or almost all) services directly to eligible recipients. The Veterans' Administration hospital and health care programs and the Indian Health Service are national programs to serve the health needs of eligible veterans and Native Americans. Nationalized health services would provide all direct services to eligible families through, for example, a Childhood Chronic Illness Service or Administration. These options could be targeted directly to childhood chronic illness or be part of an effort at universal health insurance or nationalized health services for all citizens.

Universal eligibility for health services will greatly improve the lot of many families with chronically ill children. The tremendous financial burdens of chronic illness affect families in all social classes, although certain groups are at special risk of inadequate health coverage (Butler and others, 1985). Young families, many people near or below the poverty level, and rural residents are all less likely than other citizens to have health insurance, public or private. And chronic illness in a child is associated with even greater likelihood that a family will be uninsured.

Although national health insurance would go a long way toward diminishing inequities in availability of medical and hospital services to children in the United States, little evidence exists that national health insurance programs will improve access to needed nonmedical services. The experience with national health insurance in Canada, England, and European countries provides little comfort that optimal school planning, respite care, genetic counseling, and family or sibling support are more available there than they are here. In Quebec, for example, where health services are sponsored by the provincial government, the broad range of services needed by chronically ill children and their families is no more available than it is south of the Canadian border. Although the Ministry of Health has the authority to mandate additional services, there has been little pressure to do so, and political and financial constraints make it unlikely that new services will be added. The evidence is that special services will be provided if they are covered or mandated by the insurance program. If services are not covered or mandated, the form of insurance (national or not) has little impact on their availability.

Much effort has gone into defining the costs of different proposals for national health insurance. As an example, in 1978 dollars, the federal cost of key proposals under consideration varied from $43 billion to $103 billion. In that most estimates are for direct costs alone, and even these estimates are difficult to make with confidence, the debate on costs is instructive to attempts to apply a realistic estimate to other options. Indirect costs and benefits, which may be more important in the long run, have been excluded from policy considerations.

Would nationalized services for families with chronically ill children work? Such services could be based on the Crippled Children's Services structure and could take responsibility for both organization and financing of needed services (with public support). Implementation might require major restructuring of modes of care, changing the location of service for most children from current private providers to services under public sponsorship. The option would allow central control of services and attention to the range of services that the program leadership deemed supportable. The large portion of costs presently borne by private sources would shift to public responsibility. Nationalized services is a relatively expensive option, although it does meet the principles of equity and could improve the similar treatment of different chronic illnesses and the range of services available to families.

National health insurance expresses the principles of universality and equity and encourages services to all children with chronic illnesses, regardless of the specific condition. Yet this option does little to broaden the range of services or to encourage better education of children with illnesses. Both public support and the political climate for national health insurance have been cyclical for several decades and are at a low ebb in the mid 1980s. Despite its long presence on the American political agenda, national health insurance has rarely gained a consensus strong enough to bring it close to passage. The lack of public resolve may reflect the difficulty of achieving consensus among special interest groups (labor, hospital industry, physicians) (Marmor and Christianson, 1982). Whatever the cause, national health insurance is unlikely to appear in the United States in the near future. From the perspective of families with chronically ill children, this reflects a minimalist option because it is neither practically nor politically feasible. Should national health insurance return actively to the public agenda, it merits consideration as a means of improving the lives of chronically ill children and their families.

Add Funds to the Present System

As indicated in Chapter Seven, investment in the care of chronically ill children has not kept pace with support for other groups, including well children or children with developmental disabilities. Additional funds to reinforce present service programs could rectify the imbalance, even without reforms in the structure of these programs. This option assumes that programs for chronically ill children have been chronically underfunded. If programs have structural integrity, all that may be needed is additional funds. Many families who could benefit from services are excluded by financial or other eligibility criteria. Additional monies would allow broadening the population of children served. More generous program funding could enlarge the Crippled Children's Services, school programs, or various health facilities, as described in the examples that follow. New funding would also allow enrollment of greater numbers of children and services for a broader variety of health conditions, thereby meeting the principles of commonality and equity.

The Crippled Children's Services is a major force in organizing and providing services to chronically ill and handicapped children in most states. Yet, most state programs suffer to some degree from limited funds, which curtails services or eligibility. More generous financial support would reverse these trends. Medicaid, too, contributes greatly to the care of chronically ill children by financing hospital and outpatient benefits that were unavailable to many children prior to establishment of that program. Yet many children below the poverty line are ineligible for Medicaid, and the uneven pattern of eligibility and benefits among the states has been exacerbated by cuts in funding during recent years. Improved funding for Medicaid could expand eligibility and the benefits available to poor chronically ill children. Increasing the federal share of program costs may also diminish state-by-state variations in access to Medicaid, improving equity through nationally defined standards of eligibility.

School systems could direct additional funds to effective school health and nursing programs. In the competition for limited funds, many school systems have disbanded their school nurse programs. Yet school nurses can play an important role in coordination of care for chronically ill children, help to ensure that children participate actively in school settings, and educate teachers about the problems of their chronically ill students. New monies could reverse this negative trend and improve the likelihood that children with chronic conditions will stay on task in school.

New monies might aid other institutions, such as academic health centers, developmental disabilities programs, University Affiliated Facilities (UAFs), and comprehensive disease specialty centers. The best of these institutions provide excellent services to children. The comprehensive hemophilia, cystic fibrosis, and sickle cell centers often provide high-quality, sophisticated, and broad-based services to children with specific health conditions. Families whose children have developmental disabilities receive comprehensive services from the University Affiliated Facilities across the country. Additional monies would support more specialty centers in the many parts of the country where comprehensive programs are unavailable. Improved funding would allow UAF services to be available to children with chronic physical health problems as well as to the children with developmental disabilities served now.

This option has the advantage of being built upon the present structure and past experience of many programs. In the Crippled Children's Services, it would build on traditional strengths, especially on standard-setting and an emphasis on quality of care. Yet the present system is highly fragmented; poor children often receive services from one provider and insured patients from another, even though their rare conditions require the same specialized services. The problems identified in previous chapters would in large part continue or be exaggerated through this option. Current services emphasize delivery of high-technology medical and surgical services to the relative neglect of other services desperately needed by families. Crippled Children's Services often maintain a narrow range of services with a medical-surgical emphasis, and in some states, its bureaucracy is outmoded and rigid. Many special disease programs exclude children with similar diseases and needs. The university affiliated programs for children with developmental handicaps have limited outreach to the community and community-based services; some are poorly coordinated with pediatric services in communities or in medical centers. Furthermore, some developmental programs implement vigorous, expensive diagnostic efforts and attend less to monitoring or ensuring implementation of services for developmentally handicapped children. Similarly, there is little assurance that a comprehensive hemophilia program can expand to care for children with other chronic illnesses or that a center that has developed excellent services for developmental problems will succeed in devising approaches to families whose children have chronic physical ailments.

This option serves mainly to make more families eligible for services now denied. Principles of equity and an appropriate range of services might be strengthened through this option. Yet the approach carries the risks of emphasizing the use of expensive and sometimes excessive high-technology services while ignoring family support, general health care, and genetic services. Because many services are now categorical—offered only to children with one or two diseases—the principle of commonality is unattended by this option. The needs of children in schools, too, will continue to be neglected. The option of relying on greater funding of existing institutions offers little assurance that many persisting gaps in services will be filled. The present system, already highly fragmented, could become more so.

Reform the Present System of Care

Reforms in the organization and financing of health services and in policies and programs for chronically ill children in schools could benefit families. Present programs through the Maternal and Child Health Block Grant, Public Law 94-142, the disease-specific state programs, Medicaid, and private health insurance would stay in place and undergo basic reform. This option assumes that changes in the organization or financing of services and in the experience of children in schools could occur together or separately. Several elements of incremental reform can be addressed; these include improved mechanisms for early identification and referral, the development of areawide communication and education programs, teamwork and case management, individualized planning for families, strengthened school policies and programs, and improvements in health insurance through high-risk pools, catastrophic coverage, and other mechanisms. A number of these reforms have been implemented, in part, in areas of the nation. They represent a variety of steps that policy makers and program people can take to improve programs for chronically ill children and their families.

This option addresses some of the basic structural weaknesses of programs for children with chronic illnesses that have been detailed in previous chapters. Incremental reforms are worthy of consideration, partly because policy makers are comfortable with step-by-step approaches to program change. Yet there are risks to an incremental effort, mainly the risks of assuming that complex issues of social policy can be resolved through one or two single reforms.

Planning and Integrating Services. Regional data systems would be developed; these would broadly incorporate information on the population of children in need of services, the number and types of services provided, and resources in the community for chronically ill children. Data would reflect medical and surgical care as well as educational, genetic, psychological, and nutritional services.

The data base would identify specialty care services and referral sources, pediatricians and other general health care providers for chronically ill children, school resources, developmental programs, and community agencies providing services to handicapped children. At the present time, even within programs such as the Crippled Children's Services, useful data are rarely collected. Data across program boundaries and areawide services, needs, and resources are unavailable. Yet such data are essential to the development of effective communitywide plans for chronically ill children in that they would support the identification of major gaps in services and allow for the monitoring of program changes.

Improved early identification and tracking of children with chronic illnesses may be aided by greater use of high-risk registries. Certain chronic conditions can be identified or at least suspected shortly after birth, and a sensitive high-risk registry, coupled with an effective referral and follow-up program, may help families find care in a timely fashion. Appropriate referral of children may also improve through continuing education and training for physicians and other health providers. Because most childhood chronic illnesses are rare, general health providers would have easy access to information on identification of unusual problems and sources of specialty care. Identification and referral systems would be available to school personnel as well because many chronic problems are identified by schools rather than in physicians' offices.

Methods of assuring effective communication between general health providers and their specialty colleagues and between the health and education sectors are essential. Well-implemented areawide communication and referral systems can ensure access to technical services yet allow the majority of care to be provided close to a child's home. In Iowa, for example, the care of children with leukemia has been decentralized to their community physicians. Personnel in academic health centers serve mainly as consultants, providing advice and basic management recommendations to the primary physicians in outlying communities. The Iowa experience emphasizes the importance of communication both to and from the medical center, and optimally, families can be referred back to providers in their community for most ongoing care.

There are compelling arguments for teamwork in the provision of services to families with chronically ill children. The needs of the families are broad, and no single type of provider can offer services of adequate breadth. Integral to the development of teamwork are the concepts of case management or coordination and of individualized planning for children and their families. Coordination of care diminishes the fragmentation of services. Any of a number of professionals, and often family members themselves, can coordinate services. Responsibilities include helping families find needed services of appropriate variety, interpreting findings and recommendations for families, ensuring that families are aware of the options available to them, helping mediate among conflicting recommendations, and advocating for the family where necessary. Rather than providing all services directly, case coordinators would ensure that the services families need are received. Individualized planning would reflect an appropriately broad range of services and would take into account the variations in the needs of individual children and families. Plans serve many functions. They permit prospective budgeting of resources by program managers. They provide mechanisms for monitoring services and the development of goals against which to measure a child's or family's progress.

Greater responsibilities for pediatricians and other general health providers in the care of chronically ill children would be encouraged through financial incentives for case management or for services different from those provided for children without long-term illnesses. These providers are usually closer to families than are specialists, both geographically and in their knowledge of the families. Although some are reluctant to assume the added responsibilities of working with families with chronically ill children, others provide excellent treatment, coordination of care, and support. The role of general health providers would be enhanced by more equitable reimbursement for the extra time they would spend meeting complex family and illness needs. Effective continuing education and improved communication of information among different providers would also help general physicians work more closely with families with ill children.

Financing Health Services. Several changes in health care financing have been proposed in the past few years. All of them attempt to meet varying and sometimes competing policy goals: assuring that citizens have access to basic health care, assuring that ruinous personal cost is avoided, and controlling inflation in the costs and expenditures in the health care sector. From the view of families with chronically ill children, these varied proposals offer both benefits and risks. Improved policy would recognize that chronicity means a financial outlay year after year rather than just for the acute episodes that typify most childhood illnesses and that the high cumulative expenses can ruin families financially. We offer here issues to be considered in improving present insurance mechanisms and new financing proposals as they affect chronically ill children and their families.

As is described in Chapter Seven, access to coverage by group private health insurance policies is linked to employment, mainly in large firms. Many families are excluded, a situation that could be remedied by extension of coverage to low-wage or seasonal employees, improved conversion privileges from group to individual policies, and mandatory coverage of dependents in family policies. Conversion privileges for dependent children would be especially helpful to those chronically ill children who reach the age at which they are no longer covered by their parents' policies. Access to insurance coverage for children with chronic illnesses would also be improved through state high-risk insurance pools in which all insurors in a state share the risk for uninsurable persons. High-risk pools, mandated in several states, could provide protection for chronically ill children and their families, although such plans may entail high annual out-of-pocket expenditures for premiums, deductibles, and coinsurance.

Most insurance plans protect against high-cost hospital and inpatient care. They tend therefore to cover only medical and surgical services or services offered under the direction of a physician. They seldom contain incentives for preventive or general health care, nor do they cover the broad range of special services and materials (outpatient drugs, tests, appliances) essential for chronically ill children.

In recent years, various forms of catastrophic health insurance have been proposed as one preferred type of national health insurance. These plans all protect against unexpected, and usually acute, very high medical costs. As described in Chapter Seven, they typically have high deductibles that are reapplied on a yearly basis. Catastrophic health insurance is frequently criticized for causing reallocation of health resources away from preventive care to higher-cost care, hospitalization, and other services that already receive disproportionate coverage and health resources. Some argue that these plans are inflationary in that they provide incentives to generate costly bills in order to move past the threshold of the deductible and make use of catastrophic benefits. Properly structured catastrophic insurance, however, may provide valuable protection to chronically ill children and their families. Catastrophic proposals address the cost of a single catastrophic event rather than solving the equally serious problem of expensive, long-term chronic illnesses. The enormous financial burden on families of children with chronic illnesses is missed by calculating only one year's expenses. Large expenses persist year after year. Most plans provide reimbursement only after sixty days of hospitalization in a year, a benefit that excludes a large number of chronically ill children whose days in the hospital may be fewer per year but whose hospitalizations recur frequently. Additionally, most proposed plans exclude reimbursement for outpatient drugs, which are often necessary in large and costly quantities for chronically ill children. Alternative provisions would include applying all major medical expenses toward a single deductible amount. Longer deductible periods, of perhaps several years, would also better address the special problems of long-term illness. A deductible amount based on family income, limiting expenditures on medical care to 10 to 15 percent of income, would help young adults with severe chronic illnesses. These young people are frequently unable to retain full-time employment yet do not qualify for Medicaid. Insurance protection related to their income would make a great difference in access to care and in financial independence.

Proposals to increase competition in the health marketplace have attracted attention in recent years. These proposals encourage different providers (hospitals, physicians, or others) to compete with each other in offering health services. Most competition proposals have incentives to cluster people who use many services (and therefore generate high costs) in the more expensive plans.

Such adverse selection could price the higher benefit plans needed by chronically ill people out of their reach. Methods to share the risk (that is, to spread out the costs associated with long-term illnesses) need to be included in competition plans. Otherwise, families will carry a burden that should be shared with society in general. A regulatory approach may be needed to ensure access of families to services they need.

Competition plans generally place limits on the percent of income or the flat dollar amount that individuals must pay out of pocket for health care before the insurance plan pays for care. Again, the narrow definitions of eligible services and of an episode of illness mean that many services used by chronically ill children are not counted in the deductible. To meet the needs of chronically ill children, the deductible would take into account all out-of-pocket medical expenses plus the price paid for the insurance premiums and be based on a reasonable percentage of income rather than the flat dollar amount. Competition approaches or the removal of present tax exemptions for insurance premiums could result in more circumscribed health insurance plans. In sum, these approaches must be designed very carefully so as to prevent isolation of families with predictably high medical care costs and ensure them access to adequate coverage.

Approaches that encourage competition may benefit people with long-term and costly illnesses, especially if the issues of access described earlier can be resolved. A balance between cost-containment and an appropriate range of services is needed. An advantage of the competitive approach is that it provides incentives for physicians and health care institutions to seek effective ways to replace costly elements of health care with less expensive alternatives. For example, health maintenance organizations have successfully diminished hospitalization rates among their enrollees and have been able to apply more resources to outpatient and preventive services. Examples of the effective use of home-based services among prepaid health programs include the administration of intravenous antibiotics to children at home rather than keeping them in the hospital just for this procedure and the use of home traction for certain families whose children have orthopedic problems. Prepaid health maintenance organizations have expanded greatly over the past two decades. Yet little evidence has been gathered about barriers to enrollment of children with chronic illnesses or about issues of cost and quality of care for children with severe ongoing health conditions who receive their health services under prepaid auspices. These issues merit careful research, although present evidence suggests that prepaid and competitive approaches offer benefits to people with severe chronic illnesses.

Children in Schools. The participation of chronically ill children in school can be enhanced through a variety of new mechanisms. Often, special education has served as a means for organizing services for children with severe chronic illnesses. Yet the relationship of special education services to services needed by children with chronic illnesses should be clarified (this relationship was discussed in Chapter Four). The chronically ill child whose condition only mildly or infrequently affects schooling (for example, the child who occasionally requires medications or who needs modified gym classes) is most appropriately served by the regular education system, with use of counseling and school health services. Special education, as defined in Public Law 94-142, would apply mainly to children who have problems of cognition or understanding that require special education services. Special education would not be extended or stretched for the purpose of including nonhandicapped children in need of related services. Instead, related services would be made available to all children, handicapped or not, if these services were essential for them to be able to participate effectively in an appropriate school program.

To ensure that the chronically ill child with a mild impairment receives the necessary services within each school district, each state would develop explicit school health codes for chronically ill children and mandate their adoption by local school systems. Codes would include policies and procedures in at least the following areas: medication procedures, case registry, emergency care, inservice training, and case coordination. School systems would adopt internal policies to coordinate regular and special education services. In the event that related services are made available to children based upon need, as we have recommended, the three sections (regular education, special education, and related services) must interact on a regular basis.

More flexible policies regarding the use of homebound and hospital instruction would be adopted. The consecutive absence period currently necessary to qualify for homebound services denies many chronically ill children important instructional services. The goals of such policies would be to see that children who had frequent brief absences stayed as current as possible with their classmates and that they returned to the classroom as soon as possible. Children undergoing long-term hospitalization or long-term care at home would have access to instruction that would also allow their best development. To achieve these goals, there would be changes in the time allocated to each child for homebound teaching and in the absence requirements used in most jurisdictions.

Within the school, training, education, and sensitization regarding chronically ill children would be directed at both school personnel and other students. For school personnel, training related to the child's specific condition would be provided under the direction of a school nurse or physician. Specific curricula or techniques to explore and modify student and teacher attitudes about chronically ill children would be developed. At times, supportive personal counseling may be needed by school personnel who are involved with the education of children with terminal or progressive illnesses.

To arrange proper placement and programming, schools need health-related information about chronically ill children. Yet the interaction between the health and educational systems is characteristically neglected. Models for linking health and education are described in Chapter Four. As with other aspects of dealing with children with rare and severe illnesses, adequate communication and interaction require time and effort. Appropriate functions for the physician are the transfer of essential information to schools and the fostering of communication between schools and physicians. Although there is a tendency for physicians to make educational recommendations and for schools to make health recommendations, it seems best to leave the recommendations within each professional realm and to encourage sharing of necessary information. In general, the physician functions more productively as a consultant than as an educational decision maker.

Summary. The reform option strengthens present grant programs to states, helping them provide services, develop areawide advocacy roles, organize case coordination, and develop important mechanisms of quality assurance. It encourages improvements in insurance and suggests opportunities to aid children in schools. The option serves as a guide to a broad series of incremental steps, any one of which may be of substantial benefit to families of chronically ill children.

Yet limiting change to a series of incremental steps carries a great risk. As with most problems in social policy, any single policy change is unlikely to solve the problem. Policies operate within dynamic systems; a change proposed in one direction is typically offset by counter forces in the system. Home care for children illustrates the problem of a piecemeal approach. The provision of adequate home care will benefit the families of chronically ill children, many of whom need specialized home nursing services as well as help in meeting the daily problems of caring for a child with a complex physical disorder. If home care can replace expensive hospital care, it should diminish the total cost of care. Yet critics note two problems that may greatly increase costs. First, a new benefit generates its own demand for the service. Thus, it is likely that, were home care widely available, many people who now do without home care reimbursement would make use of the benefit, including many whose need for home care is marginal. Second, freeing hospital beds may lead to more hospitalization of other children rather than simply reducing the number of children hospitalized. Empty hospital beds might be filled with new cases, creating additional expense. Home care, especially if implemented without careful attention to the implications for increasing demand, may raise health care costs. Home-care approaches should set limitations both on recipients and on the types of services provided and should incorporate methods of keeping unfilled beds empty. There is merit, then, to each step in the incremental option, although piecemeal efforts are likely to have unintended, undesirable results.

The reforms chosen by policy makers will determine which of the principles of Chapter Eleven are met. Coordination of care and development of individualized planning, as examples, help support the central nature of the family in caring for its own child. Some of the recommendations for financing and insurance will help improve access and thus meet the criterion of equity. The recommendations regarding schools will improve opportunities for children with severe chronic illnesses to obtain an adequate education. Many of the recommendations can be implemented so that programs are based on broad definitions of chronic illness that stress the commonalities among conditions.

A National Community-Based Program for Chronically Ill Children and Their Families

The complex special needs of families with chronically ill children could be met through a new national effort to develop community-based care. This option calls for the development of a network of community programs for the families of children with chronic illnesses. It offers a coordinated approach, emphasizing family and community efforts most strongly and bringing together many of the individual program elements described in the reform option. Systems of community-based care would arise through a federally mandated, state-based program that would emphasize coordinated areawide efforts, provide services as close to the child's home as possible, and ensure universal access to all children with chronic illness. The national effort would set program standards with explicit goals and objectives and measurable outcomes. The standards would support careful monitoring and review of the attainment of policy objectives. Services provided in each area would be characterized by comprehensiveness, continuity of care, and excellent communication among providers and between providers and families.

The system would be based on a network of areawide programs that would emphasize a community base of services. The size of areawide programs would vary according to the needs and resources of communities. Areas would be small enough that those coordinating the areawide efforts could be knowledgeable about a broad array of services and large enough that most needed specialty services would be available. In most cases, areas would be smaller than a single state. Most states would have several areawide programs, and in larger cities, there might be several such programs.

Range of Services. Each areawide program would define a broad set of services to be available to each child with a chronic condition. The need for a broad range of services is clear. Setting priorities among competing services will require careful judgment, especially because high-cost technology plays an important role in the treatment of childhood chronic illness. Programs would avoid technology of unproven value, nor would they support high technology at the expense of community-based services. Equal access to needed services, including high technology, would characterize programs.

The range of services would vary according to area needs and capacities; moreover, each family requires an idiosyncratic set of services. Available services would include high-quality general and specialized health services; educational planning; specialized nursing services, especially to provide families with skills in home care; other support for the family's ability to carry out most care for their child at home; nutritional services; a variety of counseling services to deal with issues of genetics, finances, prognosis, and child development; and psychological counseling to strengthen families' abilities to cope with the additional stress created by chronic illness in a child. Family support services, including homemakers, self-help groups, and respite care, are essential and go well beyond the provision of counseling efforts. Other services, such as physical and occupational therapy, are needed by children who have some conditions. Most families with chronically ill children require only a limited number of services. Various levels of service would be available throughout an area because few families require the most intensive, costly, and comprehensive services.

Planning and Coordinating Care. Access to needed services could be aided with the development of a plan for functional improvement for each child and family. The plan, developed with the family's involvement, would outline services to be provided, including attention to education, family support services, and counseling as well as medical and surgical services. The family service plan would have explicit allocation of responsibilities to providers for carrying out elements of the plan and would allow for periodic monitoring and updating.

Each plan would define a specific person as the coordinator of care for the child and family. Many types of people can coordinate care for a family, including family members themselves, social workers, nurses, lay counselors, physicians, school personnel, and others. There is little evidence that one profession coordinates a great deal better than others. The discipline of the coordinator is much less important than having a specific person assigned the function of care coordination.

The Community Base of Areawide Programs. An effective organized system of care for children with chronic illnesses would include services in local communities, in core areawide coordinating staffs, and in specialty centers. It would require some centralized services, some that are decentralized, and some activities to bridge the two.

The distinction between centralized and decentralized (or community-based) programs is key. A centralized program emphasizes the development of excellent specialty services in one central location, usually an academic health center. A decentralized program emphasizes the development of a broad range of health services in many locations and is usually accompanied by close contacts with the surrounding community. The community-based option would incorporate elements of both a decentralized and a centralized program.

The centralized aspects of this option would necessarily hinge on assuring selected specialty services (unavailable in other area sites) in the technologically sophisticated medical centers. Although a community-based program would include centralized services, its emphasis would be on decentralized efforts and on effective liaison between the two. The decentralized efforts would foster appropriate services within a community for children with a chronic illness (regardless of their diagnosis) and for their families. Liaison responsibilities would fall to an areawide coordinating group.

The development of areawide programs would target sizable resources for increasing high-quality services at the community level. It is at this level that resources for families with chronically ill children are most sparse. Community-level efforts include the identification of health and other service providers, the development of community workers called chronic illness generalists, and the organization of community education efforts.

Those health providers, especially physicians and nurses, who can provide excellent, ongoing general health care for chronically ill children would be identified. At the community level, a group of personnel—chronic illness generalists—would be developed. They would help find resources in their communities; help ensure communication among families, health providers, and schools; coordinate services for some families; and collaborate with other generalists elsewhere in a larger area. Local chronic illness generalists would also foster the development of groups of parents and children to provide mutual help and education. Such groups may include families with a variety of illnesses, especially in communities where the numbers of children with individual illnesses are small.

Many communities, large and small, have personnel, especially nurses, who could be well trained as chronic illness generalists. A nursing background may be especially suited to coordinating health services with the goal of improving the functioning of families. In some communities, a pediatrician may take on these responsibilities. In others, concerned lay citizens could be trained as effective generalists. In all cases, chronic illness generalists would work from community health settings, such as a health department, a community practice, or a community agency. Various models of this approach exist, including the lay counselor project of Pless and Satterwhite and the use of nurse practitioners in Project REACH and in the Pediatric Home Care Program in the Bronx. Local chronic illness generalists can effectively help families with the needs arising from a child's chronic illness.

A vital activity in local communities would be the development of educational programs to increase awareness of chronic illness in childhood and to improve the integration of children into the mainsteam of community life. The generalists would provide information and consultation to community institutions involved with children, especially to schools. Community health providers, too, need continuing education in issues of childhood chronic illness, and this is a process that would be best provided close to the site of practice, likely under the sponsorship of areawide coordinating staff.

A core of professionals knowledgeable about a broad range of issues related to chronic illness and handicapping conditions in childhood rather than specialists in specific diseases would provide leadership at the areawide level. At least five main groups of professional skills would be available in the core group: pediatric, nursing, social work, mental health, and education. Related skills, especially in genetics and nutrition, have special importance for many families and may be included as well. The area group might consist of a pediatrician, a nurse (with a public health or nurse specialist background), a social worker, a psychologist, and a teacher, although in some locales, more than one discipline could be covered by a single individual. Parents of children with chronic illnesses would also be group members. Depending on the size of the area and the number of affected children, professional staff could be supplemented with nonprofessional colleagues.

Core group responsibilities would include implementing some of the organizational reforms described previously: (1) developing and monitoring a data base, (2) developing identification and referral systems for children, (3) implementing systems of communication among levels of care, (4) developing regional education programs, and (5) assuring the development and implementation of family service plans. Depending on area needs, the core group may provide some services directly.

Areawide education programs for school personnel, health providers, and the community at large would be organized by areawide staff, which would join forces with personnel in the local community. Because many coordinating services are now carried out by local health care providers, teachers, or school nurses, the expansion of coordination at the local level would be encouraged. The chronic illness generalists would be closely linked to the areawide core group and, in many cases, would be responsible to the core team.

An important opportunity exists for Crippled Children's Services agencies to provide leadership in areawide programs. Some state CCS agencies are leaders in moving in this direction. CCS agencies frequently must decide between either applying their resources to paying for direct services to eligible children or channeling resources to make maximum use of other agencies' efforts and of financing available through other sources. Although CCS has traditionally emphasized direct service, organizing orthopedic clinics and paying for needed surgery, the context in which the program operates has changed. For example, far more children now have public or private health insurance coverage than was true twenty or thirty years ago. Moreover, the growth in the financial resources of CCS nationwide has been slight in comparison with that of many other publicly supported programs, and CCS now plays a much smaller role in the care of children. Resources available to the Crippled Children's Services, with some supplementation, could be used to support the development of areawide programs as described here.

Areawide programs could be implemented within any of a number of existing structures, such as Title V agencies, certain school districts, academic health centers or university affiliated facilities, or local or regional health departments. Where no effective agency exists, a new organization might offer leadership. Both areawide coordinating groups and chronic illness generalists would be housed in agencies that allow for close collaboration and effective communication. In some parts of the country, private or voluntary agencies would likely fill these roles. In other areas, public agencies would be more likely to succeed. Implementation will require effective intermingling of public and private resources. The option calls for building a service infrastructure, with primary attention to the community base. Structures would likely vary from area to area and would depend on the strengths of different agencies and on their abilities to coordinate a broad range of services for chronically ill children.

The challenge for a program straddling the distance between specialized medical centers and local communities is to avoid the tendency to become too centralized and overly dependent on the medical centers. Characteristically, greater expertise is available to design sophisticated centers, and past attempts at organizing regional systems of care have typically been more successful in improving the resources of the specialized medical center than in increasing the capacity to meet needs and provide services at the local community level. Indeed, some critics have charged that regionalization of care allows the specialty medical centers to shift resources away from general community health care. Centralization in the care of high-risk newborns, for example, consists of the development of excellent intensive care nursery programs in academic health centers with attention to strengthening prenatal care and services in smaller community hospitals where most children are born. As Miller (1980) states eloquently:

> Neonatal intensive care units appear to be flourishing in ways that community based routine prenatal care is not. Critics of regionalized perinatal care charge that it has become a device for capturing limited resources for major obstetric centers, contributing to a burden of unproven high technology that overlaps much of maternity care. . . . In some states community hospitals report a diminished capacity to render appropriate maternity and neonatal care because limited resources have been channeled to tertiary centers that expand their technological capabilities but limit the number of people they serve. Routine early and continuous prenatal care, a procedure that might decrease the risk of low birth weight, has not been improved or extended in all areas [p. 6].

Miller warns against the form of regionalization that allows the strong partners to garner most resources.

Eligibility and Access. This option utilizes a generic definition of childhood chronic illness: a health condition that leads to hospitalization for more than one month in a year or interferes with the child's ability to carry out usual daily tasks for more than three months in the year or, at the time of diagnosis, is considered likely to do so (for example, leukemia and certain birth defects). Many children without chronic illnesses but with other handicaps could also benefit from community-based programs. This generic definition is used not to exclude other disabled or handicapped children but rather to assure that all children with chronic illnesses are included. A family-centered policy would treat all illnesses similarly rather than selecting out certain diseases for special consideration. Because childhood chronic illnesses are relatively rare and because there is need for specialized and scarce resources, it makes little sense to develop chronic disease programs in the public sector separate from those in the private sector. Therefore, the areawide program would be available to all families with chronically ill children regardless of their financial status.

This definition of eligibility includes a large number of children in the United States. If 10 percent of the childhood population has an ongoing chronic condition, then one in ten children in the nation become eligible. Most of these children have mild chronic illnesses and will not need the broad range of services offered in the areawide programs. Rather, we envision such services made available and their use dictated by the needs of families in the area.

Financing. Financial support for the community-based program for families with chronically ill children could take various forms. One option is for full public support, either federal or by a combination of federal and state revenues. Yet major new public funding for direct programs is unlikely in the near future. Moreover, a fully funded public program avoids the opportunity to make maximum use of other resources (both public and private) applied to the care of families with chronically ill children. More likely, support could come from a combination of public sources, public and private health insurance mechanisms, and direct fees. Each areawide program will likely need core support to build and maintain the community and areawide infrastructure. Such support could come in the form of grants from private or public sources. For most direct health services, support could come from a number of insurance mechanisms, including prepayment plans for chronically ill children. Children presently covered by third-party payors, who became eligible for the program by meeting the generic definition of chronic illness, would have access to the range of services defined in the areawide plan. The cost of most services would be borne by the original insuror. Additional public monies would still be needed in two areas: first, to support essential services not covered by present insurors and, second, to prepay or finance insurance for the 10 to 25 percent of families who have no third-party coverage. Optimal financing would include funneling all resources through one unit, the areawide coordinating group.

There are numerous obstacles to the development of effective areawide programs, and they extend beyond the limitations in financial resources available in the 1980s and 1990s. The development of such programs runs counter to several themes underlying much of health care policy in the United States. The community-based program requires regulation to determine what services will be provided, by whom, and in what locations and what the referral patterns will be. Yet there are decreased national governmental support for regulation and continuing dissatisfaction in the medical community with constraints on medical initiatives from the private sector. Similarly, such systems need planning, yet health planning is presently out of vogue. There is also a danger that areawide systems of care would support the prerogatives of professionals already active in the marketplace, here predominantly physicians. Yet the very nature of services needed by families of chronically ill children calls for the greater involvement of nonphysician providers, especially public health nurses, nurse practitioners, nutritionists, therapists of various kinds, and lay counselors. Their increasing participation in the delivery of services would be fostered in the development of any areawide programs.

The special problems accompanying chronic illness in childhood are complex and unlikely to be met by piecemeal solutions. Great potential lies in the establishment of effective areawide programs that emphasize comprehensiveness of services, coordination, continuity, and communication together with attention to local communities. Such programs could enable families to support the growth of their children and to encourage the development of their best capacities. This option appears most responsive to the principles of Chapter Eleven. The roles of families and community are central; the commonalities among conditions are addressed; it gives attention to children with illnesses in schools; it stresses justice and equity.

Summary

In this chapter, we have examined a series of options available for the organization and financing of services for chronically ill children and their families. We see benefits to several of these options and expect that they may provide guidance to policy makers as they approach the complex task of improving the lives of chronically ill children and their families.

Chronically ill children face a mixed response from the American public. Their lives have been greatly enhanced by advances in medical care and, for many, in the distribution of costly technical services. Yet families are frequently burdened with high costs, with the daily caring for their child with illness, and with the lack of help to integrate their child into the community and to share the tasks involved in helping that child grow to the fullest capacity. For the United States, the challenge and opportunity now are to find ways of supporting families. Rather than taking responsibility away from families, a family-centered, community-based approach will assist families to meet their own needs. It will work to create as much independence as possible for the child afflicted with a severe chronic health condition.

We judge that these results will emerge most productively through renewed national efforts to develop consistent services of high quality for families. Elements of the reform option can move the nation along several important steps to a national program. But the complex special needs of families with chronically ill children will be best met through a national community-based program. The nation's attention should be brought to bear on the special problems families face when their child is born with or develops a serious, long-lasting health condition. With renewed attention, children can come out of the shadow to become full participants in our society.

References

Abildgaard, C. F. "Progress and Problems in Hemophilia and von Willebrand's Disease." *Advances in Pediatrics,* 1984, *31,* 137–178.

Ader, R., and Cohen, N. "Behaviorally Conditioned Immunosuppression." *Psychosomatic Medicine,* 1975, *37,* 333–340.

Ad Hoc Committee Task Force on Neonatal Screening. "Neonatal Screening for Cystic Fibrosis." *Pediatrics,* 1983, *72,* 741–745.

Agle, D. "Psychiatric Studies of Patients with Hemophilia and Related States." *Archives of Internal Medicine,* 1964, *114,* 76–82.

Aledort, L. M. "Lessons from Hemophilia." *New England Journal of Medicine,* 1982, *306,* 607–608.

Alexander, J., and Adelenstein, A. "Affective Responses to the Concept of Death in a Population of Children and Early Adolescents." *Journal of Genetic Psychology,* 1958, *93,* 167–177.

Allan, J., Townley, R., and Phelen, P. "Family Response to Cystic Fibrosis." *Australian Pediatrics Journal,* 1974, *10,* 136–146.

Altenstetter, C., and Bjorkman, J. "Policy, Politics, and Child Health: Four Decades of Federal Initiative and State Response." *Journal of Health Politics, Policy, and Law,* 1978, *3,* 196–234.

American Academy of Pediatrics. *Child Health Financing Report,* 1984a, *1* (3), entire issue.

American Academy of Pediatrics. "DRGs: Implications for Pediatrics." *Child Health Financing Report,* 1984b, *1* (4), 1–8.

American Medical Association, Judicial Council. *Opinions and Reports.* Chicago: American Medical Association, 1977.

Association of American Medical Colleges. *1981 Medical Student Graduation Questionnaire Survey.* Washington, D.C.: Association of American Medical Colleges, 1981.

Azarnoff, P. "Parents and Siblings of Pediatric Patients." *Current Problems in Pediatrics,* 1984, *14* (3), 6-40.

Baird, S. M., and Ashcroft, S. C. "Need-Based Educational Policy for Chronically Ill Children." In N. Hobbs and J. M. Perrin (Eds.), *Issues in the Care of Children with Chronic Illness: A Sourcebook on Problems, Services, and Policies.* San Francisco: Jossey-Bass, 1985.

Baird, S. M., Ashcroft, S., and Dy, E. "Survey of Educational Provisions for Chronically Ill Children." *Peabody Journal of Education,* 1984, *61,* 75-90.

Baldwin, S., Godfrey, C., and Staden, F. "Childhood Disablement and Family Income." Unpublished manuscript, Social Policy Research Unit, University of York (England), 1983.

Banting, F. G., and Best, C. H. "Pancreatic Extracts." *Journal of Laboratory and Clinical Medicine,* 1922, 7, 464-472.

Barnes, C. M. "Training Nurses to Care for Chronically Ill Children." In N. Hobbs and J. M. Perrin (Eds.), *Issues in the Care of Children with Chronic Illness: A Sourcebook on Problems, Services, and Policies.* San Francisco: Jossey-Bass, 1985.

Barraclough, W. "Mental Reactions of Normal Children to Physical Illness." *American Journal of Psychiatry,* 1937, *93,* 865-877.

Battle, C. U. "The Role of the Pediatrician as Ombudsman in the Health Care of the Young Handicapped Child." *Pediatrics,* 1972, *50,* 916-922.

Battle, S. F. "Genetic Disorders: Implications for Social Policy and the Delivery of Comprehensive Services." Paper presented at annual meeting of the National Conference on Social Welfare, Washington, D.C., June 1981.

Becker, A. B., Nelson, N. A., and Simons, F.E.R. "Inhaled Salbutamol (Albuterol) vs. Injected Epinephrine in Treatment of Acute Asthma in Children." *Journal of Pediatrics,* 1983, *102,* 465-469.

Bellamy, G. T., and others. "Education and Career Preparation for Youth with Disabilities." Paper presented at Adolescent Pregnancy Program Conference, "Youth with Disabilities: The Transition Years." University of Minnesota, Wayzata, June 1984.

Benton, B., Feild, T., and Millar, R. *Social Services: Federal Legislation vs. State Implementation*. Washington, D.C.: Urban Institute, 1978.

Berki, S. E., and Ashcraft, M.L.F. "HMO Enrollment: Who Joins What and Why. A Review of the Literature." *Milbank Memorial Fund Quarterly*, 1980, *58*, 588-632.

Beverly, B. "The Effect of Illness upon Emotional Development." *Journal of Pediatrics*, 1936, *7*, 533-543.

Bibace, R., and Walsh, M. E. "Development of Children's Concepts of Illness." *Pediatrics*, 1980, *66*, 912-917.

Bibace R., and Walsh, M. "Children's Conceptions of Illness." In R. Bibace and M. Walsh (Eds.), *New Directions for Child Development: Children's Conceptions of Health, Illness, and Bodily Functions*. San Francisco: Jossey-Bass, 1981.

Blendon, R. J. "Paying for Medical Care for Children: A Continuing Financial Dilemma." *Advances in Pediatrics*, 1982, *29*, 229-246.

Bock, R., and others. "There's No Place like Home." *Children's Health Care*, 1983, *12* (2), 93-96.

Bok, S. *Lying: Moral Choice in Public and Private Life*. New York: Vintage Books, 1979.

Bonhag, R. C., and others. *A Description of the Health Financing Model: A Tool for Cost Estimation*. Washington, D.C.: Department of Health and Human Services, Office of the Assistant Secretary for Planning and Evaluation, 1981.

Borman, L. D. "Self-Help Mutual Aid Groups." In N. Hobbs and J. M. Perrin (Eds.), *Issues in the Care of Children with Chronic Illness: A Sourcebook on Problems, Services, and Policies*. San Francisco: Jossey-Bass, 1985.

Bove, E. L., and others. "Congenital Heart Diseases in the Neonate: Results of Surgical Treatment." *Archives of Diseases of Childhood*, 1983, *58*, 137-141.

Bozeman, M., Orbach, C., and Sutherland, A. "Psychological Impact of Cancer and Its Treatment: The Adaptation of Mothers to the Threatened Loss of Their Children Through Leukemia." *Cancer*, 1955, *8*, 1-33.

Bracht, N. F. *Social Work in Health Care.* New York: Haworth Press, 1978.

Brent, R. L. "Radiation and Other Physical Agents." In J. G. Wilson and F. L. Fraser (Eds.), *Handbook of Teratology.* New York: Plenum, 1977.

Breslau, N. "The Contribution of Pediatric Nurse Practitioners to Child Health Care." *Advances in Pediatrics,* 1982, *29,* 387-408.

Breslau, N. "Care of Disabled Children and Women's Time Use." *Medical Care,* 1983, *21,* 620-629.

Breslau, N., and Mortimer, E. A. "Seeing the Same Doctor: Determinants of Satisfaction with Specialty Care for Disabled Children." *Medical Care,* 1981, *19,* 741-758.

Breslau, N., Weitzman, M., and Messenger, K. "Psychological Functioning of Siblings of Disabled Children." *Pediatrics,* 1981, *67,* 344-353.

Bronfenbrenner, U. "Toward an Experimental Ecology of Human Development." *American Psychologist,* 1977, *32,* 513-531.

Browne, W., Mally, M., and Kane, R. "Psychosocial Aspects of Hemophilia: A Study of Twenty-Eight Hemophilia Children and Their Families." *American Journal of Orthopsychiatry,* 1960, *30,* 730-740.

Bruch, H. "Physiologic and Psychologic Interrelationships in Diabetes in Children." *Psychosomatic Medicine,* 1948, *11,* 200-210.

Bruhn, J. "Effects of Chronic Illness on the Family." *Journal of Family Practice,* 1977, *4,* 1057-1060.

Budetti, P., Butler, J., and McManus, P. "The Medicaid Gap, Block Grants and Increased State Discretion." Unpublished manuscript, Health Policy Program, University of California at San Francisco, Washington, D.C., 1981.

Burton, L. *The Family Life of Sick Children.* London: Routledge & Kegan Paul, 1975.

Butler, J., and others. "Health Care Expenditures for Children with Chronic Illnesses." In N. Hobbs and J. M. Perrin (Eds.), *Issues in the Care of Children with Chronic Illness: A Sourcebook on Problems, Services, and Policies.* San Francisco: Jossey-Bass, 1985.

Cairns, A., Sussman, M., and Weil, W. "Family Interaction, Diabetes, and Sibling Relationships." *International Journal of Social Psychiatry,* 1966, *12,* 35-43.

Campbell, J. D., and Campbell, A. R. "The Social and Economic Costs of End-Stage Renal Disease: A Patient's Perspective." *New England Journal of Medicine*, 1978, *299*, 386-392.

Carlton, W. *In Our Professional Opinion: The Primacy of Clinical Judgment over Moral Choice*. Notre Dame, Ind.: University of Notre Dame Press, 1978.

Carpenter, E. "Children's Health Care and the Changing Role of Women." *Medical Care*, 1980, *18*, 1208-1218.

Case, J., and Matthews, S. "CHIP: The Chronic Health Impaired Program of the Baltimore City Public School System." *Children's Health Care*, 1983, *12* (2), 97-99.

Caskey, C. T., and White, R. (Eds.), *Recombinant DNA Applications to Human Disease*. New York: Cold Spring Harbor Press, 1983.

Cerreto, M. C. "Sibling Relationships: Effects on Development of Normal and Handicapped Children from Three Cultures." Department of Health and Human Services, Administration for Children, Youth, and Families, Grant no. 90CW646. Washington, D.C., 1981.

Chan, J., and Leff, P. "Parenting the Chronically Ill Child in the Hospital: Issues and Concerns." *Children's Health Care*, 1982, *11*, 9-16.

Chesler, M., and Yoak, M. "Self-Help Groups for Parents of Children with Cancer." In H. Roback (Ed.), *Helping Patients and Their Families Cope with Medical Problems: A Guide to Therapeutic Group Work in Clinical Settings*. San Francisco: Jossey-Bass, 1984.

Children's Bureau. "One in Three Hundred . . . Children Served by the Crippled Children's Program in 1948." *Statistical Series*, Number 10. Washington, D.C.: Federal Security Agency, Social Security Administration, 1951.

Chodoff, P., Friedman, S., and Hamburg, D. "Stress, Defense, and Coping Behavior: Observations in Parents of Children with Malignant Disease." *American Journal of Psychiatry*, 1964, *120*, 743-749.

Cleveland, T. "The Family—A Critical Factor in Prevention." In W. Hall, G. St. Denis, and C. Young (Eds.), *Proceedings. The Family: A Critical Factor in Prevention*. Washington, D.C.: U.S. Department of Health and Human Services, 1983.

Clewell, W. H., and others. "A Surgical Approach to the Treatment of Fetal Hydrocephalus." *New England Journal of Medicine,* 1982, *306,* 1320–1325.

Cluff, L. E. "Medical Schools, Clinical Faculty, and Community Physicians." *Journal of the American Medical Association,* 1982, *247,* 200–202.

Cohen, F., and Lazarus, R. S. "Coping with the Stresses of Illness." In G. C. Stone, F. Cohen, and N. E. Adler (Eds.), *Health Psychology—A Handbook: Theories, Applications, and Challenges of a Psychological Approach to the Health Care System.* San Francisco: Jossey-Bass, 1979.

Comptroller General of the United States. "Disparities Still Exist in Who Gets Special Education." Report to the Chairman, Subcommittee on Select Education, Committee on Education and Labor, U.S. House of Representatives. Washington, D.C.: U.S. Government Printing Office, 1981.

Congressional Budget Office. "Profile of Health Care Coverage: The Haves and Have-Nots." Publication no. 41-570-0-79-2. Washington, D.C.: U.S. Government Printing Office, 1979.

Coser, L. A. *Men of Ideas.* New York: Free Press, 1965.

Coser, R. L. *Training in Ambiguity.* New York: Free Press, 1979.

Coupey, S., and Cohen, M. "Special Considerations for the Health Care of Adolescents with a Chronic Illness." *Pediatric Clinics of North America,* 1984, *31,* 211–220.

Covelli, P. *Borrowing Time: Growing Up with Juvenile Diabetes.* New York: Crowell, 1979.

Covington, R. "Handicapped vs. Public Schools." *Suburban Woman,* 1980, p. 10–11.

Cutter, F. *Maternal Behavior and Childhood Allergy.* Washington, D.C.: Catholic University, 1955.

Cystic Fibrosis Foundation. *Over-21 Survey.* Washington, D.C.: Cystic Fibrosis Foundation, 1979.

Cystic Fibrosis Foundation. *Cost of Cystic Fibrosis Survey: Report, Part I.* Washington, D.C.: Cystic Fibrosis Foundation, 1981.

Daeschner, C. W., and Cerreto, M. C. "Training Physicians to Care for Chronically Ill Children." In N. Hobbs and J. M. Perrin (Eds.), *Issues in the Care of Children with Chronic Illness: A Sourcebook on Problems, Services, and Policies.* San Francisco: Jossey-Bass, 1985.

Day, D. "Craniofacial Birth Defects." In N. Hobbs and J. M. Perrin (Eds.), *Issues in the Care of Children with Chronic Illness: A Sourcebook on Problems, Services, and Policies.* San Francisco: Jossey-Bass, 1985.

Debuskey, M. (Ed.). *The Chronically Ill Child and His Family.* Springfield, Mass.: Thomas, 1970.

Deford, F. A. *Thé Life of a Child.* New York: Viking Press, 1983.

Dimsdale, J. E., and Moss, A. J. "Plasma Catecholamines in Stress and Exercise." *Journal of the American Medical Association,* 1980, *243,* 340-342.

Division of Maternal and Child Health, U.S. Public Health Service. "Collaborative Projects for the Health and Educational Care of Handicapped Children." Washington, D.C.: U.S. Government Printing Office, 1981.

Dorner, S. "Psychological and Social Problems of Families of Adolescent Spina Bifida Patients: A Preliminary Report." *Developmental Medicine and Child Neurology,* 1973, *15* (6), Supplement no. 29, 24-26.

Dorner, S. "Adolescents with Spina Bifida: How They See Their Situation." *Archives of Disease in Childhood,* 1976, *51,* 439-444.

Drash, A., and Berlin, N. "Juvenile Diabetes." In N. Hobbs and J. M. Perrin (Eds.), *Issues in the Care of Children with Chronic Illness: A Sourcebook on Problems, Services, and Policies.* San Francisco: Jossey-Bass, 1985.

Drotar, D., and Bush, M. "Mental Health Issues and Services." In N. Hobbs and J. M. Perrin (Eds.), *Issues in the Care of Children with Chronic Illness: A Sourcebook on Problems, Services, and Policies.* San Francisco: Jossey-Bass, 1985.

Drotar, D., and others. "The Adaptation of Parents to the Birth of an Infant with a Congenital Malformation: A Hypothetical Model." *Pediatrics,* 1975, *56,* 710-717.

Drotar, D., and others. "Psychological Functioning of Children with Cystic Fibrosis." *Pediatrics,* 1981, *67,* 338-343.

Duff, R. S. "Counseling Families and Deciding Care of Severely Defective Children: A Way of Coping with 'Medical Vietnam.'" *Pediatrics,* 1981, *67,* 315-320.

DuHamel, T., and others. "Early Parental Perceptions and the High-Risk Neonate." *Clinical Pediatrics,* 1974, *13,* 1052-1056.

Edelston, H. "Separation Anxiety in Young Children: Study of Hospital Cases." *Genetic Psychology Monographs,* 1943, *28,* 3-95.

Egbuonu, L., and Starfield, B. "Child Health and Social Status." *Pediatrics,* 1982, *69,* 550-557.

Eland, J., and Anderson, J. "The Experience of Pain in Children." In A. Jacox (Ed.), *Pain: A Source Book for Nurses and Other Health Professionals.* Boston: Little, Brown, 1977.

Ellsworth, R., and Ellsworth, S. *CAAP Scale: The Measurement of Child and Adolescent Adjustment.* Palo Alto, Calif.: Consulting Psychologists Press, 1982.

Encyclopedia of Social Work. Vol. 1. "Health Services: Social Workers In." Washington, D.C.: National Association of Social Workers, 1977.

Enthoven, A. *Health Plan: The Only Practical Solution to the Soaring Cost of Medical Care.* Reading, Mass.: Addison-Wesley, 1980.

Erikson, E. *Childhood and Society.* New York: Norton, 1964.

Farrow, F., and Rogers, C. "Effective Policies in the Provision of Related Services." A Report of the Handicapped Public Policy Analysis Project. Washington, D.C.: Center for the Study of Social Policy, 1983.

Fireman, P., and others. "Teaching Self-Management Skills to Asthmatic Children and Their Parents in an Ambulatory Care Setting." *Pediatrics,* 1981, *68,* 341-348.

Firth, M., and others. "Interviews with Parents of Boys Suffering from Duchenne Muscular Dystrophy." *Developmental Medicine and Child Neurology,* 1983, *25,* 466-471.

Fitzelle, G. "Personality Factors and Certain Attitudes Toward Child Rearing Among Parents of Asthmatic Children." *Psychosomatic Medicine,* 1959, *21,* 208-217.

Fost, N. "Counseling Families of Children with Severe Congenital Anomaly." *Pediatrics,* 1981, *67,* 321-324.

Fost, N. "Putting Hospitals on Notice." *Hastings Center Report,* 1982, *12,* 5-8.

Fox, H. B., and Bartlett, L. "Memorandum II to State Maternal and Child Health and Crippled Children's Services Program Directors *Re:* Medicaid Options for Financing the Health Care of Handicapped and Chronically Ill Children." Unpublished manuscript. Washington, D.C., 1984a.

Fox, H. B., and Bartlett, L. "Memorandum III to State Maternal and Child Health and Crippled Children's Services Directors *Re:* Medicaid Freedom-of-Choice Waiver Programs." Unpublished manuscript. Washington, D.C., 1984b.

Fox, R. C. *Experiment Perilous: Physicians and Patients Facing the Unknown,* Philadelphia: University of Pennsylvania Press, 1974.

Fox, R. C. "Training for Uncertainty." In R. C. Fox, *Essays in Medical Sociology.* New York: Wiley, 1979.

Fox, R. C. "The Evolution of Medical Uncertainty." *Milbank Memorial Fund Quarterly,* 1980, *58,* 1-49.

Fraiberg, S. *Insights from the Blind.* New York: Basic Books, 1977.

Frederickson, D. L., and others. "Biomedical Research in the 80s." *New England Journal of Medicine,* 1981, *304,* 509-517.

Freidson, E. *The Profession of Medicine.* New York: Dodd, Mead, 1970.

Freud, A. "The Role of Bodily Illness in the Mental Life of Children." *Psychoanalytic Study of the Child,* 1952, *7,* 69-81.

Friedman, S., and others. "Behavioral Observations on Parents Anticipating the Death of a Child." *Pediatrics,* 1963, *32,* 610-624.

Fullerton, W. D. "Improving Private Health Insurance Coverage for Children." Paper presented at Conference on State Action to Improve Child Health, Washington, D.C., May 1982.

Fyler, D. C. "Congenital Heart Disease." In N. Hobbs and J. M. Perrin (Eds.), *Issues in the Care of Children with Chronic Illness: A Sourcebook on Problems, Services, and Policies.* San Francisco: Jossey-Bass, 1985.

Galant, S. P. "Current Status of Beta-Adrenergic Agonists in Bronchial Asthma." *Pediatric Clinics of North America,* 1983, *30,* 931-942.

Gamble, D. R. "The Epidemiology of Insulin-Dependent Diabetes." *Epidemiological Reviews,* 1980, *2,* 49-70.

Garr, A. *A Comprehensive Survey of the Hemophilia and Related Hemorrhagic Disordered Population.* Nashville, Tenn.: Cumberland Chapter of the National Hemophilia Foundation, 1978.

Garrard, S., and Richmond, J. B. "Psychological Aspects of the Management of Chronic Diseases and Handicapping Conditions in Childhood." In H. Lief, K. Lief, and N. Lief (Eds.), *The Psychological Basis of Medical Practice*. New York: Harper & Row, 1963.

Gesten, E. L. "A Health Resources Inventory." *Journal of Consulting and Clinical Psychology*, 1976, *44*, 775–780.

Gilgoff, I., and Dietrich, S. L. "Neuromuscular Diseases." In N. Hobbs and J. M. Perrin (Eds.), *Issues in the Care of Children with Chronic Illness: A Sourcebook on Problems, Services, and Policies*. San Francisco: Jossey-Bass, 1985.

Glaser, N., and others. "Education and Vocational Attainments of Adolescents and Young Adult Survivors with Spina Bifida." Unpublished manuscript. School of Medicine, Case Western Reserve University, 1980.

Gliedman, J., and Roth, W. *The Unexpected Minority: Handicapped Children in America*. New York: Harcourt Brace Jovanovich, 1980.

Goldberg, R., Isralsky, M., and Shwachman, H. "Vocational Development and Adjustment of Adolescents with Cystic Fibrosis." *Archives of Physical and Medical Rehabilitation*, 1979, *60*, 369–374.

Gortmaker, S. L. "Demography of Chronic Childhood Diseases." In N. Hobbs and J. M. Perrin (Eds.), *Issues in the Care of Children with Chronic Illness: A Sourcebook on Problems, Services, and Policies*. San Francisco: Jossey-Bass, 1985.

Gortmaker, S., and Sappenfield, W. "Chronic Childhood Disorders: Prevalence and Impact." *Pediatric Clinics of North America*, 1984, *31*, 3–18.

Green, M. "Care of the Child with Long-Term Life-Threatening Illness: Some Principles of Management." *Pediatrics*, 1967, *39*, 441–445.

Green, M., and Haggerty, R. (Eds.). *Ambulatory Pediatrics II*. Philadelphia: Saunders, 1975.

Green, M., and Hoekelman, R. A. "Trends in the Education of Pediatricians." *Advances in Pediatrics*, 1982, *29*, 325–350.

Greenberg, H. "The Emotional Problems and Education of Hospitalized Children." *Journal of Pediatrics*, 1949, *34*, 213–218.

Guyer, B., and Walker, D. "School Health Services in Flint Elementary Schools." Boston: Community Child Health Studies, Harvard School of Public Health, 1980.

Haggerty, R. J., Roghmann, K. J., and Pless, I. B. *Child Health and the Community.* New York: Wiley, 1975.

Hamburg, D. A., Elliott, G., and Parron, D. *Health and Behavior: Frontiers of Research in the Biobehavioral Sciences.* Washington, D.C.: National Academy Press, 1982.

Harder, L., and Bowditch, B. "Siblings of Children with Cystic Fibrosis: Perceptions of the Impact of the Disease." *Children's Health Care,* 1982, *10,* 116–120.

Harding, R., Heller, J., and Kesler, R. "The Chronically Ill Child in the Primary Care Setting." *Primary Care,* 1979, *6* (2), 311–324.

Harkey, J. "Epidemiology of Childhood Chronic Illness: An In-Depth Analysis." Unpublished staff paper. Vanderbilt Institute for Public Policy Studies, Nashville, Tenn., 1981.

Health Care Financing Administration. *HCFA Statistics.* Health Care Financing Administration publication no. 03155. Baltimore, Md.: U.S. Department of Health and Human Services, September 1983a.

Health Care Financing Administration. *The Medicare and Medicaid Data Book.* Health Care Financing Administration publication no. 03156. Baltimore, Md.: U.S. Department of Health and Human Services, December 1983b.

Heisel, J. S. "Life Changes as Etiologic Factors in Juvenile Rheumatoid Arthritis." *Journal of Psychosomatic Research,* 1972, *16,* 411–420.

Hilgartner, M., Aledort, L., and Giardina, P.J.V. "Thalassemia and Hemophilia." In N. Hobbs and J. M. Perrin (Eds.), *Issues in the Care of Children with Chronic Illness: A Sourcebook on Problems, Services, and Policies.* San Francisco: Jossey-Bass, 1985.

Hippolitus, P. "Employment Opportunities and Services for Youth with Chronic Illness." In N. Hobbs and J. M. Perrin (Eds.), *Issues in the Care of Children with Chronic Illness: A Sourcebook on Problems, Services, and Policies.* San Francisco: Jossey-Bass, 1985.

Hobbs, N. *The Futures of Children: Recommendations of the Project on Classification of Exceptional Children.* San Francisco: Jossey-Bass, 1975.

Hobbs, N., and Perrin, J. M. (Eds.). *Issues in the Care of Children with Chronic Illness: A Sourcebook on Problems, Services, and Policies.* San Francisco: Jossey-F ,ss, 1985.

Hoffstein, P. A., Krueger, K. K., and Wineman, R. J. "Dialysis Costs: Results of a Diverse Sample Study." *Kidney International,* 1976, *9,* 286–293.

Holtzman, N. A. "Routine Screening of Newborns for Cystic Fibrosis: Not Yet." *Pediatrics,* 1984, *73,* 98–99.

Holtzman, N. A., and Richmond, J. "Genetic Strategies for Preventing Chronic Illnesses." In N. Hobbs and J. M. Perrin (Eds.), *Issues in the Care of Children with Chronic Illness: A Sourcebook on Problems, Services, and Policies.* San Francisco: Jossey-Bass, 1985.

Hughes, G. "The Emotional Impact of Chronic Illness." *American Journal of Diseases of Children,* 1976, *130,* 1199–1203.

Hunt, P. *Stigma: The Experience of Disability.* London: Chapman, 1966.

Hymovich, D. P. "Nursing Services." In N. Hobbs and J. M. Perrin (Eds.), *Issues in the Care of Children with Chronic Illness: A Sourcebook on Problems, Services, and Policies.* San Francisco: Jossey-Bass, 1985.

Iglehart, J. K. "Cutting Costs of Health Care for the Poor in California." *New England Journal of Medicine,* 1984, *311* (11), 745–748.

Ipswitch, E. *Scott Was Here.* New York: Delacorte Press, 1979.

Ireys, H. T. *The Crippled Children's Services: A Comparative Analysis of Four State Programs.* Mental Health Policy Monograph Series, No. 7. Nashville, Tenn.: Vanderbilt Institute for Public Policy Studies, 1980.

Ireys, H. T. *Survey of State Directors of Crippled Children's Services Programs.* Unpublished data, Vanderbilt Institute for Public Policy Studies, Nashville, Tenn., 1981.

Ireys, H. T., Hauck, R. J.-P., and Perrin, J. "Variability Among State Crippled Children's Service Programs: Pluralism Thrives." *American Journal of Public Health,* 1985, *75* (4), 375–381.

Ireys, H. T., and Merkens, M. "Supplemental Security Income Programs as They Relate to Children." Unpublished manuscript, Vanderbilt Institute for Public Policy Studies, Nashville, Tenn., 1981.

Jackson, D. "The Adolescent and the Hospital." *Pediatric Clinics of North America*, 1973, *20* (4), 901–910.

Jackson, E. "Treatment of the Young Child in the Hospital." *American Journal of Orthopsychiatry*, 1942, *12*, 70–106.

Jackson, R. C. "Developing Networks in a State-Based System of Health Care for Families." In E. L. Watkins (Ed.), *Social Work in a State-Based System of Child Health Care*. Based on the Proceedings of the 1980 Tri-Regional Workshop for Social Workers in Maternal and Child Health Services, University of North Carolina, Chapel Hill, June 1980.

Jay, S. M., and Wright, L. "Training Psychologists to Work with Chronically Ill Children." In N. Hobbs and J. M. Perrin (Eds.), *Issues in the Care of Children with Chronic Illness: A Sourcebook on Problems, Services, and Policies*. San Francisco: Jossey-Bass, 1985.

Jessop, D., and Stein, R. "Uncertainty and Its Relation to the Outcomes of Chronic Childhood Illness." Paper presented at the Annual Meetings of the Eastern Sociological Society, Baltimore, Md., March 1983.

Jetter, L. "Some Emotional Aspects of Prolonged Illness in Children." *Survey*, 1948, *84*, 165.

Johnson, B., and Steele, B. "Community Networking for Improved Services to Children with Chronic Illnesses and Their Families." *Children's Health Care*, 1983, *12* (2), 100–102.

Johnson, M. "Support Groups for Parents of Chronically Ill Children." *Pediatric Nursing*, 1982, *8*, 160–163.

Kalnins, I. "Cross-Illness Comparisons of Separation and Divorce Among Parents Having a Child with a Life-Threatening Illness." *Children's Health Care*, 1983, *12*, 72–77.

Kanthor, H., and others. "Areas of Responsibility in the Health Care of Multiply Handicapped Children." *Pediatrics*, 1974, *54*, 779–788.

Katz, G. "Regionalization Among Children's Hospitals." *Hospital and Health Services Administration*, 1980, *25* (4), 56–72.

Kisker, C. T., and others. "Health Outcomes of a Community-Based Therapy Program for Children with Cancer." *Pediatrics*, 1980, *66*, 900–906.

Klaus, M., and Kennell, J. *Maternal Infant Bonding: Impact of*

Early Separation or Loss on Family Development. St. Louis, Mo.: Mosby, 1976.

Klerman, L. V. "Interprofessional Issues in Delivering Services to Chronically Ill Children and Their Families." In N. Hobbs and J. M. Perrin (Eds.), *Issues in the Care of Children with Chronic Illness: A Sourcebook on Problems, Services, and Policies.* San Francisco: Jossey-Bass, 1985.

Koocher, G., and O'Malley, J. *The Damocles Syndrome: Psychological Consequences of Surviving Childhood Cancer.* New York: McGraw-Hill, 1981.

Kopelman, L. "Paternalism and Autonomy in the Care of Chronically Ill Children." In N. Hobbs and J. M. Perrin (Eds.), *Issues in the Care of Children with Chronic Illness: A Sourcebook on Problems, Services, and Policies.* San Francisco: Jossey-Bass, 1985.

Korsch, B. M. "Research and Patient Care." George Armstrong Lecture, Ambulatory Pediatric Association, San Francisco, May 1973.

Korsch, B. M., and Barnett, H. "The Physician, the Family, and the Child with Nephrosis." *Journal of Pediatrics,* 1961, *58,* 707–715.

Korsch, B. M. and Fine, R., "Chronic Kidney Diseases." In N. Hobbs and J. M. Perrin (Eds.), *Issues in the Care of Children with Chronic Illness: A Sourcebook on Problems, Services, and Policies.* San Francisco: Jossey-Bass, 1985.

Kovar, M., and Meny, D. *Better Health for Our Children: A National Strategy.* Vol. 3: *A Statistical Profile.* Washington, D.C.: U.S. Government Printing Office, 1981.

Kubany, A., Danowski, T., and Moses, C. "The Personality and Intelligence of Diabetics." *Diabetes,* 1956, *5,* 462–467.

Kurland, I. "A Staff-Directed Outpatient Group for Parents of Children with Arthritis." In P. Azarnoff and C. Hardgrove (Eds.), *The Family in Child Health Care.* New York: Wiley, 1981.

Langford, W. "Physical Illness and Convalescence: Their Meaning to the Child." *Journal of Pediatrics,* 1948, *33,* 242–250.

Lansky, S., and others. "Childhood Cancer: Nonmedical Costs of the Illness." *Cancer,* 1979, *43,* 403–408.

Lascari, A., and Stehbens, J. "The Reactions of Families to Childhood Leukemia." *Clinical Pediatrics,* 1976, *12,* 210–215.

Laurence, K. M. "Neural Tube Defects: A Two-Pronged Approach to Primary Prevention." *Pediatrics,* 1982, *70,* 648–650.

Lavigne, J., and Ryan, M. "Psychological Adjustment of Siblings of Children with Chronic Illness." *Pediatrics,* 1979, *63,* 616–627.

Leffert, F. "Asthma." In N. Hobbs and J. M. Perrin (Eds.), *Issues in the Care of Children with Chronic Illness: A Sourcebook on Problems, Services, and Policies.* San Francisco: Jossey-Bass, 1985.

Leikin, S. L. "Minors' Assent or Dissent to Medical Treatment." *Journal of Pediatrics,* 1983, *102,* 169–176.

Lesser, A. J. "Health Services—Accomplishments and Outlook." *Children,* 1960, *7,* 142–149.

Lesser, A. J. "Public Programs for Crippled Children." In N. Hobbs and J. M. Perrin (Eds.), *Issues in the Care of Children with Chronic Illness: A Sourcebook on Problems, Services, and Policies.* San Francisco: Jossey-Bass, 1985.

Levine, P. H. "Efficacy of Self-Therapy in Hemophilia: A Study of 72 Patients with Hemophilia A and B." *New England Journal of Medicine,* 1974, *291,* 1381–1384.

Lewis, C. E., and others. "A Randomized Trial of A.C.T. (Asthma Care Training) for Kids." *Pediatrics,* 1984, *74,* 478–486.

Lewis, I. J., and Sheps, C. G. *The Sick Citadel: The American Academic Medical Center and the Public Interest.* Cambridge, Mass: Oelgeschlager, Gunn, and Hain, 1983.

Lewiston, N. J. "Cystic Fibrosis." In N. Hobbs and J. M. Perrin (Eds.), *Issues in the Care of Children with Chronic Illness: A Sourcebook on Problems, Services, and Policies.* San Francisco: Jossey-Bass, 1985.

Lieberman, M., Borman, L., and Associates. *Self-Help Groups for Coping with Crisis: Origins, Members, Processes, and Impacts.* San Francisco: Jossey-Bass, 1979.

Linney, D., and Lazerson, J. "Hemophilia: Cost Considerations for Prescribing Therapeutic Materials." *Transfusion,* 1979, *19,* 57–59.

Lipson, J. "Effects of a Support Group on the Emotional Impact of Caesarean Birth." *Prevention in Human Services,* 1982, *1* (3), 17–30.

Little, S., and Cohen, L. "Goal-Setting Behavior of Asthmatic

Children and of Their Mothers for Them." *Journal of Personality*, 1951, *19*, 376-389.

Lowit, I. "Social and Psychological Consequences of Chronic Illness in Children." *Developmental Medicine and Child Neurology*, 1973, *15*, 75-90.

Luft, H. S. *Health Maintenance Organizations: Dimensions of Performance.* New York: Wiley, 1981.

Lund, D. *Eric.* New York: Lippincott, 1974.

Lurie, N., and others. "Termination from Medi-Cal: Does It Affect Health?" *New England Journal of Medicine,* 1984, *311* (7), 480-484.

McAnarney, E., and others. "Psychological Problems of Children with Chronic Juvenile Arthritis." *Pediatrics,* 1974, *53*, 523-528.

McCarthy, M. "Social Aspects of Treatment in Childhood Leukemia." *Social Science and Medicine,* 1975, *9*, 263-269.

McCollum, A. "Cystic Fibrosis: Economic Impact upon the Family." *American Journal of Public Health,* 1971, *61*, 1335-1340.

McCrae, W., and others. "Cystic Fibrosis: Parents' Response to the Genetic Basis of the Disease." *Lancet,* 1973, *2*, 141-143.

McInerny, T. "The Role of the General Pediatrician in Coordinating the Care of Children with Chronic Illness." *Pediatric Clinics of North America,* 1984, *31* (1), 199-210.

McKeever, P. "Fathering the Chronically Ill Child: A Neglected Area in Family Research." *American Journal of Maternal and Child Nursing,* 1981, *6*, 124-128.

McKeever, P. "Siblings of Chronically Ill Children: A Literature Review with Implications for Research and Practice." *American Journal of Orthopsychiatry,* 1983, *53*, 209-218.

McLaughlin, J., and Shurtleff, D. "Management of the Newborn with Myelodysplasia." *Clinical Pediatrics,* 1979, *18*, 463-476.

McNicol, K. N., and Williams, H. E. "Spectrum of Asthma in Children. I. Clinical and Physiological Components." *British Medical Journal,* 1973, *4*, 7-11.

MacQueen, J. "Forward." In R. McPhillips (Ed.), *Proceedings of the First National Conference of State Directors for Crippled Children.* Baltimore, Md.: Johns Hopkins University, 1974.

Magrab, P. R. "Psychosocial Development of Chronically Ill Children." In N. Hobbs and J. M. Perrin (Eds.), *Issues in the Care of Children with Chronic Illness: A Sourcebook on Problems, Services, and Policies.* San Francisco: Jossey-Bass, 1985.

Markowitz, M., and Gordis, L. "A Family Pediatric Clinic at a Community Hospital." *Children,* 1967, *14* (1), 25–30.

Marmor, T. R., and Christianson, J. B. *Health Care Policy: A Political Economy Approach.* Beverly Hills, Calif.: Sage, 1982.

Martin, R. "Legal Issues and Interpretation of P.L. 94–142." In Association for Care of Children's Health (Ed.), *Home Care for Children with Severe Handicapping Conditions: A Report of a Conference.* Houston, Tex.: Association for Care of Children's Health, 1984.

Martinson, I., and Jorgens, C. "Report of a Parent Support Group." In I. Martinson (Ed.), *Home Care for the Dying Child.* East Norwalk, Conn.: Appleton-Century-Crofts, 1976.

Mason, E. "The Hospitalized Child: His Emotional Needs." *New England Journal of Medicine,* 1965, *272,* 406–414.

Massie R., and Massie, S. *Journey.* New York: Knopf, 1976.

Massie, R. K., Jr. "The Constant Shadow: Reflections on the Life of a Chronically Ill Child." In N. Hobbs and J. M. Perrin (Eds.), *Issues in the Care of Children with Chronic Illness: A Sourcebook on Problems, Services, and Policies.* San Francisco: Jossey-Bass, 1985.

Mattsson, A. "Long-Term Physical Illness in Childhood: A Challenge to Psychosocial Adaptation." *Pediatrics,* 1972, *50,* 801–811.

Mattsson, A., Gross, S., and Hall, T. W. "Psychoendocrine Study of Adaptation in Hemophiliacs." *Psychosomatic Medicine,* 1971, *33,* 215–225.

Mauksch, I. G. "Nurse-Physician Collaboration: A Changing Relationship." *Journal of Nursing Administration,* 1981, *11,* 35–38.

Mearig, J. S. "Cognitive Development of Chronically Ill Children." In N. Hobbs and J. M. Perrin (Eds.), *Issues in the Care of Children with Chronic Illness: A Sourcebook on Problems, Services, and Policies.* San Francisco: Jossey-Bass, 1985.

Meyerowitz, J. H., and Kaplan, H. B. "Family Responses to Stress: The Case of Cystic Fibrosis." *Social Science and Medicine,* 1967, *1,* 249–266.

Mikkelsen, C., Waechter, E., and Crittenden, M. "Cystic Fibrosis: A Family Challenge." *Children Today*, 1978, July–Aug., pp. 22–26.

Miller, D. R. "Acute Lymphoblastic Leukemia." *Pediatric Clinics of North America*, 1980, *27*, 269–292.

Milofsky, C., and Elworth, J. T. "Charitable Associations." In N. Hobbs and J. M. Perrin (Eds.), *Issues in the Care of Children with Chronic Illness: A Sourcebook on Problems, Services, and Policies*. San Francisco: Jossey-Bass, 1985.

Minde, K., and others. "Self-Help Groups in a Premature Nursery: A Controlled Evaluation." *Journal of Pediatrics*, 1980, *96*, 933–940.

Minuchin, S. *Psychosomatic Families*. Cambridge, Mass.: Harvard University Press, 1978.

Mishler, E. G., and others. *Social Contexts of Health, Illness, and Patient Care*. New York: Cambridge University Press, 1981.

Myers, G., and Millsap, M. "Spina Bifida." In N. Hobbs and J. M. Perrin (Eds.), *Issues in the Care of Children with Chronic Illness: A Sourcebook on Problems, Services, and Policies*. San Francisco: Jossey-Bass, 1985.

Nadas, A. S. "Update on Congenital Heart Disease." *Pediatric Clinics of North America*, 1984, *31*, 153–164.

Nader, P. "The School Health Service: Making Primary Care Effective." *Pediatric Clinics of North America*, 1974, *21*, 57–73.

Nader, P. (Ed.). *Options for School Health: Meeting Community Needs*. Germantown, Md: Aspen, 1978.

Nader, P., Emmel, A., and Charney, E. "The School Health Service: A New Model." *Pediatrics*, 1972, *49*, 805–813.

Natanson v. *Kline*, 186 Kan. 393, 350, P.2d 1093, 1960.

National Association of Children's Hospitals and Related Institutions. "An Analysis of Children's Hospitals' Medicare, Medicaid, and Self-Pay Revenues and Receipts." *NACHRI Reports*. Wilmington, Del.: National Association of Children's Hospitals and Related Institutions, 1981.

National Center for Health Statistics. *Vital Statistics of the United States, 1950*: Vol. 3. Washington, D.C.: U.S. Department of Health, Education, and Welfare, 1953.

National Center for Health Statistics. "Final Mortality Statistics— 1977." *Monthly Vital Statistics Report*, Supplement, Vol. 28, no. 1. Hyattsville, Md.: U.S. Department of Health, Education, and Welfare, 1979a.

National Center for Health Statistics. *Vital Statistics of the United States.* Vol. 2: *Mortality, Part A.* Hyattsville, Md.: U.S. Department of Health, Education, and Welfare, 1979b.

National Health Policy Forum. *Recent and Proposed Changes in State Medicaid Programs: A Fifty-State Survey.* Washington, D.C.: National Health Policy Forum, 1981.

National Institutes of Health. *Antenatal Diagnosis.* Bethesda, Md.: U.S. Department of Health, Education, and Welfare, 1979.

National Joint Practice Commission. *Guidelines for Establishing Joint or Collaborative Practices in Hospitals.* Chicago: National Joint Practice Commission, 1981.

National Public Health Program Reporting Service. *Selected Title V Programs, Crippled Children's Services, Fiscal Year 1978.* Silver Spring, Md.: National Public Health Program Reporting Service, 1979.

National Public Health Program Reporting Service. *Selected Title V Programs, Crippled Children's Services, Fiscal Year 1980.* Silver Spring, Md.: National Public Health Program Reporting Service, 1981.

Natterson, J., and Knudson, A. "Observations Concerning the Fear of Death in Fatally Ill Children and Their Mothers." *Psychosomatic Medicine,* 1960, *22,* 456–465.

Neuhaus, E. "A Personality Study of Asthmatic and Cardiac Children." *Psychosomatic Medicine,* 1958, *20,* 181–186.

Newacheck, P. W., Budetti, P. P., and McManus, P. "Trends in Childhood Disability." *American Journal of Public Health,* 1984, *74,* 232–236.

New England Regional Infant Cardiac Program. "Report of the New England Regional Infant Cardiac Program." *Pediatrics,* 1980, *65* (Supplement), 375–461.

Norris, C. "Self-Care." In B. W. Spradley (Ed.), *Readings in Community Health Nursing.* Boston: Little, Brown, 1982.

Nyhan, W. L. "Promising Directions in Pediatric Research." *Advances in Pediatrics,* 1983, *30,* 1–12.

Office of Inspector General. *Adoption Assistance: A National Program Inspection.* New York: New York Department of Health and Human Services, 1984.

Osterweis, M., and others. "HMO Development for Primary Care

Team Teaching of Medical and Nursing Students." *Journal of Medical Education,* 1980, *55,* 743-750.

Outka, G. "Social Justice and Equal Access to Health Care." *Journal of Religious Ethics,* 1974, *2,* 11-32.

Outka, G. "Social Justice and Equal Access to Health Care." *Perspectives in Biology and Medicine,* 1975, *18,* 185-203.

Palfrey, J. S., Levy, J. C., and Gilbert, K. L. "Use of Primary Care Facilities by Patients Attending Specialty Clinics." *Pediatrics,* 1980, *65,* 567-572.

Palfrey, J., Mervis, R., and Butler, J. "New Directions in the Evaluation and Education of Handicapped Children." *New England Journal of Medicine,* 1978, *298,* 819-824.

Pantell, R. H., and others. "Physician Communication with Children and Parents." *Pediatrics,* 1982, *70,* 396-402.

Parcel, G. S., and others. "A Comparison of Absentee Rates of Elementary School Children with Asthma and Non-Asthmatic Schoolmates." *Pediatrics,* 1979, *64,* 878-881.

Pearson, D. A., Stranova, T. J., and Thompson, J. D. "Patient and Program Costs Associated with Chronic Hemodialysis Care." *Injury,* 1976, *13,* 23-28.

Pediatric Ambulatory Care Division. *Issues in the Care of Children with Special Health Needs.* Bronx, N.Y.: Albert Einstein College of Medicine, Department of Pediatrics, 1983. (Videotape.)

Pendergrass, T. W., Chard, R. L., and Hartmann, J. R. "Leukemia." In N. Hobbs and J. M. Perrin (Eds.), *Issues in the Care of Children with Chronic Illness: A Sourcebook on Problems, Services, and Policies.* San Francisco: Jossey-Bass, 1985.

Perrin, E. C., and Gerrity, P. S. "There's a Demon in Your Belly: Children's Understanding of Illness." *Pediatrics,* 1981, *67,* 841-849.

Perrin, E. C., and Gerrity, P. S. "Development of Children with a Chronic Illness." *Pediatric Clinics of North America,* 1984, *31,* 19-32.

Perrin, E. C., and Perrin, J. M. "Clinicians' Assessment of Children's Understanding of Illness." *American Journal of Diseases of Children,* 1983, *137,* 874-878.

Perrin, J. M. "Special Problems of Chronic Childhood Illness in Rural Areas." In N. Hobbs and J. M. Perrin (Eds.), *Issues in the*

Care of Children with Chronic Illness: A Sourcebook on Problems, Services, and Policies. San Francisco: Jossey-Bass, 1985.

Perrin, J. M., and Ireys, H. T. "The Organization of Services for Chronically Ill Children and Their Families." *Pediatric Clinics of North America,* 1984, *31,* 235-258.

Perrin, J. M., and MacLean, W. E. "Education and Stress Management in Chronic Childhood Illness: Intervention Strategies." Research proposal. Nashville, Tenn.: Vanderbilt University School of Medicine, 1982.

Peterson, I. "Inequity Reported in Welfare Survey." *New York Times,* Sept. 28, 1981, p. A15.

Piaget, J., and Inhelder, B. *The Psychology of the Child.* New York: Basic Books, 1969.

Pierce, P., and Freedman, S. "The REACH Project: An Innovative Health Delivery Model for Medically Dependent Children." *Children's Health Care,* 1983, *12* (2), 86-89.

Plank, E. *Working with Children in Hospitals.* Cleveland, Ohio: Western Reserve Press, 1962.

Platt Committee. *The Welfare of Children in Hospitals.* London: Her Majesty's Stationary Office, 1959.

Pless, I. B. "The Changing Face of Primary Pediatrics." *Pediatric Clinics of North America,* 1974, *21,* 223-244.

Pless, I. B. "The Agenda for Research: A Response to the Vanderbilt Findings." Paper presented at the Institute of Medicine, Washington, D.C., April 1983.

Pless, I. B. "Clinical Assessment: Physical and Psychological Functioning." *Pediatric Clinics of North America,* 1984, *31,* 33-46.

Pless, I. B., and Perrin, J. M. "Issues Common to a Variety of Illnesses." In N. Hobbs and J. M. Perrin (Eds.), *Issues in the Care of Children with Chronic Illness: A Sourcebook on Problems, Services, and Policies.* San Francisco: Jossey-Bass, 1985.

Pless, I. B., and Pinkerton, P. *Chronic Childhood Disorder: Promoting Patterns of Adjustment.* Chicago: Year Book Medical Publishers, 1975.

Pless, I. B., and Roghmann, K. J. "Chronic Illness and Its Consequences: Some Observations Based on Three Epidemiological Surveys." *Journal of Pediatrics,* 1971, *79,* 351-359.

Pless, I. B., and Satterwhite, B. B. "Chronic Illness in Children:

Selection, Activities, and Evaluation of Non-Professional Family Counselors." *Clinical Pediatrics*, 1972, *11*, 403-410.

Pless, I. B., and Satterwhite, B. B. "A Measure of Family Functioning and Its Application." *Social Science and Medicine*, 1973, 7, 613-621.

Pless, I. B., and Satterwhite, B. B. "The Family Counselor." In R. J. Haggerty, K. Roghmann, and I. B. Pless, *Child Health and the Community*. New York: Wiley, 1975.

Pless, I. B., Satterwhite, B. B., and VanVechten, D. "Division, Duplication, and Neglect: Patterns of Care for Children with Chronic Disorders." *Child Care, Health and Development*, 1978, *4*, 9-19.

Pless, I. B., and Zvagulis, I. "The Health of Children with Special Needs." In L. Klerman (Ed.), *Research Priorities in Maternal and Child Health: Report of a Conference*. Waltham, Mass.: Brandeis University, 1981.

Pool, J. G., and Shannon, A. E. "Production of High-Potency Concentrates of Antihemophilic Globulin in a Closed Bag System: Assay in Vitro and in Vivo." *New England Journal of Medicine*, 1965, *273*, 1443-1447.

President's Commission for the Study of Ethical Problems in Medicine and Biomedical and Behavioral Research. *A Report on the Ethical and Legal Implications of Informed Consent in the Patient-Practitioner Relationship*. Washington, D.C.: U.S. Government Printing Office, 1982.

Preventive Intervention Research Center. "Family Advocate Coordination Effort." Unpublished document, Albert Einstein College of Medicine, Bronx, N. Y., 1985.

Prugh, D., and others. "A Study of the Emotional Reactions of Children and Families to Hospitalization and Illness." *American Journal of Orthopsychiatry*, 1953, *23*, 70-106.

Ramsey, P. *The Patient as Person: Explorations in Medical Ethics*. New Haven, Conn.: Yale University Press, 1970.

Richards, S., and Wolff, E. "The Organization and Function of Play Activities in the Setup of a Pediatric Department: A Report of a 3-year Experiment." *Mental Hygiene*, 1940, *24*, 229-237.

Richmond, J., and Waisman, H. A. "Psychologic Aspects of Management of Children with Malignant Diseases." *American Journal of Diseases of Children,* 1955, *89,* 42-47.

Robertson, J. *A Two-Year-Old Goes to the Hospital.* New York: New York University Film Library, 1952. (Film.)

Robertson, J. *Going to Hospital with Mother.* New York: New York University Film Library, 1958. (Film.)

Robinson, T. "School Nurse Practitioners on the Job." *American Journal of Nursing,* 1981, *81* (9), 1674-1676.

Rogers, D. E., Blendon, R. J., and Moloney, T. W. "Who Needs Medicaid?" *New England Journal of Medicine,* 1982, *307* (1), 13-18.

Roghmann, K. J., and others. "The Selective Utilization of Prenatal Genetic Diagnosis." *Medical Care,* 1983, *21,* 1111-1125.

Rosenbloom, A. "Primary and Subspecialty Care of Diabetes Mellitus in Children and Youth." *Pediatric Clinics of North America,* 1984, *31* (1), 107-118.

Roskies, E., and Lazarus, R. S. "Coping Theory and the Teaching of Coping Skills." In P. O. Davidson and S. M. Davidson (Eds.), *Behavioral Medicine: Changing Health and Lifestyles.* New York: Brunner/Mazel, 1980.

Ross, J. "Coping with Childhood Cancer: Group Intervention as an Aid to Parents in Crisis." *Social Work in Health Care,* 1978, *4,* 381-391.

Rowland, D., and Gaus, C. R. "Medicaid Eligibility and Benefits: Current Policies and Future Choices." Paper for the 1981 Commonwealth Fund Forum, "Medical Care for the Poor: What Can States Do in the 1980s?" Lake Bluff, Ill., August 1981.

Rudolph, C., Andrews, V., Ratcliff, K., and Downes, D. "Training Social Workers to Aid Chronically Ill Children and Their Families." In N. Hobbs and J. M. Perrin (Eds.), *Issues in the Care of Children with Chronic Illness: A Sourcebook on Problems, Services, and Policies.* San Francisco: Jossey-Bass, 1985.

Rutter, M., Tizard, J., and Whitmore, K. (Eds.). *Education, Health, and Behavior.* London: Longman, 1970.

Rymer, M., and others. *Survey of Blind and Disabled Children Receiving Supplemental Security Income Benefits.* Social Security Administration publication no. 13-11728. Washington, D.C.: U.S. Department of Health, Education, and Welfare, 1980.

Sabbeth, B. "Understanding the Impact of Chronic Childhood Illness on Families." *Pediatric Clinics of North America,* 1984, *31,* 47-58.

Sabbeth, B., and Leventhal, J. "Marital Adjustment to Chronic Childhood Illness: A Critique of the Literature." *Pediatrics,* 1984, *73,* 763-768.

Santos, G. W. "Bone Marrow Transplantation: Current Results in Leukemia." *Yale Journal of Biology and Medicine,* 1982, *55,* 477-485.

Schorr, L. B. "Social Policy Issues in Improving Child Health Services: A Child Advocate's View." *Pediatrics,* 1978, *62,* 370-376.

Select Panel for the Promotion of Child Health. *Better Health for our Children: A National Strategy.* Department of Health and Human Services publication no. 79-55071. Washington, D.C.: U.S. Government Printing Office, 1981.

Selvin, S., and others. "Selected Epidemiologic Observations of Cell-Specific Leukemia Mortality in the United States, 1969-1977." *American Journal of Epidemiology,* 1983, *117,* 140-152.

Senn, M. "Emotional Aspects of Convalescence." *The Child,* 1945, *10,* 24-28.

Shapiro, G. G. "Corticosteroids in the Treatment of Allergic Disease." *Pediatric Clinics of North America,* 1983, *30,* 955-972.

Shayne, M. "Medicaid: Financing the Health Care of Poor Chronically Ill Children." Unpublished manuscript, Vanderbilt Institute for Public Policy Studies, Nashville, Tenn., 1981.

Shayne, M., and Cerreto, M. "Notes on Parent Group Meetings." Unpublished staff paper, Vanderbilt Institute for Public Policy Studies, Nashville, Tenn., 1981.

Shepard, S. "No Time to Dream." *Reader,* 1981, *10* (23), 1-16.

Shore, M., and Goldston, S. "Mental Health Aspects of Pediatric Care: Historical Review and Current Status." In P. Magrab (Ed.), *Psychological Management of Pediatric Problems.* Vol. 1: *Early Life Conditions and Chronic Diseases.* Baltimore, Md.: University Park Press, 1978.

Shurtleff, D. B., and others. "Myelodysplasia: Decision for Death or Disability." *New England Journal of Medicine,* 1974, *291,* 1005-1011.

Sloan, F. A., Cromwell, J., and Mitchell, J. B. *Private Physicians and Public Programs.* Lexington, Mass.: Lexington Books, 1978.

Smith, P. S., Keyes, N. C., and Forman, E. N. "Socioeconomic Evaluation of a State-Funded Comprehensive Hemophilia-Care Program." *New England Journal of Medicine,* 1982, *306,* 575–579.

Smith, P. S., and Levine, P. H. "The Benefits of Comprehensive Care of Hemophilia: A Five-Year Study of Outcomes." *American Journal of Public Health,* 1984, *74,* 616–617.

Smithells, R. W., and others. "Apparent Prevention of Neural Tube Defects by Periconceptional Vitamin Supplements." *Archives of Disease in Childhood,* 1981, *56,* 911.

Solnit, A., and Green, M. "Psychologic Considerations in the Management of Deaths on Pediatric Hospital Services: The Doctor and the Child's Family." *Pediatrics,* 1959, *24,* 106–112.

Solnit, A., and Stark, M. "Mourning and the Birth of a Defective Child." *Psychoanalytic Study of the Child,* 1961, *16,* 523–537.

Solomon, G. F., and Amkraut, A. A. "Psychoneuroendocrinological Effects on the Immune Response." *Annual Reviews of Microbiology,* 1981, *35,* 155–184.

Sourkes, B. "Siblings of the Pediatric Cancer Patient." In V. Kellerman (Ed.), *Psychological Aspects of Childhood Cancer.* Springfield, Ill.: Thomas, 1981.

Spiegelberg, H. "Good Fortune Obligates: Albert Schweitzer's Second Ethical Principle." *Ethics,* 1975, *85,* 227–234.

Spina Bifida Association of the Delaware Valley. "Study of the Costs of Spina Bifida." Wilmington, Del.: Spina Bifida Association of the Delaware Valley, 1979.

Spitz, B. "Medicaid HMOs: A Long Way from Salvation." Paper for the 1981 Commonwealth Fund Forum, "Medical Care for the Poor: What Can States Do in the 1980s?" Lake Bluff, Ill., August 1981a.

Spitz, B. *State Guide to Medicaid Cost Containment.* Washington, D.C.: Intergovernmental Health Policy Project, George Washington University, and Center for Policy Research, National Governors' Association, 1981b.

Spitz, R. "Hospitalism: An Inquiry into the Genesis of Psychiatric

Conditions in Early Childhood." *Psychoanalytic Study of the Child*, 1946, *2*, 313-342.

Starfield, B. "Health Services Research: A Working Model." *New England Journal of Medicine*, 1973, *289*, 132-136.

Starfield, B. "Measurement of Outcome: A Proposed Scheme." *Milbank Memorial Fund Quarterly*, 1974, *52*, 39-50.

Starfield, B. "Patients and Populations: Necessary Links Between the Two Approaches to Pediatric Research." *Pediatric Research*, 1981, *15*, 1-5.

Starfield, B. "Family Income, Ill Health, and Medical Care of U.S. Children." *Journal of Public Health Policy*, 1982, *3*, 244-259.

Starfield, B. "The State of Research on Chronically Ill Children." In N. Hobbs and J. M. Perrin (Eds.), *Issues in the Care of Children with Chronic Illness: A Sourcebook on Problems, Services, and Policies*. San Francisco: Jossey-Bass, 1985.

Starfield, B., and others. "Continuity and Coordination in Primary Care: Their Achievement and Utility." *Medical Care*, 1976, *14*, 625-636.

Starfield, B., and others. "Morbidity in Children: A Longitudinal View." *New England Journal of Medicine*, 1984, *310*, 824-829.

Stein, R.E.K. "Preventive Intervention Research Center for Child Health." Proposal submitted to National Institute of Mental Health. Bronx, N.Y., Department of Pediatrics, Albert Einstein College of Medicine, 1982.

Stein, R.E.K. "A Home Care Program for Children with Chronic Illness." *Children's Health Care*, 1983, *12* (2), 90-92.

Stein, R.E.K., and Jessop, D. J. "A Noncategorical Approach to Chronic Childhood Illness." *Public Health Reports*, 1982a, *97*, 354-362.

Stein, R.E.K., and Jessop, D. J. "What Diagnosis Does *Not* Tell: The Case for a Non-Categorical Approach to Chronic Physical Illness." Paper presented at the Annual Meeting of the Society for Pediatric Research, Washington, D.C., May 1982b.

Stein, R.E.K., and Jessop, D. J. "Relationship Between Health Status and Psychological Adjustment Among Children with Chronic Conditions." *Pediatrics*, 1984, *73*, 169-174.

Stein, R.E.K., and Jessop, D. J. "Delivery of Care to Inner-City Children with Chronic Conditions." In N. Hobbs and J. M.

Perrin (Eds.), *Issues in the Care of Children with Chronic Illness: A Sourcebook on Problems, Services, and Policies.* San Francisco: Jossey-Bass, 1985.

Stein, R.E.K., Jessop, D. J., and Ireys, H. T. *Education of Pediatricians for the Ongoing Care of Children with Special Health Needs.* Conference Report, Department of Pediatrics, Albert Einstein College of Medicine, Bronx, N.Y., 1984.

Stein, R.E.K., and Riessman, C. "The Development of an Impact-on-Family Scale: Preliminary Findings." *Medical Care,* 1980, *18,* 465-472.

Stein, S. C., and others. "Is Myelomeningocele a Disappearing Disease?" *Pediatrics,* 1982, *69,* 511-514.

Steinhauer, P., Muskin, D., and Rae-Grant, Q. "Psychological Aspects of Chronic Illness." *Pediatric Clinics of North America,* 1974, *21,* 825-840.

Stevens, R. *American Medicine and the Public Interest.* New Haven, Conn.: Yale University Press, 1971.

Stevens, R., and Stevens, R. *Welfare Medicine in America: A Case Study of Medicaid.* New York: Free Press, 1974.

Strain, J. "The American Academy of Pediatrics Comments on the 'Baby Doe II' Regulations." *New England Journal of Medicine,* 1983, *309,* 443-444.

Strayer, F., Kisker, C. T., and Fethke, C. "Cost-Effectiveness of a Shared-Management Delivery System for the Care of Children with Cancer." *Pediatrics,* 1980, *66,* 907-911.

Stroup, C. "The Tiniest Newborns." *Hastings Center Report,* 1983, *13,* 14-19.

Sultz, H., and others. *Long-Term Childhood Illness.* Pittsburgh, Pa.: University of Pittsburgh, 1972.

Sutherland, D.E.R., and others. "Pancreas Transplantation." *Pediatric Clinics of North America,* 1984, *31,* 735-750.

Tamborlane, W. V., and Sherwin, R. S. "Diabetes Control and Complications: New Strategies and Insights." *Journal of Pediatrics,* 1983, *102,* 805-813.

Tamborlane, W. V., and others. "Insulin Infusion Pump Treatment of Diabetes." *New England Journal of Medicine,* 1981, *305,* 303-307.

Task Force on Pediatric Education. *The Future of Pediatric Education.* Evanston, Ill.: Task Force on Pediatric Education, 1978.

Tatara, T. *Characteristics of Children in Substitute and Foster Care.* Washington, D.C.: American Public Welfare Association, December 1983.

Tew, B., and Laurence, K. "Mothers, Brothers, and Sisters of Patients with Spina Bifida." *Developmental Medicine and Child Neurology,* 1975, *15* (Supplement 29), 69–76.

Thornton, A., and Freedman, O. "The Changing American Family." *Population Bulletin,* 1983, *38* (4), 1–44.

Tiller, J., Ekert, H., and Richards, W. "Family Reactions in Childhood Acute Lymphoblastic Leukemia in Remission." *Australian Pediatric Journal,* 1977, *13,* 176–181.

Tisza, V. "Management of the Parents of the Chronically Ill Child." *American Journal of Orthopsychiatry,* 1962, *32,* 53–59.

Title V of the Social Security Act of 1935. Chapter 531, Statutes at Large, XLIX, Part 1, p. 631.

Titmuss, R. M. *The Gift Relationship.* New York: Vintage Books, 1972.

Toch, R. "Management of the Child with a Fatal Disease." *Clinical Pediatrics,* 1964, *3,* 418–427.

Travis, G. *Chronic Illness in Children: Its Impact on Child and Family.* Stanford, Calif.: Stanford University Press, 1976.

Turk, J. "Impact of Cystic Fibrosis on Family Functioning." *Pediatrics,* 1964, *34,* 67–71.

U.S. Bureau of the Census. *Projections of the Population of the U.S.: 1977 to 2050,* no. 704. In *Current Population Reports,* Series P-25. Washington, D.C.: U.S. Government Printing Office, 1977.

U.S. Department of Health and Human Services. *Technical Notes: Summaries and Characteristics of States' Title XX Social Services Plans for Fiscal Year 1980.* Washington, D.C.: U.S. Department of Health and Human Services, n.d.

U.S. Department of Health, Education, and Welfare. *Assessment of Cooley's Anemia Research and Treatment.* Publication no. 79-1653. Washington, D.C.: U.S. Government Printing Office, 1979.

United States General Accounting Office. *Maternal and Child Health Block Grant: Program Changes Emerging Under State Administration.* Washington, D.C.: U.S. Government Printing Office, 1984.

Vance, V., and Taylor, W. "The Financial Cost of Chronic Child-hood Asthma." *Annuals of Allergy*, 1971, *29*, 455-460.

Vaughan, G. F. "Children in Hospital." *Lancet*, 1957, *1*, 1117-1120.

Vaughn, J. C. "Educational Preparation for Nursing—1979." *Nursing and Health Care*, 1980, *1*, 80-86.

Veatch, R. M. "What Is 'Just' Health Care Delivery?" In R. M. Veatch and R. Branson (Eds.), *Ethics and Health Policy*. Cambridge, Mass.: Ballinger, 1976.

Veatch, R. M. *Case Studies in Medical Ethics*. Cambridge, Mass.: Harvard University Press, 1977.

Veatch, R. M. *A Theory of Medical Ethics*. New York: Basic Books, 1981.

Vernick, J., and Karon, M. "Who's Afraid of Death on a Leukemia Ward?" *American Journal of Diseases of Children*, 1965, *109*, 395-397.

Walker, D. K., Gortmaker, S. L., and Weitzman, M. *Chronic Illness and Psychological Problems Among Children in Genesee County*. Boston: Community Child Health Studies, Harvard School of Public Health, 1981. (Mimeographed.)

Walker, D. K., and Jacobs, F. "Public School Programs for Chronically Ill Children." In N. Hobbs and J. M. Perrin (Eds.), *Issues in the Care of Children with Chronic Illness: A Sourcebook on Problems, Services, and Policies*. San Francisco: Jossey-Bass, 1985.

Walker, D. K., and others. "Health and Educational Services Received by Special Needs Children." Paper presented at Annual Meeting, American Public Health Association, Anaheim, Calif., November 1984.

Walker, J., Thomas, M., and Russell, I. "Spina Bifida and the Parents." *Developmental Medicine and Child Neurology*, 1971, *13* (4), 462-476.

Weeks, K. "Private Health Insurance and Chronically Ill Children." In N. Hobbs and J. M. Perrin (Eds.), *Issues in the Care of Children with Chronic Illness: A Sourcebook on Problems, Services, and Policies*. San Francisco: Jossey-Bass, 1985.

Weisman, M. *Intensive Care: A Family Love Story*. New York: Random House, 1982.

Weitzman, M. "Medical Services." In N. Hobbs and J. M. Perrin

(Eds.), *Issues in the Care of Children with Chronic Illness: A Sourcebook on Problems, Services, and Policies.* San Francisco: Jossey-Bass, 1985.

Whitten, C. F., and Nishiura, E. N. "Sickle Cell Anemia." In N. Hobbs and J. M. Perrin (Eds.), *Issues in the Care of Children with Chronic Illness: A Sourcebook on Problems, Services, and Policies.* San Francisco: Jossey-Bass, 1985.

Whitten, C., Waugh, D., and Moore, A. "Unmet Needs of Parents of Children with Sickle Cell Anemia." In J. Hercules and others (Eds.), *Proceedings of the First National Symposium on Sickle Cell Disease.* Bethesda, Md.: National Heart, Lung, and Blood Institute, 1974.

Williams, H. E., and McNicol, K. N. "The Spectrum of Asthma in Children." *Pediatric Clinics of North America,* 1975, *22,* 43–52.

Wilson, J. G. "Embryotoxicity of Drugs in Man." In J. G. Wilson, and F. C. Fraser (Eds.), *Handbook of Teratology.* New York: Plenum, 1977.

Windham, G. C., and Edmonds, L. D. "Current Trends in the Incidence of Neural Tube Defects." *Pediatrics,* 1982, *70,* 333–339.

Yalom, I. *The Theory and Practice of Group Psychotherapy.* (2nd ed.) New York: Basic Books, 1975.

Yordy, K. D. "Federal Administrative Arrangements for Maternal and Child Health." In Select Panel for the Promotion of Child Health, *Better Health for Our Children: A National Strategy,* Vol. 4: *Background Papers.* Department of Health and Human Services publication no. 79-55071. Washington, D.C.: U.S. Department of Health and Human Services, 1981.

Zaner, R. M. "Chance and Morality: The Dialysis Phenomenon." In V. Kestenbaum (Ed.), *Phenomenology of Physical Illness.* Knoxville: University of Tennessee Press, 1982.

Zook, C., and Moore, F. "The High-Cost Users of Medical Care." *New England Journal of Medicine,* 1980, *302,* 996–1002.

Zook, C., Moore, F., and Zeckhauser, R. "Catastrophic Health Insurance: A Misguided Prescription?" *The Public Interest,* 1981, *62,* 66–81.

Name Index

Abildgaard, C. F., 259, 361
Adelenstein, A., 65, 361
Ader, R., 268, 361
Agle, D., 66, 361
Aledort, L. M., 13, 33, 178, 265, 361, 371
Alexander, J., 65, 361
Allan, J., 90, 92, 93, 361
Altenstetter, C., 222, 361
Amkraut, A. A., 268, 385
Anderson, J., 77, 368
Andrews, V., 148, 232, 239, 249, 383
Ashcraft, M.L.F., 204, 363
Ashcroft, S. C., xxvi, 47, 104, 111, 114, 115, 121, 122-123, 249, 250, 362
Azarnoff, P., 93, 362

Baird, S. M., xxvi, 47, 104, 111, 114, 115, 121, 122-123, 249, 250, 362
Baldwin, S., 184, 362
Banting, F. G., 43, 362
Barnes, C. M., 233, 239, 244, 247, 254, 362
Barnett, H., 66, 374
Barraclough, W., 64, 362
Bartlett, L., 215, 216, 368-369
Battle, C. U., 132, 362
Battle, S. F., 225, 362
Bauer, M., 279
Becker, A. B., 258, 362
Bellamy, G. T., 123, 362-363

Benton, B., 151, 363
Berki, S. E., 204, 363
Berlin, N., 6, 259, 265, 367
Best, C. H., 43, 362
Beverly, B., 64, 363
Bibace, R., 71, 269, 271, 363
Bjorkman, J., 222, 361
Blendon, R. J., 214, 243, 363, 383
Bock, R., 128, 164, 165, 363
Bok, S., 292-293, 363
Bonhag, R. C., 192n, 363
Borman, L. D., 155, 156, 157, 268, 363, 375
Bove, E. L., 259, 363
Bowditch, B., 93, 94-95, 371
Bozeman, M., 66, 363
Bracht, N. F., 144, 364
Brent, R. L., 50, 364
Breslau, N., 93, 183, 184, 265, 271, 364
Bronfenbrenner, U., 271, 364
Browne, W., 66, 364
Bruch, H., 65, 364
Bruhn, J., 132, 364
Budetti, P., 41, 214, 364, 379
Burr, C., xxvi, 149
Burton, L., 63, 93, 94, 364
Bush, M., 68, 93, 232, 245, 367
Butler, J., 3, 103, 116, 152, 153, 172, 190, 191, 194, 199, 210, 211, 214, 217, 224, 227, 337, 364, 380

Cairns, A., 93, 364
Campbell, A. R., 179, 181, 365

Campbell, J. D., 179, 181, 365
Carlton, W., 239, 291, 365
Carpenter, E., 183, 365
Case, J., 122, 365
Caskey, C. T., 261, 365
Cerreto, M. C., 83, 84, 86, 87, 96, 99,
    157, 170, 213, 233, 235, 240, 247,
    248, 271, 365, 366, 384
Chan, J., 87, 365
Chard, R. L., 11, 44, 258, 262, 380
Charney, E., 119, 378
Chesler, M., 85, 86, 87, 155, 156, 157,
    365
Chodoff, P., 66, 365
Christianson, J. B., 339, 377
Cleveland, T., 98-99, 365
Clewell, W. H., 48, 366
Cluff, L. E., 242, 366
Cohen, F., 271, 280, 366
Cohen, L., 66, 375-376
Cohen, M., 72, 79, 366
Cohen, N., 268, 361
Coser, L. A., 278, 366
Coser, R. L., 244, 366
Coupey, S., 72, 79, 366
Covelli, P., 77-78, 243, 366
Covington, R., 114, 366
Crittenden, M., 63, 82, 378
Cromwell, J., 214, 385
Cutter, F., 66, 366

Daeschner, C. W., 233, 235, 240, 247,
    248, 366
Danowski, T., 66, 374
Day, D., 10, 367
Debuskey, M., 65, 367
Deford, A., 76, 101
Deford, F. A., 63, 76, 101, 367
Dietrich, S. L., 17, 370
Dimsdale, J. E., 268, 367
Dorner, S., 79, 90, 367
Downes, D., 148, 232, 239, 249, 383
Drash, A., 6, 259, 265, 367
Drotar, D., 68, 79, 83, 93, 232, 245,
    367
Duff, R. S., 287, 296, 367
DuHamel, T., 74, 367
Dy, E., 121, 250, 362

Edelston, H., 64, 368
Edmonds, L. D., 263, 390

Egbuonu, L., 175, 368
Ekert, K., 90, 388
Eland, J., 77, 368
Elliott, G., 268, 371
Ellsworth, R., 275, 368
Ellsworth, S., 275, 368
Elworth, J. T., 86, 153-154, 226, 228,
    378
Emmel, A., 119, 378
Enthoven, A., 176, 368
Erikson, E., xiii, 71, 368

Farrow, F., 113, 115, 368
Feild, T., 151, 363
Fethke, C., 175, 177, 181, 266, 387
Fine, R., 14, 20, 44, 85, 288, 374
Fireman, P., 258, 368
Firth, M., 82, 368
Fitzelle, G., 66, 368
Forman, E. N., 178, 182, 385
Fost, N., 287, 368
Fox, H. B., 215, 216, 368-369
Fox, R. C., 244, 289, 369
Fraiberg, S., 269, 369
Frederickson, D. L., 272, 369
Freedman, O., 67, 80-81, 388
Freedman, S., 123, 159, 161, 162, 186,
    222, 381
Freidson, E., 294, 369
Freud, A., 64, 369
Friedman, S., 65, 66, 365, 369
Fullerton, W. D., 201, 369
Fyler, D. C., 10, 259, 369

Galant, S. P., 44-45, 258, 369
Gamble, D. R., 51, 369
Garr, A., 182, 369
Garrard, S., 65, 370
Gaus, C. R., 214, 383
Gerrity, P. S., 71, 72, 269, 271, 290,
    380
Gesten, E. L., 275, 370
Giardina, P.J.V., 13, 33, 371
Gilbert, K. L., 266, 380
Gilgoff, I., 17, 370
Glaser, N., 124, 370
Gliedman, J., 4, 235, 268, 370
Godfrey, C., 184, 362
Goldberg, R., 123, 124, 370
Goldston, S., 65, 77, 384

Gordis, L., 146–147, 377
Gortmaker, S. L., 2, 36–37, 38n, 41, 42, 107n, 264, 370, 389
Green, M., 65, 109, 239, 242, 245, 370, 385
Greenberg, H., 64, 370
Gross, S., 267, 377
Guyer, B., 119, 371

Haggerty, R., 109, 370
Haggerty, R. J., xxvi, 39, 41, 42n, 273, 371
Hall, T. W., 267, 377
Hamburg, D., 66, 365
Hamburg, D. A., 268, 371
Harder, L., 93, 94–95, 371
Harding, R., 132, 371
Harkey, J., xxvi, 37n, 371
Harris, L., 290
Hartmann, J. R., 11, 44, 258, 262, 380
Hauck, R. J.-P., xxvii, 139, 219, 300, 372
Heisel, J. S., 267, 371
Heller, J., 132, 371
Hilgartner, M., 13, 33, 371
Hippolitus, P., 123, 371
Hobbs, N., xi–xv, xxvii–xxviii, 5, 25, 70, 241, 271, 371–372
Hoekelman, R. A., 239, 242, 245, 370
Hoffstein, P. A., 181, 372
Holtzman, N. A., 47, 49, 142, 262, 372
Hughes, G., 132, 372
Hunt, P., 307, 372
Hymovich, D. P., 247, 372

Iglehart, J. K., 215, 372
Inhelder, B., 71, 381
Ipswitch, E., 291–292, 372
Ipswitch, S., 291–292
Ireys, H. T., xv, 132, 139, 194, 219, 221, 222, 224, 249, 265, 299, 300, 372, 381, 387
Isralsky, M., 123, 124, 370

Jackson, D., 130, 373
Jackson, E., 64, 373
Jackson, R. C., 146, 373
Jacobs, F., 4, 103, 104, 106, 108, 109, 111, 112–113, 114, 115, 116, 119, 120, 236, 250, 389
Jay, S. M., 245, 251, 373
Jessop, D. J., 19, 93, 131, 132, 141, 142, 175, 249, 260, 273–274, 373, 386–387
Jetter, L., 64, 373
Johnson, B., 128, 373
Johnson, M., 155, 373
Jorgens, C., 155, 377

Kalnins, I., 92, 93, 373
Kane, R., 66, 364
Kanthor, H., 130, 136, 137, 373
Kaplan, H. B., 90, 377
Karon, M., 66, 389
Katz, G., 176, 373
Keller, H., 70
Kennell, J., 74, 373–374
Kesler, R., 132, 371
Keyes, N. C., 178, 182, 385
Kisker, C. T., 136, 175, 177, 181, 258, 266, 373, 387
Klaus, M., 74, 373–374
Klerman, L. V., 137–138, 374
Knudson, A., 65, 379
Koocher, G., 124, 374
Kopelman, L., 288, 293, 294–295, 302, 374
Korsch, B. M., 14, 20, 44, 66, 85, 288, 296, 374
Kovar, M., 42, 172, 374
Krueger, K. K., 181, 372
Kubany, A., 66, 374
Kurland, I., 155, 374

Langford, W., 64, 374
Lansky, S., 181, 184, 229, 374
Lascari, A., 93, 374
Laurence, K. M., 93, 263, 375, 388
Lavigne, J., 93, 375
Lazarus, R. S., 271, 280, 366, 383
Lazerson, J., 178, 375
Leff, P., 87, 365
Leffert, F., 7, 51, 258, 375
Leikin, S. L., 269, 288, 294, 375
Lesser, A. J., 45, 219, 300, 375
Leventhal, J., 92, 268, 384
Levine, P. H., 178, 182, 228, 265, 375, 385

Levy, J. C., 266, 380
Lewis, C. E., 258, 375
Lewis, I. J., 130, 133, 134, 135, 375
Lewiston, N. J., 16, 46, 375
Lieberman, M., 157, 375
Lincoln, A., 70
Linney, D., 178, 375
Lipson, J., 155, 375
Little, S., 66, 375-376
Lowit, I., 65, 376
Luft, H. S., 204, 376
Lund, D., 63, 77, 87, 93, 100, 376
Lund, E., 87
Lurie, N., 214, 376

McAnarney, E., 34, 376
McCarthy, M., 93, 376
McCollum, A., 89, 376
McCrae, W., 93, 376
McInerny, T., 130, 131, 132, 265, 376
McKeever, P., 85, 90, 93, 95, 376
McLaughlin, J., 182, 376
MacLean, W. E., 69, 381
McManus, P., 41, 214, 364, 379
McNicol, K. N., 7, 34, 376, 390
MacQueen, J., 222, 376
Magrab, P. R., 71, 240, 376-377
Mally, M., 66, 364
Markowitz, M., 146-147, 377
Marmor, T. R., 339, 377
Martin, R., 114, 377
Martinson, I., 155, 377
Mason, E., 64, 65, 377
Massie, R., 77, 82, 86, 93, 94, 98, 377
Massie, R. K., Jr., 70, 74-75, 79-80,
    94, 98, 303, 377
Massie, S., 77, 82, 86, 93, 94, 98, 377
Matthews, S., 122, 364
Mattsson, A., 65, 267, 377
Mauksch, I. G., 240, 377
Mearig, J. S., 18, 118, 377
Meny, D., 42, 172, 374
Merkens, M., xxvi, 224, 372
Mervis, R., 103, 116, 380
Messenger, K., 93, 271, 364
Meyerowitz, J. H., 90, 377
Mikkelsen, C., 63, 82, 378
Millar, R., 151, 363
Miller, D. R., 258, 357, 378
Millsap, M., 9, 20, 45, 182, 378

Milofsky, C., 86, 153-154, 226, 228,
    378
Minde, K., 155, 378
Minuchin, S., 271, 378
Mishler, E. G., 270, 378
Mitchell, J. B., 214, 385
Moloney, T. W., 214, 383
Moore, A., 85, 390
Moore, F., 172, 206, 390
Mortimer, E. A., 265, 364
Moses, C., 66, 374
Moss, A. J., 268, 367
Muskin, D., 65, 387
Myers, G., 9, 20, 45, 182, 378

Nadas, A. S., 259, 378
Nader, P., 119, 120, 378
Natterson, J., 65, 379
Nelson, N. A., 258, 362
Neuhaus, E., 66, 379
Newacheck, P. W., 41, 379
Nishiura, E. N., 15, 52, 390
Norris, C., 232, 379
Nyhan, W. L., 261, 379

O'Malley, J., 124, 374
Orbach, C., 66, 363
Osterweis, M., 233, 379-380
Outka, G., 309, 310, 380

Palfrey, J. S., 103, 116, 266, 380
Pantell, R. H., 239, 380
Parcel, G. S., 7, 109, 380
Parron, D., 268, 371
Pearson, D. A., 89, 179, 380
Pendergrass, T. W., 11, 44, 258, 262,
    380
Perrin, E. C., 71, 72, 239, 269, 271,
    290, 380
Perrin, J. M., xv, 5, 19, 25, 69, 70,
    131, 139, 140, 141, 219, 239, 241,
    265, 280, 300, 372, 380-381, 382
Peterson, I., 141, 381
Phelen, P., 90, 92, 93, 361
Piaget, J., 71, 235, 271, 381
Pierce, P., 128, 159, 161, 186, 222,
    381
Pinkerton, P., 2, 33, 106, 109, 259,
    382
Plank, E., 65, 381

Name Index

395

Pless, I. B., xxv, 2, 5, 19, 33, 36, 39, 41, 42n, 66, 106, 109, 130, 136, 234, 254-255, 259, 267, 271, 273, 275, 279, 280, 354, 371, 381-382
Pool, J. G., 44, 382
Prugh, D., 64, 382

Rae-Grant, Q., 65, 387
Ramsey, P., 310, 382
Ratcliff, K., 148, 232, 239, 249, 383
Richards, S., 64, 382
Richards, W., 90, 388
Richmond, J. B., xi-xvi, 47, 49, 65, 66, 370, 372, 382-383
Riessman, C., 66, 275, 387
Robertson, J., 64, 383
Robinson, T., 120, 383
Rogers, C., 113, 115, 368
Rogers, D. E., 214, 383
Roghmann, K. J., 2, 39, 41, 42n, 52, 273, 371, 382, 383
Rosenbloom, A., 128, 383
Roskies, E., 271, 280, 383
Ross, J., 155, 383
Roth, W., 4, 235, 268, 370
Rowland, D., 214, 383
Rudolph, C., 148, 232, 239, 249, 383
Russell, I., 93, 389
Rutter, M., 106, 109, 273, 275, 383
Ryan, M., 93, 375
Rymer, M., 224, 383

Sabbeth, B., 87, 92, 268, 384
Santos, G. W., 258, 262, 384
Sappenfield, W., 38n, 370
Satterwhite, B. B., 66, 130, 136, 234, 254-255, 354, 381-382
Schorr, L. B., xxvi, 237, 384
Schweitzer, A., 304, 307
Selvin, S., 258, 384
Senn, M., 64, 384
Shannon, A. E., 44, 382
Shapiro, G. G., 258, 384
Shayne, M. W., xxvii, 83, 84, 86, 87, 96, 99, 157, 170, 213, 384
Shepard, S., 62-63, 384
Sheps, C. G., 130, 133, 134, 135, 375
Sherwin, R. S., 259, 262, 387
Shore, M., 65, 77, 384
Shurtleff, D. B., 182, 287, 376, 384

Shwachman, H., 123, 124, 370
Simons, F.E.R., 258, 362
Sloan, F. A., 214, 385
Smith, P. S., 178, 182, 385
Smithells, R. W., 9, 385
Solnit, A., 63, 65, 83, 385
Solomon, G. F., 268, 385
Sourkes, B., 93, 385
Spiegelberg, H., 304, 385
Spitz, B., 213, 215, 385
Spitz, R., 64, 385-386
Staden, F., 184, 362
Starfield, B., 42, 173, 175, 260, 265, 270, 272, 274, 275, 280, 368, 386
Stark, M., 63, 83, 385
Steele, B., 128, 373
Stehbens, J., 93, 374
Stein, R.E.K., 19, 66, 69, 93, 128, 131, 132, 141, 142, 162, 163, 175, 249, 260, 273-274, 275, 373, 386-387
Stein, S. C., 9, 387
Steinhauer, P., 65, 387
Stevens, R., 209, 212, 285, 286, 387
Stevens, R., 209, 212, 387
Strain, J., 287, 387
Stranova, T. J., 89, 179, 380
Strayer, F., 175, 177, 181, 266, 387
Stroup, C., 287, 387
Sultz, H., 109, 387
Sussman, M., 93, 364
Sutherland, A., 66, 363
Sutherland, D.E.R., 259, 387

Tamborlane, W. V., 259, 262, 387
Tatara, T., 149, 388
Tatro, A., 114
Taylor, W., 182, 228, 389
Tew, B., 93, 388
Thomas, M., 93, 389
Thompson, J. D., 89, 179, 380
Thornton, A., 67, 80-81, 388
Tiller, J., 90, 388
Tisza, V., 65, 388
Titmuss, R. M., 304, 388
Tizard, J., 106, 109, 273, 275, 383
Toch, R., 66, 388
Townley, R., 90, 92, 93, 361
Travis, G., 95-96, 130, 144, 145, 388
Turk, J., 66, 388

Vance, V., 182, 228, 389
VanVechten, D., 130, 136, 382
Vaughan, G. F., 64, 389
Vaughn, J. C., 241, 389
Veatch, R. M., 285, 288, 298, 308, 389
Vernick, J., 66, 389

Waechter, E., 63, 82, 378
Waisman, H. A., 66, 382-383
Walker, D. K., 4, 41, 103, 104, 106,
    107n, 108, 109, 111, 112-113, 114,
    115, 116, 119, 120, 236, 250, 264,
    371, 389
Walker, J., 93, 389
Walsh, M. E., 71, 269, 271, 363
Waugh, D., 85, 390
Weeks, K., xxvii, 27, 199, 206, 389
Weil, W., 93, 364
Weisman, M., 86, 87-88, 389
Weisman, P., 87-88

Weitzman, M., 41, 93, 107n, 130, 264,
    271, 364, 389-390
White, R., 261, 365
Whitmore, K., 106, 109, 273, 275, 383
Whitten, C. F., 15, 52, 85, 390
Williams, H. E., 7, 34, 376, 390
Wilson, J. C., 50, 390
Windham, G. C., 263, 390
Wineman, R. J., 181, 372
Wolff, E., 64, 382
Wright, L., 245, 251, 373

Yalom, I., 156, 390
Yoak, M., 85, 86, 87, 155, 156, 157,
    365
Yordy, K. D., 218, 390

Zaner, R. M., 307, 390
Zeckhauser, R., 206, 390
Zook, C., 172, 206, 390
Zvagulis, I., 66, 267, 271, 382

Subject Index

Academic medical centers: and research, 273; services from, 130, 133-135

Ad Hoc Committee Task Force on Neonatal Screening, 262, 361

Adoption Assistance and Child Welfare Act of 1980 (P.L. 96-272), 150

Aetna, 200

Aid for Dependent Children (ADC), 208

Aid to Families with Dependent Children (AFDC): and payment pattern, 196, 208, 210, 214; and services, 46, 148, 150

Aid to the Aged, 223

Aid to the Blind, 223

Aid to the Permanently and Totally Disabled, 223

Albert Einstein College of Medicine, and service delivery, 162

Alcoholics Anonymous, 155

American Academy of Pediatrics, 157, 172, 203, 217, 361

American Hospital Association, 144

American Medical Association, Judicial Council, 284, 361

American Public Health Association, Maternal and Child Health Section of, 158

Amniocentesis, issues for, 52

Arizona, Medicaid in, 210

Arkansas, University of, professional training at, 249-250

Arthritis: and education, 105; prevalence of, 107; and professional training, 247; research on, 257, 274; services for, 136, 137, 162; severity of, 34; treatment centers for, 46; and viruses, 51

Arthritis Foundation, 257

Association for the Care of Children's Health (ACCH), 65, 158

Association of American Medical Colleges, 285, 362

Association of Directors of State Maternal and Child Health/ Crippled Children's Programs, 158

Association of Special Educators, 158

Asthma: combating, 44-45; costs of, 175, 176, 182; described, 5, 6-8, 18-19; and education, 102, 105, 108, 109, 110, 112, 113; impact of, 66, 72, 96-97; and infections, 51; as marker disease, 2; payment pattern for, 202, 219; as polygenic, 50; prevalence of, 38, 39, 42, 107; and public policy, 316, 320, 323; research on, 258, 267, 274; services for, 133, 140, 162; severity of, 34; and values, 290, 300

Baltimore, Chronic Health Impaired Project (CHIP) in, 122-123, 126

Blue Cross/Blue Shield, 200

397

Bronx Municipal Hospital Center, and service delivery, 162-164

Canada, national health insurance, in, 338
Cancer. *See* Leukemia
Centre Technique des Etudes et Recherches National sur les Handicaps et les Inadaptations, 279
Childhood Chronic illness: achievements in combating, 43-47; analysis of, 1-31; background on, 2-5; care for, 20; challenges ahead for, 56-57; changing patterns of, 32-61; chronicity and severity of, 33-35; community impact of, 95-100; concept of, 33; control and treatment of, 43-45; costs of, 19-20, 56-57, 89; degeneration in, 20-21; described, 5-18; diagnosis of, responding to, 81-83; effects of, 62-101; and families, 63-64, 68, 79-95; functional impairment from, 40-41, 107; future trends in, 42-43; genetic component in, 20; health services provision for, 45-47; impact of, 62-79; impact of, research on, 64-66, 259-260; integrated treatment for, 21-22; and mortality rates, 35-39; pain and discomfort in, 21; policy analysis for, 23-30; prevalence of, 37-42, 107; prevention of, 47-56; psychological impacts of, 63-66; research on, 257-281; resource allocation for, 22, 298-313; summary on, 30-31, 57-58
Children, chronically ill: in adolescence, 72, 75, 79, 85, 123, 316; advocacy for, xi-xv; as class, 18-23; commonalities in needs of, 318-320, 329; costs of care for, 169-188; decision-making competence of, 294-295, 327; developmental tasks of, 71-72; education for, 102-126; and friends, 77-79; frustration, boredom, and pain for, 75-77; illness distinct from, 55-56; impact of illness on, 70-79; in infancy, 71, 74; intrinsic value

of, 302; policy choices for, 331-360; preschool, 72, 74; and professionals, 286-287; public policy on, 314-360; research involving, 296; resource allocation to, 302-308; of school age, 72, 74-75; and separation from home and family, 73-75; service delivery for, 127-168; stress for, 67-68, 73; as toddlers, 71-72
Children's Bureau, xi, 219, 365
Children's Hospital National Medical Center, 164-165
Chronic Childhood Illness Service, recommended, 337
Cleft palate: costs of, 175, 176; described, 5, 9-10; impact of, 73; as marker disease, 2; payment pattern for, 202; as polygenic, 50; prevalence of, 38, 42; and radiation, 50; and values, 300
Cleveland, Ohio, research in, 264
Community: concepts of, 97, 317; impact of illness on, 95-100; life of, 97-100; responsibilities of, 317-318, 329
Comprehensive Genetics Program, 225-226, 227
Comptroller General of the United States, 113, 366
Congenital heart disease. *See* Heart disease, congenital
Congressional Budget Office, 212, 366
Connecticut General, 200
Costs: analysis of, 169-188; background on, 169-171; concept of, 171; and economies of scale, 176-177; estimates of, for marker diseases, 180-183; and home care, 186-187; indirect, 183-184; and new treatment development and diffusion, 177-180; and organization of services, 177; payment patterns for, 189-230; and perceived need for services, 175; research on, 266-267; scope and nature of, 171-180; and service availability and access, 173, 175; and source of payment, 176; sources of sav-

ings in, 185-187; summary on, 187-188

Craniofacial anomalies. *See* Cleft palate

Crippled Children's Services (CCS): analysis of role of, 219-223, 355-356; development of, 45; and education, 125; evaluation for, xviii; and financial concerns, 89; and payment patterns, 191, 194, 196, 216, 218, 219-223, 224-225, 227, 339-340, 341; and policy analysis, 26, 28; and professional training, 237; and resource allocation, 298, 299-302, 325; and service issues, 139, 152, 338, 343

Cystic fibrosis: as autosomal recessive disorder, 60; combating, 45; costs of, 180; described, 5, 16-17, 18; and education, 109, 110, 118; impact of, 62-63, 66, 76, 79, 82, 94-95, 96, 99; as marker disease, 2; painful treatment for, 21; payment pattern for, 223, 225, 227, 228; prevalence of, 38; and professional training, 236, 237, 248, 251; research on, 257, 262; services for, 131, 135-136, 140, 144, 152-153; treatment centers for, 46; and values, 300, 306

Cystic Fibrosis Foundation, 135, 152-153, 180, 227, 228, 257, 366

Decision making: by committees and courts, 295-296; values on, 293-297

Deficit Reduction Act of 1984, 210

Developmental Disabilities program, 46

Developmentally Disabled Assistance and Bill of Rights Act of 1975, 26, 123

Diabetes: combating, 44; costs of, 175, 183; described, 5, 6; and education, 105, 109, 110, 112, 120; and functional impairment, 41, 107; and heredity, 6, 20; impact of, 65, 66, 72, 73, 77-78, 79; as marker disease, 2; painful treatment for, 21; payment pattern

for, 194-196, 219; as polygenic, 50; prevalence of, 38, 42, 107; and professional training, 235-236, 237, 243, 246-247; and public policy, 322; research on, 259, 262, 274; services for, 130, 133, 138, 140, 144, 151, 153, 162; severity of, 33, 34; and values, 290, 295, 300, 305, 311; and viruses, 51

Diagnosis Related Groups (DRGs), and Medicare, 217

Disability, concept of, 48

Disclosure and truth-telling, value of, 289-293, 326-327

Disease, concept of, 48, 236. *See also* Childhood chronic illness; Illness

District of Columbia, service delivery in, 164-165

Division of Maternal and Child Health, 115, 120, 367

Down's syndrome: and chromosomal defects, 59; and leukemia, 51-52

Duchenne's muscular dystrophy: described, 17-18; as sex-linked recessive disorder, 61. *See also* Muscular dystrophy

Early and Periodic Screening, Diagnosis, and Treatment (EPSDT) program, 143, 211

Ecosystem, and tertiary prevention, 53-55

Education: and absenteeism, 109; for adolescents, 123; analysis of, 102-126; background on, 102-104; for functional impairments, 107-108, 112; by home- or hospital-bound instruction, 121-123; and individualized education program (IEP), 114-116; for intellectual or perceptual impairment, 105-106, 112; and limited alertness and stamina, 109-110; needs for, 105-111; for nonimpaired children, 108-111, 112; participation in, public policy on, 320-321, 329; placements for, 111-120; and psychological health, 110-111; public policy on, 348-349; regu-

lar programs of, 116–120; and
related services, 113–114; and
school nurses, 103–104, 119–120;
in special programs, 112–116;
summary on, 125–126; by vocational training, 123–124
Education of All Handicapped Children Act of 1975 (P.L. 94–142):
and chronic illness, 4, 27, 47; and
education, 103, 104, 112–116, 121,
123, 125; and professional training, 237; and public policy, 342,
348
Elementary and Secondary Education Act (ESEA), 122
End-stage renal disease (ESRD). See
Kidney disease
Environment, and prevention, 49–53
Epidemiology: concept of, 35; and
research, 263–265
Ethics. See Values
Etiology, concept of, 35

Families: Asian, 98–99; changes in,
67, 80–81; and divorce, 92; effects
of illness on, 63–64, 68, 79–95;
financial concerns of, 89–90; foster or adopting, 149–151; knowledge sought by, 84–87; maintaining equilibrium of, 90–93; and
pain and fear of child, 87–89;
payment by, 228–229; policy
choices for, 331–360; and professionals, 286–287; public policy
on, 315–317, 329; and responses to
diagnosis, 81–83; support groups
for, 86, 87, 268
Flint, Michigan, functional impairment study in, 41, 107, 264
Florida, service delivery in, 159–162
Florida Department of Health and
Rehabilitative Services, Children's Medical Services (CMS) of,
159–160
Florida Health Center, University
of, and service delivery, 160
France, research center in, 279
Functional impairment: from
chronic illnesses, 40–41, 107; concept of, 35; education for, 107–

108, 112; and payment patterns,
193

Genetic Disease Act of 1976, 223, 225
Genetics: and autosomal dominant
disorders, 60–61; and autosomal
recessive disorders, 60; and changing patterns of childhood illness,
45, 47; and chronic illnesses, 20;
issues in providing services in,
142–144; and prevention, 49–53;
primer on, 58–61; and public
policy, 319, 322; research on,
261–262; and sex-linked recessive
disorders, 61

Handicap, concept of, 48–49
Harvard Community Child Health
Studies, 264
Health Care Financing Administration, 208, 213, 371
Health maintenance organization
(HMO), and payment pattern,
203–204, 215
Heart disease, congenital: costs of,
175, 181, 183; described, 5, 10–11,
19; and education, 108, 112, 118;
and functional impairment, 41,
107; and heredity, 20; impact of,
73, 79; as marker disease, 2; payment pattern for, 202, 206, 219; as
polygenic, 50; prevalence of, 38,
107; and professional training,
251; and radiation, 50; research
on, 259, 273; services for, 133; and
values, 300
Hemophilia: combating, 44; costs
of, 177–179, 182, 186–187; described, 5, 12–14, 18; and education, 105, 108, 110, 112; and
heredity, 12–13, 20; impact of, 66,
71, 73, 82, 94; as marker disease,
2; painful treatment for, 21; payment pattern for, 225, 226, 227,
228; prevalence of, 38; and professional training, 236, 251; and
public policy, 323; research on,
259, 267, 273, 274; services for,
136, 138, 144, 152; severity of,
33–34; as sex-linked recessive dis-

order, 61; treatment centers for, 46; and values, 301, 305, 306
Hemophilia Diagnostic and Treatment Center Act of 1976, 223, 226
Hogg Foundation, xii
Home care: piecemeal approach to, 350; research on, 267
Home Health Care Team (HCT), 159, 164–165
Homozygous genes, 59
Hospitalism, 64

Illinois, supplemental security income in, 224
Illness: concept of, 357; distinct from child, 55–56. *See also* Childhood chronic illness
Incidence, concept of, 35
Indian Health Service, 337
Indiana, home instruction in, 121
Individual practice association (IPA), and payment patterns, 203
Insurance: catastrophic, 206–207, 345–346; competitive approaches for, 205–206; and coverage of dependents, 200–202; and employment, 123–124; and family stress, 89–90; and high-risk pools, 207; history of, 199–200, 208–210; and nonmedical services, 202; in payment patterns, 189–190, 192, 193–227; and prepaid health care, 203–204; private, 194–196, 199–207; public, 196–197, 207–227; public policy on, 336–339; reforms proposed for, 204–207, 345–346
Iowa, leukemia care in, 266

Japan, leukemia in, 50
Johnson Foundation, Robert Wood, xix, 159
Juvenile Diabetes Foundation (JDF), 151, 153

Kerr-Mills Act of 1960, 209
Kidney disease: combating, 44; costs of, 19–20, 175, 179, 181; described, 5, 14–15; and education, 108, 109, 110, 118; impact of, 66; as marker disease, 2; payment pattern for, 219; prevalence of, 38, 107; resources for, 27, 46; services for, 133, 134; and values, 228, 295, 298, 306

Lay workers, training for, 254–256
Leukemia: combating, 44; costs of, 177, 180, 181, 184; described, 11–12, 19; and education, 105, 109, 112; genetic and environmental factors in, 50, 51–52; and heredity, 20; impact of, 66, 67, 73, 79, 85, 87, 93, 100; as marker disease, 2; payment pattern for, 219, 228–229; prevalence of, 38; and professional training, 234, 251; and public policy, 323; research on, 258, 262, 266, 268; services for, 133, 134, 159, 162; and values, 289, 291, 300, 305

March of Dimes Birth Defects Foundation, 151, 152
Massachusetts, research in, 264
Maternal and Child Health (MCH) Block Grant, 45, 158, 222, 224, 226, 342
Medicaid: analysis of role of, 207–219; and cost containment, 213–215; and costs, 176; in ecosystem, 53; and education, 115; eligibility for, 210–211, 214; evaluation of, 217–219; and financial concerns, 89; history of, 208–210; and home and community care, 216; ineligibility for, 22, 139, 197, 210, 346; management of, 212–213; and medically needy children, 212; and payment patterns, 191, 196, 198, 204, 207–219, 340; and policy review, 27; and prepaid plans, 215; and primary care case management, 215–216; and professional training, 237; and prospective reimbursement, 217; restructuring of, 214–217, 342; and service issues, 46, 139, 141, 142, 143, 150; and state options, 211–212; and vendor-payment system, 209, 211

Medical services: from academic medical centers, 130, 133–135; analysis of structure of, 129–144; communication problem in, 136–137, 166–167; in community hospitals, 132–133; comprehensive programs for, 135–136; continuing care in, 132; distance issue for, 136; entry point to, 131; genetic, 142–144; interprofessional issues in, 137–139; referral to, 131; in rural areas, 139–141, 159–162; shared-management approach to, 177; from specialty clinics, 135, 154, 157, 166, 167; for urban poor, 141–142, 162–164
Medicare, 27, 46, 209, 337
Monroe County, New York, prevalence rates in, 42
Montana, home instruction in, 121
Morbidity, concept of, 35
Mortality, concept of, 35
Mortality rates, improved, 35–39
Multifactorial conditions, 50
Muscular dystrophy: costs of, 187; described, 5, 17–18, 19; and ecosystem, 54; and education, 105, 108, 118; and heredity, 17–18, 20; impact of, 72, 87–88, 91, 100; as marker disease, 2; painful treatment for, 21; prevalence of, 38; services for, 143, 144, 151, 152, 153–154, 159
Muscular Dystrophy Association, 151, 152, 153–154
Myelomeningocele. See Spina bifida

Natanson v. Kline, on disclosure and truth-telling, 289, 378
National Association of Children's Hospitals and Related Institutions (NACHRI), 65, 218, 378
National Cancer Institute, 12
National Center for Clinical Infant Programs, 158
National Center for Health Care Technology, 263
National Center for Health Services Research and Development, 277
National Center for Health Statistics, 35, 40n, 378–379

National Council on the Aging, 256
National health care, public policy on, 336–339
National Health Interview Survey, 172; Child Health Supplement to, 39–40
National Health Policy Forum, 212, 379
National Hemophilia Foundation, 136, 152
National Institute for Aging, 279
National Institute of Child Health and Human Development (NICHD), 27, 278–279
National Institute of Chronic Diseases, 279
National Institute of Handicapped Research (NIHR), 277
National Institute of Mental Health (NIMH), 277
National Institutes of Health (NIH), 36, 379; and research, 27, 155, 257, 272, 273, 276–279
National Joint Practice Commission, 240, 379
National Organization for Rare Disorders (NORD), 152
National Public Health Program Reporting Service, 219, 220, 379
National Sickle Cell Anemia Control Act of 1972, 47
Nevada, Medicaid in, 210
New England Regional Infant Cardiac Program 181, 379
New York, Medicaid in, 210

Office of Human Development Services (OHDS), 277
Office of Inspector General, 150, 379
Office of Maternal and Child Health (OMCH), 218, 277
Office of Technology Assessment, 263
Omnibus Budget Reconciliation Act of 1981, 213
Organizations: analysis of efforts of, 151–158; development of, 65; disease-oriented voluntary, 152–155, 227–228; professional, 157–158; self-help, 155–157

Payment for care: additional funds for, 339–342; analysis of, 189–230; background on, 189–191; costs, and source of, 176; with Crippled Children's Services, 219–223; and disease-oriented organizations, 227–228; by families, 228–229; on fee-for-service basis, 200; financial implications for, 198–199; with insurance, 189–190, 192, 193–227; without insurance, 197–198; issues in, 189–190; with Medicaid, 207–219; options for, 358–359; with other public programs, 223–227; overview of, 191–199; with private insurance, 194–196, 199–207; with public insurance, 196–197, 207–227; reforms in, 344–348; summary on, 229–230

Pediatric Ambulatory Care Division, 87, 96–97, 157, 170, 380

Pediatric Home Care Program (PHC), 159, 162–164, 253, 354

Platt Committee, 64, 381

Policy analysis: assessing merits of options in, 28–29; described, 23–30; and options identification, 27–28; problem definition in, 24–26; recommendations, implementation, and evaluation in, 29–30; and review of existing policies, 26–27. See also Public policy

Poliomyelitis, changing patterns of, 36, 45–46, 47

Polygenic conditions, 50

Preferred Provider Organization (PPO), and payment pattern, 205

Prepaid group practice (PGP), and payment pattern, 203

President's Commission for the Study of Ethical Problems in Medicine and Biomedical and Behavioral Research, 238–239, 240, 285, 288, 290, 296, 382

President's Commission on Mental Health, 155–156

Prevalence: concept of, 35; estimates of, 37–42, 107

Prevention: analysis of, 47–56; and cost savings, 185–186; and genetic services, 52; genetics and environment in, 49–53; of malformations, 50–51; primary, 48, 49–53; public policy on, 321–322; secondary, 48, 49–53; tertiary, 48–49, 53–56

Preventive Intervention Research Center, 254, 382

Professional training: analysis of, 231–256; areas of knowledge in, 234–238; background on, 231–234; for caring and curing, 233; education for, 241–254; interdisciplinary, 233, 249, 250, 251, 253; and lay workers, 254–256; for nurses, 244–245, 247, 248, 251, 354; for pediatricians, 245–249, 250–251; for physicians, 242–244; in psychology, 245, 251–252; recommendations for, 253–254; for school teachers, 249–250; settings for, 252; in skills, 238–241; for social workers, 249; summary on, 256

Professionals: and children and families, 286–287; fiduciary relationship of, 285–286; relationships of, 284–287; skills for, 355; standards of practice for, 284–286; training of, 231–256; values of, 282–313, 326–328, 330

Project REACH, 159–162, 354

Prudential, 200

Psychology and development, research on, 267–269

Public Law 94–142. See Education of All Handicapped Children Act

Public Law 96–272, 150

Public policy: on additional funds, 339–342; analysis of, 23–30; assessing options in, 314–330; background on, 314–315, 331–333; choices in, 331–360; on commonalities in needs of children, 318–320, 329; on community-based program, 351–359; on community responsibility, 317–318, 329; on education, 348–349; on family centrality, 315–317, 329; greatest-

good option in, 333–335; on national health care, 336–339; on
professional values, 326–328, 330;
recommended, 329–330; on research, 328, 330; research only
option of, 335–336; on resource
allocation justice and equity,
324–326, 329; on school participation, 320–321, 329; on service
range and quality, 321–324, 329;
on service reform, 342–351; summary on, 328–330, 359–360; and
values, 297–308

Quality, standards of, 324

REACH Project (Rural Efforts to
Assist Children at Home), 159–
162, 354
Recessive genes, 59
Research: analysis of, 257–281; biomedical, 261–263; characteristics
of, 269–276; children involved in,
296; clinical, 263; epidemiological, 263–265; on health services,
265–267; history of, 257–260;
measurement problems in, 274–
276; multidisciplinary, 278; policy on emphasizing, 335–336;
population characteristics for,
271–272; principles for, 280–281;
promising areas for, 260–269; on
psychology and development,
267–269; public policy on, 328,
330; public support of, 276–279;
and recombinant DNA tech-
niques, 259, 261–262; single-
disease character of, 272–274;
theories underlying, 269–271; on
values, 269
Resource allocation: for compassion
and community, 303–305; compromise in, 312–313; for economics, 305–306; justice in, 308–313;
for knowledge, 306; by merit,
309–310; for moral discovery,
306–308; by need, 311–312; for
prudence, 305; public policy on,
324–326, 329; on random basis,
312; rationale for, 302–308; by

societal allocation, 310–311; by
states, 299–302; value conflicts in,
298–299
Rhode Island, hemophilia costs in,
178
Rochester Child Health Studies, 41,
273

Scandinavia, spina bifida screening
in, 8
Select Panel for the Promotion of
Child Health, xiii, 22, 39, 103,
175, 190, 319, 333, 384
Services: analysis of, 127–168; areawide, community base of, 353–
357; availability and access issues
in, 173, 175; background on, 127–
129; for chronic illnesses, 45–47;
community-based, policy on,
351–359; competition in, 346–347;
costs of, 169–188; delivery of, and
impact of illness, 68–69; eligibility and access reforms in, 357–358;
financing, reforms in, 344–348;
general and specialty, 322–323;
and home care, 350; innovative
programs for, 158–165; medical
and nursing, 129–144; nationalized, and public policy, 337, 338;
organizational issues of, 177, 265–
266; from organizations, 151–158;
paying for, 189–230; perceived
need for, 175; planning and integrating, 342–343, 352–353; problems in, 166–167; public policy
on range and quality of, 321–324,
329; range of, 352; reform of,
public policy on, 342–351; research on, 265–267; in schools,
348–349; from social agencies,
144–151; summary on, 165–168;
teamwork for, 327–328, 344
Severity, factors in, 33–34, 274
Siblings: effects of illness on, 63,
93–95; and family centrality, 316–
317
Sickle cell anemia: as autosomal recessive disorder, 60; described, 5,
15–16; and education, 109, 112,
and heredity, 15–16, 20; impact

of, 73, 85, 98; as marker disease, 2; painful treatment for, 21; payment pattern for, 197–198, 225; prevalence of, 38; and professional training, 236; research on, 268; services for, 136, 143, 144, 154, 162; treatment centers for, 46
Sickle Cell Anemia Foundation, 154
Social Security Act: programs under, 207, 208; and provision of services, 46; Title IV-A of, 147–148; Title IV-E of, 150; Title XVIII of, 27; Title XIX of, 207; Title XX of, 147, 148. See also Supplemental Security Income Program; Title V. . . .
Social services: access to, 144–146; analysis of, 144–151; categories of, 146; for foster care or adoption, 149–151; fragmentation of, 146–147; national programs of, 147–149
Social Services Block Grant (SSBG), 146, 147–149
Social support, for families, 86, 87, 268
Society for School Nurse Practitioners, 157
Society of Pediatric Psychology (SPP), 65, 158
South Carolina, home instruction in, 121
Spina bifida: costs of, 20, 173, 180, 181, 182, 185–186; described, 5, 8–9, 19; and ecosystem, 54–55; and education, 105, 106, 108, 109, 114, 124; impact of, 73, 100; as marker disease, 2; payment pattern for, 196, 206, 219, 228; as polygenic, 50; prevalence of, 38; and professional training, 237; research on, 262–263; services for, 132, 138, 140, 143, 144–145, 162; and values, 287, 289, 300, 311
Spina Bifida Association of the Delaware Valley, 182, 385
Stress, and research, 267–268, 271
Supplemental Security Income/ Disabled Children's Program (SSI/DCP), 223, 224–225

Supplemental Security Income (SSI) Program: and payment pattern, 196, 208, 210, 216, 223–224; and services, 27, 46, 148, 150; support from, 266
Survey of Income and Education, 192n

Task Force on Pediatric Education, 247, 387
Tatro v. Texas, and related services, 114
Tax Equity and Fiscal Responsibility Act of 1982, 213
Tennessee, hemophilia costs in, 182
Texas, home instruction in, 121
Title V of the Social Security Act of 1935, 26, 219, 356, 388
Training. See Professional training
Treatment, ethics of, 297

Understanding Handicapped Program, 250
United Kingdom: blood supply in, 304; costs study in, 184; enuresis treatment in, 270; national health insurance in, 338; research in, 273
U.S. Bureau of the Census, 43, 388
U.S. Department of Health and Human Services, 148, 192n, 210, 388; Office of Maternal and Child Health in, xix, 218, 277
U.S. Department of Health Education, and Welfare, 228, 388
U.S. General Accounting Office, 222, 388
U.S. Public Health Service, 213. See also Division of Maternal and Child Health
United Way, 146
University Affiliated Facilities, xii, 125, 240, 340–341

Values: analysis of role of, 282–313; and Baby Doe boards, 287–288; background on, 282–284; concept of, 283; on decision making, 293–297; of disclosure and truthtelling, 289–293, 326–327; in extreme and in daily situations, 287-297; impact of, 283-284; of justice in resource allocation, 308-313; and professional relationships, 284-287; public policy on, 297-308, 326-328, 330; research on, 269; and resource allocation, 298-299; and standards of practice, 284-286; summary on, 313

Vanderbilt Institute for Public Policy Studies, Center for the Study of Families and Children in, xiv, 25-26

Veterans Administration, 337

Vocational Rehabilitation Act, Section 504 of, 126

Washington, home instruction in, 121

Welfare Administration, 213

Wisconsin, home instruction in, 121

Wyoming, Supplemental Security Income in, 224